Decisions
of the
United States
Supreme Court

1981-82 TERM

by

The Editorial Staff
United States Supreme Court Reports,
Lawyers' Edition

THE LAWYERS CO-OPERATIVE PUBLISHING CO.
Rochester, New York 14694

BANCROFT-WHITNEY CO.
San Francisco, California 94107

PREFACE

This volume is designed to serve as a quick-reference guide to the work of the United States Supreme Court during its 1981–1982 Term. Its important features are described below.

The Court's Personnel. A list of the operating personnel of the Court is accompanied by photographs and biographical sketches of each Justice serving during the Term.

Survey of the Term. A succinct narrative statement outlines the high spots of the Term.

Summaries of Decisions. Every important decision of the Supreme Court is individually summarized. These summaries (reprinted from Vols. 70–73 L Ed 2d) describe the manner in which the case came before the Court, the facts involved and issues presented, the holding of the Court and the reasons supporting that holding, the name of the Justice who wrote the opinion of the majority, and the names and views of those of the Justices who concurred or dissented.

The Summaries are printed in the order in which the cases were decided by the Court. Notations to Summaries indicate the volume and page at which the full opinion of the Court may be found in the official reports (US) published by the Federal Government, and the privately published United States Supreme Court Reports, Lawyers' Edition (L Ed 2d), and Supreme Court Reporter (S Ct).

Following each Summary is a listing of the attorneys who acted in behalf of the litigants.

Glossary. A glossary of common legal terms defines, in laymen's language, various legal words and phrases frequently used in the Supreme Court's decisions.

Table of Cases. A complete Table of Cases makes possible the location of the Summary of any case through the name of a party litigant.

Index. A detailed, alphabetical word index makes possible the location of the Summary of any case by consulting the index entries for appropriate factual and conceptual terms.

THE COURT'S PERSONNEL

JUSTICES

OF THE

SUPREME COURT OF THE UNITED STATES

1981–82 Term

Chief Justice

HON. WARREN E. BURGER

Associate Justices

HON. WILLIAM J. BRENNAN, Jr.

HON. BYRON R. WHITE

HON. THURGOOD MARSHALL

HON. HARRY A. BLACKMUN

HON. LEWIS F. POWELL, Jr.

HON. WILLIAM H. REHNQUIST

HON. JOHN P. STEVENS

HON. SANDRA DAY O'CONNOR

BIOGRAPHIES OF THE
JUSTICES

Chief Justice Burger was born in St. Paul, Minnesota, on September 17, 1907, the son of Charles Joseph and Katharine B. (Schnittger)[2] Burger. He married Elvera Stromberg on November 8, 1933. They have two children, Wade Allan and Margaret Elizabeth.

After attending the public schools of St. Paul, Chief Justice Burger was a student at the University of Minnesota from 1925 to 1927. He later attended the St. Paul College of Law, receiving an LL.B. degree, magna cum laude, in 1931. After becoming admitted to the Minnesota Bar, he joined the St. Paul law firm of Boyesen, Otis and Faricy (subsequently Faricy, Burger, Moore and Costello) as an associate in 1931, and he became a partner in the firm in 1935. While practicing law in St. Paul, he also was a member of the faculty of the William Mitchell College of Law, and he was, at various times, president of the Junior Chamber of Commerce, president of the Council on Human Relations, a member of the Emergency War Labor Board, and a member of the Governor's Interracial Commission.

In 1953, Chief Justice Burger was appointed Assistant Attorney General in charge of the Civil Division of the Department of Justice, and in 1956,

he was appointed to a judgeship on the United
States Court of Appeals for the District of Columbia
Circuit. He has been not only a member but also a
committee chairman of the American Bar Association.

Chief Justice Burger was nominated by President
Nixon to be Chief Justice of the United States, and
took office on June 23, 1969.

Justice Brennan was born in Newark, New Jersey, on April 25, 1906, the son of William Joseph Brennan, Sr. and Agnes (McDermott) Brennan. He married Marjorie Leonard on May 5, 1928. They have three children, William Joseph III, Hugh Leonard, and Nancy.

Justice Brennan attended public schools in Newark, and graduated from the University of Pennsylvania in 1928 with a B.S. degree. He earned his LL.B. degree from Harvard University in 1931.

Justice Brennan was admitted to the New Jersey Bar in 1932, after joining the Newark law firm of Pitney, Hardin & Skinner. Following that, for 10 years, he practiced law in Newark.

In March, 1942, he entered the Army as a Major in the legal division of the Ordnance Department, leaving with the rank of Colonel in September, 1945.

Returning to Newark, he rejoined his law firm and became a name partner in Pitney, Hardin, Ward & Brennan. In 1949 he became a trial judge in the New Jersey Superior Court. After two years, he was elevated to a judgeship in the Appellate Division of the same court, and in March, 1952, he was appointed as an Associate Justice of the New Jersey Supreme Court.

President Eisenhower appointed him an Associate Justice of the United States Supreme Court on October 15, 1956, and he took his seat on the Court on October 16, 1956.

Justice Brennan is a member of the American, New Jersey, Essex County, Hudson County and Monmouth County (N.J.) Bar Associations.

Justice White was born in Ft. Collins, Colorado, on June 8, 1917, the son of Alpha Albert White and

Maud Burger White. He married Marion Lloyd Stearns on June 15, 1946. They have two children, Charles Byron and Nancy Pitkin.

Justice White attended elementary and high schools at Wellington, Colorado. He graduated from the University of Colorado in 1938 with a B.A. degree, and attended Oxford University, Oxford, England, as a Rhodes Scholar, from January, 1939 until October, 1939. From October, 1939 to October, 1941, and from February, 1946 to November, 1946, he attended Yale University Law School, receiving an LL.B. degree, magna cum laude.

Justice White volunteered for service in the United States Navy in July 1941 and received a commission as an ensign. During World War II, he served in the Pacific as an intelligence officer, and was honorably discharged as a Lieutenant Commander in 1946.

Upon graduation from Yale, Justice White served from 1946 to 1947 as law clerk to Chief Justice Vinson, Supreme Court of the United States.

In 1947, he joined the law firm of Lewis, Grant, Newton, Davis and Henry (now Davis, Graham and Stubbs), in Denver, Colorado. He became a partner and remained with that firm until January 1961, when he was appointed Deputy Attorney General of the United States by President Kennedy.

Justice White was nominated by President Kennedy as Associate Justice of the Supreme Court of the United States on April 3, 1962, and took his seat on April 16, 1962.

He is a member of the American Bar Association and the Colorado Bar Association.

Justice Marshall was born in Baltimore, Maryland on July 2, 1908, the son of William C. Marshall and

Norma A. Marshall. His first wife, the former Vivian Burey, whom he married on September 4, 1929, died in February, 1955. On December 17, 1955, the Justice married Cecilia A. Suyat. Justice Marshall has two sons, Thurgood, Jr., and John William.

After attending public schools in Baltimore, Justice Marshall attended Lincoln University, where, in 1930, he received his A.B. degree. He earned his LL.B. in 1933 from Howard University Law School.

The Justice was admitted to the Maryland Bar in 1933 and was engaged in private practice until 1937. He served as Assistant Special Counsel to the National Association for the Advancement of Colored People between 1936–1938 and as Special Counsel until 1950. He directed the N.A.A.C.P.'s Legal Defense and Educational Fund between 1940–1961.

In 1961, Justice Marshall was appointed United States Circuit Judge for the Second Judicial Circuit, a position he left in 1965 to become Solicitor General of the United States.

President Johnson appointed him Associate Justice of the United States Supreme Court on June 13, 1967, and he took his seat on October 2, 1967.

He is a member of the American Bar Association, the National Bar Association, the Association of the Bar of the City of New York, the New York City County Lawyers Association, and the Bar Association of the District of Columbia.

Justice Blackmun was born in Nashville, Illinois, on November 12, 1908, the son of Corwin M. and  Theo H. Blackmun. He married Dorothy E. Clark on June 21, 1941. They have three daughters: Nancy Clark, Sally Ann, and Susan Manning.

After attending Van Buren Grade School and Mechanic Arts High School in St. Paul, Minnesota, Justice Blackmun attended Harvard College, where, in 1929, he received his A.B. degree, summa cum laude. He earned his LL.B. degree from Harvard Law School in 1932.

He then served for two years as law clerk for Judge John B. Sanborn of the United States Court of Appeals for the Eighth Circuit.

In 1934, he joined the law firm then known as Dorsey, Colman, Barker, Scott & Barber, in Minneapolis, Minnesota. He became a general partner of that firm in 1943 and remained with it until 1950. During this same period he was also an instructor at St. Paul College of Law (now William Mitchell College of Law) (1935–1941), and taught at the University of Minnesota Law School (1945–1947).

In 1950 he became resident counsel of the Mayo Clinic in Rochester, Minnesota, and held that position until 1959, when he was appointed a judge of the United States Court of Appeals for the Eighth Circuit by President Eisenhower.

Justice Blackmun was nominated by President Nixon as Associate Justice of the United States Supreme Court on April 14, 1970, and took his seat on June 9, 1970.

He is a member of the American Bar Association, the Minnesota State Bar Association, the Third

Judical District (Minnesota) Bar Association, the Olmsted County, Minnesota, Bar Association, and the American Judicature Society.

Justice Powell was born in Suffolk, Virginia, on September 19, 1907. He married Josephine Pierce  Rucker in 1936. They have four children, Mrs. Richard S. Smith, Mrs. Basil T. Carmody, Mrs. Christopher J. Sumner, and Lewis F. Powell, III.

Justice Powell attended Washington and Lee University, receiving his B.S. degree, magna cum laude, in 1929, and his LL.B. degree in 1931. In 1932 he earned an LL.M. degree from Harvard Law School.

In 1932, Justice Powell commenced the private practice of law, later becoming a senior partner in the law firm of Hunton, Williams, Gay, Powell & Gibson, in Richmond, Virginia. He also served, at various times, on several national committees and commissions, including the National Commission on Law Enforcement and Administration of Justice, and the National Advisory Committee on Legal Services to the Poor. At the state and local levels, he was a member of various boards and commissions, including the Virginia State Board of Education (President, 1968–1969), the Virginia State Library Board, and the Richmond Public School Board (Chairman, 1952–1961).

During World War II, Justice Powell entered the United States Army Air Force as a First Lieutenant, and served as a combat and staff intelligence officer from 1942 to 1946, including service as Chief of Operational Intelligence for U.S. Strategic Air Forces in Europe. He attained the rank of Colonel, and was awarded the Legion of Merit, the Bronze Star, and France's Croix de Guerre with Palm.

Justice Powell was appointed to the position of Associate Justice of the United States Supreme Court by President Nixon on October 21, 1971, and took office on January 7, 1972.

Justice Powell is a member of the American Bar Association (President, 1964–1965), the American College of Trial Lawyers (President, 1969–1970), the American Bar Foundation (President, 1969–1971), the American Law Institute, the Association of the Bar of the City of New York, and the Virginia Bar Association.

Justice Rehnquist was born in Milwaukee, Wisconsin, on October 1, 1924, the son of William B. and Margery P. Rehnquist. He married Natalie Cornell in 1953. They have three children, James, Janet, and Nancy.

Justice Rehnquist attended public schools in Shorewood, Wisconsin, and received his B.A. degree, with great distinction, and an M.A. degree from Stanford University in 1948. He also earned an M.A. degree from Harvard University in 1950, and then returned to Stanford University, where he received his LL.B. degree in 1952.

From 1952 to 1953, he served as law clerk for Justice Robert H. Jackson, Supreme Court of the United States. From 1953 to 1969, Justice Rehnquist engaged in private practice in Phoenix, Arizona, and in 1969, he was appointed Assistant Attorney General, Office of Legal Counsel, by President Nixon.

Justice Rehnquist served in the United States Army Air Corps as a weather observer from 1943 to 1946, including service in North Africa, and was discharged with the rank of sergeant.

Justice Rehnquist was appointed to the position of Associate Justice of the United States Supreme Court by President Nixon on October 21, 1971, and took office on January 7, 1972.

Justice Rehnquist's professional activities have included membership in the American Bar Association, the Arizona Bar Association, the Maricopa County (Arizona) Bar Association (President, 1963), the National Conference of Lawyers and Realtors, the National Conference of Commissioners of Uniform State Laws, and the Council of the Administrative Conference of the United States.

Justice Stevens was born in Chicago, Illinois, on April 20, 1920. He is married to Maryan Mulholland

Stevens and has four children, John Joseph, Kathryn Stevens Tedlicka, Elizabeth Jane, and Susan Roberta.

Justice Stevens received an A.B. degree from the University of Chicago in 1941 and a J.D. degree from Northwestern University School of Law in 1947.

During the 1947–1948 Term of the United States Supreme Court, he was a law clerk to Justice Wiley Rutledge, and in 1949, he was admitted to practice law in Illinois. In 1951 and 1952, Justice Stevens was Associate Counsel to the Subcommittee on the Study of Monopoly Power of the Judiciary Committee of the United States House of Representatives, and from 1953 to 1955 he was a member of the Attorney General's National Committee to Study Anti-trust Law. From 1970 to 1975 he served as a Judge of the United States Court of Appeals for the Seventh Circuit.

Justice Stevens served in the United States Navy from 1942 to 1945.

Justice Stevens was appointed to the position of Associate Justice of the United States Supreme Court by President Ford on December 17, 1975, and took his seat on December 19, 1975.

Justice O'Connor was born in El Paso, Texas on March 26, 1930, the daughter of Harold A. Day and

Ada Mae Wilkey Day. She married John Jay O'Connor III in 1952. They have three children, Scott, Brian, and Jay.

Justice O'Connor graduated from Stanford University in 1950 with a B.A. degree, magna cum laude. She earned her LL.B. degree at Stanford in 1952.

Justice O'Connor served as a deputy county attorney in San Mateo County, California from 1952 to 1953, and as a civilian attorney for the Quartermaster Market Center in Frankfurt, Germany from 1954 to 1957. She was in the private practice of law in Maryvale, Arizona from 1958 to 1960, and served as an Assistant Attorney General in Arizona from 1965 to 1969.

Justice O'Connor was a member of the Arizona State Senate from 1969 to 1975. She was a judge of the Maricopa County Superior Court in Phoenix, Arizona from 1975 to 1979, and served on the Arizona Court of Appeals from 1979 to 1981.

Justice O'Connor was appointed to the position of Associate Justice of the United States Supreme Court by President Reagan on July 7, 1981, and took office on September 26, 1981.

SURVEY OF THE 1981–1982 TERM

by

Kenneth May, J.D.

§ 1. In General; statistics

The Supreme Court of the United States heard argument in 184 cases during its October Term, 1981, which began on October 5, 1981 and lasted until October 4, 1982. Of these cases, 170 were decided by signed opinions, 10 were decided by per curiam opinions, and 4 were set for reargument in the October Term, 1982.

Justice Sandra Day O'Connor took office on September 26, 1981, replacing Justice Potter Stewart.

§ 2. Landmark decisions

During its 1981-82 term, the court handed down a number of well-publicized landmark decisions. For

example, on June 24, 1982, the court held that the
President of the United States is entitled to absolute
immunity from damages liability predicated on his
official acts and that this immunity extends to all
acts within the outer perimeter of his duties of
office, and that the President may not be held civilly
liable for the wrongful dismissal of an administrative
employee. In an opinion by Powell, J., it was held
that the President's absolute immunity is a functionally mandated incident of his unique office, rooted
in the constitutional tradition of separation of powers and supported by the nation's history, and that
while the separation of powers doctrine does not
bar every exercise of jurisdiction over the President,
a court, before exercising jurisdiction, must balance
the constitutional weight of the interest to be served
against the dangers of intrusion on the authority
and functions of the Executive Branch, and the
exercise of jurisdiction is not warranted in the case
of merely private suits for damages based on the
President's official acts. [Nixon v Fitzgerald (1982,
US) 73 L Ed 2d 349, 102 S Ct 2690.]

In another landmark decision, the court considered whether a state could withhold from local
school districts any state funds for the education of
children not legally admitted in the United States.
In an opinion by Brennan, J., it was held, on June
15, 1982, that such a state statute violated the equal
protection clause of the Fourteenth Amendment,
since neither the undocumented status of the alien
children vel non, nor the state's asserted interest in
the preservation of its limited resources for the
education of its lawful residents furthered some
substantial goal of the state in order to establish a
sufficient rational basis for the discrimination con-

tained in the statute. [Plyler v Doe (1982, US) 72 L Ed 2d 786, 102 S Ct 2382.]

On June 25, 1982, the court rendered a decision which provoked considerable comment in the media. The court decided, without agreeing on an opinion, that a local school board did not have unlimited discretion to remove books from high school and junior high school libraries, and remanded for a trial on the merits a case where a local school board had done so. Brennan, J., announced the judgment of the court and delivered an opinion expressing the view that the First Amendment imposed limitations upon a local school board's exercise of its discretion to remove books from library shelves and that books may not be removed from the shelves simply because the local board disliked the ideas contained in those books and sought by the removal to prescribe what shall be orthodox in politics, nationalism, religion, or other matters of opinion. Blackmun, J., concurred in part and in the judgment, and expressed the view that a proper balance between the limited constitutional restriction imposed on state officials by the First Amendment and the broad state authority to regulate education, would have been struck by holding that state officials may not remove books from school libraries for the purpose of restricting access to the political ideas or social perspectives discussed in the books, when that action is motivated simply by officials' disapproval of the ideas involved. White, J., agreed that there should have been a trial to resolve the factual issues, and expressed the view that there was no necessity at this point for discussing the extent to which the First Amendment limited the school board's discretion to remove books from the school libraries. [Board of Education v Pico (1982, US) 73 L Ed 2d 435, 102 S Ct 2799.]

On January 13, 1982, the court decided a very significant case involving the question of what powers of a municipality were exempt from scrutiny under the federal antitrust laws. In an opinion by Brennan, J., it was held that a city's ordinance prohibiting an operator of a cable television business from expanding its business to areas not currently served by it for 3 months so that the city could draft a new cable television ordinance and invite new businesses to enter the market under the terms of that ordinance was not exempt from antitrust scrutiny as "state action," as the direct delegation of powers to the city through a home-rule amendment in the state constitution did not render the ordinance an act of government performed by the city acting as the state in local matters. [Community Communications Co. v Boulder (1982, US) 70 L Ed 2d 810, 102 S Ct 835, 1982-1 CCH Trade Cases ¶ 64448.]

In a case arising from a conflict between the Federal Home Loan Bank Board's regulation providing that a federal savings and loan association has the power to include in its loan instrument a "due-on-sale" clause, a clause which permits the association to declare the entire balance of the loan immediately due and payable if the property securing the loan is sold or otherwise transferred without the association's prior consent, and a state limitation on that practice, Blackmun, J., on June 28, 1982, authored an opinion in which the court held that the Board's regulation pre-empted the state limitation. [Fidelity Federal Sav. & Loan Asso. v De La Cuesta (1982, US) 73 L Ed 2d 664.]

On May 17, 1982, in an opinion by Blackmun, J.,
it was held that employment discrimination came
within the prohibition of Title IX of the Education
Amendments of 1972 (20 USCS §§ 1681 et seq.)
against sex discrimination and therefore that regulations promulgated under Title IX, which proscribe
discrimination on the basis of sex with respect to
employment in federally funded education programs, were valid since employment discrimination
came within the prohibitions of § 901(a) (20 USCS
§ 1681(a)), and that section's broad directive that
"no person" may be discriminated against on the
basis of gender included employees as well as students. [North Haven Bd. of Education v Bell (1982,
US) 72 L Ed 2d 299, 102 S Ct 1912, 28 BNA FEP
Cas 1393, 28 CCH EPD ¶ 32675.]

Lastly, on June 28, 1982, the court held that the
Bankruptcy Reform Act's broad grant of jurisdiction
to bankruptcy judges violated Art III of the United
States Constitution. In a plurality opinion by Brennan, J., it was held that (1) the judicial power of the
United States must be exercised by judges who,
unlike bankruptcy judges, have the attributes of life
tenure and protection against salary diminution
specified by Art III, (2) Art III barred Congress
from establishing under its Art I powers legislative
courts to exercise jurisdiction over all matters arising under the bankruptcy laws, and (3) 28 USCS
§ 1471, which established the bankruptcy court jurisdiction, impermissibly removed most, if not all, of
the essential attributes of the judicial power from
the Art III District Courts and vested these attributes in a non-Art III adjunct; this holding was
applied only prospectively since the grant of jurisdiction in question presented an unprecedented

question of interpretation of Art III, and retroactive application would not have furthered the operation of the holding. [Northern Pipeline Constr. Co. v Marathon Pipe Line Co. (1982, US) 73 L Ed 2d 598, 102 S Ct 2858, 9 BCD 67, 6 CBC2d 785, CCH Bankr L Rptr ¶ 68698.]

§ 3. Admiralty and maritime matters

The Supreme Court held that although federal admiralty tort jurisdiction is limited by the requirement that the wrong must bear a significant relationship to traditional maritime activity, there is no requirement that the maritime activity be an exclusively commercial one, and a complaint alleging a collision between two vessels on navigable waters properly stated a claim within the federal admiralty jurisdiction even though the collision was between two pleasure boats. [Foremost Ins. Co. v Richardson (1982, US) 73 L Ed 2d 300, 102 S Ct 2654.]

In a case concerning the application of 46 USCS § 596, which requires certain masters and vessel owners to pay seamen promptly after their discharge and authorizes seamen to recover double wages for each day that payment is delayed without sufficient cause, the court held that the imposition of the penalty is mandatory for each day that payment is withheld in violation of § 596 and Federal District Courts have no discretion to limit the period during which the wage penalty is assessed. [Griffin v Oceanic Contractors, Inc. (1982, US) 73 L Ed 2d 973.]

§ 4. Antitrust

In addition to the significant decision involving antitrust law which is discussed in § 2, supra (Community Communications Co. v Boulder (1982, US) 70 L Ed 2d 810, 102 S Ct 835, 1982-1 CCH Trade Cases ¶ 64448), the Supreme Court rendered several other noteworthy decisions in the antitrust area. In one case, the court held that a nonprofit association of mechanical engineers engaged in, among other things, the promulgation and publication of codes and standards for areas of engineering in the industry was civilly liable under the federal antitrust laws for the antitrust violations of its agents committed with apparent authority. [American Soc. of Mechanical Engineers, Inc. v Hydrolevel Corp. (1982, US) 72 L Ed 2d 330, 102 S Ct 1935, 1982-2 CCH Trade Cases ¶ 64730.]

The court held that a state's alcoholic beverage control statute, providing that "a licensed importer shall not purchase or accept delivery of any brand of distilled spirits unless he is designated as an authorized importer of such brand by the brand owner or his authorized agent," was not invalid on its face as being pre-empted by the Sherman Act (15 USCS §§ 1 et seq.) since the statute merely enforced a distiller's decision to restrain intrabrand competition and did not require the distiller to impose vertical restraints of any kind and did not limit the number of importers which may be designated by the distillers, and any anticompetitive effect when applied in concrete factual situations was insufficient to declare the statute itself void on its face. [Rice v Norman Williams Co. (1982, US) 73 L Ed 2d 1042, 1982-2 CCH Trade Cases ¶ 64816.]

The court also decided three antitrust cases relating to the provision of health care. The court held that maximum-fee agreements imposed by medical societies on participating physicians, establishing the maximum fees that the physicians may claim in full payment for health services provided the policyholders of specified insurance plans, were per se unlawful under § 1 of the Sherman Act (15 USCS § 1) as price-fixing agreements. [Arizona v Maricopa County Medical Soc. (1982, US) 73 L Ed 2d 48, 102 S Ct 2466, 1982-2 CCH Trade Cases ¶ 64792.] Additionally, the court held that a prepaid group health plan subscriber, who subscribed to a plan which provided reimbursement for services performed by psychiatrists but not by psychologists unless the treatment was supervised by and billed through a physician, had standing to sue for conspiracy to exclude psychologists from the psychotherapy market. [Blue Shield of Virginia v McCready (1982, US) 73 L Ed 2d 149, 102 S Ct 2540, 1982-2 CCH Trade Cases ¶ 64791.] Finally, the court held that an insurance company's use of a review committee of a state association of chiropractors to determine whether particular chiropractors' treatments and fees were necessary and reasonable, so that the insurance company could ascertain its liability under a policy limiting liability to reasonable charges for necessary medical care and services, did not constitute the "business of insurance" within the meaning of § 2(b) of the McCarran-Ferguson Act (15 USCS § 1012(b)), and thus was not exempt from antitrust scrutiny. [Union Labor Life Ins. Co. v Pireno (1982, US) 73 L Ed 2d 647, 1982-2 CCH Trade Cases ¶ 64802.]

§ 5. Attorneys and attorneys' fees

The Supreme Court decided a number of cases involving issues relating to attorney discipline and attorneys' fees during its 1981–82 term. In one case involving attorney disciplinary proceedings, the court held that a federal court should abstain from considering a challenge to the constitutionality of attorney disciplinary rules that were the subject of a pending state disciplinary proceeding within the jurisdiction of a state's highest court, where (1) the state court considered its bar disciplinary proceedings as judicial in nature, (2) the state had an extremely important interest in maintaining and assuring the professional conduct of the attorneys it licensed, especially those involved in the administration of criminal justice, (3) the attorney had an opportunity to raise and have timely decided by a competent state tribunal the federal issues involved, and (4) no bad faith, harassment, or other exceptional circumstances dictated to the contrary. [Middlesex County Ethics Committee v Garden State Bar Asso. (1982, US) 73 L Ed 2d 116, 102 S Ct 2515.]

In the case of an attorney who violated a state disciplinary rule regulating the advertising by attorneys by publishing advertisements which listed areas of practice in language other than that specified in the rule and who had, in contravention of the rule, listed courts in which he was admitted to practice and had mailed announcement cards to persons other than those individuals permitted by the rule, the court held that, as applied to the attorney, the rule's restrictions could not be sustained since (1) the listings of areas of practice published by the attorney were not shown to be misleading and the state suggested no substantial interest promoted by the rule's restrictions limiting attorneys to specify listings in areas of practice, (2) the listing of jurisdictions in which the lawyer had obtained a license to practice was not misleading on its face and the state had suggested no substantial interest in barring this information, and (3) there was no indication that, with respect to announcement cards, an inability to supervise was the reason the state restricted the potential audience of the cards nor was it clear that a prohibition was the only solution to the problem, there being no indication of a failed effort to proceed along a less restrictive path. [Re J. (1982, US) 71 L Ed 2d 64, 102 S Ct 929.]

The court also considered two cases relating to attorneys' fees and held, in one case, that a post-judgment request for an award of attorneys' fees under the Civil Rights Attorneys' Fees Awards Act (42 USCS § 1988) is not a "motion to alter or amend the judgment" subject to the timeliness standard of Rule 59(e) of the Federal Rules of Civil Procedure which would have required that such a motion be served not later than 10 days after entry of the judgment. [White v New Hampshire Dept. of Employment Secur. (1982, US) 71 L Ed 2d 325, 102 S Ct 1162, 33 FR Serv 2d 829]. Additionally, the court held that attorneys' fees incurred during proceedings before the National Labor Relations Board are not a proper element of damages under § 303(b) of the Labor Management Relations Act (29 USCS § 187(b)). [Summit Valley Industries v United Brotherhood of Carpenters & Joiners (1982, US) 72 L Ed 2d 511, 102 S Ct 2112, 110 BNA LRRM 2441, 94 CCH LC ¶ 13533.]

§ 6. Bankruptcy

In addition to the significant decision involving the constitutionality of the Bankruptcy Reform Act's conferring of Art III judicial power upon bankruptcy judges which is discussed in § 2, supra (see Northern Pipeline Constr. Co. v Marathon Pipe Line Co.

(1982, US) 73 L Ed 2d 598, 102 S Ct 2858, 9 BCD 67, 6 CBC2d 785, CCH Bankr L Rptr ¶ 68698), the court held that a petition seeking relief under Chapter XI of the Bankruptcy Act of 1898 (former 11 USCS §§ 701 et seq.) may not be dismissed in order to allow the debtor to file under Chapter XI of the Bankruptcy Code (11 USCS §§ 1101 et seq.), since (1) Rule 11-42(a) of the Rules of Bankruptcy Procedure provides no authority for such a procedure, the language of the rule contemplating a voluntary dismissal which results in an adjudication of the debtor's bankruptcy or one which revests title of all property in the debtor and removes it from the protection of the bankruptcy laws, and not contemplating a dismissal which neither declares the debtor bankrupt nor restores the creditors' rights against the debtor's property, but simply holds matters in abeyance while the debtor files its petition under a new law, and (2) the language of § 403(a) of the Bankruptcy Reform Act is unequivocal and makes no exception for petitions to be refiled under the Code, even if the refiling would not actually prejudice the creditors and even if consolidation of the debtor's petition with those filed under the Code by its subsidiaries and affiliate corporations would serve the best interest of the estate or would conserve judicial resources. [Central Trust Co. v Official Creditors' Committee of Geiger Enterprises, Inc. 454 US 354, 70 L Ed 2d 542, 102 S Ct 695, 8 BCD 623, 5 CBC2d 1085, CCH Bankr L Rptr ¶ 68476.]

For a case dealing with the constitutionality of specific legislation relating to a specific railroad reorganization, see Railway Labor Executives' Assn. v Gibbons (1982, US) 71 L Ed 2d 335, 102 S Ct

1169, 8 BCD 966, 6 CBC2d 125, CCH Bankr L Rptr ¶ 68557, reh den (US) 72 L Ed 2d 459, 102 S Ct 1997, infra § 43.

§ 7. Civil Rights

Two cases decided by the court during its 1981-82 term involved issues relating to school desegregation. The court held that a state initiative, drafted to terminate the use of mandatory busing for purposes of racial integration and to prohibit school boards from requiring any student to attend a school other than the one geographically nearest or next nearest to his home unless a student required a special educational program, or if the nearest, or next nearest school was overcrowded or unsafe, or if the school lacked necessary physical facilities, violated the equal protection clause. [Washington v Seattle School Dist. (1982, US) 73 L Ed 2d 896.] In the second case, the court held that an amendment to a state constitution which provided that state courts could not order mandatory pupil assignment or transportation unless a federal court would have been permitted under federal decisional law to do so to remedy a violation of the equal protection clause did not in itself violate the equal protection clause. [Crawford v Board of Education (1982, US) 73 L Ed 2d 948.]

The Supreme Court reaffirmed its earlier decisions and held that exhaustion of state administrative remedies is not a prerequisite to an action under 42 USCS § 1983 for damages or injunctive relief. [Patsy v Board of Regents (1982, US) 73 L Ed 2d 172, 102 S Ct 2557, 29 BNA FEP Cas 12, 29 CCH EPD ¶ 32821.]

Finally, it was held that a state statute requiring "peace officers" (including probation officers) to be

United States citizens was valid even as applied to lawfully admitted permanent resident aliens, probation officers sufficiently partaking of the sovereign's power to exercise coercive force over the individual that they may be required to be citizens. [Cabell v Chavez-Salido (1982) 454 US 432, 70 L Ed 2d 677, 102 S Ct 735, 27 BNA FEP Cas 1129, 27 CCH EPD ¶ 32310.]

For cases involving job discrimination claims under federal civil rights statutes, see § 30, infra. With regard to a civil rights action alleging misuse or abuse of a state law governing garnishment and prejudgment attachment procedures, see Lugar v Edmondson Oil Co. (1982, US) 73 L Ed 2d 482, 102 S Ct 2744, infra § 12. For a decision involving a request for injunctive relief under 42 USCS § 1983 in regard to the suspension of a student found on school premises while under the influence of alcohol, see Board of Education v McCluskey (1982, US) 73 L Ed 2d 1273, infra § 15. For a case involving standing under the Fair Housing Act of 1968 (42 USCS §§ 3601 et seq.) see Havens Realty Corp. v Coleman (1982, US) 71 L Ed 2d 214, 102 S Ct 1114, infra § 27. With respect to whether a public defender acted "under color of state law" within the meaning of 42 USCS § 1983, see Polk County v Dodson (1981) 454 US 312, 70 L Ed 2d 509, 102 S Ct 445, infra § 41. For a decision involving the availability of a remedy under 42 USCS § 1983 to redress the allegedly unconstitutional administration of a state tax system, see Fair Assessment in Real Estate Asso. v McNary (1981) 454 US 100, 70 L Ed 2d 271, 102 S Ct 177, infra § 51.

§ 8. Commodity regulation

In one case, the court held that a private party may maintain an action for damages caused by a violation of the Commodity Exchange Act (7 USCS §§ 1 et seq.), and that this included purchasers and sellers of future contracts asserting violation of the statutory prohibition against fraudulent and deceptive practices and of the provisions designed to prevent price manipulation. [Merrill Lynch, Pierce, Fenner & Smith, Inc. v Curran (1982, US) 72 L Ed 2d 182, 102 S Ct 1825.]

§ 9. Confessions and incriminating statements

The court held that a defendant's confession should have been suppressed as the fruit of an illegal arrest, where (1) it was obtained through custodial interrogation after an illegal arrest, and (2) the defendant was arrested without probable cause and confessed thereafter without any meaningful intervening event. [Taylor v Alabama (1982, US) 73 L Ed 2d 314, 102 S Ct 2664.]

§ 10. Conflict of laws

The court held that the judgment of an Indiana state court in rehabilitation proceedings brought against an Indiana insurer—in which a North Carolina insurance guaranty association holding a $100,-000 deposit required by North Carolina law from the Indiana insurer, for the benefit of North Carolina policyholders, intervened—should have been treated, under the full faith and credit clause (Art IV, § 1), as res judicata in a subsequent action in a North Carolina state court brought by the guaranty association, seeking a declaratory judgment that the association was entitled to use the deposit to fulfill prerehabilitation contractual obligations to North Carolina policyholders which had been settled in the Indiana rehabilitation proceeding. [Underwriters

Nat. Assur. Co. v North Carolina Life & Acci. & Health Ins. Guaranty Assn. (1982, US) 71 L Ed 2d 558, 102 S Ct 1357.]

§ 11. Counsel

In the one case decided by the court during its 1981-82 term involving an individual's right to counsel under the Federal Constitution, it was held that a defendant was not deprived of the effective assistance of counsel by his retained counsel's failure to file on time an application for certiorari in the state's highest court, since the defendant had no absolute right to appeal his conviction to that court and thus had no constitutional right to counsel to pursue that appeal. [Wainwright v Torna (1982, US) 71 L Ed 2d 475, 102 S Ct 1300.]

§ 12. Creditors' rights

The court held that insofar as a debtor alleged only misuse or abuse of a state law governing garnishment and prejudgment attachment procedures by a private creditor, he did not state a cause of action under 42 USCS § 1983, since the challenged conduct was not under color of state law; however, where the debtor's complaint challenged a state attachment statute as being procedurally defective under the due process clause, he presented a valid cause of action under § 1983 since the statutory scheme was a product of state action, and the private party's joint participation with state officials in the seizure of disputed property was sufficient to characterize that party as a "state actor" for purposes of the Fourteenth Amendment. [Lugar v Edmondson Oil Co. (1982, US) 73 L Ed 2d 482, 102 S Ct 2744.]

§ 13. Criminal law and procedure

Two cases involving the circumstances surrounding arrests were decided by the court during the term. The court held that a private citizen had no judicially cognizable right to prevent state officials from presenting information, through intervention of a state solicitor, that would assist a magistrate in determining whether to issue an arrest warrant. [Leeke v Timmerman (1981) 454 US 83, 70 L Ed 2d 65, 102 S Ct 69, reh den (US) 71 L Ed 2d 322, 102 S Ct 1041.] It was also held that the decision in Payton v New York (1980) 445 US 573, 63 L Ed 2d 639, 100 S Ct 1371, in which the Fourth Amendment was held to prohibit the police from making a warrantless and nonconsensual entry into a suspect's home to make a routine felony arrest, would be applied retroactively to a defendant whose case was pending on direct appeal when Payton v New York was decided. [United States v Johnson (1982, US) 73 L Ed 2d 202, 102 S Ct 2579.]

The court, in a highly publicized decision, held that the period in excess of 4 years between the dismissal of military charges against a defendant and his subsequent indictment on civilian federal criminal charges arising from events during his tenure in the military should not be considered in determining whether delay in bringing the defendant to trial violated his rights under the speedy trial clause of the Sixth Amendment. [United States v MacDonald (1982) 456 US 1, 71 L Ed 2d 696, 102 S Ct 1497.]

In a case where, during a trial, a juror submitted an employment application to the district attorney's office and the prosecutors in the case, upon being informed of the application, withheld this fact from the trial court and defense counsel until after the trial, the court held that the defendant was not entitled to have the verdict set aside on the ground that he was denied due process of law either by virtue of "implied" juror bias, or because of prosecutorial misconduct, since (1) the posttrial hearing in which the defendant was permitted to prove the juror's "actual" bias was sufficient to decide allegations of juror partiality, and neither the District Court nor the Federal Court of Appeals took issue with the findings of the trial judge, and (2) the prosecutors' failure to disclose a juror's job application, although requiring a posttrial hearing on juror bias, did not deprive the defendant of the fair trial guaranteed by the due process clause. [Smith v Phillips (1982, US) 71 L Ed 2d 78, 102 S Ct 940.]

The court also held that in the absence of the sort of affirmative assurances concerning a suspect's silence embodied in the Miranda warnings, a state does not violate due process of law by permitting cross-examination of a criminal defendant as to postarrest silence when a defendant chooses to take the stand, and that a state is entitled in such situations to leave to the judge and jury, under its own rules of evidence, the resolution of the extent to which postarrest silence may be deemed to impeach a criminal defendant's own testimony. [Fletcher v Weir (1982, US) 71 L Ed 2d 490, 102 S Ct 1309, on remand (CA6 Ky) 680 F2d 437.]

The court held that a state statute which precluded jury instructions on lesser included offenses in capital murder cases did not prejudice a defendant whose own evidence at trial negated the possibility that a lesser included offense instruction might have been warranted. [Hopper v Evans (1982, US) 72 L Ed 2d 367, 102 S Ct 2049.]

The Supreme Court decided two cases relating to double jeopardy during its 1981–82 term. The court held that where a state appellate court's reversal of a murder and rape conviction in a jury trial was based on the weight of the evidence, a retrial would not be barred by the double jeopardy clause of the Fifth and Fourteenth Amendments, since a reversal based on the weight of evidence, unlike a reversal based on insufficient evidence, did not mean that acquittal was the only proper verdict. [Tibbs v Florida (1982, US) 72 L Ed 2d 652, 102 S Ct 2211.] The court also held that a criminal defendant who successfully moved for a mistrial because of prosecutorial or judicial misconduct may not invoke the bar of the double jeopardy clause against a second trial except in those cases in which the prosecutorial or judicial conduct giving rise to the successful motion for mistrial was intended to provoke the defendant into moving for a mistrial. [Oregon v Kennedy (1982, US) 72 L Ed 2d 416, 102 S Ct 2083.]

In another case discussing allegations of prosecutorial misconduct, the court held that a presumption of prosecutorial vindictiveness was not warranted in a case in which a criminal defendant decided not to plead guilty to misdemeanor charges and requested a trial by jury, whereupon the defendant was indicted and convicted on a felony charge arising out of the same facts as the misdemeanor charges, and that absent such a presumption no violation of the due process clause was established. The presumption of an improper vindictive motive, the court held is applicable only where reasonable likelihood of vindictiveness exists, a change in the prosecutor's charging decision made before trial being less likely to be improperly motivated than such a decision made after an initial trial, the mere fact that the defendant refused to plead guilty and force the government to prove its case being insufficient to warrant a presumption that subsequent changes in the charging decision were vindictive, and the fact that the defendant requested a jury trial not compelling a special presumption of prosecutorial vindictiveness. [United States v Goodwin (1982, US) 73 L Ed 2d 74, 102 S Ct 2485.]

In a case involving substantive criminal law, it was held that the depositing of "bad checks" into federally insured banks as part of a "check kiting" scheme was not proscribed by 18 USCS § 1014 since the action of depositing a "bad check" did not technically involve the making of a false statement as to the value of any land, property, or security which was necessary for conviction under 18 USCS § 1014. [Williams v United States (1982, US) 73 L Ed 2d 767.]

In a case concerning prosecution for knowingly transporting an illegal alien in violation of 8 USCS § 1324(a)(2), the court held that no violation of either the Fifth Amendment right to due process or the Sixth Amendment right to compulsory process for obtaining witnesses occurred by the deportation of other illegal aliens present at the time the offense occurred since no evidence was presented by the defendant to show that the testimony of these witnesses would have been both material and favorable to the defense. [United States v Valenzuela-Bernal (1982, US) 73 L Ed 2d 1193.]

Finally, it was held that 18 USCS § 2314, which prohibits the transportation in interstate commerce of forged securities, knowing them to be forged, does not require proof that the securities were forged before being taken across state lines, and therefore, in a prosecution for violation of § 2314, a Federal District Court's jury instructions to the effect that in order to convict the jury had to find that the defendant transported the securities in a forged condition in "interstate commerce," but that such transportation could take place entirely within one state if it was a "continuation of movement that began out of state," were correct. [McElroy v United States (1982, US) 71 L Ed 2d 522, 102 S Ct 1332.]

For cases involving criminal punishment and sentencing, see § 14, infra. For cases involving the grant of the writ of habeas corpus, see § 25, infra.

§ 14. Criminal punishment and sentencing

The court considered two cases dealing with the death penalty during the 1981–82 term. The court held that a death sentence imposed on a 16 year old who was convicted of first-degree murder after being tried as an adult must be vacated as it was imposed without the type of individualized consideration of mitigating factors required by the Eighth and Fourteenth Amendments in capital cases, where the trial judge refused, as a matter of law, to consider in mitigation the substantial evidence which the defendant proffered of a turbulent family history, of beatings by a harsh father, and of serious emotional disturbance. [Eddings v Oklahoma (1982, US) 71 L Ed 2d 1, 102 S Ct 869.] It was also held that the imposition of the death penalty upon a person who aided and abetted in the commission of a felony in which a murder occurred but who did not aid in the killing or attempt or intend to take a life himself was inconsistent with the Eighth and

Fourteenth Amendments. [Enmund v Florida (1982, US) 73 L Ed 2d 1140.]

In the case of a sentence imposed by a state jury of 40 years imprisonment for the two crimes of possession with intent to distribute and distribution of marijuana, the court held that the sentence was not so grossly disproportionate to the crime that it violated the ban on cruel and unusual punishment of the Eighth and Fourteenth Amendments even though the case involved possession of less than 9 ounces of marijuana, since the state statutes under which conviction was obtained authorized prison terms of not less than 5, and no more than 40, years for each of the offenses. [Hutto v Davis (1982) 454 US 370, 70 L Ed 2d 556, 102 S Ct 703, reh den (US) 72 L Ed 2d 156, 102 S Ct 1742.]

Finally, in a case relating to parole rescission, it was held that the rescission without hearing of a prisoner's parole by the parole authority did not violate the prisoner's right to due process of law under the Fourteenth Amendment, neither the state law relating to parole nor the expectation resulting from the notification given to the prisoner that a parole release had been ordered in his case being sufficient to create a liberty interest within the meaning of the Amendment. [Jago v Van Curen (1981) 454 US 14, 70 L Ed 2d 13, 102 S Ct 31.]

For a decision involving sentencing under the Youth Corrections Act (18 USCS § 5010(c)), see Ralston v Robinson (1981) 454 US 201, 70 L Ed 2d 345, 102 S Ct 233, reh den (US) 71 L Ed 2d 472, 102 S Ct 1293, infra § 31.

§ 15. Education and schools

In addition to the significant decisions involving the rights of illegal aliens' children to public educa-

tion [Plyler v Doe (1982, US) 72 L Ed 2d 786, 102 S
Ct 2382] and school board censorship of high
school and junior high school libraries [Board of
Education v Pico (1982, US) 73 L Ed 2d 435, 102 S
Ct 2799] which are discussed in § 2, supra, the
Supreme Court rendered several other noteworthy
decisions in the education area. The court held that
a state university's policy of categorically denying
domiciled nonimmigrant aliens who held G-4 visas
(visas issued to nonimmigrant aliens who are officers or employees of certain international organizations and to members of their immediate families)
in-state status under which preferential treatment
was given to domiciled citizens and immigrant aliens
for purposes of tuition and fees was invalid under
the supremacy clause. [Toll v Moreno (1982) 458
US 1, 73 L Ed 2d 563.]

The court also decided two cases relating to relief
under 42 USCS § 1983 sought by students and
school employees. In a case requesting injunctive
relief under § 1983 for suspension of a student
found on school premises while under the influence
of alcohol, it was held that the District Court and
Court of Appeals erred in replacing the school
board's construction of a board regulation requiring
suspension of any student found on school premises
under the influence of "drugs" as including suspension of students under the influence of alcohol with
their own notion as to the definition of "drugs"
intended by the board regulation. [Board of Education v McCluskey (1982, US) 73 L Ed 2d 1273.] The
court further held that receipt of public funds by a
privately operated school did not make the school's
employee discharge decisions actions under color of
state law subject to claims for relief under 42 USCS

§ 1983 where discharge decisions were not compelled or influenced by any state regulation. [Rendell-Baker v Kohn (1982, US) 73 L Ed 2d 418, 102 S Ct 2764.]

§ 16. Elections and voting rights

Several cases involving voting rights issues in elections were decided by the court during the term. With regard to the Voting Rights Act of 1965 (42 USCS §§ 1973 et seq.), the court held that a state court has the power to decide whether § 5 of the Act (42 USCS § 1973c)—which requires a declaratory judgment by the United States District Court for the District of Columbia or preclearance from the Attorney General of the United States before changes in voting procedures may be implemented —applies to a change in local election procedures. [Hathorn v Lovorn (1982, US) 72 L Ed 2d 824, 102 S Ct 2421.] It was also held that a county's letter to the United States Attorney General which informed him that a referendum had approved an at-large method of election for the county's council was a request for reconsideration of the Attorney General's previous objection to that method and not a new effort to obtain preclearance for that method under § 5 of the Act. [Blanding v Du Bose (1982) 454 US 393, 70 L Ed 2d 576, 102 S Ct 715.]

With regard to reapportionment, the court held that a Federal District Court could not devise its own districts for unchallenged portions of a state's reapportionment plan, but rather had to defer to the legislative judgments the plan reflected in the absence of a finding that the plan offended either the United States Constitution or the Voting Rights Act (42 USCS §§ 1973 et seq.). [Upham v Seamon

(1982, US) 71 L Ed 2d 725, 102 S Ct 1518, reh den (US) 72 L Ed 2d 461, 102 S Ct 2001.]

With regard to the Federal Election Campaign Act (2 USCS §§ 431 et seq.), the court decided two cases during the term. The court held that § 441a(d)(3) of the Act (2 USCS § 441a(d)(3)) did not foreclose a state committee of a political party from designating the national senatorial campaign committee of that party as its agent for the purpose of making expenditures allowed by the Act, and accordingly, the Federal Election Commission acted within the authority vested in it by Congress when it determined to permit such agency agreements. [Federal Election Com. v Democratic Senatorial Campaign Committee (1981) 454 US 27, 70 L Ed 2d 23, 102 S Ct 38.] The court also held that trade associations and political action committees could not bring an expedited challenge to the validity of a section of the Act under § 310(a) of the Act (2 USCS § 437h(a)) as only parties meeting the express requirements of § 310(a) may invoke its procedures, there being no showing of such "clear expression" or "clear evidence" of congressional intent to make the procedures available to categories of plaintiffs other than those listed in § 310(a). [Bread Political Action Committee v Federal Election Com. (1982, US) 71 L Ed 2d 432, 102 S Ct 1235].

Finally, the court decided a number of cases relating to the validity of state and local election laws. In regard to a local government's ordinance placing a limit of $250 on contributions to committees formed to support or oppose ballot measures submitted to a popular vote but no limit on individuals acting alone in regard to such measures, the court held that the restraint imposed on the right of association and in turn on individual and collective rights of expression contravened both the right of association and the speech guarantees of the First Amendment. [Citizens against Rent Control/Coalition for Fair Housing v Berkeley (1981) 454 US 290, 70 L Ed 2d 492, 102 S Ct 434.] In a case that received wide media attention, the court held that a provision of a state statute prohibiting a candidate for office from offering material benefits to voters in consideration for their votes violated the First Amendment's protection of freedom of speech when applied so as to void an election for county commissioner based on one candidate's promise, later retracted, that committed him to lower commissioners' salaries if elected. [Brown v Hartlage (1982, US) 71 L Ed 2d 732, 102 S Ct 1523.] The court also held that a Puerto Rico statute which vested in a political party the initial authority to appoint an interim replacement for one of its members who vacated a position as a district senator or representative did not violate the United States Constitution. [Rodriguez v Popular Democratic Party (1982) 457 US 1, 72 L Ed 2d 628, 102 S Ct 2194.] The court also held that a Federal District Court applied the proper legal standard in its determination that an at-large system of election of a county board of commissioners violated the Fourteenth Amendment where, although the policy behind an at-large electoral system was "neutral in origin," it was being maintained for invidious purposes to prevent a substantial body of persons from effectively participating in the political process by insuring vote dilution, and that the relief provided by the District Court—division of counties into single-member districts—was proper. [Rogers v Lodge (1982, US) 73 L Ed 2d 1012.] Finally, the court held that a provision in a state constitution, interpreted by the state court to mean that a holder of public office must complete his current term, if it overlaps the legislature's term, before he may be eligible to serve in the state legislature, and another constitutional provision, which provides that if holders of certain state or county offices whose unexpired term exceeds one year become candidates for any other state or federal office, they are deemed to have automatically resigned from the office then held, did not violate the First Amendment. [Clements v Fashing (1982, US) 73 L Ed 2d 508, 102 S Ct 2836.]

§ 17. Eminent domain

The court held that a state statute providing that a landlord must permit a cable television company to install its equipment upon his property and may not demand payment from the company in excess of the amount determined by a state commission to be reasonable worked a taking of a portion of the landlord's property for which she was entitled to just compensation under the Fifth Amendment, as made applicable to the states by the Fourteenth Amendment. [Loretto v Teleprompter Manhattan CATV Corp. (1982, US) 73 L Ed 2d 868.]

§ 18. Environmental protection

During the term, the court decided two cases involving environmental issues. The court held that § 102(2)(C) of the National Environmental Policy Act of 1969 (42 USCS § 4332(2)(C)), which requires all federal agencies, "to the fullest extent possible," to include an Environmental Impact Statement in proposals for major federal actions significantly affecting the environment, did not require the Navy to prepare and release to the public a "Hypothetical

Environmental Impact Statement" with respect to its construction of a facility capable of storing nuclear weapons since the Act's public disclosure requirements were expressly governed by the Freedom of Information Act (5 USCS § 552), so that the public's interest in insuring that federal agencies comply with the Act must give way to the government's need to preserve military secrets. [Weinberger v Catholic Action of Hawaii/Peace Education Project (1981) 454 US 139, 70 L Ed 2d 298, 102 S Ct 197.] The court also held that the Federal Water Pollution Control Act (33 USCS §§ 1251 et seq.) did not require a Federal District Court to enjoin immediately all discharges that did not comply with the Act's permit requirements, but rather permitted a District Court to order that relief it considered necessary to secure prompt compliance with the Act, such relief including, but not being limited to, an order of immediate cessation. [Weinberger v Romero-Barcelo (1982, US) 72 L Ed 2d 91, 102 S Ct 1798.]

§ 19. Federal jurisdiction

The Supreme Court dismissed for want of jurisdiction an appeal from the decision of a state's highest court invalidating a university regulation prohibiting the distribution of materials on the university campus by members of the public, the appeal being brought by the state and the university, where the university's amendment of its rules rendered its appeal moot and with regard to the state, the state's jurisdictional statement urging the Supreme Court to review the case but taking no position on the merits did not provide a sound jurisdictional basis for undertaking to decide the constitutional issues presented. [Princeton University v Schmid (1982, US) 70 L Ed 2d 855, 102 S Ct 867.]

With regard to appellate jurisdiction, it was held that a Federal Court of Appeals lacked jurisdiction of an appeal from the decision of a Federal District Court holding unconstitutional the application of the Fair Labor Standards Act (29 USCS §§ 201 et seq.) to employees of a mental health facility operated by a county association for retarded citizens, the right under 28 USCS § 1252 of a party to pursue a direct appeal to the Supreme Court from a federal court order holding a federal statute unconstitutional serving to deprive the Court of Appeals of jurisdiction and 28 USCS § 1291 providing that "[t]he Courts of Appeals shall have jurisdiction of appeals from all final decisions of the District Courts of the United States . . . except where direct review may be had in the Supreme Court." [Donovan v Richland County Asso. for Retarded Citizens (1982) 454 US 389, 70 L Ed 2d 570, 102 S Ct 713.] Additionally, it was held that a Federal Court of Appeals was without jurisdiction to review a Federal District Court's interlocutory order refusing to dismiss an indictment on grounds of prosecutorial vindictiveness. [United States v Hollywood Motor Car Co. (1982, US) 73 L Ed 2d 754.]

The court held that Rule 37(b)(2)(A) of the Federal Rules of Civil Procedure—providing that a Federal District Court, as a sanction for failure to comply with a discovery order, may order that the matters regarding which the discovery order was made or any other designated facts shall be taken to be established for the purposes of the action in accordance with the claim of the party obtaining the order—did not violate due process when applied to enable a Federal District Court, as a sanction for failure to comply with a discovery order directed at establishing jurisdictional facts, to proceed on the basis that personal jurisdiction over the recalcitrant party had been established. [Insurance Corp. of Ireland, Ltd. v Compagnie des Bauxites de Guinea (1982, US) 72 L Ed 2d 492, 102 S Ct 2099.]

The court held that it was an abuse of discretion for a Federal Court of Appeals to decline to resolve a pendent state law claim, in an action alleging that a school board affirmative action plan for contractors violated both the United States Constitution and state law, since if the affirmative action plan was invalid under state law, the Court of Appeals need not have reached the federal constitutional issue. [Schmidt v Oakland Unified School Dist. (1982, US) 73 L Ed 2d 245, 102 S Ct 2612.]

Finally, the court held that it had jurisdiction under 28 USCS § 1252 to hear an appeal from a Federal District Court which involved the constitutionality of a provision of the Federal Unemployment Tax Act (26 USCS § 3309(b)), exempting from mandatory state coverage employees of church organizations, but that the District Court was deprived of jurisdiction to grant injunctive or declaratory relief to block the collection of state unemployment taxes from such organizations by virtue of the Tax Injunction Act (28 USCS § 1341), since the taxpayers had a plain, speedy and efficient state court remedy and, accordingly, the Supreme Court could not reach the taxpayers' constitutional claims, because no federal trial court had jurisdiction of the case. [California v Grace Brethren Church (1982, US) 73 L Ed 2d 93, 102 S Ct 2498.]

For a case relating to federal courts' jurisdiction over a civil action brought by a former military exchange employee, see Army & Air Force Exchange Service v Sheehan (1982, US) 72 L Ed 2d 520, 102 S Ct 2118, infra § 36.

§ 20. Food, drugs, and cosmetics

The court held that on review of a Federal District Court's finding that generic drug manufacturers were not vicariously liable for infringement of a trademark by pharmacists of a trademarked drug where the pharmacists dispensed the generic drug under the trademark, the Federal Court of Appeals erred in setting aside findings of fact that were not clearly erroneous. [Inwood Laboratories, Inc. v Ives Laboratories, Inc. (1982, US) 72 L Ed 2d 606, 102 S Ct 2182, 214 USPQ 1.]

§ 21. Forum non conveniens

In a wrongful death action brought by a representative of the estates of several Scottish citizens and residents who were killed in an airplane crash in Scotland, against the United States manufacturers of the airplane and of its propellers, it was held that (1) the plaintiffs may not defeat a motion to dismiss on the ground of forum non conveniens merely by showing that the substantive law that would be applied in the alternative forum was less favorable to the plaintiffs than that of the chosen forum, and (2) the Federal District Court did not abuse its discretion in weighing the private and public interests and granting the defendants' motion to dismiss in making the forum non conveniens determination that Scotland was the appropriate forum. [Piper Aircraft Co. v Reyno (1981) 454 US 235, 70 L Ed 2d 419, 102 S Ct 252, reh den (US) 71 L Ed 2d 474, 102 S Ct 1296.]

§ 22. Freedom of Information Act

During its 1981–82 term, the court handed down three decisions construing provisions of the Freedom of Information Act (5 USCS § 552). The court held that lists of addresses collected and utilized by the Bureau of the Census were not subject to disclosure under the Act or the discovery provisions of the Federal Rules of Civil Procedure. [Baldrige v Shapiro (1982, US) 71 L Ed 2d 199, 102 S Ct 1103, 33 FR Serv 2d 835.]

The court also held that a newspaper's request filed with the Department of State for documents indicating whether certain Iranian nationals held valid United States passports satisfied the "similar files" requirement of Exemption 6 of the Freedom of Information Act (5 USCS § 552(b)(6))—providing that the Act's disclosure requirements do not apply to "personnel and medical files and similar files the disclosure of which would constitute an unwarranted invasion of personal privacy,"—and therefore the State Department's denial of the request should have been sustained upon a showing by the government that release of the information constituted a clearly unwarranted invasion of personal privacy, the phrase "similar files" not being limited to files containing "intimate details" and "highly personal" information. [United States Dept. of State v Washington Post Co. (1982, US) 72 L Ed 2d 358, 102 S Ct 1957.]

Finally, the court held that information initially contained in a record made for law enforcement purposes continues to meet the official requirements of Exemption 7(C) of the Act (5 USCS § 552(b)(7)(C))—which exempts from disclosure "investigatory records compiled for law-enforcement purposes" when the release of such records would "constitute an unwarranted invasion of personal privacy"—when the recorded information is reproduced or summarized in a new document prepared for a non-law-enforcement purpose. [Federal Bureau of Investigation v Abramson (1982, US) 72 L Ed 2d 376, 102 S Ct 2054.]

§ 23. Freedom of religion

During the term, the court decided a number of cases involving freedom of religion issues. The court held that a state university's regulation prohibiting the use of the university buildings or grounds for purposes of religious worship or religious teaching violated the fundamental principle under the First Amendment that a state regulation of speech should be content-neutral, the university being required to show that its regulation was necessary to serve a compelling state interest and that it was narrowly drawn to achieve that end, it being permissible to characterize the university's interest in complying with its constitutional obligations under the establishment clause of the First Amendment as compelling, but an "equal access" policy under which university facilities were open to groups and speakers of all kinds not being incompatible with that clause, and the state's interest in achieving greater separation of church and state than is already insured under the establishment clause not being sufficiently "compelling" to justify content-based discrimination against religious speech of the student group in question. [Widmar v Vincent (1981) 454 US 263, 70 L Ed 2d 440, 102 S Ct 269.]

Additionally, the court held that the imposition of social security taxes was not unconstitutional as applied to individuals who objected on religious grounds to receipt of public insurance benefits and to payment of taxes to support public insurance funds. [United States v Lee (1982, US) 71 L Ed 2d 127, 102 S Ct 1051, 82-1 USTC ¶ 9205.]

Finally, the court held that a state charitable contribution statute exempting only those religious organizations which receive more than 50 percent of their total contributions from members or affiliated organizations who are exempt from its registration and reporting requirements violated the establishment clause of the First Amendment, in that it set up precisely the sort of official denominational preference forbidden by that Amendment. [Larson v Valente (1982, US) 72 L Ed 2d 33, 102 S Ct 1673, reh den (US) 73 L Ed 2d 1323, 102 S Ct 2916.]

§ 24. Freedom of speech

In addition to the significant decision involving local school board censorship of books in high school and junior high school libraries which is discussed in § 2, supra (see Board of Education v Pico (1982, US) 73 L Ed 2d 435, 102 S Ct 2799), the court decided a number of other cases relating to freedom of speech and associated First Amendment rights. In another highly publicized case, the court held that the nonviolent elements of a boycott of merchants by the National Association for the Advancement of Colored People (NAACP) were entitled to First Amendment protection despite the fact that some individuals threatened violence or acted violently in connection with the boycott and that neither the NAACP as an organization nor individual members were liable in damages for the consequences of their nonviolent, protected activity.

NAACP v Claiborne Hardware Co. (1982, US) 73 L
Ed 2d 1215.]

The court decided two cases involving obscenity
in this term. It was held that a city, in a public
nuisance abatement action brought against a mo-
tion-picture theater, did not need to prove beyond a
reasonable doubt that the motion pictures at issue
were obscene, the choice of whether to require
proof beyond a reasonable doubt in an obscenity
case being solely a matter of state law and not a
requirement of the First and Fourteenth Amendments. [Cooper v Mitchell Bros' Santa Ana Theater
(1981) 454 US 90, 70 L Ed 2d 262, 102 S Ct 172,
reh den (US) 72 L Ed 2d 181, 102 S Ct 1779.] The
court also held that a state statute prohibiting persons from knowingly promoting a sexual performance by a child under the age of 16 by distributing
materials which depict such performance and which
statute defines "sexual performance" as any performance that includes sexual conduct by such a child
does not violate the First Amendment as applied to
the states through the Fourteenth Amendment.
[New York v Ferber (1982, US) 73 L Ed 2d 1113.]

Finally, the court held that a state statute, which
as construed by the state's highest court required
trial judges, at trials for specified sexual offenses
involving a victim under the age of 18, to exclude
the press and general public from the courtroom
during the testimony of that victim, violated the
First Amendment as applied to the states through
the Fourteenth Amendment, since the statute could
not be justified on the basis of either the state's
interest in protecting minor victims of sex crimes
from further trauma and embarrassment or its interest in encouraging such victims to come forward

lv

and testify in a truthful and credible manner. [Globe Newspaper Co. v Superior Court for County of Norfolk (1982, US) 73 L Ed 2d 248, 102 S Ct 2613.]

For a case involving the permissibility of the restrictions on First Amendment rights in a rule adopted by a state's highest court to regulate attorney advertising, see Re J. (1982, US) 71 L Ed 2d 64, 102 S Ct 929, supra § 5.

§ 25. Habeas corpus

During its 1981–82 term, the court handed down a number of decisions involving 28 USCS § 2254, the federal habeas corpus statute. The court held that a Federal Court of Appeals was obligated to dismiss a state prisoner's federal habeas corpus petition, since a claim of ineffective assistance of counsel in the petition had never been raised in state court or before the Federal District Court, there being no exception to the requirement of 28 USCS § 2254(b) that state remedies be exhausted for "clear violations" of a defendant's rights. [Duckworth v Serrano (1981) 454 US 1, 70 L Ed 2d 1, 102 S Ct 18.] The court also held that under 28 USCS § 2254(b) and (c), a Federal District Court must dismiss a petition for a writ of habeas corpus that contained any claims that had not been exhausted in the state courts, thereby leaving the prisoner with the choice of returning to state court to exhaust his claims or of amending or resubmitting the habeas petition to present only exhausted claims to the District Court, since such a total exhaustion rule promoted comity and not unreasonably impaired the prisoner's right to relief. [Rose v Lundy (1982, US) 71 L Ed 2d 379, 102 S Ct 1198.]

It was held that a Federal Court of Appeals erred when it issued a writ of habeas corpus requiring a

state trial court either to grant the prisoner a new
trial or to demonstrate by appropriate findings that
there was a rational basis for its seemingly facially
inconsistent verdicts, there being no federal requirement that a state trial judge explain his reasons for
acquitting a defendant in a state criminal trial, and
any error from the resting of such an acquittal on
an improper ground did not create a constitutional
defect in a guilty verdict which was supported by
sufficient evidence and which was the product of a
fair trial. [Harris v Rivera (1981) 454 US 339, 70 L
Ed 2d 530, 102 S Ct 460.] The court also held that
petitioners were barred from asserting in a federal
habeas corpus proceeding their constitutional
claims, which were forfeited before state courts
because of their failure to comply with the state's
contemporaneous objection rule. [Engle v Isaac
(1982, US) 71 L Ed 2d 783, 102 S Ct 1558, reh den
(US) 73 L Ed 2d 1296, 102 S Ct 2286.]

In regard to a collateral challenge brought under
28 USCS § 2255 to a criminal conviction for murder
based on the defendant's challenge, not made by
direct appeal or prior motion, to jury instructions, it
was held that the "plain error" standard of Rule
52(b) of the Federal Rules of Criminal Procedure
did not apply on a collateral challenge to a criminal
conviction brought under 28 USCS § 2255, the
proper standard for review of a motion under
§ 2255 for vacation of a sentence being the "cause
and actual prejudice" standard under which to obtain collateral relief based on trial errors to which
no contemporaneous objection was made, a convicted defendant must show both "cause" excusing
his procedural default, and "actual prejudice" resulting from the errors of which he complains, a

standard which the defendant failed to meet. [United States v Frady (1982, US) 71 L Ed 2d 816, 102 S Ct 1584, reh den (US) 73 L Ed 2d 1296, 102 S Ct 2287.]

Finally, the court held that 28 USCS § 2254(a), which requires a Federal District Court to entertain an application for a writ of habeas corpus on behalf of "a person in custody" pursuant to a state court judgment in alleged violation of the Federal Constitution, does not confer jurisdiction on federal courts to consider collateral challenges to state court judgments involuntarily terminating parental rights. [Lehman v Lycoming County Children's Services Agency (1982, US) 73 L Ed 2d 928.]

§ 26. Handicapped persons

The court held that the Education for All Handicapped Children Act of 1975 (20 USCS §§ 1401 et seq.) did not require the provision of a sign-language interpreter to a deaf student attending a public school where there was no evidence to support a conclusion that the child's educational program failed to meet the Act's requirement that a child be given a "free appropriate public education" since that requirement was met whenever the state provided personalized instruction with sufficient support services to permit the handicapped child to benefit educationally from that instruction, and it was not necessary for the state to maximize the potential of each handicapped child commensurate with the opportunity provided nonhandicapped children or to achieve strict equality of opportunity of service for handicapped and nonhandicapped children. [Board of Education v Rowley (1982, US) 73 L Ed 2d 690.]

§ 27. Housing

In addition to the significant decision involving
savings and loan associations which is discussed in
§ 2, supra [see Fidelity Federal Sav. & Loan Asso. v
de La Cuesta (1982, US) 73 L Ed 2d 664], the court
held that (1) a "tester"—an individual who, without
an intent to rent or purchase a home or apartment,
poses as a renter or purchaser—who had been the
object of a misrepresentation as to the availability of
a dwelling violative of § 804(d) of the Fair Housing
Act of 1968 (42 USCS § 3604(d)) had standing
under § 812 of the Act (42 USCS § 3612) to maintain a claim for damages, (2) a nonprofit open
housing organization had standing under § 812 to
challenge an apartment complex owner's racial
steering practices where the organization had alleged that the practices had perceptively impaired
its ability to provide counseling and referral services, and (3) a complaint filed by a plaintiff who,
pursuant to the Act, alleged not just one incident of
conduct violative of the Act, but an unlawful practice that continued into the Act's 180-day limitations
period (42 USCS § 3612(a)), was timely when it was
filed within 180 days of the last asserted occurrence
of that practice. [Havens Realty Corp. v Coleman
(1982, US) 71 L Ed 2d 214, 102 S Ct 1114.]

For a case involving a state statute permitting
service of process in public housing projects by
posting a summons in a conspicuous place on the
premises, see Greene v Lindsey (1982, US) 72 L Ed
2d 249, 102 S Ct 1874, infra § 47.

§ 28. Illegitimate children

In a case relating to a state statute providing that
a paternity suit to establish the natural father of an
illegitimate child must be brought before the child
is one year old, it was held that the statute denied

illegitimate children the equal protection of law, since the state—by not allowing illegitimate children a period for obtaining support sufficiently long in duration to present a reasonable opportunity for those with an interest in such children to assert claims on their behalf—had failed to provide the children with an adequate opportunity to obtain support, and the unrealistically short time limitation was not substantially related to the state's interest in avoiding the prosecution of stale or fraudulent claims. [Mills v Habluetzel (1982, US) 71 L Ed 2d 770, 102 S Ct 1549.]

§ 29. Interstate commerce

The court held that a common carrier's violation of the credit regulations issued by the Interstate Commerce Commission did not bar the carrier's collection of its lawful freight charge from a shipper-consignor since (1) the carrier established a prima facie case of the consignor's liability by proving that the consignor had failed to sign a "nonrecourse clause" in the applicable bills of lading, and (2) the carrier's violation of the credit regulations did not provide the consignor with an equitable, affirmative defense, such an interpretation being consistent with the statutory and regulatory silence on the issue, legislative and administrative history of the regulations, and public policy disfavoring judicial implication of such a defense. [Southern Pacific Transp. Co. v Commercial Metals Co. (1982, US) 72 L Ed 2d 114, 102 S Ct 1815.]

§ 30. Job discrimination

The Supreme Court decided numerous cases involving job discrimination issues during the 1981-82

term. In addition to the significant decision involving the construction of Title IX of the Education
Amendments of 1972 which is discussed in § 2,
supra [see North Haven Bd. of Education v Bell
(1982, US) 72 L Ed 2d 299, 102 S Ct 1912, 28 BNA
FEP Cas 1392, 28 CCH EPD ¶ 32675], the court
held that an employer charged with job discrimination in hiring under Title VII of the Civil Rights Act
of 1964 (42 USCS §§ 2000e et seq.) can toll the
accrual of backpay liability under § 706(g) of Title
VII (42 USCS § 2000e-5(g)) by unconditionally offering the claimant the job previously denied, and is
not required to offer seniority retroactive to the
date of the alleged discrimination and, absent special circumstances, the rejection of an employer's
unconditional job offer ends the accrual of potential
backpay liability. [Ford Motor Co. v EEOC (1982,
US) 73 L Ed 2d 721, 29 BNA FEP Cas 121, 29 CCH
EPD ¶ 32852.]

The court decided a number of cases relating to
procedures under job discrimination acts. The court
held that the right of a complainant to use a state
fair employment practices act's adjudicatory procedures was a species of property protected by the
due process clause of the Fourteenth Amendment,
and in a case where the state act deprived a complainant of that property interest by depriving the
state commission of jurisdiction to consider a charge
when the commission failed to comply with the state
act's requirement of convening a factfinding conference within 120 days after filing of the claim, the
claimant was entitled to have the commission consider the merits of his charge before deciding
whether to terminate his claim. [Logan v Zimmerman Brush Co. (1982, US) 71 L Ed 2d 265, 102 S
Ct 1148, 28 BNA FEP Cas 9, 28 CCH EPD

¶ 32433.] The court also held, in an employment discrimination class action under Title VII of the Civil Rights Act of 1964 (42 USCS §§ 2000e et seq.), that the filing of a timely charge of discrimination with the Equal Employment Opportunity Commission is not a jurisdictional prerequisite to suit in federal court, but a requirement that, like a statute of limitations, is subject to waiver, estoppel, and equitable tolling, and, accordingly, a Federal District Court had authority to award retroactive seniority to a subclass of flight attendants whose claims were not timely filed as well as those whose claims were within the prescribed time limits. [Zipes v Trans World Airlines, Inc. (1982, US) 71 L Ed 2d 234, 102 S Ct 1127, 28 BNA FEP Cas 1, 28 CCH EPD ¶ 32432, reh den (US) 72 L Ed 2d 461, 102 S Ct 2001, 28 CCH EPD ¶ 32613.] Additionally, it was held that the limitations period for filing a complaint in a Federal District Court alleging job discrimination violative of 42 USCS § 1983 in regard to a decision to terminate educational administrators began to run at the time they were notified of the decision and not at the time their appointments ended. [Chardon v Fernandez (1981) 454 US 6, 70 L Ed 2d 6, 102 S Ct 28, 27 BNA FEP Cas 57, 27 CCH EPD ¶ 32205, reh den (US) 71 L Ed 2d 322, 102 S Ct 1042.] Finally, the court held that, for purposes of permitting a Mexican-American employee to maintain a class action on behalf of Mexican-American job applicants, it was error for a Federal District Court to presume that the employee's claim was typical of other claims against the employer by other Mexican-American employees and applicants for employment, in the absence of any specific presentation identifying the questions of law or fact that were common to the claims of the

employee and of the members of the class he
sought to represent, the employee's complaint providing an insufficient basis for concluding that the
adjudication of his claim of discrimination in promotion would require the decision of any common
question concerning the failure of the employer to
hire more Mexican-Americans. [General Tel. Co. v
Falcon (1982, US) 72 L Ed 2d 740, 102 S Ct 2364,
28 BNA FEP Cas 1745, 29 CCH EPD ¶ 32781.]

The court also decided two cases relating to the
relationship between international agreements and
job discrimination statutes. The court held that the
word "treaty" as used in a provision of 5 USCS
§ 7201 note, prohibiting employment discrimination
against United States citizens in overseas military
bases unless permitted by treaty, includes executive
agreements, such as one which provided for the
preferential employment of Filipino citizens at
United States military bases in the Philippines, and
was not limited to those international agreements
concluded by the President with the advice and
consent of the Senate pursuant to the treaty clause
of the United States Constitution (Art II, § 2, cl 2).
[Weinberger v Rossi (1982, US) 71 L Ed 2d 715,
102 S Ct 1510, 28 BNA FEP Cas 585, 28 CCH EPD
¶ 32535.] The court also held that a New York
corporation which was a wholly owned subsidiary of
a Japanese general trading company was not a
company of Japan and thus was not protected under
Article VIII(1) of the Friendship, Commerce and
Navigation Treaty between the United States and
Japan, providing that companies of either country
be permitted to engage, within the territories of the
other party, certain specified types of employees of
their choice, and therefore that the corporation was

not exempt from the bar against sex discrimination in employment under Title VII. [Sumitomo Shoji America, Inc. v Avagliano (1982, US) 72 L Ed 2d 765, 102 S Ct 2374, 28 BNA FEP Cas 1753, 29 CCH EPD ¶ 32782.]

In a case where a state agency selected candidates for promotion to supervisor in such a way that the "bottom line" percentage of blacks selected was nondiscriminatory, the court held that the nondiscriminatory results of the employer's selection process did not preclude complaining employees from establishing a prima facie case of discrimination violative of Title VII of the Civil Rights Act of 1964 (42 USCS §§ 2000e et seq.) nor did it provide the employer with a defense in such a case. [Connecticut v Teal (1982, US) 73 L Ed 2d 130, 102 S Ct 2525, 29 BNA FEP Cas 1, 29 CCH EPD ¶ 32820.]

The court decided two cases relating to seniority systems. It held that § 703(h) of Title VII (42 USCS § 2000e-2(h))—which exempts "bona fide" seniority systems from Title VII prohibition against discriminatory practices even if they perpetuate past discrimination, so long as the systems were not framed with an intent to discriminate—is not limited in its application to only those seniority systems adopted prior to the effective date of the Act, and that an interpretation of § 703(h) which would construe the statute as protecting the post-Act application of a bona fide seniority system, but not the post-Act adoption of the seniority system or an aspect of a seniority system, is insupportable. [American Tobacco Co. v Patterson (1982, US) 71 L Ed 2d 748, 102 S Ct 1534, 28 BNA FEP Cas 713, 28 CCH EPD ¶ 32561.] The court also held that for purposes of § 703(h) of the Act, a discriminatory intent is required in order to invalidate a seniority system. [Pullman-Standard, Div. of Pullman, Inc. v Swint (1982, US) 72 L Ed 2d 66, 102 S Ct 1781, 28 BNA FEP Cas 1073, 28 CCH EPD ¶ 32619, 33 FR Serv 2d 1501.]

The court held that a Federal District Court was required under 28 USCS § 1738 to give preclusive effect to a state court's decision upholding a state administrative agency's rejection of an employment discrimination claim as meritless, where, under state law, the state court's determination precluded the bringing of any other action based upon the same grievance in state court and § 1738 required federal courts to afford the same full faith and credit to state court judgments that would apply in the state's own courts. [Kremer v Chemical Constr. Corp. (1982, US) 72 L Ed 2d 262, 102 S Ct 1883, 28 BNA FEP Cas 1412, 28 CCH EPD ¶ 32674.]

In a claim brought seeking redress for alleged racial discrimination in the operation of an exclusive hiring hall established in collective bargaining contracts between local unions and employers and in the operation of an apprenticeship program established by the unions and trade associations and administered by a joint committee, half of whose members were appointed by the unions and half by the trade associations, the court held that liability may not be imposed under 42 USCS § 1981 without proof of intentional discrimination and that employers and trade associations may not be held vicariously liable for the discriminatory conduct of unions. [General Bldg. Contractors Asso. v Pennsylvania (1982, US) 73 L Ed 2d 835, 29 BNA FEP Cas 139, 29 CCH EPD ¶ 32855.]

For a case deciding whether the receipt of public funds by a privately operated school made the school's employee discharge decisions actions under color of state law subject to claims for relief under 42 USCS § 1983, see Rendell-Baker v Kohn (1982, US) 73 L Ed 2d 418, 102 S Ct 2764, supra § 15. For a case involving the standing of the Commonwealth of Puerto Rico to maintain a suit alleging that there was discrimination against the hiring of Puerto Ricans, see Alfred L. Snapp & Sons, Inc. v Puerto Rico (1982, US) 73 L Ed 995, 29 CCH EPD ¶ 32867, infra § 50.

§ 31. Juvenile delinquents

The court held that the Youth Corrections Act (18 USCS §§ 5005 et seq.) did not require that a person who has been sentenced under the Act must receive treatment pursuant to the Act for the remainder of that sentence where a judge who imposed a subsequent adult sentence determined that such treatment would not benefit the offender further. [Ralston v Robinson (1981) 454 US 201, 70 L Ed 2d 345, 102 S Ct 233, reh den (US) 71 L Ed 2d 472, 102 S Ct 1293.]

§ 32. Labor

In keeping with its practice in recent terms, the court decided numerous cases involving labor law issues during the 1981–82 term. In cases relating to union elections, it was held that members of a union who had been discharged from their positions as business agents for the union after the union president won election over a candidate supported by the discharged members failed to establish a violation of the Labor-Management Reporting and Disclosure Act of 1959 (29 USCS §§ 401 et seq.), the Act being intended to protect rank-and-file union members, not the job security or tenure of union officers or employees as such. [Finnegan v Leu (1982, US) 72 L Ed 2d 239, 102 S Ct 1867, 110 BNA LRRM 2321, 93 CCH LC ¶ 13483.] In addition, the court held that a union "outsider rule" which prohibited candidates for union office from accepting campaign contributions from nonmembers and created a committee to enforce the rule, the committee's decisions being final and binding, violated neither § 101(a)(2) of the Labor-Management Reporting and Disclosure Act (29 USCS § 411(a)(2)), giving every union member the right to assemble freely with other members and to express at union meetings his views about union candidates or any business properly before that meeting, nor § 101(a)(4) of that Act (29 USCS § 411(a)(4)), providing that a union may not limit the rights of members to institute an action in any court or administrative agency. [United Steel Workers of America v Sadlowski (1982, US) 72 L Ed 2d 707, 102 S Ct 2339, 110 BNA LRRM 2609, 94 CCH LC ¶ 13561.]

In a case that received attention in the media, the court held that a refusal by an American longshoremen's union to unload cargo shipped from the Soviet Union, in protest against the Soviet invasion of Afghanistan, constituted an illegal secondary boycott prohibited by § 8(b)(4) of the National Labor Relations Act (29 USCS § 158(b)(4)), the union's activity being "in commerce" and thus within the scope of the Act § 8(b)(4)(B) containing no exception for "political" secondary boycotts, and the application of § 8(b)(4) not infringing upon the First Amendment rights of the union and its members. [International Longshoremen's Asso. v Allied International, Inc. (1982, US) 72 L Ed 2d 21, 102 S Ct

1656, 110 BNA LRRM 2001, 93 CCH LC ¶ 13383.] In another case arising out of the same boycott, the court held that (1) the plain language of the Norris-LaGuardia Act (29 USCS §§ 101 et seq.), prohibiting injunctions in "any" labor dispute and defining "labor dispute" to include "any controversy concerning terms or conditions of employment," does not except labor disputes having their genesis in political protests, and the existence of noneconomic motives does not make the Act inapplicable, and (2) a politically motivated work stoppage may not be enjoined pending an arbitrator's ruling on the legality of the strike under a no-strike clause of a collective bargaining agreement where the underlying dispute is not arbitrable under the agreement. [Jacksonville Bulk Terminals, Inc. v International Longshoreman's Asso. (1982, US) 73 L Ed 2d 327, 102 S Ct 2673, 110 BNA LRRM 2665, 94 CCH LC ¶ 13582.]

The Supreme Court held that there is a reasonable basis in law for the practice of the National Labor Relations Board of excluding from collective bargaining units only those "confidential" employees with a "labor nexus"—employees who act in a confidential capacity to persons formulating and effectuating management policies in the area of labor relations—while rejecting any claim that all employees with access to confidential information are beyond the reach of the definition of "employee" in § 2(3) of the National Labor Relations Act (29 USCS § 152(3)). [NLRB v Hendricks County Rural Electric Membership Corp. (1981) 454 US 170, 70 L Ed 2d 323, 102 S Ct 216, 108 BNA LRRM 3105, 92 CCH LC ¶ 13098.] Additionally, it was held that a bargaining impasse between a truck-

drivers' union and an association of employers did
not justify the unilateral withdrawal of one of the
association's members from the multiemployer bargaining unit formed by the association, and that the
withdrawing member's subsequent refusal to sign an
agreement which was concluded between the union
and the association was an unfair labor practice
violative of § 8(a)(1) and (5) of the National Labor
Relations Act (29 USCS § 158(a)(1) and (5)), even
though the union initiated a selective strike against
that member when the impasse was reached.
[Charles D. Bonanno Linen Service, Inc. v NLRB
(1982) 454 US 404, 70 L Ed 2d 656, 102 S Ct 720,
109 BNA LRRM 2257, 92 CCH LC ¶ 13127.] With
regard to the "construction industry proviso" to
§ 8(e) of the National Labor Relations Act (29 USCS
§ 158(e))—exempting certain agreements between a
union and an employer in the construction industry
from § 8(e)'s proscription of secondary agreements
between unions and employers—it was held that (1)
the proviso ordinarily shelters union signatory subcontracting clauses sought and negotiated in the
context of a collective bargaining relationship, even
when not limited in application to particular jobsites
and which both union and nonunion workers are
employed, and (2) a Federal Court of Appeals was
without jurisdiction to consider whether a union
violated § 8(b)(4)(A) of the Act (29 USCS
§ 158(b)(4)(A)) when it picketed to obtain a lawful
subcontracting clause since the issue was not raised
during the proceedings before the NLRB. [Woelke
& Romero Framing, Inc. v NLRB (1982, US) 72 L
Ed 2d 398, 102 S Ct 2071, 110 BNA LRRM 2377,
94 CCH LC ¶ 13504.] The court also held that
§ 13(c) of the Urban Mass Transportation Act of
1964 (49 USCS § 1609(c))—requiring a state or

local government to make arrangements to preserve transit workers' existing collective bargaining rights before that government may receive federal aid for the acquisition of a privately owned transit company —does not provide a transit workers' union with federal causes of action for alleged breaches of § 13(c) agreements or collective bargaining contracts, the legislative history indicating that Congress intended that such agreements be governed by state law in state courts. [Jackson Transit Authority v Amalgamated Transit Union (1982, US) 72 L Ed 2d 639, 102 S Ct 2202, 110 BNA LRRM 2513.] And, in a case relating to United States Government employees, the court held that the "two-step increase" rule relating to the effect of promotion to a higher grade on the pay of federal employees under 5 USCS § 5334(b) does not apply to promotions of employees from the prevailing rate wage system to the General Schedule System. [United States v Clark (1982) 454 US 555, 70 L Ed 2d 768, 102 S Ct 805.]

Finally, the court decided two cases relating to employee benefits. It was held that § 302(c)(5) of the Labor Management Relations Act (29 USCS 186(c)(5)) did not authorize federal courts to review for reasonableness the provisions of a collective bargaining agreement which allocated health benefits among potential beneficiaries of an employee benefit trust fund. [United Mine Workers of America Health & Retirement Funds v Robinson (1982, US) 71 L Ed 2d 419, 102 S Ct 1226, 109 BNA LRRM 2865, 93 CCH LC ¶ 13253.] The court also held that a coal producer which is a signatory to a collective bargaining agreement with a mine workers' union, containing a clause requiring producers to report their purchases of coal from producers not under union contract and to make contributions to the union's health and retirement funds, is entitled, in a federal court action by trustees of the funds to enforce the reporting and contribution requirements, to plead and have adjudicated its defense that the clause violates the antitrust prohibitions of §§ 1 and 2 of the Sherman Act (15 USCS §§ 1 and 2) and the "hot-cargo" provision of § 8(e) of the National Labor Relations Act (29 USCS § 158(e)), which forbids contracts between a union and an employer whereby the employer agrees to cease doing business with or to cease handling the products of another employer. [Kaiser Steel Corp. v Mullins (1982, US) 70 L Ed 2d 833, 102 S Ct 851, 109 BNA LRRM 2268, 92 CCH LC ¶ 13128, 1982-1 CCH Trade Cases ¶ 64455.]

For labor cases dealing with job discrimination, see § 30, supra. For a case dealing with whether attorneys' fees incurred during proceedings before the National Labor Relations Board were a proper element of damages under § 303(b) of the Labor Management Relations Act (29 USCS § 187(b)), see Summit Valley Industries v United Brotherhood of Carpenters & Joiners (1982, US) 72 L Ed 2d 511, 102 S Ct 2112, 110 BNA LRRM 2441, 94 CCH LC ¶ 13533, supra § 5. And for a case involving Congress' authority to regulate labor relations in a state-owned railroad engaged in interstate commerce, see United Transp. Union v Long Island R. R. Co. (1982, US) 71 L Ed 2d 547, 102 S Ct 1349, 109 BNA LRRM 3017, 93 CCH LC ¶ 13297, infra § 43.

§ 33. Licenses

The court decided two cases relating to the constitutionality of municipal licensing ordinances during the 1981–82 term. In a case that received considerable media attention, the court held that a village ordinance requiring a business to obtain a license if it sold any items "designed or marketed for use" with illegal drugs was not facially overbroad or vague but was reasonably clear in its application to a business which sold a variety of merchandise, including "roach clips" and specially designed pipes which could be used to smoke marijuana. [Hoffman Estates v Flipside, Hoffman Estates, Inc. (1982, US) 71 L Ed 2d 362, 102 S Ct 1186, reh den (US) 72 L Ed 2d 476, 102 S Ct 2023.] In the other case, it was held that a city's licensing ordinance governing coin-operated amusement establishments was not unconstitutionally vague, where it directed the city's chief of police to consider whether a license applicant had any "connections with criminal elements" and to make a recommendation to the city manager, but where the phrase "connections with criminal elements" was not the standard for approval or disapproval of the application, the Federal Constitution not precluding a city from giving vague or ambiguous directions to officials who are authorized to make investigations and recommendations. [Mesquite v Aladdin's Castle, Inc. (1982, US) 71 L Ed 2d 152, 102 S Ct 1070.]

§ 34. Limitation of actions

The court held that a state statute which tolls the limitation period of an action against a foreign corporation that "is not represented" in the state by anyone upon whom process may be served did not violate the equal protection clause of the Fourteenth Amendment. [G. D. Searle & Co. v Cohn (1982, US) 71 L Ed 2d 250, 102 S Ct 1137.]

§ 35. Mental retardation

It was held that a mentally retarded individual has liberty interests under the due process clause of the Fourteenth Amendment which requires a state to provide him minimally adequate or reasonable training to insure safety and freedom from undue restraint, and that a state is under a duty to provide him with such training as an appropriate professional would consider reasonable to insure him safety and to facilitate his ability to function free from bodily restraints. [Youngberg v Romeo (1982, US) 73 L Ed 2d 28, 102 S Ct 2452.]

§ 36. Military

The court held that a beneficiary designation by an insured military service member under a policy issued pursuant to the Servicemen's Group Life Insurance Act of 1965 (38 USCS §§ 765 et seq.) prevailed over a constructive trust imposed upon the policy proceeds by a state court decree, the person named in the beneficiary designation being the insured's spouse at the time of his death and the constructive trust having been imposed for the benefit of the children from an earlier marriage involving the insured and in furtherance of a divorce decree dissolving the earlier marriage. [Ridgway v Ridgway (1981) 454 US 46, 70 L Ed 2d 39, 102 S Ct 49.]

Additionally, the court held that a provision of the Tucker Act (28 USCS § 1346(a)(2)), which gives federal courts jurisdiction over certain suits against the United States based upon an express or implied contract, did not confer jurisdiction over a civil action for monetary damages brought by a former military exchange employee contesting the validity of his discharge, where (1) his employment with the exchange was the result of an appointment rather than an employment contract, and (2) the military exchange's regulations governing dismissal of employees did not specifically authorize money damage awards and thus did not create an implied in-fact contract. [Army & Air Force Exchange Service v Sheehan (1982, US) 72 L Ed 2d 520, 102 S Ct 2118.]

For a case discussing the effect of a previous military charge on the rights of speedy trial of a defendant in a subsequent civilian indictment based on the same events, see United States v MacDonald (1982) 456 US 1, 71 L Ed 2d 696, 102 S Ct 1497, supra § 13. For a case involving the Navy's obligation to prepare an environmental impact statement with respect to construction of a facility capable of storing nuclear weapons, see Weinberger v Catholic Action of Hawaii/Peace Education Project (1981) 454 US 139, 70 L Ed 2d 298, 102 S Ct 197, supra § 18.

§ 37. Natural resources

The Supreme Court held that the Outer Continental Shelf Lands Act Amendments of 1978 (43 USCS §§ 1331 et seq.) did not require the Secretary of the Interior to use non-cash-bonus bidding systems in leasing tracts on the outer continental shelf for the exploration for, and development of, mineral resources, and that the language of the Amendments (43 USCS §§ 1337, 1344) required experimentation with at least some of the new bidding systems specified in those Amendments but left the details to the Secretary's discretion. [Watt v Energy Action Educational Foundation (1981) 454 US 151, 70 L Ed 2d 309, 102 S Ct 205.]

In regard to a state statute which (1) provides that a severed mineral interest that is not used for a period of 20 years automatically lapses and reverts to the current surface owner of the property unless the mineral owner within the specified time files a statement of claim in the local county recorder's office and (2) contains an exception providing that if an owner of 10 or more mineral interests in the same county files a statement of claim that inadvertently omits some of the interests, the omitted interests may be preserved by a supplemental filing made within 60 days of receiving notice of the lapse, it was held that (1) the statute did not take property without just compensation in violation of the Fourteenth Amendment, (2) the statute did not unconstitutionally impair the obligation of contracts, (3) the statute did not extinguish the property rights of persons whose unused mineral interest lapsed upon the expiration of the specified time for filing a statement of claim in violation of their due process rights, and (4) the exception for owners of 10 or more interests did not violate the equal protection clause of the Fourteenth Amendment. [Texaco, Inc. v Short (1982) 454 US 516, 70 L Ed 2d 738, 102 S Ct 781.]

§ 38. Parent and child

The court held that a state statute permitting the state to terminate the rights of parents in a natural child upon finding by a "fair preponderance of the evidence" that the child is "permanently neglected" violated the due process clause of the Fourteenth Amendment, and that, before a state may sever completely and irrevocably the rights of parents in a natural child, due process requires that the state support its allegations by at least clear and convincing evidence. [Santosky v Kramer (1982, US) 71 L Ed 2d 599, 102 S Ct 1388.]

§ 39. Poverty and welfare laws

In regard to a provision of the Social Security Act's Supplemental Security Income program (42 USCS § 1396a(a)(17)) permitting a state which operates a Medicaid plan under the program to "deem," under certain circumstances, the income of an applicant's spouse as available to the applicant for purposes of eligibility for benefits, the court held that (1) a Federal District Court order in an action involving a class of plaintiffs including SSI recipients as well as the "optional categorically needed"— those who are eligible, but do not receive, SSI benefits—conflicted with the Act insofar as it permitted the state to deny Medicaid benefit to SSI recipients and forbid "deeming" under any circumstances, and (2) a regulation promulgated by the Secretary of Health and Human Services setting time limitations on the number of months a state could "deem" a spouse's income as available to an optional categorically needed applicant once the spouse and applicant are no longer living together did not exceed the broad authority granted the Secretary under § 1396a(a)(17)(B) and was not arbitrary and capricious. [Herweg v Ray (1982, US) 71 L Ed 2d 137, 102 S Ct 1059.] In another Medicaid case, the court held that, as applied in Massachusetts, § 1903(f) of the Social Security Act (42 USCS § 1396b(f)) did not violate constitutional principles of equal treatment, even though the statute as applied resulted in a distribution of Medicaid benefits to recipients of Supplemental Security Income that was more generous than the distribution of such benefits to persons who were self-supporting. [Schweiker v Hogan (1982, US) 73 L Ed 2d 227, 102 S Ct 2597.] Finally, in a third Medicaid case, the court held that nursing homes' decisions to discharge or transfer Medicaid patients to facilities providing lower levels of care, without notice or hearing, did not constitute "state action" for purposes of the Fourteenth Amendment. [Blum v Yaretsky (1982, US) 73 L Ed 2d 534, 102 S Ct 2777.]

Finally, the court held that a state Emergency Assistance Program, which is federally funded under the Social Security Act (42 USCS § 603(a)(5)) and which precludes the furnishing of cash from the program to persons receiving or eligible for Aid to Families with Dependent Children (AFDC) or of program assistance in any form to replace a lost or stolen AFDC grant, was invalid under the supremacy clause (Art VI, cl 2) insofar as provisions of the state program conflicted with a valid federal regulation promulgated by the Secretary of Health, Education, and Welfare proscribing inequitable treatment of individuals or groups under an Emergency Assistance Program. [Blum v Bacon (1982, US) 72 L Ed 2d 728, 102 S Ct 2355.]

§ 40. Prisons and prisoners' rights

The court held that (1) the pro se complaint of a state prisoner stated a cause of action, even though it was crudely written, where it alleged that the prisoner had been placed in solitary confinement without any notice of charges or any hearing, that he was threatened with violence when he asked what the charges were, and that he was still in the "hole" a week later, and (2) such a complaint did not become moot when the prisoner was transferred to another facility. [Boag v MacDougall (1982) 454 US 364, 70 L Ed 2d 551, 102 S Ct 700.]

§ 41. Public officers and employees

In addition to discussing presidential immunity issues in the much publicized case of Nixon v Fitzgerald (1982, US) 73 L Ed 2d 349, 102 S Ct 2690, treated in § 2, supra, the court, in a case arising from the same alleged conspiracy as in the Nixon Case, held that public policy did not require blanket recognition of absolute immunity for presidential aides and that such aides were generally entitled only to good faith or qualified immunity. [Harlow v Fitzgerald (1982, US) 73 L Ed 2d 396, 102 S Ct 2727.]

It was held that, for purposes of a civil rights action under 42 USCS § 1983, a public defender did not act "under color of state law" when performing a lawyer's traditional functions as counsel to a defendant in a criminal proceeding, and therefore a complaint by a convicted state criminal that the public defender representing him had violated § 1983 by failing to represent him adequately in his appeal should be dismissed, especially since (1) although the employment relationship between the state and a public defender paid by the state was a relevant factor, it was insufficient to establish that a public defender acted under color of state law within the meaning of § 1983, and (2) the traditional adversarial functions performed by the public defender were private in nature and were not in the nature of those performed under color of state law. [Polk County v Dodson (1981) 454 US 312, 70 L Ed 2d 509, 102 S Ct 445.]

Finally, the court held that the Eleventh Amendment did not bar, in an admiralty in rem action, the issuance of a warrant to arrest property held by state officials (oceanic artifacts collected by a petitioning salvage company), since (1) the action to gain possession was directed against individual state officials who did not have a colorable claim to the possession of the artifacts rather than at the state or an agency thereof and, (2) the warrant sought possession of specific property and did not seek attachment of state funds and would not burden the state treasury. [Florida Dept. of State v Treasure Salvors, Inc. (1982, US) 73 L Ed 2d 1057.]

§ 42. Public utilities

The court decided two cases relating to public utilities during the 1981–82 term. The court held that an order of a state's public utilities commission which required a privately owned public utility which generated and transmitted electricity at wholesale from several plants within the state to arrange to sell previously exported hydroelectric energy solely within the state restricted the flow of privately owned and produced electricity in interstate commerce in a manner inconsistent with the commerce clause (Art I § 8, cl 3), and that the "savings clause" in § 201(b) of the Federal Power Act (16 USCS § 924(b))—which provides that the Act's provisions delegating exclusive authority to the Federal Energy Regulatory Commission to regulate the transmission and sale at wholesale of electric energy in interstate commerce "shall not . . . deprive a State or State Commission of its lawful authority now exercised over the exportation of hydroelectric energy which is transmitted across a State line"—did not provide an affirmative grant of authority to a state to issue such an order. [New

England Power Co. v New Hampshire (1982, US) 71 L Ed 2d 188, 102 S Ct 1096.]

The court also held that Titles I and III and § 210 of Title II of the Public Utility Regulatory Policies Act of 1978 (16 USCS §§ 2611 et seq.; 15 USCS §§ 3201 et seq.; 16 USCS § 824a-3), encouraging the adoption of certain retail regulatory practices in the energy field and the development of "cogeneration" and small power production facilities, were within Congress' power under the commerce clause (Art I § 8, cl 3) and did not trench on state sovereignty in violation of the Tenth Amendment. [Federal Energy Regulatory Com. v Mississippi (1982, US) 72 L Ed 2d 532, 102 S Ct 2126.]

§ 43. Railroads

The court decided two cases relating to railroads in its 1981–82 term. It was held that the employee protection provisions, §§ 106 and 110 of the Rock Island Railroad Transition and Employee Assistance Act (45 USCS §§ 1005, 1008), were repugnant to the bankruptcy clause of the United States Constitution (Art I § 8, cl 4), which empowers Congress to enact uniform laws on the subject of bankruptcies throughout the United States, the Act not being a response either to the particular problems of major railroad bankruptcies or to any geographically isolated problem, and the Act applying only to one regional bankrupt railroad. [Railway Labor Executives' Assn. v Gibbons (1982, US) 71 L Ed 2d 335, 102 S Ct 1169, 8 BCD 966, 6 CBC2d 125, CCH Bankr L Rptr ¶ 68557, reh den (US) 72 L Ed 2d 459, 102 S Ct 1997.]

The court also held that (1) the Tenth Amendment did not prohibit application of the Railway

Labor Act (45 USCS §§ 151 et seq.) to a state-owned railroad engaged in interstate commerce since the operation of a railroad engaged in interstate commerce was not an integral part of traditional state activities generally immune from federal regulation, and federal regulation of a state-owned railroad, whether freight or passenger, did not impair a state's ability to function as a state, and (2) in view of the fact that Congress has the authority to regulate labor relations in the railroad industry in general, application of this authority to a state-owned railroad did not so impair the ability of a state to carry out its constitutionally preserved sovereign function as to come in conflict with the Tenth Amendment, especially given that the states, merely by acquiring functions previously performed by the private sector, may not erode federal authority in areas traditionally subject to federal statutory regulation. [United Transp. Union v Long Island R. R. Co. (1982, US) 71 L Ed 2d 547, 102 S Ct 1349, 109 BNA LRRM 3017, 93 CCH LC ¶ 13297.]

§ 44. Residency requirements

In a well-publicized case, the court held that a state dividend distribution plan, under which the state distributed from a permanent fund into which 25 percent of its annual mineral income was deposited each year one dividend unit per adult resident for each year of residency subsequent to 1959, violated the equal protection clause of the Fourteenth Amendment, since the state had shown no valid state interests which were rationally served by the distinction it made between citizens who established residency before 1959 and those who have become residents since then. [Zobel v Williams (1982, US) 72 L Ed 2d 672, 102 S Ct 2309.]

§ 45. Search and seizure

The court decided two cases relating to search and seizure issues during its 1981–82 term. The court held that (1) it is not "unreasonable" under the Fourth Amendment for a police officer, as a matter of routine, to monitor the movements of an arrested person, as his judgment dictates, following an arrest, (2) such surveillance is not an impermissible invasion of the privacy or personal liberty of an individual who has been arrested, and accordingly, an officer could, consistently with the Fourth Amendment, accompany a student to his dormitory room and enter the room upon observing suspected contraband in plain view, such entry from a public corridor not requiring a showing of exigent circumstances, and (3) the Fourth Amendment did not prohibit the seizure of contraband which was in plain view, it being of no legal significance whether the officer was in the room, on the threshold, or in the hallway at the time he observed the contraband since he had a right to be in any of these places as an incident of a valid arrest. [Washington v Chrisman (1982) 455 US 1, 70 L Ed 2d 778, 102 S Ct 812.]

It was also held that police officers who have legitimately stopped an automobile and who have probable cause to believe that contraband is concealed somewhere in it may conduct a warrantless search of the vehicle that is as thorough as a magistrate could authorize by warrant. [United States v Ross (1982, US) 72 L Ed 2d 572, 102 S Ct 2157.]

§ 46. Securities regulation

The court held that neither a certificate of deposit which was pledged by depositors to a federally regulated bank to guarantee a loan made to a third-party company nor an agreement whereby other depositors, in exchange for a loan guaranty, were to receive a share of the company's profits and other compensation was a "security" within the meaning of § 3(a)(10) of the Securities Exchange Act of 1934 (15 USCS § 78c(a)(10)) subject to the antifraud provisions of § 10(b) of the Act (15 USCS § 78j(b)). [Marine Bank v Weaver (1982, US) 71 L Ed 2d 409, 102 S Ct 1220, CCH Fed Secur L Rep ¶ 98471.]

The court also held that a state business takeover statute, under which any takeover offer for the shares of a target company must be registered with the state's Secretary of State, was unconstitutional under the commerce clause of the United States Constitution (Art I § 8, cl 3), since it imposed a substantial burden on interstate commerce which outweighed its putative local benefits. [Edgar v Mite Corp. (1982, US) 73 L Ed 2d 269, 102 S Ct 2629, CCH Fed Secur L Rep ¶ 98728.]

For cases dealing with criminal offenses involving securities, see § 13, supra.

§ 47. Service of process

The court held that a state statute, permitting service of process in forcible entry and detainer actions to be made by posting a summons in a conspicuous place on the premises if the defendant or a member of the defendant's family over the age of 16 cannot be found, failed to afford tenants of a public housing project with adequate notice of eviction proceedings against them before the issuance of final orders of eviction, and that the state thus deprived them of property without due process of law as required by the Fourteenth Amendment since, in a significant number of instances, reliance on posting pursuant to the provisions of the statute resulted in a failure to provide actual notice to the tenants concerned. [Greene v Lindsey (1982, US) 72 L Ed 2d 249, 102 S Ct 1874.]

§ 48. Sex discrimination

The court held that the policy of a state-supported university, which has from its inception limited its enrollment to women, of denying otherwise qualified males the right to enroll for credit in its School of Nursing violated the equal protection clause of the Fourteenth Amendment since the single-sex admission policy could not be justified on the asserted grounds that it compensated for discrimination against women and, therefore, constituted educational affirmative action since the policy, rather than compensating for discriminatory barriers faced by women, tended to perpetuate the stereotyped view of nursing as an exclusively woman's job and the university's policy of permitting men to attend classes in the school as auditors fatally undermined its claim that women, at least those in the School of Nursing, were adversely affected by the presence of men. [Mississippi University for Women v Hogan (1982, US) 73 L Ed 2d 1090, 29 CCH EPD ¶ 32868.]

§ 49. Social security

The Supreme Court decided two cases relating to the Medicare program during the 1981–82 term. The court held that hearing procedures provided for under Part B of the Medicare program, which provides medical insurance benefits covering a portion of the cost of certain physician services, outpatient physical therapy, X-rays, laboratory tests, and other medical and health care, may, consistently with due process, be held by private insurance carriers, without a further right of appeal where (1) the hearing officers appointed by the carriers who preside over the claim disputes at oral hearings do not have any disqualifying interests for due process purposes in view of the fact that the carriers pay claims from federal funds and not out of their own funds, the salaries of the hearing officers are paid by the Federal Government, and the carriers operate under contracts that require compliance with standards prescribed by the statute and the Secretary of Health and Human Services, and (2) the fact that the hearing officer must be either an attorney or another "qualified" individual who must have a "thorough knowledge" of the Medicare program undermines the contention that procedures prescribed by Congress and the Secretary are not fair or that different or additional procedures would reduce the risk of erroneous deprivation of Part B benefits. [Schweiker v McClure (1982, US) 72 L Ed 2d 1, 102 S Ct 1665.]

Additionally, the court held that the United States Court of Claims had no jurisdiction to review determinations by private insurance carriers of the amounts payable pursuant to Part B of the Medicare program. [United States v Erika, Inc. (1982, US) 72 L Ed 2d 12, 102 S Ct 1650.]

For cases dealing with Medicaid issues, see § 39, supra.

§ 50. Standing to sue

The court decided three issues relating to standing in the last term. The court held that an organization dedicated to the separation of church and state and several of its employees did not have standing, either in their capacity as taxpayers or as citizens, to challenge the conveyance of a tract of property formerly used as a military hospital to a church-related college as "surplus property" under the Federal Property and Administrative Services Act of 1949 (40 USCS §§ 471 et seq.) even though the plaintiffs alleged that the conveyance violated the establishment clause of the First Amendment and that each member of the organization would be deprived of the fair and constitutional use of his or her tax dollars. [Valley Forge Christian College v Americans United for Separation of Church & State, Inc. (1982) 445 US 464, 70 L Ed 2d 700, 102 S Ct 752.]

The court also held that Medicaid patients eligible to receive care in private nursing homes, which were designated as either "skilled nursing facilities" or "health related facilities," with the latter providing less extensive, and generally less expensive, medical care than the former, had standing to challenge the procedural adequacy of facility-initiated discharges and transfers to lower levels of care since the threat of transfer was not imaginary or speculative but was realistic, however, the court held that the threat of transfers to higher levels of care was not of sufficient immediacy and reality to give the patients standing to seek an adjudication of procedures attending such transfers. [Blum v Yaretsky (1982, US) 73 L Ed 2d 534, 102 S Ct 2777.]

Finally, the court held that Puerto Rico had parens patriae standing to maintain a suit alleging that there was discrimination against the hiring of Puerto Ricans in favor of foreign laborers in violation of the Wagner-Peyser Act (29 USCS §§ 49 et seq.) and the Immigration and Nationality Act of 1952 (8 USCS §§ 1101 et seq.), which required that United States workers, including citizens of Puerto Rico, be given preference over temporary foreign workers for jobs that became available within the United States. [Alfred L. Snapp & Sons, Inc. v Puerto Rico (1982, US) 73 L Ed 2d 995, 29 CCH EPD ¶ 32867.]

For a decision involving various individuals' and organizations' standing to sue under § 812 of the Fair Housing Act of 1968 (42 USCS § 3612), see Havens Realty Corp. v Coleman (1982, US) 71 L Ed 2d 214, 102 S Ct 1114, supra § 27.

§ 51. Tax matters

Issues arising from various forms of taxation were before the court in a number of cases during the 1981–82 term. The court held that a regulation of the Department of the Treasury interpreting the term "brother-sister controlled group" in § 1563(a)(2) of the Internal Revenue Code of 1954 (26 USCS § 1563(a)(2)) to mean two or more corporations if the same five or fewer persons own "singly or in combination" the two statutorily prescribed percentages of voting power or total value in each corporation was invalid as not being a reasonable interpretation of the statute, the language, structure, and legislative history of the statute indicating that the term was intended to apply only where each person owns stock in each corporation of the group. [United States v Vogel Fertilizer Co. (1982, US) 70 L Ed 2d 792, 102 S Ct 821, 82-1 USTC ¶ 9134.]

With regard to the gift tax, it was held that a donor who makes a gift of property on condition that the donee pay the resulting gift tax realizes taxable income to the extent that the gift tax paid by the donee exceeds the donor's adjusted basis in the property. [Diedrich v Commissioner (1982, US) 72 L Ed 2d 777 102 S Ct 2414, 82-1 USTC ¶ 9419.] In regard to a regulation of the Department of the Treasury (26 CFR § 25.2511-1(c)) excepting from the federal gift tax (26 USCS §§ 2501, 2511) a refusal to accept ownership of an interest in property transferred by will if such refusal is effective under local law and is made within a reasonable time after knowledge of the existence of the transfer, it was held that the disclaimers by the trust beneficiary of a contingent interest in a testamentary trust 33 years after that trust was created, while it was still contingent, were indirect transfers of property by gift within the meaning of 26 USCS §§ 2501(a)(1) and 2511(a), and were not excepted from the federal gift tax under the regulation, the "transfer" referred to in the regulation occurring when the interest was created, not at a later time when the interest either vested or became possessory, and that the disclaimers, although effective under local law, were thus not made "within a reasonable time" after the interest was created. [Jewett v Commissioner (1982, US) 71 L Ed 2d 170, 102 S Ct 1082.]

It was also held that the Eleventh Amendment barred a statutory interpleader action in Federal District Court by the administrator of the estate of Howard Hughes arising out of a dispute between Texas and California in which both states asserted the right to levy death taxes on the estate, the taxing officials of both states claiming that Hughes was domiciled in the state at the time of his death. [Cory v White (1982, US) 72 L Ed 2d 694, 102 S Ct 2325.]

The court also decided a number of cases relating to state taxation. The court held that (1) taxpayers were barred by the principle of comity from bringing in federal court a damages action under 42 USCS § 1983 to redress the allegedly unconstitutional administration of state taxes, where there were plain, adequate, and complete state remedies whereby the taxpayers could seek protection of their federal rights, since the very maintenance of the suit itself, as well as any federal court determination of a constitutional violation, would intrude on the enforcement of the state scheme, and (2) the principle of comity is not restricted by the Tax Injunction Act (28 USCS § 1341) to limit federal court deference to actions enumerated in the Act. [Fair Assessment in Real Estate Asso. v McNary (1981) 454 US 100, 70 L Ed 2d 271, 102 S Ct 177.] The court also (1) vacated a judgment of the Temporary Emergency Court of Appeals holding that a state's tax on the gross receipts of oil companies from their activities within that state which was established in June, 1980 conflicted with, and was therefore pre-empted by, federal price control authority under the Emergency Petroleum Allocation Act (15 USCS §§ 751 et seq.), and (2) remanded the case to the Court of Appeals for reconsideration in light of the expiration of federal price control authority under the Act. [Tully v Mobil Oil Corp. (1982, US) 71 L Ed 2d 120, 102 S Ct 1047.] Additionally, the court held that government contractors using an "advance funding" procedure whereby a contractor's costs are paid out of a special bank account into which federal funds are deposited—so that only federal funds are expended when the contractor meets his obligations—were taxable entities independent of the United States, so that (1) the state's use tax could be applied to the contractors without offending the notion of federal sovereignty, the contractors not being "constituent parts" of the Federal Government, (2) the gross receipts tax could be applied to the funds received by the contractors to meet salaries and internal costs, and (3) the state could tax receipts of a vendor selling tangible property to the United States through the contractors, such sales to the contractors not being sales to the "United States itself," since the contractors made purchases in their own names, the vendors were not informed that the government was the only party with an independent interest in the purchases, and the government disclaimed any formal intention to denominate the contractors as purchasing agents. [United States v New Mexico (1982, US) 71 L Ed 2d 580, 102 S Ct 1373.] The court held that a state's tax on a portion of the dividends received by a nondomiciliary corporate taxpayer from its foreign subsidiaries and that state's efforts to tax the "gross up" income, income that the corporation never actually received from its foreign subsidiaries but that the Federal Government (for purposes of calculating a foreign tax credit) deemed it to have received, both contravened the due process clause. [F. W. Woolworth Co. v Taxation & Revenue Dept. (1982, US) 73 L Ed 2d 819.] Finally, in regard to another state's effort to tax income of a nondomiciliary parent corporation's subsidiary corporation, it was held that a state may not constitutionally include within the taxable income of a nondomiciliary parent corporation doing some business in the state a portion of intangible income (dividends, interest payments, and capital gains from the sale of stock) that the corporation received from subsidiary corporations having no other connection with the state. [AS-ARCO Inc. v Idaho State Tax Com. (1982, US) 73 L Ed 2d 787.]

For a case discussing the jurisdiction of the Supreme Court to hear an appeal from a Federal District Court involving the constitutionality of a provision of the Federal Unemployment Tax Act (26 USCS § 3309(b)), see California v Grace Brethren Church (1982, US) 73 L Ed 2d 93, 102 S Ct 2498, supra § 19. For a case regarding whether the requirement that an employer must pay social security taxes violated the free exercise clause of the First Amendment in certain situations, see United States v Lee (1982, US) 71 L Ed 2d 127, 102 S Ct 1051, 82-1 USTC ¶ 9205, supra § 23.

§ 52. Waters

The court held that ground water is an article of commerce subject to congressional regulation and that a state statute which required any person intending to withdraw ground water from any well located in the state and transport it for use in an adjoining state to obtain a permit from the state Department of Water Resources, issuance of which was subject to the condition that the adjoining state gave reciprocal rights to permit transportation of water to the initial state, violated the commerce clause (Art I § 8, cl 3) by imposing an impermissible burden on interstate commerce. [Sporhase v Nebraska (1982, US) 73 L Ed 2d 1254.]

For a case discussing a Federal District Court's discretion in enforcing the Federal Water Pollution Control Act (33 USCS §§ 1251 et seq.), see Weinberger v Romero-Barcello (1982, US) 72 L Ed 2d 91, 102 S Ct 1798, supra § 18.

§ 53. Workmen's compensation

It was held that § 20(a) of the Longshoremen's and Harbor Workers' Compensation Act (33 USCS § 920(a))—providing for the presumption, in the absence of evidence to the contrary, that a claim for compensation under the Act does in fact come within its provisions—did not apply to an employee's claim for disability benefits stemming from pain suffered at home one day after the employee engaged in heavy lifting while on the job, since (1) the § 20(a) presumption could not support a claim the employee did not make, the employee having claimed that he was injured at work and not that the injury occurred at home and that it was somehow "employment-bred," and (2) the "injury" having arisen at home, it did not arise "in the course of employment," as required to make out the prima facie case under the Act to which the § 20(a) presumption refers. [U. S. Industries/Federal Sheet Metal, Inc., v Director, Office of Workers' Compensation Programs, etc. (1982, US) 71 L Ed 2d 495, 102 S Ct 1312.]

SUMMARIES OF DECISIONS

JACK DUCKWORTH, Warden, Petitioner,

v

ISADORE SERRANO

454 US 1, 70 L Ed 2d 1, 102 S Ct 18

Decided October 19, 1981.

Decision: Federal Court of Appeals' consideration of issue of ineffective assistance of counsel of state defendant on federal habeas corpus petition, held erroneous where issue was not raised in state court or Federal District Court.

SUMMARY

An individual was convicted of murder in the Superior Court, Criminal Division, Lake County, Indiana, and the Supreme Court of Indiana affirmed (266 Ind 126, 360 NE2d 1257). The defendant then filed a petition for habeas corpus in the United States District Court, but it was dismissed. On appeal to the United States Court of Appeals for the Seventh Circuit, the defendant claimed that since his attorney had represented a prosecution witness in an unrelated case, the defendant had received ineffective assistance of counsel. The Court of Appeals agreed, reversing the District Court's dismissal on the grounds that the defendant's attorney's representation of the prosecution witness constituted a per se violation of the Sixth Amendment guarantee

1

of effective representation and that while the ineffective assistance argument had never been presented to the state court, in view of the clear violation of the defendant's rights and in the interest of judicial economy, there was no reason to await the state court's consideration of the issue.

Granting certiorari, the United States Supreme Court reversed and remanded. In a per curiam opinion, expressing the view of BURGER, Ch. J., and BRENNAN, WHITE, BLACKMUN, POWELL, REHNQUIST, STEVENS, and O'CONNOR, it was held that the Federal Court of Appeals was obligated to dismiss the state prisoner's federal habeas corpus petition, since the claim of ineffective assistance of counsel had never been raised in state court or before the Federal District Court, there being no exception to the requirement of 28 USCS § 2254(b) that state remedies be exhausted for "clear violations" of a defendant's rights.

MARSHALL, J., dissented.

CARLOS CHARDON, individually, et al.,
Petitioners,

v

RAFAEL RIVERA FERNANDEZ, et al.

454 US 6, 70 L Ed 2d 6, 102 S Ct 28

Decided November 2, 1981.

Decision: Limitations period applicable to employment discrimination action under 42 USCS
§ 1983, held to run from time of notice that
appointment would terminate rather than from
termination date.

SUMMARY

On June 19, 1978, several non-tenured administrators in the Puerto Rico Department of Education
filed a complaint in the United States District Court
for the District of Puerto Rico alleging that the
termination of their appointments violated 42 USCS
§ 1983. The District Court dismissed the suit, holding that the action had accrued on the date the
administrators received letters notifying them that
their appointments would be terminated, and the
claims were therefore barred by the applicable one-
year statute of limitations, since the letters had been
received prior to June 18, 1977, notifying the administrators of a termination at a specified date
between June 30 and August 8, 1977. The United
States Court of Appeals for the First Circuit reversed on the ground that the limitations period did
not begin running until the administrators' appointments ended.

Granting certiorari, the United States Supreme Court reversed and remanded. In a per curiam opinion, expressing the view of BURGER, Ch. J., and WHITE, BLACKMUN, POWELL, REHNQUIST, and O'CONNOR, JJ., it was held that the claims by the administrators that the termination of their appointments violated 42 USCS § 1983 were barred by the applicable one-year statute of limitations, since the operative decision for purposes of the running of the statute of limitations had been made, and notice given, in advance of the designated date on which employment terminated.

BRENNAN, J., joined by MARSHALL, J., dissented, expressing the view that because the Supreme Court's decision was potentially far-reaching in its impact, the issue should be decided only upon plenary review, the court's summary reversal being particularly inappropriate.

STEVENS, J., joined by BRENNAN and MARSHALL, JJ., dissented, agreeing with the Court of Appeals that the letters notifying the employees of their discharges were not actions in themselves comparable to the denial of tenure, so that the limitations period began with the discharge and not the notice and that a prior Supreme Court decision holding that for a tenured position the limitations period began running with the notice of denial of tenure and not with the subsequent termination of employment was not dispositive and should not be followed.

A. R. JAGO, Former Superintendent, Southern
Ohio Correctional Facility, et al., Petitioners,

v

GEORGE D. VAN CUREN

454 US 14, 70 L Ed 2d 13, 102 S Ct 31

ˮ Decided November 9, 1981.

Decision: Rescission without hearing of prisoner's
parole by Ohio Adult Parole Authority, held not
violative of due process under Fourteenth
Amendment.

SUMMARY

A prisoner, who had been notified by the Ohio
Adult Parole Authority that the parole board was
ordering a parole release in his case, but whose
parole had been rescinded without a hearing by the
Authority, filed a petition for a writ of habeas
corpus in the United States District Court for the
Southern District of Ohio claiming that the rescission without hearing violated his right to due process of law under the Fourteenth Amendment. The
District Court ultimately denied the writ, determining that early release from prison in Ohio is a
matter of grace and holding therefore that the
rescission of parole without hearing did not violate
due process. On appeal, the United States Court of
Appeals for the Sixth Circuit reversed, concluding
that a liberty interest protected by the Fourteenth
Amendment's guarantee of due process arose from
mutually explicit understandings created when the

Authority notified the prisoner that it was ordering a parole release in his case (641 F2d 411).

Granting certiorari, the United States Supreme Court reversed. In a per curiam opinion, expressing the view of BURGER, Ch. J., and WHITE, POWELL, REHNQUIST, and O'CONNOR, JJ., it was held that the rescission without hearing of the prisoner's parole by the Parole Authority did not violate the prisoner's right to due process of law under the Fourteenth Amendment, neither Ohio law relating to parole nor the expectation resulting from the notification given to the prisoner that a parole release had been ordered in his case being sufficient to create a liberty interest within the meaning of the Amendment.

BLACKMUN, J., concurring in the result, expressed the view that under Ohio law, state parole authorities have the clear right to rescind a parole order before it becomes effective and therefore the prisoner's expectation of release was no more than a unilateral one to which no due process rights attached, and that, in any event, no mutual expectation existed under the circumstances in as much as the parole board's order was based on the prisoner's untruths.

Stevens, J., joined by BRENNAN and MARSHALL, JJ., dissenting, expressed the view that the state's formal decision, conveyed to the prisoner, to grant him parole creates an interest protected by the due process clause of the Fourteenth Amendment.

FEDERAL ELECTION COMMISSION, Petitioner,

v

DEMOCRATIC SENATORIAL CAMPAIGN
COMMITTEE (No. 80-939)

NATIONAL REPUBLICAN SENATORIAL
COMMITTEE, Petitioner,

v

DEMOCRATIC SENATORIAL CAMPAIGN
COMMITTEE (No. 80-1129)

454 US 27, 70 L Ed 2d 23, 102 S Ct 38

Argued October 6, 1981.
Decided November 10, 1981.

Decision: Designation by political party's state committees of national senatorial campaign committee as agent for purposes of making campaign
expenditures, held not foreclosed by provision
of Federal Election Campaign Act (2 USCS
§ 441a(d)(3)).

SUMMARY

Section 441a(d)(3) of the Federal Election Campaign Act of 1971 (2 USCS § 441a(d)(3)) limits the
amount of money that the national and state committees of a political party may spend in connection
with the general election campaign of a candidate
for the Senate or House of Representatives. The
National Republican Senatorial Campaign Committee (NRSC), which is a political committee organized specifically to support Republican candidates

7

in elections for the U. S. Senate, is authorized by
§ 441a(h) of the Act (2 USCS § 441a(h)) to make
contributions to candidates. However, the NRSC is
not given authority under § 441a(d) of the Act (2
USCS § 441a(d)) to make expenditures on behalf of
such candidates, and the Federal Election Commission takes the position that the NRSC may not do
so on its own account. The Commission has permitted the NRSC to act as the agent of national and
state party committees in making expenditures on
their behalf. After certain state Republican party
committees designated the NRSC as their agent for
§ 441a(d)(3) expenditure purposes, the Democratic
Senatorial Campaign Committee (DSCC) filed a
complaint with the Commission asserting that the
NRSC's agreements with the state committees were
contrary to § 441a(d)(3). The Commission unani-
mously dismissed the complaint, and the DSCC then
petitioned for review in the United States District
Court for the District of Columbia, which granted
the Commission's motion for summary judgment.
On appeal, the United States Court of Appeals for
the District of Columbia Circuit reversed, concluding that the plain language of § 441a(d)(3) precludes agency agreements between state committees
and the NRSC.

On certiorari, the United States Supreme Court
reversed. In an opinion by White, J., expressing the
unanimous view of the court, it was held that (1)
§ 441a(d)(3) of the Federal Election Campaign Act
does not foreclose a state committee of a political
party from designating the national senatorial campaign committee of that party as its agent for the
purpose of making expenditures allowed by the Act,
and (2) accordingly, the Federal Election Commission acted within the authority vested in it by Con-

8

gress when it determined to permit such agency agreements, this determination by the Commission not being contrary to law in view of the absence of a prohibition on the agency arrangements at issue, the lack of a clearly enunciated legislative purpose to that effect, and the countervailing existence of a transfer mechanism in the statutory scheme.

STEVENS, J., concurring, expressed the view that (1) the agency relationship employed in the case at bar does not violate the Federal Election Campaign Act (2 USCS §§ 431 et seq.) and (2) it was not entirely certain that the expenditures at issue would otherwise be impermissible were it not for the statutory authorization in § 441a(d) of the Act (2 USCS § 441a(d)).

COUNSEL

Charles Nevett Steele argued the cause for the Federal Election Commission.

Jan W. Baran argued the cause for the National Republican Senatorial Committee.

Robert F. Bauer argued the cause for respondents.

DONNA RIDGWAY and PRUDENTIAL
INSURANCE COMPANY OF AMERICA,
Petitioners,

v

HAYLEY D. RIDGWAY et al.

454 US 46, 70 L Ed 2d 39, 102 S Ct 49

Argued October 7, 1981.
Decided November 10, 1981.

Decision: Insured serviceman's beneficiary designation under life policy issued pursuant to Servicemen's Group Life Insurance Act (38 USCS
§§ 765 et seq.), held to prevail over constructive trust imposed upon proceeds by state
court.

. SUMMARY

A career sergeant in the United States Army
obtained a divorce from his wife, and the Maine
state court divorce judgment ordered the serviceman, among other things, to keep in force the
insurance policies then outstanding for the benefit
of the couple's three children. At the time, his life
was insured under a life policy issued pursuant to
the Servicemen's Group Life Insurance Act of 1965
(38 USCS §§ 765 et seq.), his first wife being the
designated beneficiary of that policy. Subsequently,
the serviceman remarried and changed the policy's
beneficiary designation to one directing that its
proceeds be paid as specified "by law," which meant
under the Act that they would be paid to his second
wife as his widow. Following his death and after

10

both wives had filed claims for the proceeds, the first wife instituted a suit in Superior Court for Androscoggin County, Maine, against the insurance company, seeking, as legal representative of the three minor children, both to enjoin the payment of the policy proceeds to the second wife, and to obtain a declaratory judgment that those proceeds were payable to the children. The second wife joined the litigation and was aligned as a plaintiff asserting a claim to the proceeds, and the first wife then filed a cross-claim against the second wife, praying for the imposition of a constructive trust, for the benefit of the children, on any policy proceeds payed to the second wife. The Superior Court rejected the first wife's claims, believing that although the terms of the judgment of divorce and the beneficiary designation were inconsistent, the imposition of a constructive trust would interfere with the operation of the Act and that such a disposition would run afoul of the supremacy clause of the United States Constitution (Art VI, cl 2). On appeal, the Supreme Judicial Court of Maine vacated the dismissal of the first wife's cross-claim and remanded the case with directions to enter an order naming the first wife as constructive trustee of the policy proceeds (419 A2d 1030).

On appeal, the United States Supreme Court reversed. In an opinion by BLACKMUN, J., joined by BURGER, Ch. J., and BRENNAN, WHITE, and MARSHALL, JJ., it was held that the serviceman's beneficiary designation under the life policy issued pursuant to the Act prevailed over the constructive trust, the provision of § 770(a) of the Act (38 USCS § 770(a)) giving the insured service member the right freely to designate the beneficiary and to alter that choice at any time by communicating the decision in writing to the proper office prevailing over and displacing inconsistent state law, and the imposition of a constructive trust being also inconsistent with the anti-attachment provision of the Act (38 USCS § 770(g)) which shields payments made under § 770(a) "from taxation" and from "claims of creditors," and states that the payments "should not be liable to attachment, levy, or seizure by or under any legal or equitable process whatever, either before or after receipt by the beneficiary." .

POWELL, J., joined by REHNQUIST, J., dissented, expressing the view that the special nature of the parental legal duty, as expressly manifested by the serviceman's negotiated bargain with his family and by the terms of his divorce decree, imposed a constructive trust upon the proceeds of the insurance for the benefit of the serviceman's children as a matter of federal law and that as the intention of Congress to supplant state law does not extend to a breach of trust, the fund impressed with the trust should be held for its agreed purposes in accordance with Maine law.

STEVENS, J., dissenting, stated that neither the strong federal interest in protecting federally-supported benefits from claims of the recipient's commercial creditors nor the federal interest in permitting a federal serviceman to designate the beneficiary of his insurance policy, as expressed in § 770(g) and § 770(a), respectively, was compromised by the decision of the state court, so that the federal statutory provisions did not preempt state law in the case.

O'CONNOR, J., did not participate.

12

COUNSEL

Stephen P. Beale argued the cause for petitioners.

Joshua I. Schwartz argued the cause for the United States as amicus curiae by special leave of court.

Curtis Webber argued the cause for respondents.

———————

WILLIAM LEEKE, etc., et al., Petitioners,

v

MELVIN LEE TIMMERMAN, et al.

454 US 83, 70 L Ed 2d 65, 102 S Ct 69

Decided November 16, 1981.

Decision: Private citizen's right to prevent state officials from presenting information that will assist magistrate in determining whether to issue arrest warrant, held not judicially cognizable.

SUMMARY

South Carolina prison inmates who claimed that they had been unnecessarily beaten by prison guards during a prison uprising sought criminal arrest warrants against the guards from a state court magistrate. After the magistrate expressed his intent to issue the warrants, the state solicitor—as a result of a meeting with the legal advisor to the state's department of corrections, the prison warden, the county sheriff, and deputy attorney—wrote the magistrate a letter which requested that the warrants not be issued and stated that the solicitor intended to ask state officials to conduct an investigation concerning the charges made against the officers involved. The magistrate did not issue the warrants, and no investigation was conducted. The inmates subsequently filed suit in the United States District Court for the District of South Carolina contending, among other claims, that the state correctional officials had conspired in bad faith to block the issu-

14

ance of the arrest warrants and thereby violated 42 USCS §§ 1983 and 1985(3). The District Court ultimately concluded that the state correctional officials denied the inmates their right to a meaningful ability to set in motion the governmental machinery, because the officials' activity stopped the machinery unlawfully, not in a proper way, as for example, upon a valid determination of lack of probable cause, and the court awarded the inmates compensatory and punitive damages. The United States Court of Appeals for the Fourth Circuit affirmed, concluding that even though a private citizen lacks a judicially cognizable interest in the prosecution or nonprosecution of another, that did not foreclose the inmates' right to seek an arrest warrant.

Granting certiorari, the United States Supreme Court reversed. In a per curiam opinion, expressing the view of Burger, Ch. J., and White, Powell, Rehnquist, Stevens, and O'Connor, JJ., it was held that a private citizen has no judicially cognizable right to prevent state officials from presenting information, through intervention of the state solicitor, that will assist the magistrate in determing whether to issue the arrest warrant.

Brennan, J., joined by Marshall and Blackmun, JJ., dissented, expressing the view that prisoners had standing in the civil action brought pursuant to 42 USCS §§ 1983 and 1985(3), since they alleged that conspiratorial acts by state officials deprived them of their right to seek an arrest warrant, and thus denied them their constitutional right of access to the courts, assured by the First and Fourteenth Amendments.

EDWARD COOPER, City Attorney of Santa Ana, California, Petitioner,

v

MITCHELL BROTHERS' SANTA ANA THEATER, ETC., et al.

454 US 90, 70 L Ed 2d 262, 102 S Ct 172

Decided November 30, 1981.

Decision: Proof, in public nuisance abatement action by city against motion picture theater, that motion pictures in question were obscene beyond reasonable doubt, held not required.

SUMMARY

A city brought a public nuisance abatement action under a state civil statute alleging that numerous films shown by certain theater operators were obscene and that this constituted a public nuisance under the state civil code. The state trial court determined that the complaint presented both equitable and legal issues and ordered that a jury trial be held on the issues of obscenity, public nuisance, and damages prior to resolution of the equitable issues by the court. After evidence pertaining to obscenity and public nuisance had been presented, the jury was instructed that they could find the films at issue obscene only if they were persuaded "beyond a reasonable doubt." Thereupon, the jury found 11 of the 17 films at issue obscene. With respect to the equitable issues, the trial court found, independently from the jury verdict and based upon its own viewing, that the same 11 films were ob-
16

scene beyond a reasonable doubt as the term obscene is defined in a provision of the state's criminal code. On appeal, the city asserted that the trial court had erred in imposing the beyond-reasonable-doubt burden of proof, but the Court of Appeal of California, Fourth Appellate District, affirmed on this issue, concluding that obscenity had to be proven "beyond a reasonable doubt" (114 Cal App 3d 923, 171 Cal Rptr 85).

Granting certiorari, the United States Supreme Court reversed and remanded. In a per curiam opinion expressing the view of Burger, Ch. J., and White, Blackmun, Powell, Rehnquist, and O'Connor, JJ., it was held that the city was not required to prove beyond a reasonable doubt that the motion pictures at issue were obscene, the choice of whether to require proof beyond a reasonable doubt in an obscenity case being solely a matter of state law and not a requirement of the First and Fourteenth Amendments.

Brennan, J., joined by Marshall, J., dissenting, expressed the view that (1) the court lacked the requisite assurance of its jurisdiction to consider the question of whether the state was required to demonstrate beyond a reasonable doubt that the communication it sought to suppress was obscene, and (2) even assuming the court possessed jurisdiction in the case at bar, the First Amendment requires the state, when it seeks to suppress otherwise constitutionally protected material, to prove that the material is obscene beyond a reasonable doubt.

Stevens, J., dissenting, expressed the view that certiorari in the case at bar should not have been granted, the jurisdiction of the United States Supreme Court to decide the case being in doubt absent a clearer indication by the lower state courts that their ruling on the standard of proof issue was required by federal law.

FAIR ASSESSMENT IN REAL ESTATE
ASSOCIATION, INC., et al., Petitioners,

v

GENE McNARY, et al.

454 US 100, 70 L Ed 2d 271, 102 S Ct 177

Argued October 5, 1981.
Decided December 1, 1981.

Decision: Taxpayer's damages action under 42
USCS § 1983 for alleged unconstitutional administration of state tax system, held barred in
federal court by principle of comity.

SUMMARY

Two taxpayers and a taxpayer's non-profit corporation filed suit in the United States District Court
for the Eastern District of Missouri under 42 USCS
§ 1983, alleging that St. Louis County and various
county and state officials had deprived them of
equal protection and due process of law by unequal
taxation of real property, and seeking actual damages in the amount of overassessments and of expenses incurred in efforts to obtain equitable property assessment for the corporation's members and
seeking punitive damages. The District Court held
that such suits were barred by both the Tax Injunction Act (28 USCS § 1341) and the principle of
comity (478 F Supp 1231), and the United States
Court of Appeals for the Eighth Circuit affirmed by
an equally divided court sitting en banc (622 F2d
415).

19

On certiorari, the United States Supreme Court affirmed. In an opinion by REHNQUIST, J., joined by BURGER, Ch. J., and WHITE, BLACKMUN, and POWELL, JJ., it was held that (1) the taxpayers were barred by the principle of comity from bringing in federal court the damages action under 42 USCS § 1983, where there were plain, adequate, and complete state remedies whereby the taxpayers could seek protection of their federal rights, since the very maintenance of the suit itself, as well as any federal court determination of a constitutional violation, would intrude on the enforcement of the states scheme, and (2) the principle of comity is not restricted by the Tax Injunction Act to limit federal court deference to actions enumerated in the Act.

BRENNAN, J., joined by MARSHALL, STEVENS, and O'CONNOR, JJ., concurred in the judgment, expressing the view that the jurisdiction of the federal courts over an action for damages brought pursuant to express congressional authority is not governed by applying a "principle of comity" granted solely on the Supreme Court's notion of an appropriate division of responsibility between federal and state judicial systems and that, as a jurisdictional matter, the federal courts have jurisdiction over claims seeking monetary relief arising from unconstitutional state taxation, but stated that the taxpayers' complaint was properly dismissed, because they failed to exhaust their administrative remedies in each tax year for which they sought damages.

COUNSEL

David J. Newburger argued the cause for petitioners.

Thomas W. Wehrle argued the cause for respondents.

———————

CASPAR W. WEINBERGER, Secretary of Defense,
et al., Petitioners,

v

CATHOLIC ACTION OF HAWAII/PEACE
EDUCATION PROJECT, et al.

454 US 139, 70 L Ed 2d 298, 102 S Ct 197

Argued October 13, 1981.
Decided December 1, 1981.

Decision: Section 102(2)(C) of the National Environmental Policy Act (42 USCS § 4332(2)(C)),
held not to require Navy to prepare and release
"Hypothetical Environmental Impact Statement" regarding nuclear weapons storage.

SUMMARY

After the Navy decided to construct several weapons storage structures capable of storing nuclear
weapons, an action was brought in the United States
District Court for the District of Hawaii, seeking an
injunction against the building of such new facilities
until an environmental impact statement had been
filed by the Navy pursuant to § 102(2)(C) of the
National Environmental Policy Act of 1969 (42
USCS § 4332(2)(C)), regarding the environmental
impact of nuclear weapons storage on the area
surrounding the new facilities. The District Court
held that the Navy was not required to file an
environmental impact statement, even though the
construction and operation of such facilities was
"major federal action" under the National Environ-

mental Policy Act (42 USCS §§ 4321 et seq.), because, given certain national security provisions of the Atomic Energy Act (42 USCS §§ 2011 et seq.) and the Navy's own regulations concerning nuclear weapons, the Navy had complied with the Act "to the fullest extent possible" (468 F Supp 190). The United States Court of Appeals for the Ninth Circuit reversed, holding that § 102(2)(C) of the Environmental Policy Act requires the Navy to prepare and release to the public a "Hypothetical Environmental Impact Statement" with regard to the operation of a facility capable of storing nuclear weapons (643 F2d 569).

On certiorari, the United States Supreme Court reversed and remanded. In an opinion by REHNQUIST, J., joined by BURGER, Ch. J., and WHITE, MARSHALL, POWELL, STEVENS, and O'CONNOR, JJ., it was held that the Navy was not required to prepare and release the hypothetical environmental impact statement ordered by the Court of Appeals, such a statement being a creature of judicial cloth, not legislative cloth, and is not mandated by the National Environmental Policy Act or other regulatory provisions, since the Act's public disclosure requirements are expressly governed by the Freedom of Information Act (5 USCS § 552), so that the public's interest in ensuring that federal agencies comply with the Act must give way to the government's need to preserve military secrets, and since due to national security reasons the Navy could neither admit nor deny that it proposed to store nuclear weapons at the facility, it had not been and could not be established that the Navy had proposed the only action that would require the preparation of an environmental impact statement dealing with the environmental consequences of nuclear weapons storage at the facility.

BLACKMUN, J., joined by BRENNAN, J., concurred in the judgment, expressing the view that the Freedom of Information Act defeats any attempt to obtain classified material and that the publishing of a hypothetical environmental impact statement would itself disclose confidential material and would therefore run afoul of Exemption 1 of the Freedom of Information Act.

COUNSEL

Solicitor General Rex E. Lee argued the cause for petitioners.

Nancy Stearns argued the cause for respondents.

JAMES G. WATT, Secretary of the Interior, et al.,
Petitioners,

v

ENERGY ACTION EDUCATIONAL
FOUNDATION et al.

454 US 151, 70 L Ed 2d 309, 102 S Ct 205

Argued October 5, 1981.
Decided December 1, 1981.

Decision: Interior Secretary's refusal to use non-
cash-bonus bidding systems in leasing oil and
gas tracts on outer continental shelf, held not
violative of Outer Continental Shelf Lands Act
Amendments (43 USCS §§ 1331 et seq.).

SUMMARY

Nine consumer groups, two state governmental
entities, and three private citizens brought suit in
the United States District Court for the District of
Columbia against several parties, including the Secretary of the Interior, alleging that the Secretary
abused his discretion under the Outer Continental
Shelf Lands Act Amendments of 1978 (43 USCS
§§ 1331 et seq.) in regard to the use of bidding
systems for the leasing of tracts on the outer continental shelf for the exploration for, and development of, mineral resources, including oil and gas.
The District Court denied all motions for summary
judgment and the plaintiffs' motion for a preliminary injunction. On appeal, the United States Court
of Appeals for the District of Columbia Circuit
concluded that the provision of the 1978 Amend-

ments (43 USCS § 1337(a)(1)), which requires the Secretary of the Interior to experiment with certain specified bidding systems for such leasing and authorizes the use of systems involving "cash bonus" bidding as well as systems involving a factor other than a cash bonus as the bidding variable, compels the Secretary to experiment with at least some of the latter type of bidding systems (654 F2d 735).

On certiorari, the United States Supreme Court reversed. In an opinion by O'CONNOR, J., expressing the unanimous view of the court, it was held that the Outer Continental Shelf Lands Act Amendments of 1978 do not require the Secretary of the Interior to use non-cash-bonus bidding systems in leasing tracts on the outer continental shelf for the exploration for, and development of, mineral resources, the language of the Amendments (43 USCS §§ 1337, 1344) requiring experimentation with at least some of the new bidding systems specified in those Amendments but leaving the details to the Secretary's discretion.

COUNSEL

Louis F. Claiborne argued the cause for petitioners.

John Silard argued the cause for respondents.

NATIONAL LABOR RELATIONS BOARD,
Petitioner,

v

HENDRICKS COUNTY RURAL ELECTRIC
MEMBERSHIP CORPORATION (No. 80–885)

HENDRICKS COUNTY RURAL ELECTRIC
MEMBERSHIP CORPORATION, Petitioner,

v

NATIONAL LABOR RELATIONS BOARD (No.
80–1103)

454 US 170, 70 L Ed 2d 323, 102 S Ct 216

Argued October 5, 1981.
Decided December 2, 1981.

Decision: National Labor Relations Board's "labor nexus" test for determining eligibility of confidential employees for inclusion in collective bargaining units, held to have reasonable basis in law.

SUMMARY

The National Labor Relations Board has a practice of excluding from collective bargaining units only those confidential employees with a "labor nexus" while rejecting any claim that all employees with access to confidential information are beyond the reach of the definition of "employee" in § 2(3) of the National Labor Relations Act (29 USCS § 152(3)). In keeping with this practice, the Board—finding that the personal secretary to a corporation's

27

general manager and chief executive officer, did not assist and act in a confidential capacity to persons who formulate, determine, and effectuate management policies in the field of labor relations—ruled that the secretary was protected by the Act (29 USCS §§ 151 et seq.) and that her discharge following her signing of a petition for reinstatement of a fellow employee constituted an unfair labor practice. The Board also ordered reinstatement of the secretary (236 NLRB 1616). The employer sought review in the United States Court of Appeals for the Seventh Circuit and the Board cross-petitioned for enforcement. Ultimately, that court refused to enforce the Board's order, holding that all secretaries working in a confidential capacity, without regard to labor relations, must be excluded from the coverage of the Act (603 F2d 25), and that the evidence in the record failed to support a finding that the secretary in question did not come within the court's broader definition of confidential secretary (627 F2d 766). In another case, the National Labor Relations Board, reviewing an employer's refusal to bargain with a unit of employees which the employer contended included confidential employees not subject to the National Labor Relations Act, accepted the view that none of the challenged employees was a confidential employee under the Board's labor nexus test, and issued a bargaining order after finding that the employer's refusal to bargain violated the Act (244 NLRB 485). On the employer's petition for review and the Board's cross-petition for enforcement, the Seventh Circuit Court of Appeals once again denied enforcement, noting that the Board's labor nexus test which the court had rejected in its earlier decision had also been utilized in the case before it. (631 F2d 734).

28

On certiorari, the United States Supreme Court reversed and remanded both decisions. In an opinion by BRENNAN, J., joined by WHITE, MARSHALL, BLACKMUN, and STEVENS, JJ., it was held that (1) the National Labor Relations Board's practice of excluding from collective bargaining units only those confidential employees with a labor nexus while rejecting any claim that all employees with access to confidential information are beyond the reach of the definition of "employee" in § 2(3) of the National Labor Relations Act has a reasonable basis in law, and therefore the Court of Appeals, in denying enforcement of the Board's order requiring reinstatement of the secretary, erred in holding that the record did not support the Board's determination that the secretary was not a confidential employee with a labor nexus, and (2) in view of the Court of Appeals' erroneous rejection of the Board's labor nexus test, the question of whether the challenged employees should have been excluded from the bargaining unit in question would be remanded for a determination as to whether the employees could be excluded from the unit for reasons entirely unrelated to whether they are confidential employees.

POWELL, J., joined by BURGER, Ch. J., REHNQUIST, J., and O'CONNOR, J., concurring in part and dissenting in part, agreed that employees in the possession of proprietary or nonpublic business information are not for that reason excluded from the National Labor Relations Act as "confidential" employees, but disagreed with the court's conclusion that the confidential secretary was not a confidential employee excluded from the Act, expressing the view that (1) the labor nexus test, as increasingly

29

narrowed by the National Labor Relations Board
and as now accepted by the court is antithetical to
any commonsense view or understanding of the role
of confidential secretaries, and (2) the Board's position that confidential employees are not excluded
from the Act as a whole but only from collective
bargaining should be rejected.

COUNSEL

Lawrence G. Wallace argued the cause for the
NLRB.

Warren D. Krebs argued the cause for Hendricks
County REMC.

Russ R. Mueller argued the cause for Malleable
Iron Range Company.

GEORGE A. RALSTON, Warden, Petitioner,

v

JOHN CARROLL ROBINSON

454 US 201, 70 L Ed 2d 345, 102 S Ct 233

Argued October 5, 1981.

Decided December 2, 1981.

Decision: Youth Corrections Act (18 USCS §§ 5005 et seq.), held not to require that youth offender sentenced to adult term while serving youth term must receive youth treatment for remainder of youth term.

SUMMARY

A 17-year old male pleaded guilty to second degree murder and was sentenced to a 10-year prison term in accordance with the Youth Corrections Act (18 USCS §§ 5005 et seq.), under which he was to be segregated from adult prisoners and receive rehabilitative treatment. While in prison, the defendant was found guilty of assaulting a federal officer with a dangerous weapon, whereupon the defendant was given an additional sentence to run consecutively with his term under the Act. The sentencing judge further found that the defendant would "not benefit any further" under the Act and sentenced him as an adult. Subsequently, the defendant was convicted of a second assault charge and received another consecutive sentence. At this point, the Bureau of Prisons classified the defendant as an adult offender and, although his Youth Corrections Act sentence had not expired, placed the defendant with the adult prison population. The defendant then filed a petition for a writ of a habeas corpus on the grounds that the Bureau had no authority to treat him as an adult offender during the remainder of his Youth Corrections Act sentence, and the writ was granted by the United States District Court for the Southern District of Illinois. The United States Court of Appeals for the Seventh Circuit affirmed, holding that the Act forbids the reevaluation of a sentence under the Act by a second judge, even if the second judge makes an explicit finding that further treatment under the Act would not benefit the offender (642 F2d 1077).

On certiorari, the United States Supreme Court reversed and remanded. In an opinion by MARSHALL, J., joined by BURGER Ch. J., and WHITE, BLACKMUN, and REHNQUIST, JJ., it was held that the Youth Corrections Act does not require that a youth offender who is sentenced to a consecutive adult term of imprisonment while serving his sentence under the Act must receive treatment under the Act for the remainder of his youth sentence if the judge imposing the subsequent adult sentence determines that the youth will not benefit from further such treatment during the remainder of his youth sentence, the Act authorizing the judge who sentences a youth offender to a consecutive adult term to require that the offender also serve the remainder of his youth sentence as an adult, and Congress not intending that the person who commits serious crimes while serving a sentence under the Act should automatically receive treatment that has proven futile.

POWELL, J., concuring in the judgment, agreed with the court's conclusion that the defendant did not have to be separated from other adult offenders for the remainder of his youth sentence, but expressed the view that the court should not have taken up the issue of whether the Bureau of Prisons was precluded by the Youth Corrections Act from deciding on its own to treat the defendant as an adult offender for the remainder of his term under the Act.

STEVENS, J., joined by BRENNAN and O'CONNOR, JJ., dissented, expressing the view that there is nothing in the Youth Corrections Act which supports the court's holding that a judge may modify a sentence under the Act after it has become final, the modification in effect increasing the severity of the original sentence.

COUNSEL

David A. Strauss argued the cause for petitioner, pro hac vice, by special leave of court.

Jerold S. Solovy argued the cause for respondent.

PIPER AIRCRAFT COMPANY, Petitioner,

v

GAYNELL REYNO, Personal Representative of the
Estate of William Fehilly, et al. (No. 80–848)

HARTZELL PROPELLER, INC., Petitioner,

v

GAYNELL REYNO, Personal Representative of the
Estate of William Fehilly, et al. (No. 80–883)

— US —, 70 L Ed 2d 419, 102 S Ct 252

Argued October 14, 1981.
Decided December 8, 1981.

Decision: Plaintiff's showing that substantive law of
alternative forum would be less favorable to
plaintiff than that of chosen forum, held not to
defeat motion to dismiss on ground of forum
non conveniens.

SUMMARY

Following an air crash that occurred in Scotland,
a California probate court appointed an administra-
tix of the estates of several Scottish citizens killed in
the accident. Subsequently, she commenced wrongful death actions against the American manufacturers of the plane and its propellers in the Superior
Court of California, claiming negligence and strict
liability. The British owner of the plane and the
Scottish operator and pilot were not parties to the
litigation. The suit was removed to the United
States District Court for the Central District of
34

California and then transferred pursuant to 28 USCS § 1404(a) to the United States District Court for the Middle District of Pennsylvania. Both defendants moved to dismiss the action on the ground of forum non conveniens, and the District Court granted the motions, concluding after balancing private interest factors affecting the convenience of the litigants and public interest factors affecting the convenience of the forum that Scotland was the appropriate forum, and explicitly rejecting the plaintiff's contention that dismissal would be unfair because Scotish law was less favorable to the plaintiffs, reasoning that the possibility that dismissal might lead to an unfavorable change in the law did not deserve significant weight (479 F Supp 727). On appeal, the United States Court of Appeals for the Third Circuit reversed, holding that the District Court abused its discretion in conducting the forum non conveniens analysis and that, in any event, dismissal is never appropriate where the law of the alternative forum is less favorable to the plaintiff (630 F2d 149).

On certiorari, the United States Supreme Court reversed. In an opinion by MARSHALL, J., joined by BURGER, Ch J., BLACKMUN, J., and REHNQUIST, J., it was held that (1) plaintiffs may not defeat a motion to dismiss on the ground of forum non conveniens merely by showing that the substantive law that would be applied in the alternative forum is less favorable to the plaintiffs than that of the chosen forum, since the possibility of a change in substantive law should ordinarily not be given conclusive or even substantial weight in the forum non conveniens inquiry, and (2) the Federal District Court did not abuse its discretion in weighing the private and public interests and granting the defendants' motion to dismiss, since the District Court (1) did not act unreasonably in concluding that fewer evidentiary problems would be posed if the trial were held in Scotland, a large proportion of the relevant evidence being located in Great Britain, (2) correctly concluded that the problems posed by the inability to implead potential third party defendants clearly supported holding the trial in Scotland, and (3) did not act unreasonably in deciding that the public interest favored trial in Scotland, the accident having occurred in its air space, all the decedents being Scottish, and apart from the manufacturers, all potential plaintiffs and defendants being either Scottish or English.

WHITE, J., concurring in part and dissenting in part, joined the court's decision that plaintiffs may not defeat a motion to dismiss by showing that the substantive law that would be applied in the alternative forum is less favorable to them, and stated that he would not proceed to deal with the issue of the District Court's discretion in handling the forum non conveniens inquiry.

STEVENS, J., joined by BRENNAN, J., dissented, agreeing that the question presented in the petition for certiorari about whether a motion to dismiss on grounds of forum non conveniens must be denied whenever the law of the alternative forum is less favorable to recovery than that which would be applied by the District Court should be answered in the negative, but stating that having decided that question, he would simply remand the case to the Court of Appeals for further consideration of the question whether the District Court correctly decided that Pennsylvania was not a convenient forum in which to litigate a claim against a Pennsylvania company that a plane was defectively designed and manufactured in Pennsylvania.

POWELL, J., and O'CONNOR, J., did not participate.

COUNSEL

James M. FitzSimons argued the cause for petitioner in No. 80-848.

Warner W. Gardner argued the cause for petitioner in No. 80-883.

Daniel C. Cathcart argued the cause for respondents in both cases.

GARY E. WIDMAR, et al., Petitioners,

v

CLARK VINCENT et al.

— US —, 70 L Ed 2d 440, 102 S Ct 269

Argued October 6, 1981.

Decided December 8, 1981.

Decision: State university's refusal to grant student religious group access to university facilities generally open to other student groups, held unjustifiable, content based exclusion of religious speech.

SUMMARY

A state university, which routinely provided university facilities for meetings of registered student organizations, excluded from the facilities a student group desiring to use them for religious worship and religious discussion. The exclusion was based on a university regulation prohibiting the use of buildings or grounds "for purposes of religious worship or religious teaching." Several students who were members of the group brought suit challenging the regulation in the United States District Court for the Western District of Missouri, alleging that the university's discrimination against religious activity and discussion violated their rights to free exercise of religion, equal protection, and freedom of speech under the First and Fourteenth Amendments of the Federal Constitution. The District Court upheld the challenged regulation, holding that the regulation was required by the establish-

38

ment clause of the federal Constitution. The court reasoned that the state could not provide facilities for religious use without giving prohibited support to an institution of religion, and rejected the argument that the university could not discriminate against religious speech on the basis of its content (480 F Supp 907). The United States Court of Appeals for the Eighth Circuit reversed, the court viewing the university regulation as a content-based discrimination against religious speech for which there was no compelling justification, and holding that the establishment clause does not bar a policy of equal assess in which facilities are open to groups and speakers of all kinds (635 F2d 1310).

On certiorari, the United States Supreme Court affirmed. In an opinion by POWELL, J., joined by BURGER, Ch. J., and BRENNAN, MARSHALL, BLACK-MUN, REHNQUIST, and O'CONNOR, JJ., it was held that the state university's exclusionary policy violated the fundamental principle that a state regulation of speech should be content-neutral, since (1) by creating a discriminatory exclusion from a public forum based on the religious content of a group's intended speech, the university was required to show that its regulation was necessary to serve a compelling state interest and that it was narrowly drawn to achieve that end, (2) while the university's interest in complying with its constitutional obligations could be characterized as compelling, a policy permitting "equal access" to the religious group would not necessarily have been incompatible with the establishment clause of the First Amendment in view of the fact that such policy would have a secular purpose, would avoid entanglement with religion, and would not have the primary effect of advancing religion, in the absence of evidence that religion would not dominate an open forum, and (3) the state's asserted interest in achieving greater separation of church and state than is already ensured under the establishment clause is limited by both the free exercise clause and the free speech clause of the First Amendment and is insufficiently compelling to justify content-based discrimination against the student group's religous speech.

STEVENS, J., concurring in the judgment, expressed the view that, while the university in the case at bar did not establish a sufficient justification for its refusal to allow the student religious group to engage in religious worship on campus, a university may nonetheless exercise a measure of control over the agenda for student use of school facilities, preferring some subjects over others, without needing to identify so-called "compelling state interests."

WHITE, J., dissenting, expressed the view that the university's application of its regulation to prevent the student religious group from holding services in university facilities did not violate the First and Fourteenth Amendments, the minimal burden imposed on the student group requiring the state to do no more than demonstrate that the regulation furthered some permissible state end which was embodied by the state's interest in avoiding claims that it was financing or otherwise supporting religious worship.

COUNSEL

Ted D. Ayres argued the cause for petitioners.
James M. Smart, Jr., argued the cause for respondents.

CITIZENS AGAINST RENT CONTROL/
COALITION FOR FAIR HOUSING, et al.,
Appellants,

v

CITY OF BERKELEY, CALIFORNIA, et al.

— US —, 70 L Ed 2d 492, 102 S Ct 434

Argued October 14, 1981.
Decided December 14, 1981.

Decision: Municipal ordinance placing $250 limitation on contributions to committees formed to support or oppose ballot measures, held violative of First Amendment rights of association and speech.

SUMMARY

Pursuant to a Berkeley, California, ordinance which placed a limitation of $250 on contributions to committees formed to support or oppose ballot measures, the city fair campaign practices commission ordered an unincorporated association formed to oppose a particular ballot measure to pay into the city treasury the amount of contributions it received in excess of the permitted amount. Two weeks before the election, the association sought and obtained from the Superior Court, Alameda County, a temporary restraining order prohibiting enforcement of the ordinance. Following the ballot measure's defeat, the Superior Court granted the association's motion for summary judgment, declaring that the ordinance was invalid on its face because it violated the state constitution and the First
42

Amendment of the Federal Constitution, and the
California Court of Appeal, First District, affirmed
that conclusion (160 Cal Rptr 448). The Supreme
Court of California reversed, concluding that the
ordinance furthered compelling governmental interests because it ensured that special interest groups
could not corrupt the initiative process by spending
large amounts to support or oppose a ballot measure and that the ordinance accomplished its goal
by the least restrictive means available (27 Cal3d
819, 614 P2d 742, 167 Cal Rptr 84).

On appeal, the United States Supreme Court
reversed and remanded. In an opinion by BURGER,
Ch. J., joined by BRENNAN, POWELL, REHNQUIST, and
STEVENS, JJ., it was held that the restraint imposed
by the ordinance on rights of association and in
turn on individual and collective rights of expression contravened both the right of association and
the speech guarantees of the First Amendment, the
ordinance not advancing a legitimate governmental
interest significant enough to justify its infringement
on First Amendment rights, since the public interest
allegedly advanced by the ordinance—identifying
the sources of support for and opposition to ballot
measures—was insubstantial, since contributors
were required to make their identities known under
another provision, and there being no significant
state or public interest in curtailing debate and
discussion of a ballot measure, whatever may be the
state interest or degree of that interest in regulating
and limiting contributions to or expenditures of a
candidate or a candidate's committee.

REHNQUIST, J., concurred, expressing the view
that the municipal ordinance was not aimed only at
corporations, but sought to impose an across-the-

43

board limitation on the sizes of contributions to committees formed to support or oppose ballot measure referenda and there was no indication that the ordinance was aimed at corporations as opposed to individuals, and that in this situation there was no state interest which could justify a limitation on the exercise of rights guaranteed under the First and Fourteenth Amendments.

MARSHALL, J., concurring in the judgment, expressed the view that governmental action limiting contributions is subject to less rigorous scrutiny than a direct restriction on expenditures and that there being no evidentiary support in the record to justify the conclusion that large contributions to ballot measure committees undermined the confidence of the citizenry in government, the state had not demonstrated a sufficient governmental interest to sustain the indirect infringement on First Amendment interests resulting from the operation of the ordinance.

BLACKMUN, J., joined by O'CONNOR, J., concurring in the judgment, expressed the view that the contribution limitation at issue encroached directly on political expression and association and could not survive constitutional challenge unless it withstood exacting scrutiny and that the city had neither proved a genuine threat to its important governmental interest in maintaining voter confidence in government nor employed means closely drawn to avoid unnecessary abridgement of protected activity.

WHITE, J., dissented, expressing the view that the ordinance represented such a negligible intrusion on expression and association that the measure should be upheld, that the ordinance did not go beyond what the First Amendment permits, the

ordinance neither controlling the quantity or content of speech nor completely prohibiting contributions and expenditures but rather by assuring that a
diversity of views would be presented to the voters
facilitated and enlarged public discussion and participation in the electoral process, goals vital to a self-
governing people, and that the limitations of the
ordinance were content-neutral and served to maximize the exchange of political discourse and to
protect the role of initiative in the state to prevent
the dominance of special interests.

COUNSEL

James R. Parrinello argued the cause for appellants.

Natalie E. West argued the cause for appellees.

POLK COUNTY, et al., Petitioners,

v

RUSSELL RICHARD DODSON

— US —, 70 L Ed 2d 509, 102 S Ct 445

Argued October 13, 1981.
Decided December 14, 1981.

Decision: Public defender performing lawyer's traditional functions, held not acting "under color of state law" for purposes of suit under 42 USCS § 1983.

SUMMARY

An individual convicted at a state criminal trial for robbery subsequently brought an action under 42 USCS § 1983 in the United States District Court for the Southern District of Iowa alleging that a public defender who was a full-time employee of the county had failed to represent him adequately in an appeal to the state's highest court. The individual asserted that the public defender—who had moved for permission to withdraw as counsel on the ground that the claims asserted on appeal were frivolous—had deprived him of his right to counsel, subjected to him to cruel and unusual punishment, and had denied him due process of law. To establish that the public defender had acted "under color of state law," a jurisdictional requisite for a § 1983 action, the individual relied on the public defender's employment by the county. In addition to the public offender, the individual also sued the county, its board of supervisors, and its offender advocate. The

District Court dismissed the claims against all the defendants, holding that the relevant actions of the public defender had not occurred under color of state law (483 F Supp 347). However, the United States Court of Appeals for the Eighth Circuit reversed (628 F2d 1104).

On certiorari, the United States Supreme Court reversed. In an opinion by POWELL, J., joined by BURGER, Ch. J., and BRENNAN, WHITE, MARSHALL, REHNQUIST, STEVENS, and O'CONNOR JJ., it was held that, for purposes of a civil rights action under 42 USCS § 1983, a public defender does not act "under color of state law" when performing a lawyer's traditional functions as counsel to a defendant in a criminal proceeding, and therefore the complaint by the convicted state criminal that the public defender representing him had violated § 1983 by failing to represent him adequately in his appeal should be dismissed, especially since (1) although the employment relationship between the state and a public defender paid by the state is a relevant factor, it is insufficient to establish that a public defender acts under color of state law within the meaning of § 1983, and (2) the traditional adversarial functions performed by the public defender are private in nature and are not in the nature of those performed under color of state law.

BURGER, Ch. J., concurring, emphasized that governmental participation in providing counsel for an accused is very limited, the government undertaking only to provide a professionally qualified advocate wholly independent of the government.

BLACKMUN, J., dissenting, expressed the view that the public defender was acting "under color of state law," since (1) the presumption that a state employee acts under color of state law when exercising his official duties is not overridden by the public defender's ethical obligations to his client, and (2) the court's attempt to draw distinctions based on the particular functions a public defender performs were unconvincing.

COUNSEL

Norman G. Jesse argued the cause for petitioners.

John D. Hudson argued the cause for respondent.

Edwin S. Kneedler argued the cause for the United States as amicus curiae, by special leave of court.

———————

DAVID R. HARRIS, Superintendent, Green Haven
Correctional Facility, Petitioner,

v

JOSE RIVERA

— US —, 70 L Ed 2d 530, 102 S Ct 460

Decided December 14, 1981.

Decision: Federal court's order in habeas corpus
proceeding that state trial court must grant
habeas petitioner new criminal trial or explain
reasons for its inconsistent verdicts, held erroneous.

SUMMARY

A person who was convicted of robbery, grand
larceny, and burglary in a state bench trial and
whose conviction was affirmed on appeal petitioned
the United States District Court for the Southern
District of New York for a writ of habeas corpus.
That court rejected several challenges by the petitioner to the conviction, describing them as varia-
tions on the claim of insufficiency of the evidence.
On appeal from that judgment, the United States
Court of Appeals for the Second Circuit concluded
that there was an apparent inconsistency in the state
trial judge's general verdicts acquitting one of the
petitioner's co-defendants and convicting the petitioner, because all defendants would have been
found guilty if the trial judge had credited all of the
testimony of the government's only witness but all
defendants would have been found not guilty if the
judge had credited all of the testimony of the

49

defense's only witness. The Court of Appeals held that the trial judge's failure to explain this inconsistency on the record violated the due process clause of the Fourteenth Amendment and therefore entered an order requiring the state trial court either to grant petitioner a new trial or to demonstrate by appropriate findings that there was a rational basis for the facially inconsistent verdicts (643 F2d 86).

Granting certiorari, the United States Supreme Court reversed. In a per curiam opinion, expressing the view of BURGER, Ch. J., and BRENNAN, WHITE, BLACKMUN, POWELL, REHNQUIST, STEVENS, and O'CONNOR, JJ., it was held that the Court of Appeals erred when it entered its order with respect to the state trial court, there being no federal requirement that a state trial judge explain his reasons for acquitting a defendant in a state criminal trial, and any error from the resting of such an acquittal on an improper ground not creating a constitutional defect in a guilty verdict that is supported by sufficient evidence and is the product of a fair trial.

MARSHALL, J., dissented, expressing the view that the court should utilize the practice of deciding cases summarily, without benefit of oral argument and full briefing with more caution than has been true in the recent past.

CENTRAL TRUST COMPANY, ROCHESTER,
N.Y., Petitioner,

v

OFFICIAL CREDITORS' COMMITTEE OF
GEIGER ENTERPRISES, INC., et al.

— US —, 70 L Ed 2d 542, 102 S Ct 695

Decided January 11, 1982.

Decision: Dismissal of Chapter XI petition filed
under 1898 Bankruptcy Act in order to refile
under Chapter 11 of 1978 Bankruptcy Code,
held not authorized by Bankruptcy Rule 11-
42(a) or § 403(a) of Bankruptcy Reform Act of
1978.

SUMMARY

On August 15, 1979, a corporation filed a petition
in the United States District Court for the Western
District of New York seeking relief under Chapter
XI of the Bankruptcy Act of 1898 (former 11 USCS
§§ 701 et seq.). Subsequently numerous creditors,
including the United States, filed claims and the
Bankruptcy Court established a creditors' committee
to represent the interests of creditors with relatively
small claims. On October 1, 1979, the Bankruptcy
Code (11 USCS §§ 101 et seq.), as enacted by the
Bankruptcy Reform Act of 1978 (92 Stat 2549)
became effective, and several of the debtor's wholly-
owned subsidiaries and affiliate corporations filed
petitions for relief under Chapter 11 of the Code
(11 USCS §§ 1101 et seq.). Soon thereafter, the
debtor moved to dismiss its Chapter XI petition on

51

the representation that if dismissal were granted it to would immediately file a petition under Chapter 11 of the Code and would seek substantive consolidation of its proceedings with the proceedings of its subsidiary and affiliate corporations. The United States, the creditors' committee, and a secured creditor opposed the motion, arguing that such dismissal was prohibited by § 403(a) of the Bankruptcy Reform Act—which provides that cases commenced under the Bankruptcy Act be conducted and determined as if the new Code had not been enacted and that the substantive rights of parties in connection with any such bankruptcy case continued to be governed by the law applicable to such case as if the Code had not been enacted. The United States Bankruptcy Court for the Western District of New York rejected this argument and granted the motion to dismiss the corporation's Chapter XI petition, relying primarily upon Rule 11-42(a) of the Rules of Bankruptcy Procedure, the court characterizing this voluntary dismissal rule as unique in that the purpose of dismissal is to permit refiling under compatible substantive law provisions and to permit substantive consolidation, and finding that consolidation of the debtor's proceedings with the proceedings of it subsidiaries and affiliates would be in the best interest of the estate. The District Court reversed, holding the plain meaning of § 403(a) to be that the Bankruptcy Court must apply the Bankruptcy Act to cases filed prior to October 1, 1979, and that such cases shall proceed as if the new Code had never been enacted, but the United States Court of Appeals for the Second Circuit reversed the District Court's decision, holding that Rule 11-42(a) must be read in conjunction with § 403(a) to permit dismissal and refiling in certain cases, and

52

that the operative test was whether the estate's best interest will be served by such procedure (635 F2d 106).

Granting certiorari, the United States Supreme Court reversed. In a per curiam opinion, expressing the view of BURGER, Ch. J., and BRENNAN, WHITE, BLACKMUN, POWELL, REHNQUIST, and O'CONNOR, JJ., it was held that a petition seeking relief under Chapter XI of the Bankruptcy Act could not be dismissed in order to allow the debtor to file a petition under Chapter 11 of the Bankruptcy Code, since (1) Rule 11-42(a) provided no authority for such a procedure, the language of the rule contemplating a voluntary dismissal which results in an adjudication of the debtor's bankruptcy or one which revests title of all property in the debtor and removes it from the protection of the bankruptcy laws, and not contemplating a dismissal which neither declares the debtor bankrupt nor restores the creditors' rights against the debtor's property, but simply holds matters in abeyance while the debtor files its petition under a new law, and (2) the language of § 403(a) of the Bankruptcy Reform Act is unequivocal and makes no exception for petitions to be refiled under the Code, even if the refiling would not actually prejudice the creditors and even if consolidation of the debtor's petition with those filed under the Code by its subsidiaries and affiliate corporations would serve the best interest of the estate or would conserve judicial resources.

STEVENS, J., joined by MARSHALL, J., dissenting, expressed the view that if a bankruptcy judge, with the consent of all parties to a proceeding commenced prior to October 1, 1979, correctly concluded that the best interest of the estate and all its creditors and the judiciary would be served by permitting the voluntary dismissal of that proceeding and the immediate commencement of a new proceeding under the new Code, that action would not be prohibited by § 403(a) of the Bankruptcy Reform Act, and that permitting the debtor in this case to dismiss its petition under the Bankruptcy Act and to file a petition under the new Code, thereby facilitating consolidation of its petition with the petitions of its numerous affiliates and subsidiaries, was perfectly consistent with the spirit of both bankruptcy statutes.

DONALD G. BOAG, Petitioner,

v

ELLIS MacDOUGALL, Director, Arizona
Department of Corrections

— US —, 70 L Ed 2d 551, 102 S Ct 700

Decided January 11, 1982.

Decision: State prisoner's crudely written, pro se
complaint alleging his placement in solitary
confinement for one-week period without any
notice of charges or any hearing, held sufficient
to state cause of action.

SUMMARY

A state prisoner filed a crudely written, pro se
complaint in the United States District Court for the
District of Arizona alleging, inter alia, that he had
been placed in solitary confinement without any
notice of charges or any hearing, that he was threatened with violence when asked what the charges
were, and that he was still in "the hole" a week
later. The District Court dismissed the complaint on
the ground that the case was moot because the
prisoner had been transferred to another facility.
On appeal, the United States Court of Appeals for
the Ninth Circuit did not endorse the District
Court's mootness rationale, but nevertheless affirmed, concluding that (1) the District Courts have
especially broad discretion to dismiss frivolous actions against prison officials under 28 USCS
§ 1915(d) and (2), the prisoner's action was frivo-

lous because it did not state a claim upon which relief can be granted.

Granting certiorari, the United States Supreme Court reversed. In a per curiam opinion, expressing the view of BRENNAN, WHITE, MARSHALL, BLACKMUN, POWELL, STEVENS, and O'CONNOR, JJ., it was held that the complaint states a cause of action and that the case did not become moot when the prisoner was transferred to another facility.

O'CONNOR, J., concurring, emphasized that nothing in the court's opinion prevents the District Court on remand from dismissing this suit under 28 USCS § 1915(d) if it finds grounds to believe that the complaint is malicious or frivolous.

REHNQUIST, J., joined by BURGER, Ch. J., and WHITE, J., dissented, expressing the view that (1) there was a sufficient basis for affirming the dismissal of the complaint, since the prisoner failed to comply with the District Court's local rules for filing a complaint, and (2) even if there were no grounds for affirmance, the case was unworthy of the court's attention, since it would have no importance beyond the facts and parties involved.

TERRELL DON HUTTO, Director, Virginia State
Department of Corrections, et al., Petitioners,

v

ROGER TRENTON DAVIS

— US —, 70 L Ed 2d 556, 102 S Ct 703

Decided January 11, 1982.

Decision: Sentence of two consecutive 20-year
prison terms and two fines of $10,000 for con-
victions of possession and distribution of 9
ounces of marijuana, held not to constitute
cruel and unusual punishment under Eighth
Amendment.

SUMMARY

An individual convicted in the Circuit Court of
Wythe County, Virginia, on separate counts of intent to distribute and the distribution of nine
ounces of marijuana was sentenced to two consecutive 20-year terms and two separate fines of
$10,000, the state's maximum penalty on each count
being $25,000 and 40 years in prison. The defen-
dant subsequently filed a petition for a writ of
habeas corpus in the United States District Court
for the Western District of Virginia. The District
Court issued the writ, holding that a 40-year sentence and $20,000 fine was so grossly out of pro-
portion to the severity of the crimes that it constituted cruel and unusual punishment in violation of
the Eighth and Fourteenth Amendments (432 F
Supp 444). A panel of the United States Court of
Appeals for the Fourth Circuit reversed, noting that

57

the Supreme Court had never found a sentence for a term of years within the limits authorized by statute to be, by itself, a cruel and unusual punishment (585 F2d 1226), but sitting en banc, the Court of Appeals reheard the case and affirmed the award of habeas relief (601 F2d 153). The United States Supreme Court granted certiorari, vacated the judgment of the Court of Appeals, and remanded the case for reconsideration in light of a subsequent Supreme Court decision (63 L Ed 2d 782), but the Court of Appeals again affirmed the District Court (646 F2d 123).

Granting certiorari, the United States Supreme Court reversed and remanded. In a per curiam opinion expressing the view of BURGER, Ch. J., and WHITE, BLACKMUN, REHNQUIST, and O'CONNOR, JJ., it was held that the defendant's sentence did not constitute cruel and unusual punishment in violation of the Eighth and Fourteenth Amendments, the presence or absence of violence in the defendant's crime, notwithstanding the purpose behind the criminal statute, a comparison of maximum penalties for similar offenses in other states, or a comparison of punishments applicable to other offenses within the state, since for such a crime classifiable as a felony, the length of a sentence actually imposed is purely a matter of legislative prerogative, and federal courts should thus be reluctant to review such legislatively mandated terms of imprisonment.

POWELL, J., concurring in the judgment, expressed the view that although the sentence was unjust and disproportionate to the offense, the Supreme Court's prior decision was controlling on the facts in the instant case.

BRENNAN, J., joined by MARSHALL and STEVENS, JJ., dissented, expressing the view that this case was

58

one of those exceedingly rare cases in which a sentence should be invalidated on Eighth Amendment grounds, and that, in any event, the case should not have been decided in summary fashion without benefit of full briefing or oral argument.

———

RAYMOND J. DONOVAN, Secretary of Labor, et
al., Appellants,

v

RICHLAND COUNTY ASSOCIATION FOR
RETARDED CITIZENS

— US —, 70 L Ed 2d 570, 102 S Ct 713

Decided January 11, 1982.

Decision: Appeal taken to Federal Court of Appeals
of District Court decision finding application of
Fair Labor Standards Act unconstitutional, held
improper under 28 USCS §§ 1252 and 1291,
and appeal to Supreme Court dismissed.

SUMMARY

A county association for retarded citizens brought
an action in the United States District Court for the
District of Montana, seeking a declaratory judgment
that the Fair Labor Standards Act (29 USCS §§ 201
et seq.) did not apply to employees of a mental
health facility operated by the association, or, in the
alternative, that an application of the Act to the
facility would be unconstitutional. The District
Court held that the Act was unconstitutional as
applied to the association in its operation of the
facility, and the United States Court of Appeals for
the Ninth Circuit affirmed.

On appeal, the United States Supreme Court
vacated the judgment and opinion of the Court of
Appeals. In a per curiam opinion, expressing the
view of BURGER, Ch. J., and BRENNAN, WHITE, MAR-
SHALL, REHNQUIST, STEVENS, and O'CONNOR, JJ., it

was held that (1) the Court of Appeals lacked
jurisdiction of the appeal from the decision of the
District Court holding the application of the Fair
Labor Standards Act unconstitutional, the right under 28 USCS § 1252 of a party to pursue a direct
appeal to the United States Supreme Court from a
federal court order holding a federal statute unconstitutional also serving to deprive the Court of
Appeals of jurisdiction, 28 USCS § 1291 providing
that "[t]he courts of appeals shall have jurisdiction
of appeals from all final decisions of the district
courts of the United States . . . except where a
direct review may be had in the Supreme Court,"
(2) the Supreme Court would dismiss the appeal
filed from the decision of the Court of Appeals,
since the government's proper course of conduct
was to file a direct appeal, but at the time of the
Supreme Court's decision, such relief was foreclosed
by 28 USCS § 2101(a), and (3) the Supreme Court
would decline to remand the matter to the District
Court for entry of a fresh decree from which a
timely appeal to the Supreme Court might be taken,
since the government, by obtaining an intermediate
decision from the Court of Appeals that had no
power to consider the case and thus failing to
pursue timely the right to immediate review conferred by § 1252, simply failed to follow the clear
commands of §§ 1252 and 1291, the fact that the
Court of Appeals also held the Act unconstitutional
not resurrecting the right created by § 1252 that
had lapsed by the government's action.

POWELL, J., joined by BLACKMUN, J., concurring in
part and dissenting in part, agreed with the court's
decision to vacate the judgment and opinion of the
Court of Appeals, but stated that he would not

simply dismiss the government's appeal, but would remand the matter to the District Court for entry of a fresh decree from which a timely appeal might be taken, Congress not intending 28 USCS § 1252 to serve the function of blocking review in the Supreme Court in such circumstances and the court's disposition defeating the fundamental purpose of § 1252 to expedite review by the Supreme Court.

LARRY BLANDING, et al., Appellants,

v

E. M. DuBOSE, et al.

— US —, 70 L Ed 2d 576, 102 S Ct 715

Decided January 11, 1982.

Decision: Letter to Attorney General advising of results of county referendum endorsing at-large method of electing county council, held to be request for reconsideration of Attorney General's prior objections to method and not pre-clearance request under Voting Rights Act (42 USCS § 1973c).

SUMMARY

Following the enactment of a 1975 South Carolina statute permitting a county to hold a referendum to select a form of local government and to choose between at-large and single-member district elections and assigning the council-administrator form of government with council members elected at-large to Sumter County if the county did not hold a referendum, Sumter County chose not to hold a referendum, and the county council passed a resolution and ordinance adopting the assigned form of government and method of election. Subsequently, in order to comply with § 5 of the Voting Rights Act of 1965 (42 USCS § 1973c)—which provides that when a covered political subdivision enacts a voting procedure different from that in effect on November 1, 1964, the political subdivision must either seek a declaratory judgment approving the procedure or submit it to the United States Attorney General for preclearance—the county administrator submitted the ordinance and a 1967 state statute which had established a new form of government for the county consisting of a seven-member county commission elected at-large to the Attorney General for preclearance. The Attorney General made a timely objection to the at-large method of election of the council, but interposed no objection to the county-administrator form of government. The county requested the Attorney General to reconsider his objection to at-large elections, and in 1978, after continuing correspondence, the Attorney General declined to withdraw the objection. Prior to the next scheduled council election, private parties and the United States brought separate suits in the United States District Court for the District of South Carolina to prevent elections under the at-large system, and a three-judge District Court permanently enjoined county elections until the requirements of the Voting Rights Act were fulfilled. That fall, the county decided to hold a referendum in which voters were asked whether they preferred that council members be elected at-large or from single-member districts and the majority endorsed the at-large method. On June 4, 1979, the Attorney General received a letter from the county advising him of the referendum results. Following a conference between county officials and representatives of the United States Department of Justice, the Attorney General, referring to the county's letter as a "request for reconsideration" under 28 CFR § 51.21(b), refused to withdraw the objection to at-large elections, but advised the county that the Department had not yet completed its review, and

64

subsequently the Attorney General again refused to withdraw his objection. County officials then moved the District Court for summary judgment, contending that the June letter was a preclearance submission, not a request for reconsideration, and that since § 5 required the Attorney General to object within 60 days of a preclearance submission and the Attorney General did not interpose an objection by August 3, the county was free under § 5 to proceed with at-large elections. A three-judge District Court was again convened and it agreed with the county officials, rejecting the Attorney General's argument that the letter was a request for reconsideration of his timely objection to at-large elections (509 F Supp 1334).

On appeal, the United States Supreme Court reversed. In a per curiam opinion expressing the view of BURGER, Ch. J., and BRENNAN, WHITE, MARSHALL, BLACKMUN, STEVENS, and O'CONNOR, JJ., it was held that the letter submitted by the county to the Attorney General advising him of the results of the referendum was not a preclearance submission under § 5 of the Voting Rights Act, but was a request under 28 CFR § 51.21(b) for reconsideration of the Attorney General's earlier objections, even though the letter was filed after the time prescribed by § 51.21(b), since the change to at-large county elections already had been submitted to the Attorney General for preclearance, the referendum merely approved the pre-existing at-large method that was previously submitted to the Attorney General and that was the subject of the outstanding objection, and the results of the referendum constituted further "explanatory information," within the meaning of § 51.21(b), concerning at-

65

large elections which the county asked the Attorney General to consider.

REHNQUIST, J., joined by POWELL, J., concurred, expressing agreement with the court's reasoning and conclusion, but stating that the record in the case illustrated the unreasonably burdensome and unrealistic control which the federal government routinely exercises over state and local governments under the Voting Rights Act.

CHARLES D. BONANNO LINEN SERVICE, INC.,
Petitioner,

v

NATIONAL LABOR RELATIONS BOARD et al.

— US —, 70 L Ed 2d 656, 102 S Ct 720

Argued October 13, 1981.
Decided January 12, 1982.

Decision: Employer's unilateral withdrawal from multiemployer bargaining unit, held not justified by bargaining impasse.

SUMMARY

A linen supply company which was a member of a multiemployer collective bargaining association was struck by the union representing its drivers after the union and the association had reached an impasse in bargaining. The company hired permanent replacements for the striking drivers and notified the association and the union that it was withdrawing from the association. Because of this purported withdrawal, the union commenced unfair labor practice proceedings before the National Labor Relations Board against the company. Subsequently, the union reached an agreement with the association. The union informed the company that it considered the company bound by the new contract, but the company denied it was so bound. The National Labor Relations Board affirmed an administrative law judge's conclusion that no unusual circumstances excused the company's withdrawal from the multiemployer unit, and ordered the company to sign and retroactively to implement the contract (243 NLRB 1093). According to the Board, the company's withdrawal, and consequent refusal to execute the new contract, constituted an unfair labor practice in violation of §§ 8(a)(5) and 8(a)(1) of the National Labor Relations Act (29 USCS §§ 158(a)(5) and 158(a)(1)). The United States Court of Appeals for the First Circuit enforced the Board's order (630 F2d 25).

On certiorari, the United States Supreme Court affirmed. In an opinion by WHITE, J., joined by BRENNAN, MARSHALL, BLACKMUN, and STEVENS, JJ., it was held that (1) an impasse in collective bargaining does not justify unilateral withdrawal from a multiemployer bargaining unit, and (2) the decision of the National Labor Relations Board ordering the linen supply company to sign and implement the contract negotiated between the multiemployer association and the union should therefore be enforced.

STEVENS, J., concurring, expressed the view that (1) the court's holding in the case at bar does not impair an employer's freedom to structure the manner in which it will conduct collective bargaining and does not preclude an employer from explicitly conditioning its participation in group bargaining on any special terms of its own design, and (2) absent an unequivocal committment to be bound by group action, an employer is free to withdraw from group negotiation at any time, or simply to reject the terms of the final group contract.

BURGER, Ch. J., joined by REHNQUIST, J., dissenting, expressed the view that while a brief cessation in bargaining, without more, does not trigger a right to withdraw from a multiemployer unit, an employer should not be prohibited from withdrawing from an impasse, such as that in the case at bar, which is characterized by a complete breakdown in negotiations coupled with a prolonged strike and walkout, especially where the union may have the opportunity to negotiate separate "interim" agreements with individual employers.

O'CONNOR, J., joined by POWELL, J., dissenting, expressed the view that (1) the Board should examine the circumstances surrounding and following an impasse to determine whether an unusual circumstance sufficient to justify withdrawal has occurred, and (2) the court's decision in the case at bar allowed both a complete breakdown in negotiations and a fragmented bargaining unit, neither of which further the goal of multiemployer bargaining to promote labor peace through strengthened collective bargaining.

COUNSEL

Sidney A. Coven argued the cause for petitioner.

Norton J. Come argued the cause for respondent NLRB.

James T. Grady argued the cause for respondents Teamsters Local Union No. 25, et al.

CLARENCE E. CABELL, et al., Appellants,

v

JOSE CHAVEZ-SALIDO et al.

— US —, 70 L Ed 2d 677, 102 S Ct 735

Argued November 3, 1981.
Decided January 12, 1982.

Decision: State statute requiring peace officers, including deputy probation officers, to be United States citizens, held not violative of equal protection clause of Fourteenth Amendment.

SUMMARY

Three lawfully admitted permanent resident aliens, after unsuccessfully applying for positions as deputy probation officers in Los Angeles County, California, filed suit in the United States District Court for the Central District of California challenging the constitutionality of a provision in the California statutes that required "peace officers," including probation officers, to be United States citizens under, inter alia, the equal protection clause of the Fourteenth Amendment. A three-judge panel of the District Court held the provision unconstitutional both on its face and as applied to the aliens (427 F Supp 158), and reaffirmed this position after reconsidering it on remand from the United States Supreme Court (490 F Supp 984).

On direct appeal, the United States Supreme Court reversed and remanded. In an opinion by WHITE, J., joined by BURGER, Ch. J., and POWELL, REHNQUIST, and O'CONNOR, JJ., it was held that the

70

statutory citizenship requirement is valid, probation officers sufficiently partaking of the sovereign's power to exercise coercive force over the individual that they may be required to be citizens.

BLACKMUN, J., joined by BRENNAN, MARSHALL, and STEVENS, JJ., dissented, expressing the view that the statutory provision violates the Fourteenth Amendment's equal protection clause by denying the aliens' right to equal treatment and an individualized determination of fitness.

COUNSEL

William F. Stewart argued the cause for appellants.

Mary S. Burdick argued the cause for appellees.

_____

VALLEY FORGE CHRISTIAN COLLEGE,
Petitioner,

v

AMERICANS UNITED FOR SEPARATION OF
CHURCH AND STATE, Inc., et al.

— US —, 70 L Ed 2d 700, 102 S Ct 752

Argued November 4, 1981.
Decided January 12, 1982.

Decision: Taxpayers' organization dedicated to separation of church and state, held to have no standing to challenge, as violative of First Amendment establishment clause, no-cost transfer of surplus United States property to religious educational institution.

SUMMARY

Pursuant to the Federal Property and Administrative Services Act of 1949 (40 USCS §§ 471 et seq.), which provides for the disposal of surplus property belonging to the United States, the Department of Health, Education, and Welfare conveyed a 77-acre tract that was part of a former military hospital to a nonprofit college-level educational institution operating under the supervision of a religious order. In accordance with a provision of the Act (40 USCS § 484(k)(1)), which authorizes the Department to take into account "any benefit which has accrued or may accrue to the United States" from the transferee's use of the property, the appraised value of the tract was discounted by the Department's computation of a 100-percent public benefit allowance,

which permitted the college to acquire the property
without making any financial payment for it. Subsequently, a nonprofit organization composed of taxpayer members committed to the constitutional
principle of separation of church and state and four
of its employees brought suit in the United States
District Court for the Eastern District of Pennsylvania to challenge the conveyance on the ground that
it violated the establishment clause of the First
Amendment, the complaint asserting that each
member would be deprived of the fair and constitutional use of their tax dollar for constitutional purposes in violation of their rights under the First
Amendment and the plaintiffs seeking a declaration
that the conveyance was null and void and an order
compelling the college to transfer the property to
the United States. On motion of the college, the
District Court granted summary judgment and dismissed the complaint, finding that the organization
and its employees lacked standing to sue as taxpayers and had failed to allege that they had suffered
an actual or concrete injury beyond a generalized
grievance common to all taxpayers. On appeal, the
United States Court of Appeals for the Third Circuit
reversed, holding that the organization and its employees had standing merely as citizens claiming
injury in fact to their shared individuated right to a
government that "shall make no law respecting the
establishment of religion," this "citizen standing"
being sufficient to satisfy the case or controversy
requirement of Article III of the United States
Constitution (619 F2d 252).

On certiorari, the United States Supreme Court
reversed. In an opinion by REHNQUIST, J., joined by
BURGER, Ch. J., and WHITE, POWELL, and O'CON-

NOR, JJ., it was held that the organization and its employees had no standing to challenge the conveyance of the surplus property, since (1) they were without standing to sue as taxpayers, the source of their complaint not being a congressional action and the property transfer about which they complained not being an exercise of authority conferred by the taxing and spending clause of the United States Constitution (Art I, § 8), the authorizing legislation rather being an exercise of Congress' power under the property clause (Art IV, § 3, cl 2), and (2) the organization and its employees had not sufficiently alleged any other basis for standing to bring the action, they having failed to identify any personal injury suffered by them as a consequence of the alleged constitutional error, other than the psychological consequences presumably produced by observation of conduct with which one disagrees.

BRENNAN, J., joined by MARSHALL and BLACKMUN, JJ., dissenting, expressed the view that the court makes a fundamental mistake when it determines that a plaintiff has failed to satisfy the two-pronged "injury-in-fact" test, or any other test of standing, without first determining whether the Constitution or a statute defines injury and creates a cause of action for redress of that injury, in precisely the circumstances presented to the court, that Article III overrides no other provision of the Constitution and the drafters of the Bill of Rights intended that the particular beneficiaries of their legacy should enjoy rights legally enforceable in courts of law, and that a taxpayer has standing at the time he learns of the government's alleged establishment clause violation to seek equitable relief in order to halt the continuing and intolerable burden on his pocketbook, his conscience, and his constitutional rights.

74

STEVENS, J., dissented, stating that the organization and its employees had standing to mount an establishment clause challenge against the government's transfer of property to the church-related college, and expressing the view that for the court to hold that their standing depended upon whether the government's transfer was an exercise of its power to spend money, on the one hand, or its power to dispose of tangible property, on the other, was to trivialize the standing doctrine.

COUNSEL

C. Clark Hodgson, Jr., argued the cause for petitioner.

Solicitor General Rex E. Lee argued the cause for federal respondents in support of the petitioner.

Lee Boothby argued the cause for non-federal respondents.

TEXACO, INC., et al., Appellants,

v

LOUISE F. SHORT et al. (No. 80–965)

———

EDEN H. POND, EDNA H. BOBE AND
CONSOLIDATION COAL COMPANY, Appellants,

v

ULYSSES G. WALDEN, Jr., et al. (No. 80–1018)

— US —, 70 L Ed 2d 738, 102 S Ct 781

Argued October 6, 1981.
Decided January 12, 1982.

Decision: State statute extinguishing unused mineral interests after 20 years unless owner files
statement of claim, held not violative of contract clause, Fifth Amendment just compensation clause, and Fourteenth Amendment due
process and equal protection.

SUMMARY

    In 1971 the Indiana Legislature enacted a statute
providing that a severed mineral interest that is not
used for a period of 20 years automatically lapses
and reverts to the current surface owner of the
property, unless the mineral owner files a statement
of claim in the local county recorder's office. The
statute also provided for a two-year grace period
from the date of its enactment, during which owners
of such mineral interests could file their statements
of claim. In addition, an exception to automatic
lapse was built into the statute whereby an owner of
76

10 or more mineral interests in the same county, under certain circumstances, was entitled to 60 days within which to file a supplemental statement of claim after having received notice of lapse or having obtained actual knowledge of the lapse. Several owners and lessees of lapsed mineral interests, all owning less than 10 such interests within one county, filed actions challenging the constitutionality of the statute, claiming that, in violation of the Fourteenth Amendment, (1) the lack of prior notice of the lapse deprived them of property without due process of law, (2) the statute effected a taking of private property without just compensation, and (3) the exception for owners of 10 or more mineral interests denied them equal protection, and that, in violation of the contract clause of the United States Constitution (Art I, § 10), the statute constituted an impairment of contracts. The Circuit Court of Gibson County, Indiana, held that the statute deprived the mineral interest owners of property without due process and was a taking of property without just compensation. On appeal, the Supreme Court of Indiana reversed, rejecting all of the claims of the mineral interest owners (406 NE2d 625).

On appeal, the United States Supreme Court affirmed. In an opinion by STEVENS, J., joined by BURGER Ch. J., and BLACKMUN, REHNQUIST, and O'CONNOR, JJ., it was held that the state statute (1) did not constitute a taking of private property without just compensation, there being no "taking" in the requirement that an owner of such a property interest come forward and file a current statement of claim, since it is the owner's failure to make use of the property, not any action by the state, which causes the lapse of the property right, (2) did not constitute an impermissible impairment of of contracts in violation of the contracts clause, the mineral owners having not executed any leases to their interests until after the statutory lapse of their mineral rights, their right to enter into such an agreement, even though impaired by the statute, being a property right and not a contract right, and the requirement that, in order to safeguard any contractual rights or obligations, a mineral owner file a statement of claim being a minimal "burden" on contractual obligations that is not beyond the scope of permissible state action, (3) did not extinguish the property rights of mineral owners without adequate notice either on the ground that the state failed adequately to notify the owners of the legal requirements of the statute, the two-year grace period in the statute foreclosing any argument that the statute was invalid because mineral owners may not have had an opportunity to become familiar with its terms, or due to the absence of a requirement that the surface owner give advance notice that the 20-year period is about to expire, the due process clause not requiring a defendant to notify a potential plaintiff that a statute of limitations is about to run, and (4) did not deny equal protection of the law under the Fourteenth Amendment to the owners of less than 10 mineral interests, the statute being rationally related to the legitimate purpose of encouraging the assembly of multiple interests in a single ownership, such owners being more likely to be able to engage in the actual production of mineral resources, and the statute having no adverse impact on owners of fewer mineral interests.

BRENNAN, J., joined by WHITE, MARSHALL, and POWELL, JJ., dissenting, expressed the view that since a form of pre-extinguishment notice, procedurally comparable to that statutorily provided with respect to owners of 10 interests or more, would be entirely consistent with the asserted legislative purpose, such notice was constitutionally required before a person, otherwise without notice of his obligations under the statute, might be deprived of his property "by operation of law."

COUNSEL

John L. Carroll argued the cause for appellants.

Verner P. Partenheimer argued the cause for appellees.

UNITED STATES, Petitioner,

v

JOSEPH J. CLARK, et al.

— US —, 70 L Ed 2d 768, 102 S Ct 805

Argued November 3, 1981.
Decided January 12, 1982.

Decision: "Two-step" pay increase rule of 5 USCS
§ 5334(b), held not to apply to federal employees promoted from prevailing wage rate system
(WS) to General Schedule (GS).

SUMMARY

Six federal civilian employees were promoted
from positions covered by the prevailing wage system (WS), which primarily applies to blue collar
employees, to the General Schedule (GS), which
applies to white collar employees. Salary treatment
for an employee shifted or hired into the GS system
is governed by the provisions of 5 USCS § 5334. An
employee's salary after promotion is determined by
reference to either the "highest previous rate" rule
of 5 USCS § 5334(a) or the "two-step increase" rule
of 5 USCS § 5334(b). The employees, upon their
promotion, were given salary increases based upon
the "highest previous rate" rule, which were much
smaller than if they had received an increase based
upon the "two-step increase" rule. The employees
filed an action in the United States Court of Claims
contending that they were entitled to a two-step
increase. Agreeing with the employees, the court
held that § 5334(b) was applicable to situations
where employees were promoted from the WS to
80

the GS, and invalidated 5 CFR § 531.204(a), which construed § 5334(b) as being limited to transfers or promotions within the GS. (599 F2d 411).

On certiorari, the United States Supreme Court reversed. In an opinion by O'CONNOR, J., expressing the unanimous view of the court, it was held that 5 USCS § 5334(b) does not apply to prevailing rate wage system employees promoted to General Schedule positions.

COUNSEL

Alan I. Horowitz argued the cause for petitioner.

John I. Heise, Jr., argued the cause for respondents.

WASHINGTON, Petitioner,

v

NEIL MARTIN CHRISMAN

— US —, 70 L Ed 2d 778, 102 S Ct 812

Argued November 3, 1981.
Decided January 13, 1982

Decision: Police officer's accompaniment of lawful arrestee to residence and subsequent seizure of contraband in plain view, held not violative of Fourth Amendment.

SUMMARY

A university police officer stopped a student who was carrying a bottle of gin and who appeared to be under the minimum age allowable for possession of alcoholic beverages. The officer asked him for identification. The student requested the opportunity to retrieve his identification from his dormitory room and the officer accompanied him there. While standing in the open doorway watching the student and his roommate, the officer noticed what he believed to be marijuana seeds and a pipe lying on a desk in the room. The officer entered the room, confirmed that the seeds were marijuana and determined that the pipe smelled of marijuana. The officer informed the students of their rights, which they indicated they were willing to waive. The student's roommate then gave the officer a box containing more marijuana and cash. After a second officer arrived, the students voluntarily consented to a search of their room which yielded more marijuana and a quantity of LSD. The roommate was later charged with possession of controlled substances and, after denial of his pretrial motion to suppress the evidence seized in the room, was convicted in a state trial court. The Court of Appeals of Washington affirmed the convictions (24 Wash App 385, 600 P2d 1316). On appeal the Supreme Court of Washington reversed, holding that the officer had no right to enter the students' room and either examine or seize contraband without a warrant (94 Wash 2d 711, 619 P2d 971.).

On certiorari, the United States Supreme Court reversed and remanded. In an opinion by BURGER, Ch. J., joined by BLACKMUN, POWELL, REHNQUIST, STEVENS, and O'CONNOR, JJ., it was held that (1) it is not "unreasonable" under the Fourth Amendment for a police officer, as a matter of routine, to monitor the movements of an arrested person as his judgment dictates following an arrest, (2) such surveillance is not an impermissible invasion of the privacy or personal liberty of an individual who has been arrested, and accordingly the officer could, consistently with the Fourth Amendment, accompany the student to his dormitory room and enter the room upon observing suspected contraband in plain view, such entry from a public corridor not requiring a showing of exigent circumstances, and (3) the Fourth Amendment did not prohibit the seizure of the contraband which was in plain view, it being of no legal significance whether the officer was in the room, on the threshold, or in the hallway at the time he observed the contraband since he had a right to be in any of these places as an incident of a valid arrest.

WHITE, J., joined by BRENNAN and MARSHALL, JJ., dissented, expressing the view that the officer could only enter the residence of the arrested person to protect himself or to maintain control over his arrestee, and therefore, in the case at bar, where the officer entered solely to confirm his suspicion that there was contraband in it, his action violated the Fourth Amendment rights of the arrestees.

COUNSEL

Ronald R. Carpenter argued the cause for petitioner.

Robert F. Patrick argued the cause for respondent.

UNITED STATES, Petitioner,

v

VOGEL FERTILIZER COMPANY

— US —, 70 L Ed 2d 792, 102 S Ct 821

Argued November 3, 1981.
Decided January 13, 1982.

Decision: Treasury Regulation (26 CFR § 1.1563-1(a)(3)) implementing statutory definition of "brother-sister controlled group" of corporations (26 USCS § 1563(a)), held unreasonable.

SUMMARY

Under § 1561(a) of the Internal Revenue Code of 1954 (26 USCS § 1561(a)), as it formerly read, a "controlled group of corporations" was limited to a single corporate surtax exemption. Section 1563(a)(2) of the Code (26 USCS § 1563(a)(2)) provides that a "controlled group of corporations" includes a "brother-sister controlled group," defined as "[t]wo or more corporations if 5 or fewer persons . . . own . . . stock possessing (A) at least 80 percent of the total combined voting power . . . or at least 80 percent of the total value . . . of each corporation, and (B) more than 50 percent of the total combined voting power . . . or more than 50 percent of the total value . . . of each corporation, taking into account the stock ownership of each such person only to the extent such stock ownership is identical with respect to each such corporation," and a Treasury Regulation (26 CFR § 1.1563-1(a)(3)) interpreting that statutory provision states

85

that the term "brother-sister controlled group" means two or more corporations if the same five or fewer persons own "singly or in combination" the two prescribed percentages of voting power or total value. A fertilizer corporation—77.49 percent of whose stock was owned by an individual who held 87.5 percent of the voting power of another corporation, and the remaining 22.51 percent of whose stock was owned by an unrelated individual who owned no stock in the second corporation—did not claim a full surtax exemption on its tax returns, believing that the Treasury regulation barred such a claim. However, the corporation subsequently filed timely claims for refunds, asserting that it and the other corporation were not members of a controlled group and that it was therefore entitled to a full surtax exemption for each taxable year. The Internal Revenue Service disallowed the claims, and the corporation brought a suit for a refund in the United States Court of Claims. The Court of Claims held that two corporations did not constitute a brother-sister controlled group within the meaning of § 1563(a)(2), that the Treasury regulation was invalid to the extent that it took into account, with respect to the 80-percent requirement, stock held by a shareholder who owns stock in only one corporation of the controlled group, and that the corporation was therefore entitled to a refund (634 F2d 497).

On certiorari, the United States Supreme Court affirmed. In an opinion by BRENNAN, J., joined by BURGER, Ch. J., and MARSHALL, POWELL, REHNQUIST, STEVENS, and O'CONNOR, JJ., it was held that the Treasury regulation was not a reasonable implementation of the statute, which, as evidenced by its

86

language, structure, and legislative history, was intended to apply only where each person whose stock is taken into account owns stock in each corporation of the group.

BLACKMUN, J., joined by WHITE, J., dissented, expressing the view that both the language and history of 26 USCS § 1563(a)(2) are ambiguous and that the Commissioner of Internal Revenue's interpretation was not unreasonable or meaningless for it insured that the stock was closely held and that, in such a situation, the choice among reasonable interpretations is for the Commissioner, not the courts.

COUNSEL

Stuart A. Smith argued the cause for petitioner.

Ronald C. Jensen argued the cause for respondent.

————————

COMMUNITY COMMUNICATIONS COMPANY,
INC., Petitioner,

v

CITY OF BOULDER, COLORADO, et al.

— US —, 70 L Ed 2d 810, 102 S Ct 835

Argued October 13, 1981.

Decided January 13, 1982.

Decision: Ordinance enacted by home-rule municipality prohibiting expansion of cable television
operator's business, held not to be "state action" eligible for exemption from federal antitrust laws.

SUMMARY

The assignee of a permit granted by a city ordinance to conduct a cable television business within
the city limits filed suit in the United States District
Court for the District of Colorado, alleging that the
city violated § 1 of the Sherman Act (15 USCS § 1)
when it enacted an "emergency" ordinance prohibiting the assignee for three months from expanding
its business to areas of the city not currently served
by it so that the city council could draft a model
cable television ordinance and invite new businesses
to enter the market under the terms of that ordinance, even though the city is a "home-rule" municipality which is granted extensive powers of self-
government in local and municipal matters by the
constitution of the state in which the city is located.
The District Court held that the city's moratorium
ordinance was not exempt from federal antitrust

laws under the "state action" doctrine of an earlier decision of the United States Supreme Court and issued a preliminary injunction (485 F Supp 1035). The United States Court of Appeals for the Tenth Circuit reversed, holding that the city's action satisfied the criteria for an exemption from antitrust liability (630 F2d 704).

On certiorari, the United States Supreme Court reversed and remanded. In an opinion by BRENNAN, J., joined by MARSHALL, BLACKMUN, POWELL, and STEVENS, JJ., it was held that the moratorium ordinance was not exempt from antitrust scrutiny under the "state action" doctrine, the direct delegation of powers to the city through a home-rule amendment in the state constitution not rendering the ordinance an act of government performed by the city acting as the state in local matters.

STEVENS, J., concurred, emphasizing that the holding that the city's action was not exempt from the antitrust laws was not tantamount to a holding that the antitrust laws have been violated.

REHNQUIST, J., joined by BURGER, Ch. J., and O'CONNOR, J., dissented, expressing the view that the question addressed in the case was not whether state and local governments are exempt from the Sherman Act, but whether statutes, ordinances, and regulations enacted as an act of government are preempted by the Sherman Act under the operation of the Federal Constitution's supremacy clause, and that the presumption is that preemption is not to be found absent the clear and manifest intention of Congress that the federal act should supersede the police powers of the states.

WHITE, J., did not participate.

COUNSEL

Harold R. Farrow argued the cause for petitioner.

Thomas P. McMahon argued the cause for the State of Colorado, et al., as amicus curiae, by special leave of court.

Jeffrey H. Howard argued the cause for respondents.

KAISER STEEL CORPORATION, Petitioner,

v

JULIUS MULLINS et al.

— US —, 70 L Ed 2d 833, 102 S Ct 851

Argued November 10, 1981.
Decided January 13, 1982.

Decision: Coal producer sued on promise to contribute to union welfare funds based on "purchased coal," held entitled to plead and have adjudicated illegality defense.

SUMMARY

A 1974 collective bargaining agreement between a mine workers' union and various coal producers included a so-called "purchased coal" clause, which required signatory employers to report purchases of coal from producers not under union contract and to contribute specified amounts to employee health and retirement funds based on the amount of coal the employers bought from the other producers. One coal producer which was a signatory to the contract failed to make the required reports and contributions, and the trustees of the union health and retirement funds sued the coal producer in the United States District Court for the District of Columbia. While the coal producer admitted its failure to report and contribute, it defended on the ground, among others, that the agreement was void and unenforceable as violative of §§ 1 and 2 of the Sherman Act (15 USCS § 1 and 2) and § 8(e) of the National Labor Relations Act (29 USCS § 158(e)), which forbids contracts between a union and an employer whereby the employer agrees to cease doing business with or to cease handling the products of another employer. The District Court did not pass on the legality of the purchased coal agreement under these statutes, but nevertheless rejected the coal producer's defense of illegality and granted the trustees' motion for summary judgment. The United States Court of Appeals for the District of Columbia Circuit affirmed, also rejecting the coal producer's defense without adjudicating the legality of the purchased coal clause (206 App DC 334, 642 F2d 1302).

On certiorari, the United States Supreme Court reversed and remanded. In an opinion by WHITE, J., joined by BURGER, Ch. J., and POWELL, REHNQUIST, STEVENS, and O'CONNOR, JJ., it was held that the coal producer was entitled, in an action in federal court by the funds' trustees to enforce the reporting and contribution allegations, to plead and have adjudicated its defense that the clause violated the antitrust prohibitions of §§ 1 and 2 of the Sherman Act (15 USCS §§ 1 and 2) and the "hot-cargo" provision of § 8(e) of the National Labor Relations Act (29 USCS § 158(e)).

BRENNAN, J., joined by MARSHALL and BLACKMUN, JJ., dissenting, expressed the view that (1) the case at bar exemplifies the very sort of abuse that Congress intended to stop with the enactment of § 306(a) of the Multiemployer Pension Plan Amendment Act of 1980 (29 USCS § 1145(a)), the statute allowing an employer to be relieved of a plan contribution obligation only when the payment at issue is inherently illegal, and (2) the coal producer's defenses, which did not attack the legality of the planned contributions themselves, were properly rejected by the lower federal courts since § 306(a) renders them irrelevant to the coal producer's obligation to make its promised contributions to the designated employee benefit funds.

COUNSEL

A. Douglas Melamed argued the cause for petitioner.

Stephen J. Pollak argued the cause for respondents.

Barbara E. Etkind argued the cause for the United States as amicus curiae by special leave of court.

_____

PRINCETON UNIVERSITY AND NEW JERSEY,
Appellants,

v

CHRIS SCHMID

— US —, 70 L Ed 2d 855, 102 S Ct 867

Argued November 10, 1981.
Decided January 13, 1982.

Decision: Appeal of decision invalidating subsequently amended university rule, held moot as to university and without jurisdictional basis as to state which sought review but refused to take position on merits.

SUMMARY

An individual was convicted in the Princeton Borough Municipal Court in New Jersey of criminal trespass due to his distributing political materials on a university campus while not being a student there. The university had, at that time, a regulation forbidding such conduct, without permission, by members of the public. A de novo trial in the New Jersey Superior Court, Law Division, also resulted in conviction. While an appeal to the New Jersey Superior Court, Appellate Division, was pending, the case was certified for review by the Supreme Court of New Jersey, which, after the university intervened as a party, reversed the conviction, holding that the individual's rights of speech and assembly under the New Jersey Constitution had been violated (84 NJ 535, 423 A2d 615).

On appeal, the United States Supreme Court dismissed. In a per curiam opinion expressing the unanimous view of the eight participating members of the court, it was held that the Supreme Court will dismiss an appeal for want of jurisdiction, where the state's jurisdictional statement to the court urging it to review the case but taking no position on the merits did not provide a sound jurisdictional basis for undertaking to decide the difficult constitutional issues presented, where the appeal was rendered moot, with respect to the university, by the fact that the regulation was amended while the case was on appeal to the state's highest court, and where the university did not have standing to invoke Supreme Court jurisdiction, even though the judgment below would deprive the university of the authority to enforce the regulation as it stood prior to amendment, the judgment not preventing the university from having the validity of its new regulation ruled upon in another enforcement action.

BRENNAN, J., did not participate.

COUNSEL

Nicholas deB. Katzenbach argued the cause for appellants.
Sanford Levinson argued the cause for appellee.

———————

MONTY LEE EDDINGS, Petitioner,

v

OKLAHOMA

— US —, 71 L Ed 2d 1, 102 S Ct 869

Argued November 2, 1981.
Decided January 19, 1982.

Decision: State trial judge's refusal to consider defendant's family history and emotional disturbance in mitigation in death penalty sentencing hearing, held violative of Eighth and Fourteenth Amendments.

SUMMARY

Ordered to stand trial as an adult, a 16-year-old youth was found guilty of murder in the first degree by the District Court of Creek County, Oklahoma, upon his plea of nolo contendere. Oklahoma's death penalty statute provides that in the sentencing proceeding, evidence may be presented as to "any mitigating circumstances" or as to any of certain enumerated aggravating circumstances. At the sentencing hearing, the state alleged three of the aggravating circumstances, and, in mitigation, the defendant presented substantial evidence of a turbulent family history, of beatings by a harsh father, and of severe emotional disturbance. The trial judge found that the state had proved each of the three alleged aggravating circumstances beyond a reasonable doubt and considered the defendant's youth as a mitigating circumstance, but found, as a matter of law, that he could not consider in mitigation the circumstances of the defendant's unhappy upbringing and emotional disturbance, and it sentenced the defendant to death. On appeal, the Court of Criminal Appeals of Oklahoma affirmed the sentence of death, finding that each of the aggravating circumstances alleged by the state had been present and agreed with the trial court that only the fact of the defendant's youth was properly considered as a mitigating circumstance (616 P2d 1159).

On certiorari, the United States Supreme Court reversed in part and remanded. In an opinion by POWELL, J., joined by BRENNAN, MARSHALL, STEVENS, and O'CONNOR, JJ., it was held that the imposition of the sentence of death on the 16 year old was done without the type of individualized consideration of mitigating factors required by the Eighth and Fourteenth Amendments in capital cases.

BRENNAN, J., concurred, expressing the view that the death penalty is in all circumstances cruel and unusual punishment prohibited by the Eighth and Fourteenth Amendments.

O'CONNOR, J., concurred, stating that the court's opinion neither altered the court's opinions establishing the constitutionality of the death penalty nor decided the issue of whether the United States Constitution permits imposition of the death penalty on an individual who committed a murder at age 16, and expressing the view that rather, by listing in detail some of the circumstances surrounding the defendant's life, the court sought to emphasize the variety of mitigating information that may not have been considered by the trial court in deciding whether to impose the death penalty or some lesser sentence.

BURGER, Ch. J., joined by WHITE, BLACKMUN, and REHNQUIST, JJ., dissenting, stated that the defendant's claim was neither presented to the state courts nor presented to the United States Supreme Court in the petition for certiorari, and that the sentencing proceedings in this case were in no sense inconsistent with prior decisions of the court, since it was incorrect to characterize the sentencing judge's action as a finding that, as a matter of law, he was unable to consider the defendant's proffered evidence in mitigation and since it was the choice of the Oklahoma courts—a choice not inconsistent with any decision of the Supreme Court—to accord relatively little weight to the defendant's family background and emotional problems as balanced against the circumstances of his crime and his potential for future dangerousness.

COUNSEL

Jay C. Baker argued the cause for petitioner.
David W. Lee argued the cause for respondent.

J. GREGORY MERRION AND ROBERT L. BAYLESS, etc., et al., Petitioners,

v

JICARILLA APACHE TRIBE, et al. (No. 80–11)

AMOCO PRODUCTION COMPANY AND MARATHON OIL COMPANY, Petitioners,

v

JICARILLA APACHE INDIAN TRIBE, et al. (No. 80–15)

— US —, 71 L Ed 2d 21, 102 S Ct 894

Argued March 30, 1981.
Reargued November 4, 1981.
Decided January 25, 1982.

Decision: Severance tax imposed on oil and gas removed from Indian reservation, held authorized by Tribe's inherent authority to tax as part of power of self-government, and held not violative of commerce clause (Art I, § 8, cl 3).

SUMMARY

Pursuant to its Revised Constitution, which had been approved by the Secretary of the Interior, the Tribal Council of the Jicarilla Apache Tribe enacted an ordinance imposing a severance tax on oil and gas production on the tribal land, the tax applying to any oil and natural gas severed, saved, and removed from tribal lands, but not applying to oil and gas consumed by lessees of the Tribe to develop their leases or received by the Tribe as in-kind royalty payments, and the ordinance was approved by the Secretary. Subsequently, several individuals and corporations who, pursuant to long-term leases previously signed with the Tribe, extracted and produced oil and gas from the Tribe's reservation lands and who paid royalties to the Tribe brought actions in the United States District Court for the District of New Mexico to enjoin enforcement of the tax by either the tribal authorities or the Secretary. The District Court consolidated the cases and permanently enjoined enforcement of the tax, ruling that the Tribe lacked the authority to impose the tax, that only state and local authorities had the power to tax oil and gas production on Indian reservations, and that the tax violated the commerce clause of the United States Constitution (Art I, § 8, cl 3). On appeal, the United States Court of Appeals for the Tenth Circuit reversed, holding that the taxing power is an inherent attribute of tribal sovereignty that had not been divested by any treaty or act of Congress (617 F2d 537).

On certiorari, the United States Supreme Court affirmed. In an opinion by MARSHALL, J., joined by BRENNAN, WHITE, BLACKMUN, POWELL, and O'CONNOR, JJ., it was held that (1) the Tribe had the inherent authority to impose the severance tax both as part of its power to govern and to pay for the costs of self-government and from its power to exclude non-Indians from the reservation, Congress not having deprived the Tribe of this authority by its enactment of the Act of May 11, 1938 (25 USCS §§ 396a et seq.) establishing the procedures for leasing oil and gas interests on tribal lands or the Act of March 3, 1927 (25 USCS § 398c) permitting state taxation of mineral production on Indian reservations, and a severance tax not conflicting with national energy policies, and (2) the Tribe's imposition of the tax did not violate the "negative implications" of the commerce clause, since Congress had affirmatively acted by providing a series of federal check-points that had to be cleared before the tribal tax could take effect and since, in any event, the tax did not discriminate against interstate commerce, the tax not treating minerals transported away from the reservation differently than it treated minerals that might be sold on the reservation, and the exemption for minerals received by the Tribe as in-kind payments on the leases and used for tribal purposes merely avoiding the administrative make-work that would ensue if the Tribe taxed the minerals that it, as a commercial partner, received in royalty payments.

STEVENS, J., joined by BURGER, Ch. J., and REHN-QUIST, J., dissented, expressing the view that the power of Indian tribes to tax nonmembers stems from the tribe's power to exclude those nonmembers, rather than from the tribe's inherent power of self-government, that any exercise of the power must be consistent with its source, and that the Jicarilla Tribe could not retroactively change the conditions of the authority granted by the Tribe to the lessees to extract oil and gas from the reservation lands by imposing the tax, since the Tribe did not retain the power in the leases to impose additional conditions.

COUNSEL

Jason W. Kellahin argued the cause for petitioners in 80-11.

John R. Cooney argued the cause for petitioners in 80-15.

Robert J. Nordhaus and Louis F. Claiborne argued the cause for respondents.

IN THE MATTER OF R. M. J., Appellant

v

— US —, 71 L Ed 2d 64, 102 S Ct 929

Argued November 9, 1981.
Decided January 25, 1982.

Decision: Missouri Supreme Court rule regulating attorney's advertising absent proof that regulated material was misleading, held violative of attorney's First Amendment rights.

SUMMARY

An attorney practicing in Missouri was charged by information in the Supreme Court of Missouri with violating Rule 4 of the Supreme Court which regulates advertising by attorneys. The attorney had published advertisements which listed areas of practice in language other than that specified in the Rule and had, in contravention of the rule, listed courts in which the attorney was admitted to practice. Additionally, the attorney had mailed announcement cards to persons other than those individuals permitted by the rule. The attorney contended that the restrictions on advertising in the Rule were unconstitutional under the First and Fourteenth Amendments, but the court upheld the Rule's constitutionality and issued a private reprimand (609 SW2d 411).

On appeal, the United States Supreme Court reversed. In an opinion by Powell, J., expressing the unanimous view of the court, it was held that, as applied to the attorney, the Rule's restrictions could

103

not be sustained because (1) the listings of areas of practice published by the attorney were not shown to be misleading and the state suggested no substantial interest promoted by the Rule's restrictions limiting attorneys to specified listings in areas of practice, (2) the listing of jurisdictions in which the lawyer had obtained a license to practice was not misleading on its face and the state had suggested no substantial interest in barring this information, and (3) there was no indication that, with respect to announcement cards, an inability to supervise was the reason the state restricted the potential audience of the cards nor was it clear that a prohibition was the only solution to the problem, there being no indication of a failed effort to proceed along a less restrictive path.

COUNSEL

Charles B. Blackmar argued the cause for appellant.

John W. Inglish argued the cause for appellee.

HAROLD J. SMITH, Superintendent, Attica
Correctional Facility,

v

WILLIAM R. PHILLIPS

— US —, 71 L Ed 2d 78, 102 S Ct 940

Argued November 9, 1982.
Decided January 25, 1982.

Decision: Juror's submission, during criminal trial,
of job application to prosecutor's office and
failure of prosecution to disclose such fact during trial, held not violative of due process.

SUMMARY

After an individual was convicted of murder and
attempted murder by a New York state court jury,
the defendant moved to vacate the conviction on
the ground that, during the trial, a juror submitted
an employment application in the district attorney's
office and that the prosecutors in the case, upon
being informed of the application, withheld this fact
from the trial court and defense counsel until after
the trial. A post-trial hearing on the motion to
vacate was held before the same judge who heard
the trial, and the motion was denied, the judge
concluding beyond a reasonable doubt that the
events giving rise to the motion did not influence
the verdict (87 Misc 2d 613, 384 NYS2d 906). The
Appellate Division of the Supreme Court, First Division, affirmed without opinion (52 App Div 2d 758,
384 NYS2d 715), and the Court of Appeals of New
York denied leave to appeal (39 NY2d 949, 386

NYS2d 1039, 352 NE2d 894). The defendant subsequently petitioned for a writ of habeas corpus in the United States District Court for the Southern District of New York on the same ground asserted in the state post-trial hearing. The District Court granted the writ, concluding that even though there was insufficient evidence to demonstrate actual bias on the part of the juror, on the ground of "imputed" bias, the average man in the juror's position would believe that the jury's verdict would directly affect the evaluation of his job application (485 F Supp 1365). The United States Court of Appeals for the Second Circuit, although not considering the issue of actual or imputed bias, affirmed on the ground that the failure of the prosecutors to disclose their knowledge of the application denied the defendant due process (632 F2d 1019).

On certiorari, the United States Supreme Court reversed. In an opinion by REHNQUIST, J., joined by BURGER, Ch. J., and WHITE, BLACKMUN, POWELL, and O'CONNOR, JJ., it was held that the defendant was not entitled to have the verdict set aside on the ground that he was denied due process of law in violation of the Fourteenth Amendment either by virtue of "implied" juror bias, or because of prosecutorial misconduct, since (1) the post-trial hearing at which the defendant was permitted to prove the juror's "actual" bias, was sufficient to decide allegations of juror partiality, and neither the District Court nor Court of Appeals took issue with the findings of the trial judge, and (2) the prosecutors' failure to disclose the juror's job application, although requiring a post-trial hearing on juror bias, did not deprive the defendant of the fair trial guaranteed by the due process clause.

O'CONNOR, J., concurred, expressing the view that the use of "implied bias" in appropriate circumstances should not be foreclosed.

MARSHALL, J., joined by BRENNAN and STEVENS, JJ., dissented, expressing the view that the defendant was denied due process on the ground that a juror who applies for employment with the office of the prosecutor and vigorously pursues that employment throughout the course of the trial is impliedly biased, and on the alternative ground that the prosecutors' improper failure to disclose during trial that the juror applied for a job prejudiced the defendant by depriving him of the opportunity to substitute an unbiased alternative juror.

COUNSEL

Robert M. Pitler argued the cause for petitioner.
William M. Kunstler argued the cause for respondent.

JAMES H. TULLY, JR., et al., Appellants,

v

MOBIL OIL CORPORATION et al.

— US —, 71 L Ed 2d 120, 102 S Ct 1047

Decided February 22, 1982.

Decision: Temporary Emergency Court of Appeals' invalidation of anti-passthrough provision of state tax statute relating to oil company revenues, vacated and remanded in light of expiration of preempting federal price control authority.

SUMMARY

In June, 1980, the state of New York established a tax on gross receipts of oil companies limited to their revenues derived from their activities within the state, and prohibited the companies from passing on the cost of the tax in the prices of their products sold in New York. If the "passthrough" prohibition was ever adjudged invalid, it was provided that the tax would cease to exist on the tenth day following the adjudication, although all tax liabilities accrued to that date would remain in effect. It was also provided that the tax would self-destruct ten days after any court issued "any order, judgment, injunction or stay" prohibiting the enforcement of the anti-passthrough provision. Several oil companies instituted suit to enjoin the anti-passthrough provision, contending that it was preempted by federal price control authority under the Emergency Petroleum Allocation Act (15 USCS

§§ 751 et seq.). The United States District Court for the Northern District of New York agreed, and enjoined enforcement of the provision (499 F Supp 888). The United States Court of Appeals for the Second Circuit ruled that appellate consideration of the preemption issue was a matter for the Temporary Emergency Court of Appeals (639 F2d 912). The Temporary Emergency Court of Appeals affirmed the District Court, noting that the federal statute would expire by its terms shortly, and that expiration "would signal the end of federal concern in this area" (653 F2d 497).

On appeal, the United States Supreme Court vacated and remanded. In a per curiam opinion expressing the view of BURGER, Ch. J., and WHITE, MARSHALL, BLACKMUN, POWELL, REHNQUIST, and O'CONNOR, JJ., it was held that the judgment of the Temporary Emergency Court of Appeals would be vacated and the case remanded to that court for reconsideration, the judgment and accompanying injunction not being appropriately framed for Supreme Court review since (1) the Emergency Petroleum Allocation Act expired by its own terms between the time of the Temporary Emergency Court of Appeals' decision and potential review of that decision in the Supreme Court, removing the only barrier to enforcement of the anti-passthrough provision, (2) the District Court's injunction did not terminate upon expiration of the federal statute, and therefore the declaration of invalidity of the state tax provision and the accompanying injunction had no current validity, requiring it to be set aside, and (3) the Temporary Emergency Court of Appeals must decide what effect, if any, the expiration of federal price authority has on such collateral matters as the state's legal authority to pass through to consumers taxes paid or accrued prior to the federal statute's expiration, and the validity of the state tax itself, such matters being relevant to the litigation in that they may constitute remaining live issues supplying the constitutional requirement of a case or controversy.

BRENNAN, J., would have set the case for oral argument.

STEVENS, J., dissenting, expressed the view that the judgment of the Temporary Emergency Court of Appeals should simply have been affirmed since any question concerning the meaning or enforceability of the state tax laws during the period after the expiration of federal price control authority was not presented by the litigation, which concerned only the question—correctly answered by the Court of Appeals—whether the then-existing federal price control authority prevented the state from fixing the economic burden of a tax imposed upon companies that sell petroleum products.

UNITED STATES, Appellant,

v

EDWIN D. LEE

— US —, 71 L Ed 2d 127, 102 S Ct 1051

Argued November 2, 1981.
Decided February 23, 1982.

Decision: Imposition of social security taxes on persons who object on religious grounds to receipt of public insurance benefits and to payment of taxes to support such benefits, held constitutional.

SUMMARY

A self-employed farmer and carpenter who was a member of the Old Order Amish religion sued in the United States District Court for the Western District of Pennsylvania for a refund of the social security taxes paid by him pursuant to 26 USCS §§ 3101 et seq. on account of his employment of other members of that religion on his farm and in his carpentry shop. He claimed that imposition of the taxes violated his First Amendment free exercise rights and those of his employees, because members of the Old Order Amish religion believe that there is a religiously based obligation to provide for their fellow members the kind of assistance contemplated by the social security system, and that therefore their religion prohibits acceptance of social security benefits and payment of social security taxes. The District Court held the statutes requiring the claimant to pay social security taxes unconstitutional as

111

applied on the basis of both an exemption provided in 26 USCS § 1402(g) for self-employed persons who conscientiously oppose acceptance of social security benefits and the First Amendment.

On direct appeal, the United States Supreme Court reversed and remanded. In an opinion by BURGER, Ch. J., joined by BRENNAN, WHITE, MARSHALL, BLACKMUN, POWELL, REHNQUIST, and O'CONNOR, JJ., it was held that (1) the exemption provided by § 1402(g), being available only to self-employed individuals, does not apply to employers or employees, and hence the complainant and his employees are not within its provisions, and (2) the imposition of social security taxes is not unconstitutional as applied to such persons as the claimant who object on religious grounds to receipt of public insurance benefits and to payment of taxes to support public insurance funds.

STEVENS, J., concurring in the judgment, emphasized that the objector must shoulder the burden of demonstrating that there is a unique reason for allowing him a special exemption from a valid law of general applicability when the clash between the objector's religious obligation and his civic obligation is irreconcilable.

COUNSEL

Lawrence G. Wallace argued the cause for appellant.

Francis X. Caiazza argued the cause for appellee.

ELVINA M. HERWEG, by her husband and next
friend, DARRELL E. HERWEG and DARRELL E.
HERWEG, etc., Petitioners,

v

ROBERT D. RAY, Governor of Iowa, et al.

— US —, 71 L Ed 2d 137, 102 S Ct 1059

Argued January 13, 1982.
Decided February 23, 1982.

Decision: State's unlimited deeming of Medicaid
applicant's spouse's income as available to applicant in determining eligibility, held barred by
42 USCS § 1396a(a).

SUMMARY

An individual who applied for Medicaid benefits
from a state Medicaid plan and who was institutionalized in a long-term care facility filed suit in the
United States District Court for the Southern District of Iowa, along with her husband, challenging
the state's practice of "deeming" the income of a
spouse as available to the applicant for an unlimited
time after an applicant and spouse are no longer
living together. The applicant was eligible for, but
was not receiving, benefits under the Supplemental
Security Income for the Aged, Blind, and Disabled
(SSI) program (42 USCS §§ 1381 et seq.) and was
thus classified by the program as "optional categorically needy." Her husband was not eligible for
Medicaid benefits. The state plan was operating
under the SSI program, which requires that (1)
under § 1902(a)(10)(A) of the Social Security Act

(42 USCS § 1396a(a)(10)(A)), all recipients of SSI benefits be provided Medicaid assistance, (2) under § 1902(a)(17)(B) of the Act (42 USCS § 1396a(a)(17)(B)), participating states must grant benefits to eligible individuals taking into account only such income and resources as are, as determined by the Secretary of Health and Human Services (HHS) available to an applicant, and (3) under § 1902(a)(17)(D) of the Act (42 USCS § 1396a(a)(17)(D)), state Medicaid plans must not take into account the financial responsibility of any individual for an applicant under the plan unless the applicant is that individual's spouse. A regulation of the Secretary of Health and Human Resources (42 CFR § 435.723(d)), promulgated under § 1902(a)(17)(B), requires a state to deem the income of an applicant's spouse as "available" for one month after the applicant and spouse are no longer living together, when the spouse is not eligible for Medicaid. The District Court certified the suit as a class action, including both SSI recipients as well as the "optional categorically needy," and held that § 1902(a)(17) requires the state's procedures to provide a factual determination in each instance of the amount of a spouse's income which is in fact reasonably available for the support of the institutionalized spouse, and that the predecessor to 42 CFR § 435.723 was inconsistent with this construction (443 F Supp 1315). In response, the state adopted a procedure for making such factual determinations, and the District Court approved the plan (481 F Supp 914). On appeal, the United States Court of Appeals for the Eighth Circuit affirmed by an equally divided court (619 F2d 1265).

On certiorari, the United States Supreme Court reversed and remanded. In an opinion by REHN-

QUIST, J., joined by BRENNAN, WHITE, MARSHALL, BLACKMUN, POWELL, and O'CONNOR, JJ., it was held that (1) section 1902(a)(17)(D) does not preclude the Secretary from promulgating regulations that impose time limitations upon a state's ability to consider the income of an institutionalized applicant's spouse in determining the applicant's eligibility for Medicaid benefits under a state plan, the Secretary being granted broad authority under § 1902(a)(17)(B) to determine what income is "available," so that, with regard to the optional categorically needy, the Secretary did not exceed his authority in promulgating 42 CFR § 435.723, and the regulation was neither arbitrary or capricious, and (2) to the extent that the District Court order permitted the state to deny Medicaid benefits to recipients of SSI benefits or prohibited the state from "deeming" under any circumstances, the order conflicted with § 1902(a)(10)(A) and could not stand.

STEVENS, J., concurring in part, expressed the view that nothing in the language of § 1902(a)(17) requires that any spousal income be deemed to be available to an applicant.

BURGER, Ch. J., dissented, expressing the view that the state deeming procedure was authorized by § 1902(a)(17)(D).

COUNSEL

Neal S. Dudovitz argued the cause for petitioners. Brent R. Appel argued the cause for respondents.

———

CITY OF MESQUITE, Appellant,

v

ALADDIN'S CASTLE, INC.

— US —, 71 L Ed 2d 152, 102 S Ct 1070

Argued November 10, 1981.
Decided February 23, 1982.

Decision: Ordinance directing city's police chief to consider applicant's "connection with criminal elements" in licensing amusement establishments, held not unconstitutionally vague.

SUMMARY

One section of a city's licensing ordinance governing coin-operated amusement establishments required the city's chief of police to consider whether a license applicant had any "connection with criminal elements," while another section prohibited a licensee from allowing children under 17 years of age to operate the amusement devices unless accompanied by a parent or a legal guardian. After a corporation proposed to open an amusement center, the city exempted from the prohibition against operation of amusement devices by unattended children certain amusement centers,—the features of which were defined in terms of the corporation's rules—as long as children under the age of seven were accompanied by an adult. However, the corporation's application for a license was refused because the chief of police concluded that the corporation's parent corporation was connected with criminal elements. After the corporation successfully

116

brought suit in a Texas state court challenging the ordinance and obtained an injunction requiring the city to issue it a license, the city adopted a new ordinance repealing the corporation's exemption and reinstating the 17-year age requirement, while defining the term "connected with criminal elements" in some detail. The Corporation commenced an action in the United States District Court for the Northern District of Texas, seeking an injunction against enforcement of the new ordinance. The District Court ruled that the language "connected with criminal elements," even as defined, was unconstitutionally vague, but upheld the age restriction (434 F Supp 473). The United States Court of Appeals for the Fifth Circuit affirmed the former holding and reversed the latter (630 F2d 1029).

On appeal, the United States Supreme Court reversed in part and remanded. In an opinion by STEVENS, J., joined by BURGER, Ch. J., and BRENNAN, MARSHALL, BLACKMUN, REHNQUIST, and O'CONNOR, JJ., it was held that (1) that portion of the ordinance which directed the chief of police to consider an applicant's "connection with criminal elements" in determining whether to grant a license was not unconstitutionally vague, the Federal Constitution not precluding a city from giving vague or ambiguous directions to officials who are authorized to make investigations and recommendations, and (2) a remand for clarification of the Court of Appeals' invalidation of the age requirement—which rested on its interpretation of the state as well as the Federal Constitution—was necessary since (a) Congress has limited the Supreme Court's jurisdiction to review, on appeal under 28 USCS § 1254(2), the Court of Appeals' interpretation of the state constitution, (b) ambiguity existed in the Court of Appeals' holding as to whether the Court of Appeals had placed independent reliance on state law or merely treated the state constitutional protections as congruent with corresponding federal provisions, and (c) the Supreme Court would therefore to decline at present to decide the federal constitutional question relating to the age limitation in view of the fact that the relevant language of the state constitutional provisions is arguably broader than corresponding federal provisions, it was unclear as to whether the Supreme Court would apply as a matter of federal law the same standards applied as a matter of state law by the Court of Appeals, and especially in view of the court's policy of avoiding adjudication of unnecessary constitutional questions.

WHITE, J., concurring in part and dissenting in part, expressed the view that (1) the city's ordinance directing the police chief to consider whether a license applicant has any "connection with criminal elements" is not void for vagueness, and (2) the challenge to the age requirement should not have been remanded since there was no reason to suspect that the Court of Appeals standards for evaluating the due process and equal protection claims under the state constitution differed in any respect from federal constitutional standards.

POWELL, J., concurring in part and dissenting in part, expressed the view that (1) the ordinance provision relating to the police chief's determination of whether a license applicant is "connected with criminal elements" is not void for vagueness, but (2) no justification existed for a remand on the issue of the age requirement's validity, especially in view of the fact that the Court of Appeals' opinion con-

118

tained no analysis of state law independent of its clear application of federal law.

COUNSEL

Elland Archer argued the cause for appellant.
Philip W. Tone argued the cause for appellee.

GEORGE F. JEWETT, JR., et ux., Petitioners,

v

COMMISSIONER OF INTERNAL REVENUE

— US —, 71 L Ed 2d 170, 102 S Ct 1082

Argued December 1, 1981.
Decided February 23, 1982.

Decision: Trust beneficiary's disclaimer of contingent interest in testamentary trust, held taxable transfer of property by gift under 26 USCS §§ 2501(a)(1) and 2511(a), not excepted from tax by 26 CFR § 25.2511-1(c).

SUMMARY

A testamentary trust established in 1939 provided that the trust income be paid to the testatrix's husband during his life, and thereafter to their son and his wife, and that upon the death of the survivor thereof, the principal was to be divided into equal shares so that there would be one share for each child of the couple then living and one share for the issue then living representing each child of the couple then dead. In 1972, a grandson of the testatrix, who was then 45 years old and whose mother was still living, executed two disclaimers which recognized that he had an interest in 50 percent of the trust estate provided that he survived his mother and in which he renounced his right to receive any of that portion of the remainder of the trust estate. He and his wife filed gift tax returns in which they advised the Commissioner of Internal Revenue of the disclaimers, but did not treat them
120

as taxable gifts. The Commissioner assessed a deficiency, concluding that the disclaimers were indirect transfers of property by gift within the meaning of §§ 2501(a)(1) and 2511(a) of the Internal Revenue Code of 1954 (26 USCS §§ 2501(a)(1) and 2511(a)), and that they were not excepted from tax under a Treasury Regulation (26 CFR § 25.2511-1(c)) which provided that a trust beneficiary's refusal to accept ownership of property is not subject to tax if it is effective under local law and made "within a reasonable time after knowledge of the transfer," because they were not made "within a reasonable time after knowledge" of his grandmother's transfer to him of an interest in the trust estate. The taxpayer then filed an action in the United States Tax Court seeking a redetermination of the deficiency, arguing that at the time the disclaimers were made he had nothing more than a contingent interest in the trust, and that the "reasonable time" in which a tax-free disclaimer could be made did not begin to run until the interest became vested and possessory upon the death of the last surviving life tenant. The Tax Court ruled in favor of the Commissioner (70 TC 430), and the United States Court of Appeals for the Ninth Circuit affirmed (638 F2d 93).

On certiorari, the United States Supreme Court affirmed. In an opinion by STEVENS, J., joined by BURGER, Ch. J., and BRENNAN, WHITE, MARSHALL, and POWELL, JJ., it was held that the disclaimers by the trust beneficiary of the contingent interest in the testamentary trust 33 years after that trust was created, but while it was still contingent, were indirect transfers of property by gift within the meaning of 26 USCS §§ 2501(a)(1) and 2511(a), and were not excepted from the federal gift tax under 26 CFR

§ 25.2511-1(c), the "transfer" referred to in the regulation occurring when the interest is created, not at a later time when the interest either vests or becomes possessory, and that the disclaimers, although effective under local law, were thus not made "within a reasonable time" after the interest was created.

BLACKMUN, J., joined by REHNQUIST and O'Connor, JJ., dissenting, expressed the view that the federal gift tax statute does not make mention of, nor provide for, a reasonable time requirement, and that any transfer in the case was not one of the grandson, but a transfer from the testatrix, so that the holder of the vested remainder interest subjected to divestiture has a reasonable time within which to disclaim after the death of the life beneficiary, there being nothing unfair or improper in allowing the remainderman to wait until the life beneficiary's death and then decide whether to accept the bequest.

COUNSEL

James D. St. Clair argued the cause for petitioners.

Stuart A. Smith argued the cause for respondent.

NEW ENGLAND POWER COMPANY, Appellant,

v

NEW HAMPSHIRE et al. (No. 80–1208)

MASSACHUSETTS, et al., Appellants,

v

NEW HAMPSHIRE et al. (80–1471)

DENNIS J. ROBERTS, II, Attorney General of the
State of Rhode Island, et al., Appellant,

v

NEW HAMPSHIRE et al. (80–1610)

— US —, 71 L Ed 2d 188, 102 S Ct 1096

Argued December 7, 1981.
Decided February 24, 1982.

Decision: State public utility commission's order
requiring privately-owned and federally-licensed
public utility to sell within state hydroelectric
energy it had been exporting, held violative of
commerce clause (Art I, § 8, cl 3).

SUMMARY

The Commonwealth of Massachusetts, the Attorney General of Rhode Island, and a privately-owned
public utility which generated and transmitted electricity at wholesale from several hydroelectric plants
within New Hampshire and which was licensed by
the Federal Energy Regulatory Commission (FERC)
pursuant to the Federal Power Act (16 USCS §§ 792

123

et seq.) appealed to the Supreme Court of New
Hampshire an order of the New Hampshire Public
Utilities Commission requiring the utility to arrange
to sell within New Hampshire hydroelectric energy
which it had previously exported to, among other
places, Massachusetts and Rhode Island. They
claimed that the order was preempted by Parts I
and II of the Act (16 USCS §§ 792–824k) and
imposed impermissible burdens on interstate commerce. The court rejected those arguments, concluding that the "savings clause" of § 201(b) of the
Act (16 USCS § 824(b))—which provides that the
Act's provisions delegating exclusive authority to
FERC to regulate the transmission and sale at
wholesale of electric energy in interstate commerce
"shall not . . . deprive a State or State Commission
of its lawful authority now exercised over the exportation of hydroelectric energy which is transmitted
across a State line"—granted New Hampshire authority to restrict the interstate transportation of
hydroelectric power generated within the state, and
holding that the New Hampshire Commission's order did not interfere with FERC's exclusive regulatory authority over rates charged for interstate sales
of electricity at wholesale (120 NH 866, 424 A2d
607).

On certiorari, the United States Supreme Court
reversed. In an opinion by BURGER, Ch. J., expressing the unanimous view of the court, it was held
that the New Hampshire Commission's order restricted the flow of privately owned and produced
electricity in interstate commerce in a manner inconsistent with the commerce clause of the Federal
Constitutional (Art I, § 8, cl 3), the "savings clause"
in § 201(b) of the Federal Power Act not providing

an affirmative grant of authority to the state to issue such an order.

COUNSEL

Samuel Huntington argued the cause for appellant in 80-1208.

Donald K. Stern argued the cause for appellants in 80-1471 and 80-1610.

Gregory H. Smith argued the cause for appellees.

————————

MALCOLM BALDRIGE, Secretary of Commerce, et al., Petitioners,

v

PETER SHAPIRO, Essex County Executive (No. 80–1436)

WILLIAM H. McNICHOLS, JR., etc., et al., Petitioners,

v

MALCOLM BALDRIGE, Secretary of the United States Department of Commerce, et al. (No. 80–1781)

— US —, 71 L Ed 2d 199, 102 S Ct 1103

Argued December 2, 1981.
Decided February 24, 1982.

Decision: Address lists compiled by Bureau of the Census, held not subject to disclosure under Freedom of Information Act (5 USCS § 552) or discovery provisions of Federal Rules of Civil Procedure.

SUMMARY

These two consolidated cases presented the question whether lists of addresses collected and utilized by the Bureau of the Census are exempt from disclosure, either by way of civil discovery or the Freedom of Information Act (5 USCS § 552), under the confidentiality provisions of §§ 8(b) and 9(a) of the Census Act (13 USCS §§ 8(b) and 9(a)). After concluding its 1980 enumeration which indicated
126

that Essex County, New Jersey, and Denver, Colorado, among other areas, had lost population, the Bureau conveyed this information to the appropriate officials in both areas. Both jurisdictions challenged the census count under Bureau procedures allowing a municipality 10 working days from receipt of the preliminary counts to challenge the accuracy of the census data, proceeding on the theory that the Bureau had erroneously classified occupied dwellings as vacant, and seeking to compel disclosure of a portion of the address lists used by the Bureau in conducting its count in the respective jurisdictions. In the first case (No. 80–1436), the Essex County Executive filed suit in the United States District Court for the District of New Jersey to compel the Bureau to release the "master address" register—compiled initially from commercial mailing address lists and census postal checks, and updated through direct responses to census questionnaires, pre- and post-enumeration canvasing by census personnel, and in some instances by a cross-check with the 1970 census data—under the Freedom of Information Act. The Bureau resisted disclosure of the list, arguing that §§ 8(b) and 9(a) prohibit disclosure of all raw census data pertaining to particular individuals, including addresses, and that it therefore could lawfully withhold the information under Exemption 3 of the Freedom of Information Act (5 USCS §§ 552(b)(3)), which provides that the Act does not apply where information is specifically exempt from disclosure by statute. The District Court concluded that the Freedom of Information Act required disclosure of the requested information, concluding that the Census Act did not provide a "blanket of confidentiality" for all census materials, that the Bureau's claim of confidentiality

127

impeded the goal of accurate and complete enumeration, and that the information sought was not derived from the questionnaires received, but rather from data available prior to the census, and it ordered the Bureau to make available the address register of all property in the county, with the proviso that all persons using the records be sworn to secrecy, and the United States Court of Appeals for the Third Circuit affirmed (636 F2d 1210). In the second case (No. 80–1781), Denver officials filed suit in the United States District Court for the District of Colorado, seeking a preliminary injunction to require the Bureau to cooperate with the city in verifying its vacancy data. The District Court granted the city's discovery request for the vacancy information contained in the updated master address registers maintained by the Bureau, concluding that the purposes of § 9 of the Census Act could be maintained without denying the city the right of discovery. On appeal, the United States Court of Appeals for the Tenth Circuit reversed, reasoning that Congress had the power to make census information immune from direct discovery or disclosure and concluding that Congress had neither made nor implied an exception covering the instant case (644 F2d 844).

On certiorari, the United States Supreme Court reversed in case No. 80–1436 and affirmed in case No. 80–1781. In an opinion by Burger, Ch. J., expressing the unanimous view of the court, it was held that (1) the master address register was not subject to disclosure under the Freedom of Information Act, since (a) §§ 8(b) and 9(a) of the Census Act qualified under Exemption 3 of the Freedom of Information Act as statutes specifically exempting the disclosure of information, §§ 8(b) and 9(a) specifically providing for the nondisclosure of certain census data and no discretion being provided to the Bureau on whether or not to disclose the information referred to in §§ 8(b) and 9(a), and (b) Congress intended that the requested raw census data be protected by §§ 8(b) and 9(a), it not being relevant that the municipalities seeking the data would use it only for statistical purposes, and (2) vacancy information contained in the updated master address registers was not subject to disclosure under the discovery provisions of the Federal Rules of Civil Procedure, since the confidentiality provisions of §§ 8(b) and 9(a) constituted a "privilege" within the meaning of Rule 26(b)(1) of the Federal Rules of Civil Procedure which provides for access to all information relevant to the subject matter involved in a pending action unless the information is privileged, even though the municipality requesting the raw census data might have important reasons for requesting the data for purposes of its civil suit against the Bureau.

COUNSEL

Elliott Schulder argued the cause for petitioners in 80-1436 and for the respondents in 80-1781.

David H. Ben-Asher argued the cause for respondent in 80-1436.

George J. Cerrone, Jr., argued the cause for petitioners in 80-1781.

HAVENS REALTY CORPORATION, et al.,
Petitioners,
v
SYLVIA COLEMAN, et al.

— US —, 71 L Ed 2d 214, 102 S Ct 1114

Argued December 1, 1981.
Decided February 24, 1982.

Decision: Black "tester" given false information about housing availability and nonprofit, open housing organization, held to have standing to challenge racial steering under Fair Housing Act (42 USCS § 3612); Act's 180-day limitation period (42 USCS § 3612(a)), held not to bar claims of continuing violation, even though some incidents alleged occur outside period.

SUMMARY

A class action was filed in the United States District Court for the Eastern District of Virginia by three individuals and a nonprofit corporation whose purpose was to make equal opportunity in housing a reality in the Richmond, Virginia metropolitan area against the owners of an apartment complex and one of its employees, alleging that the defendants engaged in "racial steering" violative of § 804 of the Fair Housing Act of 1968 (42 USCS § 3604) and seeking declaratory, injunctive, and monetary relief. One of the individuals was a black "renter" who, attempting to rent an apartment from the owners, inquired about the availability of an apartment at the complex and was falsely told that no apartments
130

were available. The other two individuals were "testers"—individuals who, without an intent to rent or purchase a home or apartment, pose as renters or purchasers for the purpose of collecting evidence of unlawful steering practices—who were employed by the organization to determine whether the owners practice racial steering. One of the testers was black and on four separate occasions on which she made inquiries as to the availability of apartments was told that no apartments were available, while the other tester was white and was told that there were vacancies. The three individual plaintiffs were all residents of Richmond or the adjacent Henrico County in which the complex was located, and they averred that they had been injured by the discriminatory acts of the defendants, the renter claiming that he had been denied the right to rent real property in Henrico County, he and the two tester plaintiffs alleging that the owners' practices deprived them of the important social, professional, business and economic, political and aesthetic benefits of interacial associations that arise from living in integrated communities free from discriminatory housing practices, and the black tester alleging that the misinformation given her by the owner concerning the availability of apartments in the complex had caused her specific injury. In addition, the organization asserted that the steering practices had frustrated its counseling and referral services, with a consequent drain on resources. On the defendants' pre-trial motion, the District Court dismissed the claims of the two testers and the organization, holding that they lacked standing and that their claims were barred by the 180-day statute of limitations of § 812(a) of the Act (42 USCS § 3612(a)). On appeal, the United States Court of Appeals for the Fourth

Circuit, reversed and remanded, holding that the allegations of injury by the two testers, both as testers and as individuals who were deprived of the benefits of residing in an integrated community, sufficed to withstand a motion to dismiss, that the organization's allegations of injury to itself were sufficient, at the pleading stage, to afford the organization standing in its own capacity, and that none of the allegations of racial steering were time-barred, because the defendants' conduct constituted a continuing violation lasting through the last reported occurrence, which was less than 180 days before the complaint was filed (633 F2d 384).

On certiorari, the United States Supreme Court affirmed in part and reversed in part. In an opinion by BRENNAN, J., expressing the unanimous view of the court, it was held that (1) a "tester" who has been the object of a misrepresentation as to the availability of a dwelling made unlawful under § 804(d) of the Act (42 USCS § 3604(d)) has suffered injury in precisely the form the Act was intended to guard against and thus has standing under § 812 of the Act (42 USCS § 3612) to maintain a claim for damages, even though the tester may have approached a real estate agent fully expecting to receive false information and without any intention of buying or renting a home, so that the black tester had suffered "specific injury" from the challenged acts of the apartment complex owner and the Federal Constitution's Article III requirement of injury-in-fact was satisfied, but that the white tester had alleged no injury to his statutory right to accurate information concerning the availability of housing and thus had no standing to sue in his capacity as a tester, (2) the nonprofit organiza-

132

tion had standing in its own right under § 812 to challenge the owner's allegedly unlawful steering practices, since the organization had alleged that the practices had perceptibly impaired its ability to provide counseling and referral services for low- and moderate-income homeseekers, the fact that the alleged injury resulted from the organization's no-neconomic interest in encouraging open housing not affecting the nature of the injury suffered, and (3) a complaint filed by a plaintiff who, pursuant to the Act, challenges not just one incident of conduct violative of the Act, but an unlawful practice that continues into the limitations period is timely when it is filed within 180 days of the last asserted occurrence of that practice, and that this continuing violation theory applied both to the claims of the organization that it had suffered injury to its counseling and referral services and to the claims of the two individuals that the apartment complex owner's continuing pattern, practice, and policy of unlawful racial steering had deprived them of the benefits of interracial association arising from living in an integrated neighborhood, but that the black tester whose claims arose from four isolated occasions on which she received false information from the owners in violation of § 804(d) could not take advantage of the continuing violation period.

POWELL, J., concurring, emphasized that distinct and palpable injury remains the minimal constitutional requirement for standing in a federal court and that in this case neither the District Court nor the counsel for the parties took appropriate action to prevent the case from reaching an appellate court with only meaningless averments concerning the disputed question of standing.

COUNSEL

Everett G. Allen, Jr., argued the cause for petitioners.

Vanessa Ruiz argued the cause for respondents.

———————

ANNE B. ZIPES, et al., Petitioners,

v

TRANS WORLD AIRLINES, INC. (No. 78–1545)

———

INDEPENDENT FEDERATION OF FLIGHT
ATTENDANTS, Petitioner,

v

TRANS WORLD AIRLINES, INC., et al. (No. 80–
951)

— US —, 71 L Ed 2d 234, 102 S Ct 1127

Argued December 2, 1981.
Decided February 24, 1982.

Decision: Filing of timely charge with Equal Employment Opportunity Commission, held not
jurisdictional prerequisite to suit under Title
VII of Civil Rights Act of 1964 (42 USCS
§§ 2000e et seq.)

SUMMARY

A union representing certain airline flight attendants brought a class action in the United States
District Court for the Northern District of Illinois
charging that an airline had practiced unlawful sex
discrimination in violation of Title VII of the Civil
Rights Act of 1964 (42 USCS §§ 2000e et seq.) by
its policy of grounding all female flight cabin attendants who became mothers, while their male coun-
terparts who became fathers were permitted to continue flying. Collective bargaining eliminated the
challenged practice prospectively, and the parties in

the case reached a tentative settlement. Although the settlement, which provided neither backpay nor retroactive seniority, was approved by the District Court, the United States Court of Appeals for the Seventh Circuit found the union to be an inadequate representative of the class, and remanded the case with instructions that individual members of the class replace the union as the class representatives (490 F2d 636). Individual members of the class were later appointed as class representatives, and the airline moved to exclude those class members who had not filed charges with the Equal Employment Opportunity Commission within the time limit specified in Title VII. However the District Court, while agreeing with the airline that the filing requirements of Title VII are jurisdictional, denied the motion on the theory that any violation by the airline continued against all class members until the airline changed the challenged policy. Furthermore, the District Court granted the motion of the class for summary judgment on the issue of the airline's liability for violating Title VII. The Court of Appeals affirmed the District Court's grant of summary judgment on liability, but declined to extend the continuing violation theory to include in the plaintiff class employees who failed to file timely charges with the EEOC. The Court of Appeals further held that timely filing of EEOC charges was a jurisdictional prerequisite (582 F2d 1142). However, the court stayed its mandate pending the filing of petitions in the United States Supreme Court, which deferred consideration of the petitions pending completion of settlement proceedings in the District Court. In connection with the settlement proceedings, the District Court divided class members into two subclasses, one of which was comprised of all individuals whose claims the Court of Appeals had found to be jurisdictionally barred for failure to satisfy the filing requirement. Another union, which currently represented the flight attendants, was permitted to intervene and to object to the proposed settlement, which included a monetary award and an award of retroactive seniority to those who had not filed timely charges. However, the District Court, noting that the Court of Appeals' had stayed its mandate in its jurisdictional decision, rejected the union's challenge to its jurisdiction over those individuals who had not complied with the Title VII filing requirement, and approved the settlement while awarding restoration of retroactive seniority. The Court of Appeals affirmed, rejecting the union's argument that, because of the Court of Appeals' earlier opinion, the District Court lacked jurisdiction to approve the settlement or to order retroactive seniority with respect to class members whose claims the Court of Appeals had found to be jurisdictionally barred for failure to satisfy the timely filing requirement (630 F2d 1164).

On certiorari, the United States Supreme Court reversed as to the filing requirement, and affirmed as to the award of retroactive seniority. In an opinion by WHITE, J., joined by BRENNAN, MARSHALL, BLACKMUN, and O'CONNOR, JJ., and joined in part (as to holding 1 below) by BURGER, Ch. J., POWELL, J., and REHNQUIST, J., it was held that (1) filing a timely charge with the Equal Employment Opportunity Commission pursuant to current § 706(e) of Title VII (42 USCS § 2000e-5(e)) is not a jurisdictional prerequisite to suit in federal court, but a requirement that, like a statute of limitations, is subject to waiver, estoppel and equitable tolling, and (2) the District Court had the authority, in connection with the settlement agreement, to award retroactive seniority to the two subclasses of employees over the objection of the union representing the flight attendants, despite the fact that the Court of Appeals had previously determined that the claims of members of one subclass were jurisdictionally barred because of their failure to file charges with the EEOC within the time limit specified by Title VII, since (a) the District Court had found unlawful discrimination against the plaintiff class as a whole prior to its division into subclasses, (b) the Court of Appeals erred in ruling that the District Court had no jurisdiction over claims by those who had not met the filing requirement, thereby removing a jurisdictional barrier to the District Court's finding of discrimination with respect to the entire class, and (c) the union's contention that retroactive seniority contrary to a collective bargaining agreement should not have been awarded over the objection of a union that had not itself been found guilty of discrimination was without merit.

POWELL, J., joined by BURGER, Ch. J., and REHNQUIST, J., concurring as to the filing requirement and concurring in the judgment as to the award of retroactive seniority, expressed the view that (1) timely filing is not jurisdictional and is subject to waiver and estoppel, (2) it should have been made clear in the court's opinion in the case at bar that a timely charge, as well as a violation of Title VII, is a prerequisite to disturbing rights under a bona fide seniority system protected by § 703(h) of Title VII (42 USCS § 2000e-2(h)), and (3) as a result of the court's ruling in the case at bar, the District Court's orders finding timely charges and class-wide discrimination were final.

138

STEVENS, J., did not participate.

COUNSEL

William A. Jolley argued the cause for petitioner in 80-951.

A. Raymond Randolph, Jr., argued the cause for petitioners in 78-1545.

Laurence A. Carton argued the cause for respondents.

G. D. SEARLE & COMPANY, Petitioner,

v

SUSAN COHN and WALTER COHN

— US —, 71 L Ed 2d 250, 102 S Ct 1137

Argued December 7, 1981.
Decided February 24, 1982.

Decision: New Jersey statute tolling limitation period for actions against unrepresented foreign corporations, held not violative of Fourteenth Amendment's equal protection clause.

SUMMARY

Two individuals brought an action in New Jersey state court against a foreign corporation which had no agent for service of process within New Jersey. The corporation was served under New Jersey's long-arm rule, but not until 11 years after the cause of action arose. The corporation removed the action to the United States District Court for the District of New Jersey and moved for summary judgment based upon New Jersey's two-year statute of limitations applicable to the suit. The plaintiffs countered with a New Jersey statute which tolls the limitation period for a cause of action against a foreign corporation that "is not represented" in New Jersey by any person or officer upon whom process may be served. The District Court held that the suit was barred, reasoning that the tolling provision had operated to preserve only causes of action against corporations not subject to in personam jurisdiction in New Jersey, that with the subsequent enactment of New Jersey's long-arm rule the rationale for the pre-existing tolling provision ceased to exist, and that the tolling provision no longer served any logical purpose and thus was invalid under the equal protection clause of the Fourteenth Amendment (447 F Supp 903). The United States Court of Appeals for the Third Circuit reversed, holding that, as a matter of New Jersey law, the tolling provision continued in force despite the advent of long-arm jurisdiction, and that the tolling provision did not violate the equal protection clause because the increased difficulty of out of state service provided a rational basis for tolling the statute of limitation in a suit against an unrepresented foreign corporation (628 F2d 801).

On certiorari, the United States Supreme Court vacated and remanded. In an opinion by BLACKMUN, J., joined by BRENNAN, WHITE, MARSHALL, REHNQUIST, and O'CONNOR, JJ., and joined in part (as to holding 1 below) by BURGER, Ch. J., and POWELL, J., it was held that (1) the tolling provision did not violate the equal protection clause of the Fourteenth Amendment, the provision having not been rendered meaningless by the state's subsequent acceptance of long-arm jurisdiction, since rational reasons supported tolling the limitation period for unrepresented foreign corporations despite the institution of long-arm jurisdiction, the unrepresented foreign corporation remaining potentially difficult to locate and the institution of long-arm jurisdiction having not made service upon the corporation the equivalent of service upon a corporation with an in-state representative, but rather having made additional conditions for effective service, but (2) the court would not pass upon a challenge under the commerce clause of the United States Constitution (Art I, § 8, cl 3), to the tolling provision, since neither the District Court nor the Court of Appeals directly addressed the issue and since the commerce clause issue was clouded by an ambiguity in state law.

POWELL, J., joined by BURGER, Ch. J., concurring in part and dissenting in part, expressed the view that the court should have decided the commerce clause issue rather than remand the case to the Court of Appeals, since the issue was addressed at length by both parties in their briefs and in oral argument.

STEVENS, J., dissented, expressing the view that there was no legitimate state purpose justifying the special burden imposed on unregistered foreign corporations by the tolling provision.

COUNSEL

William P. Richmond argued the cause for petitioner.

Walter R. Cohn argued the cause for respondents.

LAVERNE L. LOGAN, Appellant,

v

ZIMMERMAN BRUSH COMPANY et al.

— US —, 71 L Ed 2d 265, 102 S Ct 1148

Argued October 14, 1981.
Decided February 24, 1982.

Decision: Termination of Illinois fair employment
practices act claimant's claim because of state's
failure to convene hearing within 120 days, held
violative of Fourteenth Amendment due process
and equal protection.

SUMMARY

A probationary employee who was discharged by
a company, purportedly because his short left leg
made it impossible for him to perform his duties as
a shipping clerk, filed a timely charge with the
Illinois Fair Employment Practices Commission alleging that his employment had been terminated
unlawfully because of his physical handicap. This
triggered the Commission's obligation under the
state fair employment practices act to convene a
factfinding conference within 120 days. Apparently
through inadvertence, the Commission scheduled
the conference 5 days after expiration of the statutory period, and when the conference date arrived,
the company moved that the complaint's charge be
dismissed because the Commission had failed to
hold the conference within the statutorily-mandated
period. However, the Commission rejected this request. On appeal, the Supreme Court of Illinois

found the legislative language to be mandatory and accordingly held that the failure to comply with the 120-day period deprived the Commission of jurisdiction to consider the complainant's charge, and it summarily rejected the complainant's argument that his due process and equal protection rights would be violated were the Commission's error allowed to extinguish his cause of action (80 Ill 2d 99, 411 NE2d 277).

On appeal, the United States Supreme Court reversed and remanded. Although unable to agree on an opinion with respect to the alleged equal protection violation, six members of the court agreed that the act's creation of two classes of claimants—those whose claims were processed within the 120 days following the filing of a claim and were accordingly given full consideration on the merits, and those whose claims were not processed within the 120 days and were accordingly terminated—violated the Fourteenth Amendment right of the claimant to equal protection of the laws. In an opinion by BLACKMUN, J., joined by BURGER, Ch. J., and BRENNAN, WHITE, MARSHALL, and STEVENS, JJ., it was held that the right of the complainant to use the state fair employment practices act's adjudicatory procedures was a species of property protected by the due process clause of the Fourteenth Amendment, and the act deprived the complainant of that property interest by depriving the Commission of jurisdiction to consider the charge when the Commission failed to comply with the act's requirement to convene a factfinding conference within 120 days after the filing of the claim, and that the claimant was entitled to have the Commission consider the merits of his charge, based upon the substantiality

144

of the available evidence, before deciding whether to terminate his claim, a postdeprivation hearing being constitutionally inadequate particularly since the state's only posttermination process came in the form of an independent tort action.

In an separate opinion, BLACKMUN, J., joined by BRENNAN, MARSHALL, and O'CONNOR, JJ., expressed the view that the Illinois scheme also deprived the complainant of his Fourteenth Amendment right to the equal protection of the laws, neither the state fair employment practices act's purpose of eliminating employment discrimination nor of protecting employers and other potential defendants from unfounded charges of discrimination being advanced by the act's deadline provision, terminating a claim that the state itself has misscheduled not being a rational way of expediting the resolution of disputes, the procedure at issue not serving generally to hasten the processing or ultimate termination of employment controversies, and the state's conversion of similarly situated claims into dissimilarly situated ones and subsequent use of this distinction as a basis for its classification being the very essence of arbitrary state action.

POWELL, J., joined by REHNQUIST, J., concurring in the judgment, expressed concern with the potential implications of the court's expansive due process analysis, and stated that the case should be decided narrowly on its unusual facts so that the challenged statute, as construed and applied in the case, failed to conform with the minimal equal protection standard that a state-created classification bear a rational relationship to legitimate governmental objectives, the challenged classification bearing no relationship to the merits of the underlying charges and being arbitrary and irrational when measured against the state's asserted purposes of redressing valid claims of discrimination and of protecting employers from frivolous law suits.

COUNSEL

Gary H. Palm argued the cause for appellant.
Jay A. Canel argued the cause for appellee.

———————

RICHARD H. WHITE, Petitioner,

v

NEW HAMPSHIRE DEPARTMENT OF
EMPLOYMENT SECURITY et al.

— US —, 71 L Ed 2d 325, 102 S Ct 1162

Argued November 30, 1981.
Decided March 2, 1982.

Decision: Postjudgment request for attorney's fees
under Civil Rights Attorney's Fees Awards Act
(42 USCS § 1988), held not subject to 10-day
timeliness standard of Rule 59(e) of Federal
Rules of Civil Procedure.

SUMMARY

Four and one-half months after approval of a
consent decree and entry of judgment by the United
States District Court for the District of New Hampshire in a suit by an individual against the New
Hampshire Department of Employment Security alleging that the Department failed to make timely
determinations of certain entitlements to unemployment compensation and thereby violated certain
federal statutory and constitutional provisions, the
claimant filed a motion requesting an award of
attorney's fees under the Civil Rights Attorney's
Fees Awards Act of 1976 (42 USCS § 1988), which
authorizes the award, in the court's discretion, of
attorney's fees to the prevailing party as part of the
costs in constitutional and civil rights litigation of
various kinds. The District Court granted attorney's
fees and denied a subsequent motion to vacate the

consent decree. On appeal, the United States Court of Appeals for the First Circuit reversed, holding that the claimant's motion for attorney's fees constituted a "motion to alter or amend the judgment" under Rule 59(e) of the Federal Rules of Civil Procedure and was governed by the Rule's requirement that such a motion be served not later than 10 days after entry of the judgment (629 F2d 697).

On certiorari, the United States Supreme Court reversed and remanded. In an opinion by POWELL, J., joined by BURGER, Ch. J., and BRENNAN, WHITE, MARSHALL, REHNQUIST, STEVENS, and O'CONNOR, JJ., it was held that a postjudgment request for an award of attorney's fees under the Civil Rights Attorney's Fees Awards Act is not a "motion to alter or amend the judgment" subject to the timeliness standard of Rule 59(e) of the Federal Rules of Civil Procedure.

BLACKMUN, J., concurring in the judgment, emphasized that Rules 54(d) and 58 of the Federal Rules of Civil Procedure should also have been held to be inapplicable to postjudgment requests for attorney's fees under the Civil Rights Attorney's Fees Awards Act.

COUNSEL

E. Richard Larson argued the cause for petitioner. Marc R. Scheer argued the cause for respondents.

RAILWAY LABOR EXECUTIVES' ASSOCIATION,
Appellant,

v

WILLIAM M. GIBBONS, Trustee, et al. (No. 80–
415)

———

RAILWAY LABOR EXECUTIVES' ASSOCIATION,
Appellant,

v

WILLIAM M. GIBBONS, Trustee, etc., et al. (No.
80–1239)

— US —, 71 L Ed 2d 335, 102 S Ct 1169

Argued December 2, 1981.
Decided March 2, 1982.

Decision: Employee protection provisions of Rock
Island Transition and Employee Assistance Act
(45 USCS §§ 1005 and 1008), held violative of
bankruptcy clause (Art I, § 8, cl 4).

SUMMARY

In 1975, a railroad company petitioned the United
States District Court for the Northern District of
Illinois for reorganization under § 77 of the Bankruptcy Act of 1898 (former 11 USCS § 205), and it
continued to operate for several more years until a
labor strike depleted its cash reserves. In 1980, the
reorganization court concluded that reorganization
was not possible and it directed the trustee of the
railroad estate to prepare a plan for liquidation.
Subsequently, various railroads and labor organiza-

149

tions representing employees of the bankrupt railroad reached an agreement as to railroad employees
hired by carriers acquiring the railroad's trackage,
the agreement covering such matters as hiring preferences, monetary protection, and seniority, but not
covering those employees who were not employed
by acquiring carriers. Subsequently, the railroad
trustee petitioned the reorganization court to confirm the railroad's abandonment of all rail lines in
operation. The court then ordered the total abandonment of the railroad system and the discontinu-
ance of its service and concluded, among other
things, that it would not allow nor require any claim
or arrangement of any kind or nature for employee
labor protection payable out of the assets of the
railroad's estate. In the meantime Congress had
responded to the crisis resulting from the demise of
the railroad by enacting the Rock Island Transition
and Employee Assistance Act (45 USCS §§ 1001 et
seq.) which was signed into law three days before
the reorganization court's abandonment order. Sections 106 and 110 of the Act (45 USCS §§ 1005,
1008) were employee protection provisions which
required that the railroad trustee provide economic
benefits to those railroad employees who were not
hired by other carriers, that benefits be paid from
the estate's assets, and that employee benefit obligations be considered administrative expenses of the
railroad estate for purposes of determining the
priority of the employees' claims to the assets of the
estate upon liquidation. A complaint was filed in the
court seeking to declare the Act unconstitutional
and to enjoin its enforcement. The court then issued a preliminary injunction prohibiting the enforcement of §§ 106 and 110, concluding that the
employee protection provisions constituted an un-

compensated taking of private property for a public purpose in violation of the just compensation clause of the Fifth Amendment, and the District Court's order was appealed to the United States Supreme Court. Congress responded to the court's injunction by enacting § 701 of the Staggers Rail Act of 1980 (94 Stat 1959), which, with certain modifications, reenacted §§ 106 and 110 of the Rock Island Act and amended that Act to provide a remedy if the labor protection provisions were found to constitute a taking. A motion was filed with the reorganization court to vacate its injunction on the basis that the passage of the Staggers Act rendered the injunction moot. The court denied the motion to vacate and issued a new order enjoining the implementation of the labor protection provisions of the Rock Island Act, as amended and reenacted, and the United States Court of Appeals for the Seventh Circuit affirmed by an equally divided vote (645 F2d 45).

On appeal, the United States Supreme Court vacated and remanded the appeal from the District Court and affirmed the appeal from the Court of Appeals. In an opinion by REHNQUIST, J., joined by BURGER, Ch. J., and WHITE, BLACKMUN, POWELL, STEVENS, and O'CONNOR, JJ., it was held that (1) the appeal from the District Court holding that the employee protection provisions constituted an un-compensated taking of private property in violation of the just compensation clause of the Fifth Amendment was rendered moot by Congress' subsequent enactment of the Staggers Act which reenacted and amended the provisions the District Court declared unconstitutional, and (2) the employee protection provisions of §§ 106 and 110 of the Rock Island Act were repugnant to the bankruptcy clause of the

United States Constitution (Art I, § 8, cl 4) which empowers Congress to enact "uniform" laws on bankruptcy, since the Act was an exercise of Congress' power under the bankruptcy clause, rather than the commerce clause of the United States Constitution (Art I, § 8, cl 3), Congress doing nothing less in the Act than to prescribe the manner in which the priority of the railroad's estate was to be distributed among its creditors, and since the Act was not uniform, the Act not being a response either to the particular problems of major railroad bankruptcies or to any geographically isolated problem, but rather being a response to the problems caused by the bankruptcy of one railroad, and only its creditors being affected by the Act's employee protection provisions and only its employees being permitted to take benefit of the arrangement.

MARSHALL, J., joined by BRENNAN, J., concurring in the judgment, expressed the view that the bankruptcy clause permits Congress to legislate with respect to the distinctive needs of a particular railroad or its employees if Congress finds that the application of a law to a single debtor, or limited class of debtors, serves a national interest apart from the economic interest of that debtor or class, and if the identified national interest justifies Congress' failure to apply the law to other debtors, but that the Rock Island Transition and Employee Assistance Act was unconstitutional since it did not satisfy this stringent test.

COUNSEL

John O'B. Clarke, Jr., argued the cause for appellant.

Elinor H. Stillman argued the cause for federal appellees in support of the appellant.

Daniel R. Murray argued the cause for non-federal appellees.

———

JAMES M. MURPHY, District Judge, Fourth Judicial
District of the State of Nebraska, Douglas County,
Appellant,

v

EUGENE L. HUNT

— US —, 71 L Ed 2d 353, 102 S Ct 1181

Argued January 18, 1982.
Decided March 2, 1982.

Decision: Claim that Nebraska's prohibition of pretrial bail to person charged with sexual offenses
violated Federal Constitution, held moot where
defendant had already been convicted of offenses.

SUMMARY

An individual was charged with first degree sexual
assault on a child and three counts of first degree
forcible sexual assault. He appeared on these
charges in Omaha Municipal Court, Nebraska,
where his request for bail was denied, and in a bail
review hearing held in Douglas County District
Court his second application for bail was denied,
the court relying upon a provision in the Nebraska
constitution allowing all persons bail except, among
other things, for violent sexual offenses. Pending
trial, the defendant filed a complaint under 42
USCS § 1983 in the United States District Court for
the District of Nebraska, claiming that the state
constitutional provision violated his federal constitutional rights to be free from excessive bail and cruel
and unusual punishment, to due process and equal

protection of the laws, and to the effective assistance of counsel under the Sixth, Eighth, and Fourteenth Amendments, but the District Court dismissed his complaint. In the meantime, in prosecutions ending both before and after the District Court decision, the defendant was convicted of several offenses, each of which he appealed to the Supreme Court of Nebraska. On appeal of the District Court's dismissal, the United States Court of Appeals for the Eighth Circuit reversed and held that the exclusion of violent sexual offenses from bail before trial violated the excessive bail clause of the Eighth Amendment (648 F2d 1148).

On appeal, the United States Supreme Court vacated and remanded. In a per curiam opinion, expressing the view of BURGER, Ch. J., and BRENNAN, MARSHALL, BLACKMUN, POWELL, REHNQUIST, STEVENS, O'CONNOR, JJ., it was held that the judgment of the Court of Appeals should be vacated and the case remanded to the Court of Appeals with instructions that the complaint be dismissed as moot, since as a result of the defendant's convictions even a favorable decision on the pretrial bail issue would not have entitled him to bail and, since he had not prayed for damages nor sought to represent a class of pretrial detainees, he no longer had a legally cognizable interest in the result in the case, the mere physical or theoretical possibility that his convictions could be overturned and he might then once again demand bail before trial not being a reasonable expectation or demonstrable probability that he would ever again be in that position, and the fact that he might have a live claim for bail pending appeal not saving from dismissal his moot claim to pretrial bail.

WHITE, J., dissenting, expressed the view that since the provision of the state constitution denying the defendant bail pending trial also served to deny the defendant bail pending appeal of his conviction, the claim was plainly presented in the United States Supreme Court that the challenged provision effectively barred bail during his appeal to the Nebraska Supreme Court, and that remand was particularly in order since the mootness issue had not been briefed and both parties agreed that the case was not moot.

COUNSEL

Terry R. Schaaf argued the cause for appellant.

Bennett G. Hornstein argued the cause for appellee.

VILLAGE OF HOFFMAN ESTATES, et al.,
Appellants,

v

FLIPSIDE, HOFFMAN ESTATES, INC.

— US —, 71 L Ed 2d 362, 102 S Ct 1186

Argued December 9, 1981.
Decided March 3, 1982.

Decision: Municipal ordinance requiring license to
sell "items designed or marketed for use with
illegal cannabis or drugs," held not unconstitutionally vague or overbroad.

SUMMARY

A village enacted an ordinance regulating the sale
of drug paraphernalia. The ordinance requires a
business to obtain a license if it sells any items that
are "designed or marketed for use with illegal cannabis or drugs". A store selling drug paraphernalia
in the village brought an action in the United States
District Court for the Northern District of Illinois
challenging the ordinance prior to its enforcement
as unconstitutionally vague and overbroad. The
District Court upheld the constitutionality of the
ordinance. On appeal, the United States Court of
Appeals for the Seventh Circuit reversed, holding
that the ordinance was impermissibly vague on its
face (639 F2d 373).

On appeal, the United States Supreme Court
reversed and remanded. In an opinion by MAR-
SHALL, J., expressing the view of BURGER, Ch. J., and
BRENNAN, BLACKMUN, POWELL, REHNQUIST, and

157

O'Connor, JJ., it was held that (1) the ordinance did not infringe upon the First Amendment rights of a merchandiser of items purported to be regulated by the ordinance and was not overbroad as inhibiting the First Amendment rights of other parties since (a) the ordinance does not restrict speech as such but simply regulates the commercial marketing of items that the labels reveal may be used for an illicit purpose and thus the ordinance does not embrace noncommercial speech, (b) insofar as any commercial speech interest was implicated, it was only the attenuated interest in displaying and marketing merchandise in the manner the retailer desires, and (c) it was irrelevant whether the ordinance had an overbroad scope encompassing other persons' commercial speech, (2) the ordinance is not impermissibly vague in all of its applications and could therefore not be challenged on its face as unduly vague in violation of due process as applied to a business engaged in selling drug paraphernalia since (a) the language "designed for use" is not unconstitutionally vague on its face insofar as it is sufficiently clear to cover at least some of the items sold by the business, and (b) the language "marketed for use" gave the business ample warning that its marketing activities required a license.

White, J., concurring in the judgment, expressed the view that the court need not have discussed the overbreadth problem in order to reach the result since the Court of Appeals did not discuss any problem of overbreadth but rather erroneously held the ordinance void for vagueness.

Stevens, J., did not participate.

COUNSEL

Richard N. Williams argued the cause for appellants.

Michael L. Pritzker argued the cause for appellee.

———————

JIM ROSE, Warden, Petitioner,

v

NOAH HARRISON LUNDY

— US —, 71 L Ed 2d 379, 102 S Ct 1198

Argued October 14, 1981.
Decided March 3, 1982.

Decision: State prisoner's habeas corpus petition
filed under 28 USCS § 2254, held required to
be dismissed by Federal District Court when it
contains both exhausted and unexhausted
claims.

SUMMARY

An individual whose conviction and imprisonment
on charges of rape and crime against nature were
affirmed by the Tennessee Court of Criminal Appeals (521 SW2d 591) was denied review by the
Supreme Court of Tennessee, and he filed an unsuccessful petition for post-conviction relief in the
Knox County Criminal Court. The prisoner subsequently filed a petition in the United States District
Court for the Middle District of Tennessee for a
writ of habeas corpus under 28 USCS § 2254, alleging four specified grounds for relief. The District
Court, although concluding that it could not consider two of the claims because the prisoner had not
exhausted his state remedies for those grounds,
granted the writ. The United States Court of Appeals for the Sixth Circuit affirmed, concluding that
the District Court properly found that the prisoner's
constitutional rights had been seriously impaired
160

and specifically rejecting the state's argument that the District Court should have dismissed the petition because it included both exhausted and unexhausted claims (624 F2d 1100).

On certiorari, the United States Supreme Court reversed and remanded. In that part of the opinion (Parts I, II, III-A, III-B, and IV) by O'CONNOR, J., which constituted the opinion of the court and which was joined by BURGER, Ch. J., and BRENNAN, MARSHALL, POWELL, and REHNQUIST, JJ., it was held that under 28 USCS § 2254(b)(c), a Federal District Court must dismiss a petition for a writ of habeas corpus containing any claims that have not been exhausted in the state courts, thereby leaving the prisoner with the choice of returning to state court to exhaust his claims or of amending or resubmitting the habeas petition to present only exhausted claims to the District Court, such a total exhaustion rule promoting comity and not unreasonably impairing the prisoner's right to relief. In the balance of her opinion (Part III-C), O'CONNOR, J., joined by BURGER, Ch. J., POWELL, J., and REHNQUIST, J., expressed the view that the total exhaustion rule would not impair the prisoner's interest in speedy federal relief on his claims since he could always amend the petition to delete the exhausted claims, rather than returning to state court to exhaust all those claims, although by invoking this procedure the prisoner would risk forfeiting consideration of his unexhausted claims in federal court under 28 USCS § 2254 Rule 9(b).

BLACKMUN, J., concurring in the judgment, expressed the view that a Federal District Court should be simply permitted to dismiss unexhausted grounds for relief and consider exhausted claims on the merits and thus would affirm the Court of Appeals' ruling that the exhaustion doctrine requires dismissal of only the unexhausted claims in a mixed habeas petition, but would remand the case for reconsideration of the merits of the prisoner's constitutional arguments.

BRENNAN, J., joined by MARSHALL, J., concurring in part and dissenting in part, agreed with the court's holding that the exhaustion requirement of 28 USCS § 2254(b)-(c) obliges a Federal District Court to dismiss, without consideration of the merits, a habeas corpus petition from a state prisoner when that petition contains claims that have not been exhausted in the state courts, but expressed the view that 28 USCS § 2254 Rule 9(b) could not be read to permit dismissal of a subsequent petition containing the previously unexhausted claims, concluding rather that when a prisoner's original, mixed habeas petition is dismissed without any examination of its claims or the merits, and when the prisoner later brings a second petition based on the previously unexhausted claims that had earlier been refused a hearing, then the remedy of dismissal for abuse of writ cannot be employed against the second petition, absent unusual factual circumstances truly suggesting abuse.

WHITE, J., concurring in part and dissenting in part, stated that he would not require a mixed petition to be dismissed in its entirety, with leave to resubmit the exhausted claims, and expressing the view that the trial judge should dismiss the unexhausted claims and rule on the exhausted claims unless they are intertwined with those he must dismiss or unless the habeas petitioner prefers to have his entire petition dismissed and that, in any event, if the judge rules on those issues that are ripe and dismisses those that are not, the petitioner should not be taxed with abuse of the writ if he returns with the latter claims after seeking state relief.

STEVENS, J., dissented, stating that he would allow federal district judges to exercise discretion to determine whether the presence of an unexhausted claim in the habeas corpus application makes it inappropriate to consider the merits of a properly pleaded exhausted claim, the total exhaustion rule adopted by the court arbitrarily denying district judges the kind of authority they need to administer their calendars effectively.

COUNSEL

John C. Zimmerman argued the cause for petitioner, pro hac vice, by special leave of court.

D. Shannon Smith argued the cause for respondent.

———————

MARINE BANK, Petitioner,

v

SAMUEL WEAVER, et ux.

— US —, 71 L Ed 2d 409, 102 S Ct 1220

Argued January 11, 1982.
Decided March 8, 1982.

Decision: Certificate of deposit from federally regulated bank and business agreement arising from pledging of certificate as guarantee for loan, held not securities for purposes of 15 USCS § 78j(b).

SUMMARY

Two individuals purchased a $50,000 certificate of deposit from a bank. They subsequently pledged the certificate of deposit to guarantee a $65,000 loan from the bank to a company which owed the bank $33,000 for prior loans and was substantially overdrawn at the bank. In consideration for guaranteeing the loan, the company's officers entered into an agreement with the purchasers of the certificate under which they were to receive a share of the company's profits and other compensation. The new loan, rather than being used as working capital by the company as the bank's officers allegedly told the purchasers it would, was applied to pay the company's overdue obligations to the bank. Subsequently, the company became bankrupt and the bank acknowledged that it intended to claim the pledged certificate of deposit. The purchasers then brought suit in the United States District Court for the

Western District of Pennsylvania alleging that the bank had violated the anti-fraud provision of § 10(b) of the Securities Exchange Act of 1934 (15 USCS § 78j(b)). The purchasers alleged that the bank's officers had solicited the loan guarantee while knowing, but not disclosing, the company's financial plight or the bank's plans to repay itself from the new loan guaranteed by the certificate of deposit. The District Court granted summary judgment in favor of the bank, holding that if a wrong occurred, it did not take place "in connection with the purchase or sale of any security" as required for liability under § 10(b). The court declined to exercise pendent jurisdiction over the state law claims. On appeal, the United States Court of Appeals for the Third Circuit reversed, holding that it could reasonably be found that either the certificate of deposit or the agreement between the purchasers and the company's owners was a security (637 F2d 157).

On certiorari, the United States Supreme Court reversed and remanded. In an opinion by BURGER, Ch. J., expressing the unanimous view of the court, it was held that (1) the certificate of deposit purchased from a federally regulated bank with a six year maturity date was not a security for purposes of the antifraud provision of § 10(b) of the Securities Exchange Act of 1934 (15 USCS § 78j(b)) since (a) a certificate of deposit is not the functional equivalent of the withdrawable capital shares of a savings and loan association, nor is a certificate of deposit similar to any other long-term debt obligation commonly found to be a security, and (b) the purchaser of a certificate of deposit is virtually guaranteed payment in full, whereas the holder of an ordinary long-term debt obligation assumes the risk of the

165

borrower's insolvency, and (2) the agreement between the purchasers of the certificate of deposit and the owners of the business was not a security for purposes of the anti-fraud provisions of § 10(b) of the Securities Exchange Act of 1934 (15 USCS § 78j(b)) since (a) the business owners distributed no prospectus to the purchasers of the certificate or to other potential investors and the agreement was not to be traded publicly, and (b) although the agreement provided for distribution of a share of the profits, that provision alone was not sufficient to make the agreement a security.

COUNSEL

Daniel L. R. Miller argued the cause for petitioner.

Andrew J. Conner argued the cause for respondents.

UNITED MINE WORKERS OF AMERICA
HEALTH AND RETIREMENT FUNDS, et al.,
Petitioners,

v

GRACIE ROBINSON and JUANITA HAGER, etc.

— US —, 71 L Ed 2d 419, 102 S Ct 1226

Argued January 13, 1982.
Decided March 8, 1982.

Decision: Collective bargaining contract allocating health benefits among potential beneficiaries of employee trust fund, held not reviewable for reasonableness under Labor Management Relations Act (29 USCS § 186(c)(5)).

SUMMARY

A collective bargaining agreement between a union representing coal miners and an employer bargaining group representing coal mine operators provided for an increase in health benefits, payable out of employee benefit trust funds financed by the operators, for widows of coal miners who died prior to the effective date of the agreement and who were receiving pensions when they died. However, benefits were not increased for those miners who died prior to the effective date of the agreement and were eligible for pensions, but who were still working when they died. Widows of coal miners in the latter category filed a class action against the trustees of the funds in the United States District Court for the District of Columbia, alleging that the requirement that a miner actually be receiving a pension for which he was eligible at the time of his death in order to make his survivors eligible for increased health benefits bore no rational relationship to the purpose of the trust funds and therefore was illegal under § 302 of the Labor Management Relations Act (29 USCS § 186). The District Court denied relief, rejecting an argument that the eligibility requirement was arbitrary and capricious, concluding that public policy dictates a limited role for the courts in reviewing collectively bargained agreements, and holding that the trustees were bound to adhere to the terms of the agreement (449 F Supp 941). The United States Court of Appeals for the District of Columbia Circuit reversed, relying on the requirement of § 302(c)(5) of the Act (29 USCS § 186(c)(5), which requires that jointly administered pension trusts be maintained for the sole and exclusive benefit of the employees of the contributing employer and their families and dependents, and holding that eligibility rules fixed by a collective bargaining agreement must meet a reasonableness standard (205 App DC 330, 640 F2d 416).

On certiorari, the United States Supreme Court reversed. In an opinion by STEVENS, J., expressing the unanimous view of the court, it was held that § 302(c)(5) of the Act does not authorize federal courts to review for reasonableness the provisions of a collective bargaining agreement allocating health benefits among potential beneficiaries of an employee benefit trust fund, neither the language, the legislative history, nor any other requirement of § 302(c)(5) embodying or supporting any such reasonableness requirement, the trustees of the fund having breached no fiduciary duties in administering the fund in accordance with the collective bargaining agreement, and a federal court having no authority to modify the substantive terms of a collective bargaining contract when neither the collective bargaining process nor its end product violates any command of Congress.

COUNSEL

E. Calvin Golumbic argued the cause for petitioners.

Larry Franklin Sword argued the cause for respondents.

BREAD POLITICAL ACTION COMMITTEE, et
al., Appellants,

v

FEDERAL ELECTION COMMITTEE, et al.

— US —, 71 L Ed 2d 432, 102 S Ct 1235

Argued January 19, 1982.
Decided March 8, 1982.

Decision: Trade associations and political action
committees, held barred from invoking expedited constitutional challenge procedures of Federal Election Campaign Act (2 USCS § 437h).

SUMMARY

Two trade associations and three political action
committees filed an action in the United States
District Court for the Northern District of Illinois,
challenging the validity of the provisions of the
Federal Election Campaign Act of 1971 limiting the
extent to which they could solicit funds for political
purposes (2 USCS § 441b(b)(4)(D)), and seeking
expedited consideration of the action under § 310(a)
of the Act (2 USCS § 437h(a))—which lists three
categories of plaintiffs who may challenge the constitutionality of any provision of the Act in a Federal
District Court action in which the District Court
must certify all questions of constitutionality to the
court of appeals sitting on banc: (1) the Federal
Election Commission, (2) the national committee of
any political party and (3) any individual eligible to
vote in any election for the office of president. The
District Court denied such consideration on the
grounds that the associations and committees were
170

not within any of the three categories listed as
eligible to invoke § 310(a)'s expedited procedures.
On an interlocutory appeal, the United States Court
of Appeals for the Seventh Circuit reversed, holding
that § 310(a) is available for use by plaintiffs
whether they belong to an enumerated category or
not (591 F2d 29). On remand, the District Court, as
required by § 310, first made findings of fact and
then certified the case back to the Court of Appeals
sitting en banc for a determination on the constitutional questions raised by the parties. The Court of
Appeals declined to overrule the earlier panel decision regarding the reach of § 310(a), and upheld the
constitutionality of the challenged provisions (635
F2d 621).

On appeal, the United States Supreme Court
reversed and remanded. In an opinion by O'CON-
NOR, J., expressing the unanimous view of the court,
it was held that the trade associations and political
action committees could not bring an expedited
challenge to the validity of a section of the Federal
Election Campaign Act under § 310(a) of the Act as
only parties meeting the express requirements of
§ 310(a) may invoke its procedures, there being no
showing of such "clear expression" or "clear evidence" of congressional intent to make the procedures available to categories of plaintiffs other than
those listed in § 310(a).

COUNSEL

Jeffrey Cole argued the cause for appellants.
Charles N. Steele argued the cause for appellees.

LOUIE L. WAINWRIGHT, Secretary, Florida
Department of Corrections, Petitioner,

v

JOSE TORNA

— US —, 71 L Ed 2d 475, 102 S Ct 1300

Decided March 22, 1982.

Decision: Retained counsel's failure to timely file
for discretionary review of state court convictions with state's highest court, held not to
deprive defendant of effective assistance of
counsel.

SUMMARY

An individual was convicted in Florida state court
on several felony counts, and his convictions were
affirmed by the Third District Court of Appeal of
Florida (358 So 2d 1109). The Supreme Court of
Florida dismissed an application for a writ of certiorari, on the ground that the application was not filed
timely (362 So 2d 1057), and a petition for rehearing and clarification was later denied. The defendant subsequently filed a petition for habeas corpus
in the United States District Court for the Southern
District of Florida, contending that he had been
denied his right to the effective assistance of counsel
by the failure of his retained counsel to file the
application for certiorari on time. The District Court
denied the petition, stating that the failure to file a
timely application for certiorari did not render
counsel's action so grossly deficient as to render the
proceedings fundamentally unfair. On appeal, the
172

United States Court of Appeals for the Fifth Circuit reversed and remanded (649 F2d 290).

Granting certiorari, the United States Supreme Court reversed. In a per curiam opinion, expressing the view of BURGER, Ch. J., and BRENNAN, WHITE, BLACKMUN, POWELL, REHNQUIST, STEVENS, and O'CONNOR, JJ., it was held that the defendant was not deprived of the effective assistance of counsel by his retained counsel's failure to file on time the application for certiorari, since the defendant had no absolute right to appeal his convictions to that court and thus had no constitutional right to counsel to pursue that appeal.

MARSHALL, J., dissenting, expressed the view that the defendant had a constitutional right to counsel to pursue discretionary state appeals, and that, in any event, the defendant was denied his right to due process by being deprived of his right to seek discretionary review by the state's highest court, since he reasonably relied on counsel's promise to seek such review.

GEORGE SUMNER, Warden, Petitioner,

v

ROBERT MATA

— US —, 71 L Ed 2d 480, 102 S Ct 1303

Decided March 22, 1982.

Decision: Federal Court of Appeals' decision holding 28 USCS § 2254(d) inapplicable to habeas petition challenging photographic identification procedures, remanded for failure to adhere to instructions of Supreme Court on prior remand.

SUMMARY

On appeal to the California Court of Appeals, a state prisoner who was convicted of the first-degree murder of a fellow inmate argued for the first time that a photographic lineup procedure used by the state police was so impermissibly suggestive as to deprive him of due process. After examining the evidence, the court rejected this assertion, concluding that the pretrial procedures had not been unfair. However, a different conclusion was reached by the United States Court of Appeals for the Ninth Circuit on appeal in a subsequent federal habeas corpus proceeding brought by the inmate (611 F2d 754). The United States Supreme Court vacated and remanded the decision of the Court of Appeals, holding that 28 USCS § 2254(d) requires federal courts in habeas proceedings to accord a presumption of correctness to state court findings of fact, that the presumption of correctness is equally applicable

174

when a state appellate court makes the finding of
fact, and that if a federal court concludes that the
presumption of correctness does not control, it
must provide a written explanation of the reasoning
that led it to conclude that one or more of the first
seven factors listed in § 2254(d) were present, or
the reasoning which led it to conclude that the state
finding was not fairly supported by the record, and
finding that the Court of Appeals had neither applied the presumption of correctness nor explained
why it had not. The Supreme Court remanded so
that the Court of Appeals could review its determination of the issue and either apply the statutory
presumption or explain why the presumption did
not apply in light of the listed factors (66 L Ed 2d
722). On remand, the Court of Appeals concluded
that § 2254(d) was irrelevant in the case because its
findings in no way differed from those of the state
court, finding that whether or not the pretrial photographic identification procedure used was impermissibly suggestive was a mixed question of law and
fact as to which the presumption of correctness do
not apply, and reinstating its conclusion that the
pretrial procedures had been impermissibly suggestive and that the inmate therefore was entitled to
release or a new trial (649 F2d 713).

Granting certiorari, the United States Supreme
Court vacated and remanded. In a per curiam opinion, expressing the view of BURGER, Ch. J., and
WHITE, BLACKMUN, POWELL, REHNQUIST, and O'CON-
NOR, JJ., it was held that although the ultimate
question as to the constitutionality of the pretrial
identification procedures used in the case is a mixed
question of law and fact that is not governed by 28
USCS § 2254(d), remand was again required, since

the Court of Appeals neither applied the statutory presumption nor explained why the presumption was not applicable in view of the factors listed in the statute, as it had been asked to do by the Supreme Court in its prior remand decision.

BRENNAN, J., joined by MARSHALL, J., dissenting, expressed the view that the opinion of the Court of Appeals accorded with the principles expressed in the court's prior opinion and restated by the court in the current opinion, § 2254(d) being inapplicable to the ultimate question whether pretrial identification procedures are impermissibly suggestive and there being no basis for disbelieving the Court of Appeals' assurance that it had accepted the factual findings of the state court and that it granted relief only because it concluded that the pretrial identification procedures employed in the case were, as a matter of law, unconstitutional.

STEVENS, J., dissented, stating that the court, although more clearly articulating its position that 28 USCS § 2254(d) applies to a basic, primary, or historical fact and that it does not apply to a mixed question of law and fact, merely delayed either the habeas corpus relief to which the Court of Appeals has held that the inmate was entitled or a consideration of the merits of the only significant question that the inmate had raised.

———

LLOYD FLETCHER, Superintendent, Bell County
Forestry Camp, Petitioner,

v

ERIC WEIR

— US —, 71 L Ed 2d 490, 102 S Ct 1309

Decided March 22, 1982.

Decision: State prosecutor's cross-examination of
defendant as to post-arrest silence, held not
violative of Fourteenth Amendment due process
in absence of Miranda warning assurances.

SUMMARY

At his trial for intentional murder in a Kentucky
state court, the defendant took the stand in his own
defense, admitting that he stabbed the victim, but
claiming, for the first time, that he acted in self-
defense and that the stabbing was accidental. The
prosecutor cross-examined the defendant as to why
he had, when arrested, failed either to advance his
exculpatory explanation to the arresting officers or
to disclose the location of the knife he had used to
stab the victim. The defendant was convicted of first
degree manslaughter, and the conviction was affirmed by the Supreme Court of Kentucky. Subsequently, the United States District Court for the
Western District of Kentucky granted the defendant
a writ of habeas corpus, and the United States Court
of Appeals for Sixth Circuit affirmed, concluding
that the defendant was denied due process of law
guaranteed by the Fourteenth Amendment when the
prosecutor used his post-arrest silence for impeach-

ment purposes, and that, although it did not appear from the record that the arresting officers had immediately read the defendant his Miranda warnings, a defendant cannot be impeached by use of this post-arrest silence even if no Miranda warnings had been given.

Granting certiorari, the United States Supreme Court reversed and remanded. In a per curiam, expressing the view of BURGER, Ch. J., and WHITE, BLACKMUN, POWELL, REHNQUIST, STEVENS, and O'CONNOR, JJ., it was held that in the absence of the sort of affirmative assurances concerning a suspect's silence embodied in the Miranda warnings, a state does not violate due process of law by permitting cross-examination of a criminal defendant as to post-arrest silence when the defendant chooses to take the stand, and that a state is entitled in such situations to leave to the judge and jury, under its own rules of evidence, the resolution of the extent to which post-arrest silence may be deemed to impeach a criminal defendant's own testimony.

BRENNAN, J., would set the case for oral argument.

MARSHALL, J., dissented from the summary reversal of the case.

U.S. INDUSTRIES/FEDERAL SHEET METAL,
INC., et al., Petitioners,

v

DIRECTOR, OFFICE OF WORKERS'
COMPENSATION PROGRAMS, UNITED STATES
DEPARTMENT OF LABOR, et al.

— US —, 71 L Ed 2d 495, 102 S Ct 1312

Argued October 6, 1981.
Decided March 23, 1982.

Decision: Presumption of compensability under
§ 20(a) of Longshoremen's and Harbor Workers' Compensation Act (33 USCS § 920(a)),
held inapplicable to claimed injury at work
where "injury" arose at home

SUMMARY

An employee who awoke one day with severe
pains in his neck, shoulders, and arms, which were
later attributed by physicians to an exacerbation of
an arthritic condition, contended that he was permanently and totally disabled by the arthritic condition.
His retained counsel filed a claim for compensation
under the Longshoremen's and Harbor Workers'
Compensation Act (33 USCS §§ 901 et seq.), the
employee alleging that he had an accident when on
the previous day while lifting duct work he felt a
sharp pain in his neck. After an evidentiary hearing,
an administrative law judge found that the employee
had sustained no injury within the meaning of § 2(2)
of the Act (33 USCS § 902(2))—which defines "injury" as an "accidental injury . . . arising out of and

179

in the course of employment"—as alleged and that the employee and a co-worker gave false testimony as to the happening of the accident. The Benefits Review Board affirmed the denial of disability benefits, holding that the administrative law judge's findings were supported by substantial evidence. However, on the employee's petition for review, the United States Court of Appeals for the District of Columbia Circuit vacated the Board's decision, holding that the employee suffered an "injury" when he awakened in pain which was sufficient to invoke § 20(a) of the Act (33 USCS § 920(a))—which provides that in any proceeding for the enforcement of a claim for compensation under the Act "it shall be presumed, in the absence of substantial evidence to the contrary . . . [t]hat the claim comes within the provisions of [the Act]"—so as to leave for remand the question whether the "injury" was "employment-bred" (627 F2d 455).

On certiorari, the United States Supreme Court reversed. In an opinion by STEVENS, J., joined by BURGER, Ch. J., and WHITE, BLACKMUN, POWELL and REHNQUIST, JJ., it was held that (1) the presumption of § 20(a) of the Act applies to a claim, and even if a claimant has an unfettered right to amend his claim to conform to the proof, the presumption by its terms cannot apply to a claim that has never been made, and the presumption does not require an administrative law judge to address and the employer to rebut every conceivable theory of recovery, so that the Court of Appeals erred in invoking the presumption on the theory that the employee had suffered an injury at home in bed which was "employment-bred" where the employee, represented by counsel, alleged in his claim that he had

180

suffered an accidental injury in the course of his employment, and (2) under the definition of "injury" in § 2(2) of the Act, arising "out of" and "in the course of" are separate elements, the former referring to injury causation, the latter to the place, time, and circumstances of the injury, so that a prima facie "claim for compensation," to which § 20(a) refers, must allege an injury that arose in the course of employment as well as out of employment, and therefore the Court of Appeals erred in using the term "injury" where the employee awoke with severe pains, this "injury" arising in bed, not in the course of employment.

BRENNAN, J., joined by MARSHALL, J., dissenting, expressed the view that § 20(a) of the Act requires the employer in a compensation hearing to offer substantial evidence refuting the existence of a causal relationship between the compensation claimant's injury and his employment, and that in the instant case, given the existence of the exacerbation to the employee's arthritic neck condition, and the statutory presumption, the relevant inquiry was whether the employer had shown the condition was not sufficiently work-related to render the employer accountable.

O'CONNOR, J., did not participate.

COUNSEL

Richard W. Galiher, Jr., argued the cause for petitioners.

James F. Green argued the cause for respondents.

MICHAEL P. LANE, Director, Illinois Department
of Corrections, Petitioner,

v

LAWRENCE WILLIAMS and OSCAR SOUTHALL

— US —, 71 L Ed 2d 508, 102 S Ct 1322

Argued December 1, 1981.
Decided March 23, 1982.

Decision: Claims of habeas corpus petitioners seeking relief on ground that failure to be advised
of mandatory parole terms before pleading
guilty violated due process, held moot after
parole terms expired.

SUMMARY

In separate cases, two individuals pleaded guilty
in Illinois state court to a charge of burglarly, an
offense punishable by imprisonment for an indeter-
minate term of years and a mandatory three-year
parole term. The defendant in neither case was
informed during the plea acceptance hearing that
the negotiated sentence included the mandatory
parole term. In each case, the defendant was discharged from prison and released on parole, but
later returned to prison as a parole violator. While
in custody, they each filed a petition for a writ of
habeas corpus in the United States District Court
for the Northern District of Illinois, alleging that
they were not informed that a mandatory parole
term had attached to their sentence until after their
discharge from prison and that their incarceration as
a result of a violation of that parole term violated

the due process clause of the Fourteenth Amendment. The cases were consolidated, and the District Court ordered their release through "specific performance" of the plea bargain, rather than nullification of the guilty pleas (447 F Supp 95). The United States Court of Appeals for the Seventh Circuit reversed on the ground that the defendants had failed to exhaust an available state remedy (594 F2d 614). On remand, the District Court reentered judgment for the defendants, but since both had been released from the custody of Illinois corrections officials, the court simply entered an order declaring void the mandatory parole terms (483 F Supp 775), and the Court of Appeals affirmed (633 F2d 71).

On certiorari, the United States Supreme Court vacated. In an opinion by STEVENS, J., joined by BURGER, Ch.J., and WHITE, POWELL, REHNQUIST, and O'CONNOR, JJ., it was held that the claims of the two defendants for habeas corpus relief were moot, since instead of asking the Federal District Court to set aside their convictions and give them an opportunity to plead anew, they elected to seek relief in the nature of "specific enforcement" of the plea agreement by eliminating the mandatory parole term, and since, after the District Court had ordered their discharge from incarceration for the parole violations, their parole terms expired, neither the doctrine that an attack on a criminal conviction is not rendered moot by the fact that the underlying sentence has expired, nor the doctrine that a case is not moot where it is capable of repetition, yet evading review, being applicable.

MARSHALL, J., joined by BRENNAN and BLACKMUN, JJ., dissented, expressing the view that the cases were not moot since there were sufficient collateral consequences flowing from parole-violation status that both the state and the defendants had a live interest in the Supreme Court's review of the holdings that the alleged constitutional violations rendered the guilty pleas void and that the defendants were entitled to specific performance of the pleas in the form of a declaration that the mandatory parole terms were void and should be expunged.

COUNSEL

Michael B. Weinstein argued the cause for petitioner.

Martha A. Mills argued the cause for respondents.

CHARLES RONALD McELROY, Petitioner,

v

UNITED STATES

— US —, 71 L Ed 2d 522, 102 S Ct 1332

Argued January 12, 1982.
Decided March 23, 1982.

Decision: Statute (18 USCS § 2314) prohibiting transport of forged securities in "interstate commerce," held not to require proof securities were forged before being taken across state lines.

SUMMARY

A federal criminal defendant was convicted in the United States District Court for the Western District of Pennsylvania of transporting in interstate commerce falsely made and forged securities in violation of 18 USCS § 2314 of the National Stolen Property Act. According to the proof at trial, several blank checks were stolen in Ohio and the defendant had attempted to use them in Pennsylvania several months later with signatures forged upon the checks. The trial judge instructed the jury that it must find, for a guilty verdict, that the defendant had transported the checks in a forged condition in "interstate commerce" and that such transportation could take place entirely within the state of Pennsylvania if it was a "continuation of movement that began out of state." After the court rejected the defendant's objection to this instruction, the defendant was convicted. The United States Court of

185

Appeals for the Third Circuit affirmed the conviction (644 F2d 274).

On certiorari, the United State Supreme Court affirmed. In an opinion by O'CONNOR, J., joined by BURGER, Ch. J., BRENNAN, WHITE, MARSHALL, BLACKMUN, POWELL, and REHNQUIST, JJ., it was held that (1) an individual may be convicted of violating 18 USCS § 2314, which prohibits the transport of forged securities in interstate commerce, absent proof that the securities had been forged before being taken across state lines since (a) § 2314 was intended to proscribe the transportation of a forged security at any and all times during the course of its movement in interstate commerce, (b) the stream of interstate commerce may continue after a state border has been crossed, and (c) the purpose underlying § 2314 indicates that federal prosecutors did not have to prove that the securities had been forged before crossing state lines, and (2) accordingly, the trial judge correctly instructed the jury that they could find the defendant guilty of violating 18 USCS § 2314 if they found that the forgeries occurred during the course of interstate commerce, which included a "continuation of a movement that began out of state," even though movement of the forged checks was restricted to one state.

STEVENS, J., dissented, expressing the view that Congress, in enacting the National Stolen Property Act, did extend its proscription beyond the interstate transportation of stolen property, and that the prosecutor in the case at bar has encroached on an area of state responsibility.

COUNSEL

Thomas S. White argued the cause for petitioner.
Carter G. Phillips argued the cause for respondents.

UNITED TRANSPORTATION UNION, Petitioner,

v

LONG ISLAND RAIL ROAD COMPANY, et al.

— US —, 71 L Ed 2d 547, 102 S Ct 1349

Argued January 20, 1981.
Decided March 24, 1982.

Decision: Application of Railway Labor Act (29
USCS §§ 151 et seq.), to state-owned railroad
engaged in interstate commerce, held not prohibited by Tenth Amendment.

SUMMARY

A state-owned passenger railroad failed to reach a
collective bargaining agreement with a union after
conducting negotiations pursuant to the Railway
Labor Act (45 USCS §§ 151 et seq.). Mediation
efforts by the National Mediation Board also failed.
The Board released the case from mediation, triggering a 30-day cooling-off period under the Act.
The union, anticipating that the state would challenge the applicability of the Act to the railroad,
filed suit one day before the expiration of the
cooling-off period in the United States District
Court for the Eastern District of New York, seeking
a declaratory judgment that the dispute was covered
by the Act and not by a state law prohibiting strikes
by public employees. The railroad then filed suit in
state court seeking to enjoin the impending strike
under the state law. Before the state court acted, the
District Court held that the railroad was a carrier
subject to the Railway Labor Act (509 F Supp

188

1300). The United States Court of Appeals for the Second Circuit reversed, holding that the operation of the railroad was an integral state governmental function, and that the Railway Labor Act displaced "essential governmental decisions" involving that function. The court also ruled that the state's interest in controlling the operation of its railroad outweighed the federal interest in having the federal statute apply (634 F2d 19).

On certiorari, the United States Supreme Court reversed and remanded. In an opinion by BURGER, Ch. J., expressing the unanimous view of the court, it was held that (1) the Tenth Amendment does not prohibit application of the Railway Labor Act to a state-owned railroad engaged in interstate commerce since the operation of a railroad engaged in interstate commerce is not an integral part of traditional state activities generally immune from federal regulation, and federal regulation of a state-owned railroad, whether freight or passenger, does not impair a state's ability to function as a state, and (2) in view of the fact that the commerce clause grants Congress the plenary authority to regulate labor relations in the railroad industry in general, application of this authority to a state-owned railroad does not so impair the ability of a state to carry out its constitutionally-preserved sovereign function as to come in conflict with the Tenth Amendment, especially given that the states, merely by acquiring functions previously performed by the private sector, may not erode federal authority in areas traditionally subject to federal or statutory regulation.

COUNSEL

Edward D. Friedman argued the cause for petitioner.

Joshua I. Schwartz argued the cause for the United States, as amicus curiae, by special leave of court.

Lewis B. Kaden argued the cause for respondent.

———————

UNDERWRITERS NATIONAL ASSURANCE
COMPANY, Petitioner,

v

NORTH CAROLINA LIFE AND ACCIDENT AND
HEALTH INSURANCE GUARANTY
ASSOCIATION, et al.

— US —, 71 L Ed 2d 558, 102 S Ct 1357

Argued November 9, 1981.
Decided March 24, 1982.

Decision: North Carolina courts' refusal to treat as
res judicata Indiana rehabilitation court's adjudication of rights to insurance company's deposit posted in North Carolina, held violative of
full faith and credit clause (Art IV, § 1).

SUMMARY

An Indiana stock insurance corporation, as required by North Carolina law to do business in the
state, joined the North Carolina Life and Accident
and Health Insurance Guaranty Association, a state-
created association of all foreign and domestic insurance companies operating in North Carolina
which was ultimately responsible for fulfilling the
policy obligations of any member that becomes
insolvent or otherwise fails to honor its obligation
to North Carolina policyholders. After determining
that the insurance company's financial condition was
questionable, the North Carolina Commissioner of
Insurance required it to post a $100,000 deposit for
the sole benefit of North Carolina policyholders,
and the company did so soon thereafter. Subse-

quently, the Indiana Department of Insurance commenced rehabilitation proceedings against the insurance company in the Superior Court for Marion
County, on the ground that its reserves were inadequate to meet its future policy obligations. The
rehabilitation court appointed the Indiana Commissioner of Insurance as rehabilitator and directed him
to take possession of the business and assets of the
insurance company, and notice of this action was
sent to all state insurance commissioners. The
North Carolina Commissioner informed the Association that the company was undergoing rehabilitation
in Indiana, and that title to all assets of the company had been transferred, and the Association later
intervened in the rehabilitation proceedings. After
extensive proceedings, the rehabilitation court ordered the adoption of a rehabilitation plan, the
court stating that it had jurisdiction over the subject
matter and over the parties, including all policyown-
ers and state insurance guaranty associations, and
no appeal was taken from this order. Afterwards,
the insurance company and the the Association
disagreed as to the effect of the plan on the deposit
previously made in North Carolina, and the Association filed suit against the insurance company, and
various North Carolina officials, in the Superior
Court of Wake County, North Carolina, seeking a
declaratory judgment that the Association was entitled to use the deposit to fulfill the prerehabilitation
contractual obligations to North Carolina policyown-
ers that had been compromised in the rehabilitation
proceeding. The insurance company answered, asserting that the Indiana judgment was res judicata
as to any prerehabilitation claims against the deposit, and therefore was entitled to full faith and
credit in the North Carolina courts. In addition, the
192

insurance company invoked the rehabilitation court's continuing jurisdiction to resolve all the questions involving the interpretation of the plan, and after a hearing at which the company and the Association appeared and presented their respective full-faith-and-credit claims, the rehabilitation court held that the plan fully adjudicated and determined that the North Carolina deposit was an asset of the insurance company, and any claim existing as of the date of the adoption of the plan was compromised, settled, and dismissed by its final order and the plan. However, on motions for summary judgment filed by both parties, the North Carolina trial court ruled in favor of the Association, reasoning that it was the only court with a requisite subject matter jurisdiction to determine the rights of North Carolina policyholders in the deposit, and noting that the Indiana courts did not have in personam jurisdiction over North Carolina officials or over the North Carolina policyholders, and the court ordered the liquidation of the deposit to reimburse the Association for satisfying the prerehabilitation claims of North Carolina policyholders. On appeal, the Court of Appeals of North Carolina affirmed, concluding that the deposit could never be an asset of the insurance company, and that the rehabilitation court's decision to the contrary was not entitled to full faith and credit (48 NC App 508, 269 SE2d 688), and the Supreme Court of North Carolina declined to grant discretionary review (301 NC 527, 273 SE2d 453).

On certiorari, the United States Supreme Court reversed and remanded. In an opinion by MAR-SHALL, J., joined by BURGER, Ch. J., and BRENNAN, BLACKMUN, REHNQUIST, and O'CONNOR, JJ., it was held that the North Carolina courts violated the full faith and credit clause of the United States Constitution (Art IV § 1) and its implementing statute (28 USCS § 1738) by refusing to treat the rehabilitation court's judgment adjudicating the rights of the various parties in the $100,000 deposit as res judicata in the subsequent proceedings brought by the Association, since the rehabilitation court fully and fairly considered whether it had subject-matter jurisdiction to settle the prerehabilitation claims of the parties before it to the deposit, the rehabilitation court had personal jurisdiction over all parties necessary to the determination that the Association could not satisfy prerehabilitation claims out of the deposit, and any argument that honoring the rehabilitation court's determination that the deposit was an asset of the insurance company would negate North Carolina's comprehensive statutory scheme to insure the protection of North Carolina policyowners had to be made in Indiana, not in North Carolina.

WHITE, J., joined by POWELL and STEVENS, JJ., concurred in the judgment, expressing the view that jurisdiction over the deposit was not relevant to the question of the res judicata effect of the rehabilitation court's judgment as to the Association, that the rehabilitation plan fully determined the nature of the claim that the Association would have against the insurance company and established the manner in which it could collect on those claims, and that, since the rehabilitation court did not fail to follow the procedural requirements of the due process clause, its decision had to be given res judicata effect by the North Carolina courts with regard to the Association.

194

COUNSEL

Theodore R. Boehm argued the cause for petitioner.

William S. Patterson argued the cause for respondents.

———————

UNITED STATES, Petitioner,

v

NEW MEXICO, et al.

— US —, 71 L Ed 2d 580, 102 S Ct 1373

Argued December 8, 1981.
Decided March 24, 1982.

Decision: Imposition of New Mexico's gross receipts and compensating use taxes on federal contractors doing business in state, held valid.

SUMMARY

Three contractors who performed management, maintenance, and construction and repair work for the United States Department of Energy at government-owned atomic laboratories located in New Mexico worked under contracts providing, among other things, for an "advanced funding" procedure to meet contractor costs whereby the contractor was allowed to pay creditors and employees with drafts drawn on a special bank account in which United States Treasury funds were deposited, so that only federal funds were expended when the contractor met its obligations. New Mexico imposes a gross receipts and a compensating use tax on those doing business in the state, the gross receipts tax operating as a tax on the sale of goods and services, and the compensating use tax functioning as an enforcement mechanism for the gross receipts tax by imposing a levy on the use of all property that has not already been taxed. The United States brought an action in the United States District Court for the

196

District of New Mexico, seeking a declaratory judgment that advanced funds were not taxable gross receipts to the contractors, that the receipts of vendors selling tangible property to the United States through the contractors could not be taxed by the state, and that the use of government-owned property by the contractors was not subject to the state's compensating use tax. The District Court granted the United States summary judgment, concluding that the contractors were procurement agents for the government and holding that the gross receipts tax could not constitutionally be applied to purchases by the contractors, that the compensating use tax as a correlative of the receipts tax was also invalid, and that advanced funds did not serve as compensation to the contractors and therefore could not be taxed as gross receipts (455 F Supp 993). The United States Court of Appeals for the Tenth Circuit reversed, concluding that the government-contractor relationship did not so incorporate the contractors into the governmental structure as to make them instrumentalities of the United States and thus immune from taxation (624 F2d 111).

On certiorari, the United States Supreme Court affirmed. In an opinion by BLACKMUN, J., expressing the unanimous view of the court, it was held that contractors conducting business with the federal government under an "advanced funding" procedure are taxable entities independent of the United States, so that (1) the state's use tax could be applied to the contractors without offending the notion of federal sovereignty, the contractors not being "constituent parts" of the federal government, (2) the gross receipts tax could be applied to

197

the funds received by the contractors to meet salaries and internal costs, and (3) the state could tax the receipts of a vendor selling tangible property to the United States through the contractors, such sales to the contractors not being sales to the "United States itself," since the contractors made purchases in their own names, the vendors were not informed that the government was the only party with an independent interest in the purchase, and the government disclaimed any formal intention to denominate the contractors as purchasing agents.

COUNSEL

George W. Jones argued the cause for petitioner, pro hac vice, by special leave of court.

Daniel H. Friedman argued the cause for respondents.

JOHN SANTOSKY II and ANNIE SANTOSKY,
Petitioners,

v

BERNHARDT S. KRAMER, Commissioner, Ulster
County Department of Social Services, et al.

— US —, 71 L Ed 2d 599, 102 S Ct 1388

Argued November 10, 1982.
Decided March 24, 1982.

Decision: Application of at least "clear and convincing evidence" standard of proof to state's parental rights termination proceeding, held required by Fourteenth Amendment due process clause.

SUMMARY

In an action brought in the Ulster County, New York, Family Court to terminate the rights of certain natural parents in their three children, the parents challenged the constitutionality of a provision of a New York statute under which the state may terminate the rights of parents in their natural child upon a finding that the child is "permanently neglected," when such a finding is supported by a fair preponderance of the evidence. The Family Court rejected the challenge, weighed the evidence under the "fair preponderance of the evidence" standard, found permanent neglect, and ultimately ruled that the best interests of the children required permanent termination of the parents' custody. The Appellate Division of the New York Supreme Court affirmed, holding application of the preponderance of the

199

evidence standard proper and constitutional (75 App Div 2d 910, 427 NYS2d 319), and the New York Court of Appeals dismissed the parents' appeal to that court.

On certiorari, the United States Supreme Court vacated and remanded. In an opinion by BLACKMUN, J., joined by BRENNAN, MARSHALL, POWELL and STEVENS, JJ., it was held that (1) process is constitutionally due a natural parent at a state's parental rights termination proceeding, and (2) the "fair preponderance of the evidence" standard prescribed by the state statute violated the due process clause of the Fourteenth Amendment, due process requiring proof by clear and convincing evidence in such a proceeding.

REHNQUIST, J., joined by BURGER, Ch. J., and WHITE and O'CONNOR, JJ., dissenting, expressed the view that the "fair preponderance of the evidence" standard prescribed by the New York statute must be considered in the context of New York's overall scheme of procedures relating to the termination of parental rights on the basis of permanent neglect, that such standard, when considered in that context, did not violate the due process clause of the Fourteenth Amendment, and that the majority decision, by holding the statutory standard unconstitutional without evaluation of the overall effect of New York's scheme of procedures for terminating parental rights, invited further federal court intrusion into every facet of state family law.

COUNSEL

Martin Guggenheim argued the cause for petitioners.

Stephen Scavuzzo argued the cause for respondents, pro hac vice, by special leave of court.

UNITED STATES, Petitioner,

v

JEFFREY R. MacDONALD

456 US 1, 71 L Ed 2d 696, 102 S Ct 1497

Argued December 7, 1981.
Decided March 31, 1982.

Decision: Time between dismissal of military charges and subsequent indictment of individual on civilian charges, held not to be considered in determining whether violation of right to speedy trial under Sixth Amendment has occurred.

SUMMARY

Approximately five years after an Army physician's wife and two daughters had been murdered on an Army base, and more than four years after murder charges brought by the military had been dismissed, the physician, who had received an honorable discharge, was indicted by a grand jury and charged with three murders. Prior to trial, the United States District Court for the Eastern District of North Carolina denied the defendant's motion to dismiss the indictment because of the denial of his Sixth Amendment right to a speedy trial. The United States Court of Appeals for the Fourth Circuit allowed an interlocutory appeal and reversed, holding that a two year delay between the submission of a military report to the Department of Justice recommending further investigation, and the actual convening of the grand jury violated the

202

physician's constitutional right to a speedy trial (531
F2d 196). The United States Supreme Court reversed, holding that a criminal defendant could not
appeal the denial of a motion to dismiss on speedy
trial clause grounds until after the trial had been
completed (435 US 850, 56 L Ed 2d 18, 98 S Ct
1547). The physician was then tried and convicted
on two counts of second-degree murder and one
count of first-degree murder. On appeal, a divided
panel of the Fourth Circuit Court of Appeals again
held that the indictment violated the physician's
Sixth Amendment right to a speedy trial and dismissed the indictment (632 F2d 258). The court
denied rehearing en banc by an evenly-divided vote
(635 F2d 1115).

On certiorari, the United States Supreme Court
reversed and remanded. In an opinion by BURGER,
Ch. J., joined by WHITE, POWELL, REHNQUIST, and
O'CONNOR, JJ., it was held that the period in excess
of four years between dismissal of military charges
against the physician and his subsequent indictment
on civilian federal criminal charges arising from
events during his tenure in the military should not
be considered in determining whether a delay in
bringing the physician to trial violated his rights
under the speedy trial clause of the Sixth Amendment since (1) criminal charges were not pending
against him during the entire period between his
arrest on military charges and later indictment on
civilian charges, (2) once the charges instituted by
the military were dismissed, the physician was legally and constitutionally in the same posture as
though no charges had been made, (3) there was no
indication that the military acted in bad faith in
dismissing the charges, nor that the Department of

Justice had acted in bad faith in not securing an indictment at an earlier date, and (4) any delay between the civilian indictment and trial was caused primarily by the physician's own legal maneuvers.

STEVENS, J., concurred in the judgment, expressing the view that (1) the physician's constitutional right to a speedy trial was not suspended in the time between the dismissal of the military charges and his subsequent indictment on civilian charges but (2) the question of whether the delay was constitutionally acceptable was "close," and the interest in allowing the government to proceed cautiously and deliberately before making a final decision to prosecute for such a serious offense was of decisive importance.

MARSHALL, J., joined by BRENNAN and BLACKMUN, JJ., dissented, expressing the view that the application of the speedy trial right was not suspended during the period between the dismissal of the military charges against the physician and his subsequent indictment on civilian charges and that—because the record in the case revealed no legitimate reason for a substantial period of pretrial delay, and because the physician may have suffered prejudice at trial and clearly suffered other forms of prejudice —his speedy trial right was violated.

COUNSEL

Alan I. Horowitz argued the cause for petitioner.

Ralph S. Spritzer argued the cause for respondent.

CASPAR W. WEINBERGER, Secretary of Defense,
et al., Petitioner,

v

ANTHONY M. ROSSI et al.

— US —, 71 L Ed 2d 715, 102 S Ct 1510

Argued February 22, 1982.
Decided March 31, 1982.

Decision: Word "treaty" in 5 USCS § 7201 note,
which exempts from certain employment discrimination requirements actions permitted by
"treaty," held to include executive agreements.

SUMMARY

The President of the United States and the Philippines negotiated a Base Labor Agreement (BLA) in
1968 which provides for the preferential employment of Filipino citizens at United States military
facilities in the Philippines. In 1971, Congress enacted 5 USCS § 7201 note, which prohibits employment discrimination against United States citizens
on military bases overseas unless permitted by
"treaty." In 1978, a number of United States citizens residing in the Philippines were notified that
their jobs at a United States naval facility were being
converted into local national positions in accordance
with the BLA, and that they would be discharged
from their employment with the Navy. After unsuccessfully pursuing an administrative remedy, they
filed suit in the United States District Court for the
District of Columbia, alleging that the preferential
employment provisions of the BLA violated 5 USCS

205

§ 7201 note. The District Court rendered summary judgment against the employees (467 F Supp 960). However, the United States Court of Appeals for the District of Columbia Circuit reversed (642 F2d 553).

On certiorari, the United States Supreme Court reversed and remanded. In an opinion by REHNQUIST, J., expressing the unanimous view of the court, it was held that the "treaty" exception in 5 USCS § 7201 note extends to executive agreements concluded by the President of the United States with a "host" country, as well as to those international agreements entered into by the President with the advice and consent of the Senate pursuant to Art II, § 2, cl 2 of the United States Constitution, especially in view of the absence of an affirmative expression of congressional intent to abrogate the United States' international obligations.

COUNSEL

Barbara E. Etkind argued the cause for petitioner. Randy M. Mott argued the cause for respondent.

CHESTER R. UPHAM, JR. and ERIC CLIFFORD,
Appellants,

v

A.M. SEAMON et al.

— US —, 71 L Ed 2d 725, 102 S Ct 1518

Decided April 1, 1982.

Decision: Federal District Court effecting interim
Texas congressional reapportionment for districts objected to by Attorney General, held
without power to redraw other districts in absence of constitutional or statutory violation.

SUMMARY

Following the 1980 census which increased Texas'
congressional delegation from 24 to 27 members,
the Texas state legislature enacted a reapportionment plan and submitted it to the United States
Attorney General for preclearance as required by
the Voting Rights Act (42 USCS §§ 1973 et seq.).
While this was pending, a suit was filed in the
United States District Court for the Eastern District
of Texas challenging the constitutionality of the
plan and its validity under § 2 of the Act (42 USCS
§ 1973). A three-judge court was empaneled, held a
hearing, and delayed any further action until after
the Attorney General acted. The Attorney General
entered an objection to the plan, specifically object-
ing to the lines drawn for two contiguous districts in
the state, but stating that the state had satisfied its
burden of demonstrating that the submitted plan
was nondiscriminatory in purpose and effect with
207

respect to the other 25 districts. Since this objection made the proposed plan unenforceable and since the prior apportionment plan was unconstitutional, the court ordered the parties to provide written submissions along with maps, plats, and other data to aid the court in reaching a court-ordered reapportionment plan. Following the hearing, the court proceeded to resolve the Attorney General's objection to the two districts. Instead of leaving all other districts of the court's plan identical to those of the state plan, the court devised its own districts for one portion of the state, one judge determining that the plan for that area was unconstitutional and another judge expressing the view that since the legislative proposal was a nullity, the entire plan had to be a court-ordered plan which must conform to stricter standards than those that must be observed by the legislature.

On direct appeal, the United States Supreme Court vacated and remanded. In a per curiam opinion, expressing the unanimous view of the court, it was held that the District Court could not devise its own districts for the unchallenged portion of the plan, but rather had to defer to the legislative judgments the plan reflected in the absence of a finding that the plan offended either the United States Constitution or the Voting Rights Act.

CARL W. BROWN, Petitioner,

v

EARL J. HARTLAGE

— US —, 71 L Ed 2d 732, 102 S Ct 1523

Argued January 20, 1982.
Decided April 5, 1982.

Decision: Kentucky statute prohibiting candidates
from offering benefits to voters in exchange for
votes, held violative of First Amendment as
applied to candidate who pledged to work at
reduced salary.

SUMMARY

A candidate for the office of Commissioner of
Jefferson County, Kentucky, publicly pledged to
lower the salaries of Commissioners if elected. That
pledge was later retracted upon learning that it
might violate a Kentucky statutory provision prohibiting a candidate from offering material benefits to
voters in consideration for their votes. After the
candidate won election, his opponent filed suit in
the Circuit Court of Jefferson County, alleging that
the candidate violated the provision and seeking to
have the election declared void. The Circuit Court
held that the candidate's promise violated the provision, but nevertheless refused to void the election
on the ground that he had been "fairly elected."
The Court of Appeals of Kentucky reversed, agreeing with the Circuit Court that the salary of commissioners was fixed by law and that the candidate's
statement was proscribed by the provision, but

209

holding that the retraction of the statement was of no consequence and that the Circuit Court did not possess the discretionary authority to balance the gravity of the violation against the disenfranchisement of the electorate that would result from declaring the election void. The Court of Appeals also rejected the candidate's First Amendment claims, holding that his statement was not constitutionally protected (618 SW2d 603).

On certiorari, the United States Supreme Court reversed and remanded. In an opinion by BRENNAN, J., joined by WHITE, MARSHALL, BLACKMUN, POWELL, STEVENS, and O'CONNOR, JJ., it was held that application of the Kentucky statutory provision to the candidate's statement limited speech in violation of the First Amendment, the application not being justified as (1) a prohibition on buying votes, since the candidate's promise to reduce his salary, insofar as it confers some ultimate benefit on the voter qua taxpayer, citizen, or member of the general public, not being beyond the reach of the First Amendment, (2) facilitating the candidacy of persons lacking independent wealth, the state, to the extent it designed the provision to further its interest in ensuring that the willingness of some persons to serve in public office without remuneration does not make gratuitous service the sine qua non of plausible candidacy, having chosen a means unacceptable under the First Amendment, or (3) an application of the state's interests and prerogatives with respect to factual misstatements, the chilling effect of the absolute accountability imposed by the state for factual misstatements made in the course of political debate being incompatible with the atmosphere of free discussion contemplated by the First Amendment in the context of political campaigns.

210

BURGER, Ch. J., concurred in the judgment.

REHNQUIST, J., concurred in the result, expressing the view that on different facts, more weight should be given to the state's interest in preventing corruption in elections.

COUNSEL

Fred M. Goldberg argued the cause for petitioner.
L. Stanley Chauvin, Jr., argued the cause as amicus curiae in support of the judgment below.

———————

AMERICAN TOBACCO COMPANY, et al.,
Petitioners,

v

JOHN PATTERSON, et al.

— US —, 71 L Ed 2d 748, 102 S Ct 1534

Argued January 19, 1982.
Decided April 5, 1982.

Decision: 42 USCS § 2000e-2(h) requiring showing
of discriminatory impact and discriminatory
purpose to invalidate seniority system, held not
limited to systems adopted before Title VII's
effective date.

SUMMARY

Certain black employees of a corporation brought
a class action under Title VII of the Civil Rights Act
of 1964 (42 USCS §§ 2000e et seq.) and 42 USCS
§ 1981 in the United States District Court of the
Eastern District of Virginia challenging, as racially
discriminatory, lines of job progression for advancement which were developed in 1968 by the corporation in agreement with the employee's union. This
action was consolidated for trial with a subsequent
Title VII action filed by the Equal Employment
Opportunity Commission alleging both race and sex
discrimination. Although the District Court initially
granted injunctive relief, finding that the seniority,
promotion, and job classification practices in question violated Title VII, the United States Court of
Appeals for the Fourth Circuit ultimately ruled that,
even if the lines of progression in question were

considered part of a seniority system for purposes of § 703(h) of Title VII (42 USCS § 2000e-2(h)—which exempts "bona fide" seniority systems from the Title VII prohibition against discriminatory practices even if they perpetuate past discrimination, so long as the systems were not framed with an intent to discriminate—Congress intended the immunity accorded a seniority system in § 703(h) to apply to seniority systems adopted after the July 2, 1965 effective date of Title VII (634 F2d 744).

On certiorari, the United States Supreme Court vacated and remanded. In an opinion by WHITE, J., joined by BURGER, Ch. J., and POWELL, REHNQUIST, and O'CONNOR, JJ., it was held that § 703(h) of Title VII is not limited in its application to only those seniority systems adopted prior to the effective date of the Act, and that an interpretation of § 703(h) which would construe the statute as protecting the post-Act application of a bona fide seniority system but not the post-Act adoption of the seniority system or an aspect of a seniority system is insupportable.

BRENNAN, J., joined by MARSHALL and BLACKMUN, JJ., dissenting, expressed the view that the court in the case at bar had ignored the fundamental distinction between challenges to the adoption and challenges to the application of seniority plans, § 703(h) of Title VII by its terms being relevant only where the application of a seniority plan is challenged.

STEVENS, J., dissenting, expressed the view that although § 703(h) of Title VII may be applied to bona fide post-Act seniority systems, that section was not available as a defense in the case at bar because the lines of progression in question—even if a seniority system—were adopted in violation of

Title VII and therefore could not be "bona fide" within the meaning of § 703(h).

COUNSEL

Henry T. Wickham argued the cause for petitioners American Tobacco Co., et al.

Ronald Rosenberg argued the cause for the petitioner Unions.

Henry L. Marsh, III argued the cause for the respondents John Patterson, et al.

David A. Strauss argued the cause for respondent EEOC, pro hac vice, by special leave of Court.

LOIS MAE MILLS, Appellant,

v

DAN HABLUETZEL

— US —, 71 L Ed 2d 770, 102 S Ct 1549

Argued January 12, 1982.
Decided April 5, 1982.

Decision: Texas statute barring paternity suits brought on behalf of illegitimate children more than one year after their birth, held violative of equal protection.

SUMMARY

The mother of a child born out of wedlock and the Texas Department of Human Resources, to which she had assigned the child's support rights, brought suit in a Texas state court on behalf of the child to establish that the putative father was the child's natural father. The father answered by asserting that the action was barred by a Texas statute providing that a paternity suit to establish the natural father of an illegitimate child must be brought before the child is one year old because the child was one year and seven months old when the suit was filed. The trial court agreed with the father and dismissed the suit. The Court of Civil Appeals of Texas, Thirteenth Supreme Judicial District, affirmed, holding that the one-year limitation was not tolled during minority and did not violate the equal protection clause of the Fourteenth Amendment, and the Texas Supreme Court denied discretionary review upon a finding of no reversible error.

215

On appeal, the United States Supreme Court reversed and remanded. In an opinion by REHNQUIST, J., joined by BURGER, Ch. J., and BRENNAN, WHITE, MARSHALL, BLACKMUN, STEVENS, and O'CONNOR, JJ., it was held that the Texas statute denied illegitimate children in Texas the equal protection of law, the state—by not allowing illegitimate children a period for obtaining support sufficiently long in duration to present a reasonable opportunity for those with an interest in such children to assert claims on their behalf—having failed to provide the children with an adequate opportunity to obtain support, and the unrealistically short time limitation not being substantially related to the state's interest in avoiding the prosecution of stale or fraudulent claims.

O'CONNOR, J., joined by BURGER, Ch. J., BRENNAN, J., and BLACKMUN, J., and joined in part (as to Part I of the opinion) by POWELL, J., concurred, expressing the view that not only birth-related circumstances compelled the conclusion that the statutory distinction between legitimate and illegitimate children was unconstitutional, and that a review of the factors used in deciding that the one-year statute of limitation could not withstand an equal protection challenge indicated that longer periods of limitation for paternity suits also could be unconstitutional, there being nothing special about the first year following birth.

POWELL, J., concurring in the judgment, stated his concern that the court's opinion could be read as prejudging the constitutionality of longer periods of limitation and that it was significant that a paternity suit is one of the few Texas causes of action not tolled during the minority of the plaintiff.

COUNSEL

Michael S. Mankins argued the cause for appellant.

Lola L. Bonner argued the cause for appellee.

———————

TED ENGLE, Superintendent, Chillicothe
Correctional Institute, Petitioner,

v

LINCOLN ISAAC

— US —, 71 L Ed 2d 783, 102 S Ct 1558

Argued December 8, 1981.
Decided April 5, 1982.

Decision: Assertions of state prisoners in federal
habeas corpus proceedings that jury instructions given at their trials violated due process,
held barred where prisoners did not comply
with state contemporaneous objection rule.

SUMMARY

Three persons who were convicted after separate
trials on unrelated charges in Ohio state courts and
who failed to comply with an Ohio court rule man-
dating contemporaneous objections to jury instructions, challenged the constitutionality of those instructions in federal habeas corpus proceedings
brought in United States District Courts in Ohio
under 28 USCS § 2254. Their trials occurred after
the effective date of an Ohio statute which placed
the burden of proving guilt beyond a reasonable
doubt upon the prosecution and provided that "the
burden of going forward with the evidence of an
affirmative defense is upon the accused, but before
the Ohio Supreme Court, in an unrelated proceeding, held that the statute changed Ohio's traditional
rule requiring defendants to carry the burden of
proving the affirmative defense of self-defense by a

218

proponderence of the evidence and placed only the burden of production, not persuasion, on the defendant, so that once the defendant produced some evidence of self-defense, the prosecutor had to disprove self-defense beyond a reasonable doubt. The appropriate Ohio Courts of Appeal affirmed the convictions of two of the petitioners before that decision, and the Ohio Supreme Court declined to review their convictions. Neither of those petitioners challenged the self-defense instruction in their appeals. When the third petitioner appealed his conviction to the intermediate appellate court, he relied upon the intervening decision to challenge the self-defense instruction given at his trial, but the court rejected the challenge as having been waived by the petitioner's failure to comply with the contemporaneous objection rule, and the Ohio Supreme Court dismissed his appeal. The District Courts denied each petitions for a writ of habeas corpus. On appeal, the United States Court of Appeals for the Sixth Circuit ruled that (1) Wainwright v Sykes (1977) 433 US 72, 53 L Ed 2d 594, 97 S Ct 2497, did not preclude consideration of the third petitioner's constitutional claims despite Wainwright's holding that a state prisoner, barred by procedural default from raising a constitutional claim on direct appeal, could not litigate that claim in federal habeas corpus proceedings under 28 USCS § 2254 without showing cause for and actual prejudice from the default, and (2) the instructions given at that petitioner's trial violated due process. Therefore the Court of Appeals reversed the District Court's order (646 F2d 1129). Subsequently, in reliance upon the decision as to the third petitioner, two panels of the Court of Appeals ordered the District Court to release the other petitioners unless the state chose to retry them within a reasonable time (635 F2d 575, 642 F2d 451).

On certiorari, the United States Supreme Court reversed and remanded. In an opinion by O'CON-NOR, J., joined by BURGER, Ch. J., and WHITE, POWELL, and REHNQUIST, JJ., it was held that all three petitioners were barred from asserting in the federal habeas corpus proceedings their constitutional claim, which was forfeited before the state courts because of their failure to comply with Ohio's contemporoneous objection rule.

BLACKMUN, J., concurred in the result.

STEVENS, J., concurring in part and dissenting in part, expressed the view that (1) neither of the claims of the first two petitioners described a violation of any constitutional right and therefore that neither justified a collateral attack on the convictions, (2) he would not bar habeas corpus relief simply as a matter of procedural foreclosure when the petitioner cannot show an absence of cause excusing his procedural default where the petitioner can show that the prejudice resulting from the errors of which he complains was so great that it should permit relief even in the absence of cause, and (3) the claim of deprivation of due process and equal protection of the laws because the Ohio Supreme Court refused to apply retroactively to the petitioners' convictions its disapproval of the challenged jury instruction was unpersuasive.

BRENNAN, J., joined by MARSHALL, J., dissenting, expressed the view that the third petitioner committed no "procedural default" in that his claim did not exist until after he was denied relief on his last direct appeal so that his habeas petition was not barred by the principles articulated in Wainwright v

220

Sykes (1977) 433 US 72, 53 L Ed 2d 594, 97 S Ct 2497, that inchoateness of the petitioners' claims constituted a "cause" sufficient under Wainwright to excuse their failure to raise those claims in compliance with Ohio's rules of procedure, and that the standard set forth in Wainwright should not be extended to cases in which the constitutional error affects the truthfinding function of the trial.

COUNSEL

Simon B. Karas argued the cause for petitioner.

James R. Kingsley argued the cause for the respondent Isaac.

Richard L. Aynes argued the cause for respondents Bell and Hughes.

UNITED STATES, Petitioner,

v

JOSEPH C. FRADY

— US —, 71 L Ed 2d 816, 102 S Ct 1584

Argued December 8, 1981.
Decided April 5, 1982.

Decision: "Cause and actual prejudice," rather than "plain error" of Rule 52(b) of Federal Rules of Criminal Procedure, held proper standard of review on motion for collateral relief under 28 USCS § 2255.

SUMMARY

An individual who was convicted of first-degree murder following trial in the United States District Court for the District of Columbia, which at the time had exclusive jurisdiction over local felonies committed in the District, and whose conviction was affirmed by the United States Court of Appeals for the District of Columbia Circuit, then acting as the local appellate court, filed a long series of collateral attacks on his sentence. Ultimately, he brought a motion in the District Court under 28 USCS § 2255, seeking the vacation of his sentence because the jury instructions used at his trial were defective and contending that the judge's instructions on malice compelled the jury to presume malice and thereby wrongfully eliminated any possibility of a manslaughter verdict, since manslaughter was defined as culpable homicide without malice. The District Court denied the prisoner's § 2255 motion, stating
222

that he should have challenged the jury instructions on direct appeal, or in one of his many earlier motions. On appeal, the Court of Appeals reversed, holding that the proper standard to apply to the prisoner's claim was the "plain error" standard governing relief on direct appeal from errors not objected to at trial of Rule 52(b) of the Federal Rules of Criminal Procedure, rather than the "cause and actual prejudice" standard governing relief on collateral attack following procedural default at trial, and finding the challenged instruction to be plainly erroneous (204 App DC 234, 636 F2d 506).

On certiorari, the United States Supreme Court reversed and remanded. In an opinion by O'CONNOR, J., joined by WHITE, POWELL, REHNQUIST, and STEVENS, JJ., it was held that (1) the "plain error" standard of Rule 52(b) of the Federal Rules of Criminal Procedure does not apply on a collateral challenge to a criminal conviction brought under 28 USCS § 2255, the proper standard for review of a motion under § 2255 for vacation of a sentence being the "cause and actual prejudice" standard under which to obtain collateral relief based on trial errors to which no contemporaneous objection was made, a convicted defendant must show both "cause" excusing his double procedural default, and "actual prejudice" resulting from the errors of which he complains, and (2) the prisoner failed to meet his burden of showing actual prejudice, since he had never presented colorable evidence indicating such justification, mitigation, or excuse that would reduce his crime from murder to manslaughter, the evidence in the record compelled the conclusion that there was malice aplenty, and there was no substantial likelihood that the same jury that

223

found the prisoner guilty of first-degree murder would have concluded, if only the malice instructions had been better framed, that his crime was only manslaughter.

STEVENS, J., concurring, expressed the view that the court's opinion in the case properly focused on the character of the prejudice to determine whether collateral relief was appropriate.

BLACKMUN, J., concurring in the judgment, expressed the view that the plain error rule of Rule 52(b) of the Federal Rules of Criminal Procedure has some applicability in a § 2255 proceeding and that recognizing a federal court's discretion to redress plain error on collateral review neither nullifies the cause and prejudice requirement nor disserves the policies underlying that requirement, but agreed with the court that the prisoner had not demonstrated that the erroneous jury instruction of which he complained so infected the entire trial that the resulting conviction violated due process.

BRENNAN, J., dissented, expressing the view that Rule 52(b) of the Federal Rules of Criminal Procedure permits, rather than directs, the courts to notice plain error and is applicable to proceedings under 28 USCS § 2255, the plain error doctrine merely allowing federal courts the discretion common to most courts to weigh the procedural defaults where justice requires.

BURGER, Ch. J., and MARSHALL, J., did not participate.

COUNSEL

Andrew L. Frey argued the cause for petitioner.

Daniel M. Schember argued the cause for respondent.

RICHARD S. SCHWEIKER, Secretary of Health
and Human Services, Appellant,

v

WILLIAM McCLURE et al.

— US —, 72 L Ed 2d 1, 102 S Ct 1665

Argued March 1, 1982.
Decided April 20, 1982.

Decision: Hearing procedures for claim disputes
under Part B of Medicare program (42 USCS
§§ 1395j et seq.), held not violative of due
process.

SUMMARY

Part B of the Medicare program provides medical
insurance benefits covering a portion of the costs of
certain physician services, outpatient physical therapy, x-rays, laboratory tests, and other medical and
health care. Congress authorized the Secretary of
Health and Human Services to contract with private
insurance carriers to administer the payment of
qualifying Part B claims. The Secretary pays the
participating carriers' costs of claims administration,
and, in return, the carriers act as the Secretary's
agents. They review and pay Part B claims for the
Secretary according to a particular process. If it
determines that the claims meets certain criteria, the
carrier pays the claim out of a government trust
fund. Should the carrier refuse on behalf of the
Secretary to pay a portion of a claim, a claimant is
entitled to a "review determination," in which
claimants submit written evidence and arguments of
226

fact and law. If the amount in dispute is $100 or more, a still-dissatisfied claimant then has a right to an oral hearing. An officer chosen by the carrier, who has not participated personally in the case prior to the hearing stage, presides over this hearing. Neither the applicable federal statute nor the regulations make provision for further review of the hearing officer's decision. Three claimants who were denied partial or total reimbursement for certain medical procedures sued to challenge the constitutional adequacy of the hearings afforded them. The United States District Court for the Northern District of California concluded that the hearing procedures violated the claimant's right to due process insofar as the final, unappealable decision regarding claims disputes is made by carrier appointees. The court concluded that due process required additional protection to reduce the risk of erroneous deprivation of benefits and that the claimants were entitled to a de novo hearing by a Social Security Administration administrative law judge. (503 F Supp 409).

On direct appeal, the United States Supreme Court reversed and remanded. In an opinion by POWELL, J., expressing the unanimous view of the court, it was held that hearings on disputed claims under Part B of Medicare may, consistently with due process, be held by private insurance carriers, without a further right of appeal where (1) the hearing officers appointed by the carriers who preside over claim disputes at oral hearings do not have any disqualifying interests for due process purposes in view of the fact that the carriers pay claims from federal funds and not out of their own funds, the salaries of the hearing officers are paid by the federal government, and the carriers operate under contracts that require compliance with standards prescribed by the statute and the Secretary, and (2) the fact that the hearing officer must be either an attorney or another "qualified" individual who must have a "thorough knowledge" of the Medicare program undermines the contention that procedures prescribed by Congress and the Secretary are not fair or that different or additional procedures would reduce the risk of erroneous deprivation of Part B benefits.

COUNSEL

Kenneth S. Geller argued the cause for appellant.
Harvey Sohnen argued the cause for appellees.

UNITED STATES, Petitioner,

v

ERIKA, INC.

— US —, 72 L Ed 2d 12, 102 S Ct 1650

Argued March 1, 1982.

Decided April 20, 1982.

Decision: Determinations by insurance carriers of amount of benefits payable under Part B of Medicare program (42 USCS §§ 1395j et seq.), held not reviewable in Court of Claims.

SUMMARY

Part B of the Medicare program (42 USCS §§ 1395j et seq.) is a federally subsidized, voluntary health insurance system for persons who are 65 or older or who are disabled. The companion Part A Medicare program covers institutional health costs such as hospital expenses and Part B supplements Part A's coverage. The Secretary of Health and Human Services is authorized to assign the task of paying Part B claims to private insurance carriers experienced in such matters. If the carrier decides that reimbursement in full is not warranted, the statute and the regulations designate an appeal procedure available to dissatisfied claimants, which ultimately could result in an oral hearing before a hearing officer designated by the carrier. Neither the statute nor the Secretary's regulations make provision for review of the hearing officer's decisions. A major distributor of kidney dialysis supplies made sales covered by the Part B program, and the purchasers assigned their Medicare Part B claims to the distributor. The distributor in turn billed a private insurance carrier which, according to its contract with the Secretary, was required to reimburse 80% of what it determined to be a "reasonable charge" for the supplies. Over a certain period of time, the carrier reimbursed the distributor's Part B invoices on the basis of catalog prices effective the preceding year. When the distributor requested the carrier to adjust past and future reimbursements to reflect price increases, the carrier, with one exception, refused. The supplier sought review before one of the carrier's hearing officers who affirmed the carrier's decision. The supplier then brought an action against the United States in the United States Court of Claims seeking reimbursement on the basis of its current charges. The Court of Claims ruled that the supplier's suit was within the jurisdictional grant of the Tucker Act (28 USCS § 1491), and decided that the carrier's calculation of the supplier's maximum allowable charges erred in several respects (634 F2d 580).

On certiorari, the United States Supreme Court reversed. In an opinion by POWELL, J., expressing the unanimous view of the court, it was held that the Court of Claims does not have jurisdiction to review determinations by private insurance carriers of the amount of benefits payable under Part B of the Medicare program since (1) in the context of the statute's precisely drawn provisions, the omission of authorization of further review for determinations of the amount of Part B awards provides persuasive evidence that Congress deliberately intended to foreclose further review of such claims, and (2) the legislative history confirms the view that Congress intended to limit judicial review of Part B determinations.

COUNSEL

Edwin S. Kneedler argued the cause for petitioner.

Stephen H. Oleskey argued the cause for respondent.

———————

INTERNATIONAL LONGSHOREMEN'S
ASSOCIATION, AFL-CIO et al., Petitioners,

v

ALLIED INTERNATIONAL, INC.

— US —, 72 L Ed 2d 21, 102 S Ct 1656

Argued January 18, 1982.
Decided April 20, 1982.

Decision: Refusal by longshoremen's union to unload cargoes shipped from Soviet Union in
protest against Afghanistan invasion, held illegal secondary boycott under 29 USCS
§ 158(b)(4).

SUMMARY

In response to the invasion of Afghanistan by the
Soviet Union, an American longshoremen's union
ordered its members to stop handling cargoes arriv-
ing from or destined for the Soviet Union. In
obedience to that order, the members refused to
service ships carrying Russian cargoes. An American
importer of Russian wood products responded to
the boycott by bringing an action in the United
States District Court for the District of Massachusetts, claiming that the boycott violated the prohibition against secondary boycotts contained in
§ 8(b)(4) of the National Labor Relations Act (29
USCS § 158(b)(4)) and seeking damages under
§ 303 of the Labor Management Relations Act (29
USCS § 187). The District Court dismissed the importer's complaint, holding that the boycott was a
purely political primary boycott of Russian goods
and as such was not within the scope of § 8(b)(4)
232

(492 F Supp 334). The United States Court of Appeals for the First Circuit reversed and remanded, holding that the boycott was "in commerce" within the meaning of the National Labor Relations Act, that the boycott, despite its political purpose, was within § 8(b)(4)'s prohibition against secondary boycotts, and that the union's action was not protected activity under the First Amendment (640 F2d 1368).

On certiorari, the United States Supreme Court affirmed. In an opinion by POWELL, J., expressing the unanimous view of the court, it was held that the union's boycott constituted an illegal secondary boycott prohibited by § 8(b)(4), since (1) the union's activity was "in commerce" and thus within the scope of the National Labor Relations Act, (2) the statutory prohibition of § 8(b)(4)(B) was applicable to activity the certain effect of which was to impose a heavy burden on neutral employers, (3) the union's action was not outside the prohibition against secondary boycotts, even though its object was not to halt business between neutral employers with respect to Russian goods but simply to free union members from the morally repugnant duty of handling such goods, there being no exception to the statutory prohibition for "political" secondary boycotts, and (4) the application of § 8(b)(4) did not infringe upon the First Amendment rights of the union and its members.

COUNSEL

Ernest L. Mathews, Jr., argued the cause for petitioners.

Duane R. Batista argued the cause for respondent.

Lawrence G. Wallace argued the cause for the United States as amicus curiae, by special leave of court.

———————

JOHN R. LARSON, etc., et al., Appellants,

v

PAMELA VALENTE et al.

— US —, 72 L Ed 2d 33, 102 S Ct 1673

Argued December 9, 1981.
Decided April 21, 1982.

Decision: Minnesota statute exempting from certain
registration and reporting requirements only
religious organizations receiving more than
50% of contributions from members, held violative of First Amendment establishment clause.

SUMMARY

Following the enactment of an amendment to
Minnesota's charitable contributions statute to exempt from the statute's registration and reporting
requirements only those religious organizations that
receive more than fifty percent of their total contributions from members or affiliated organizations,
the Minnesota Department of Commerce notified
the Holy Spirit Association for the Unification of
World Christianity (Unification Church) that it was
required to register under the statute because of the
newly enacted provision. Several persons claiming
to be followers of the tenets of the Church responded by bringing an action in the United States
District Court for the District of Minnesota, seeking
a declaration that the statute, on its face and as
applied to them through the fifty percent rule,
constituted an abridgement of their First Amendment rights of expression and free exercise of reli-

235

gion, as well as a denial of their rights to equal
protection of the laws, guaranteed by the Fourteenth Amendment, and seeking temporary and
permanent injunctive relief. The Church was later
joined as a plaintiff by stipulation of the parties, and
the action was transferred to a United States Magistrate. Following the issuance of a preliminary injunction, the Church and its followers moved for
summary judgment. After finding that the "overbreadth" doctrine gave the parties standing to challenge the statute's constitutionality, the magistrate
held that the statute was facially unconstitutional
with respect to religious organizations, and was
therefore entirely void as to such organizations,
because the 50 percent rule violated the establishment clause of the First Amendment. The magistrate recommended, among other things, that the
plaintiffs be granted the declaratory and permanent
injunctive relief that they had sought, namely a
declaration that the statute was unconstitutional as
applied to religious organizations and their members and an injunction against enforcement of the
statute as to any religious organization. Accepting
these recommendations, the District Court entered
summary judgment. On appeal, the United States
Court of Appeals for the Eighth Circuit affirmed the
District Court's application of the overbreadth doctrine and affirmed the District Court's holding that
the religious classification embodied in the 50 percent rule violated the establishment clause, but
disagreed with the District Court's conclusion that
the Church and others should enjoy the religious
organization exemption from the statute merely by
claiming to be such organizations and accordingly
vacated the judgment and remanded the action for
236

entry of a modified injunction and further proceedings (637 F2d 562).

On appeal, the United States Supreme Court
affirmed. In an opinion by BRENNAN, J., joined by
MARSHALL, BLACKMUN, POWELL, and STEVENS, JJ., it
was held that (1) the Church and its followers had
standing under Article III of the United States
Constitution to raise their claims that the charitable
contributions statute violated the establishment
clause of the First Amendment, despite the state's
argument that the Church was not a "religious
organization" within the meaning of the statute,
since, the state having chose to apply the statute
and its fifty percent rule as the sole statutory authority requiring the Church to register under the
statute, at least for purposes of the suit, the Church
was a religious organization within the meaning of
the statute, the threatened application of the statute
and its fifty percent rule to the Church amounted to
a distinct and palpable injury to it and its followers,
there was a fairly traceable causal connection between the claimed injury and the challenged conduct, that is between the claimed disabling and
threatened application of the statute and its fifty
percent rule, and the fact that the church could be
compelled, ultimately, to register under the statute
on some other grounds than the fifty percent rule
did not detract from the palpability of the particular
and discreet injury caused, and (2) the statute's
exemption of certain religious organizations from
the statute's registration and reporting requirements
violated the establishment clause of the First
Amendment, the state clearly granting denominational preferences forbidden by the First Amendment and the fifty percent rule not being closely

fitted to further any compelling interest the state may have in protecting its citizens from abusive practices in the solicitation of funds for charity, despite the argument that members of a religious can and will exercise supervision and control over the organization's solicitation activities when membership contributions exceed fifty percent, that membership control is an adequate safeguard against abusive solicitations of the public by the organization, and that the need for public disclosure rises in proportion with the percentage of non-member contributions.

STEVENS, J., concurring, agreed that the parties had standing to challenge the fifty percent rule, since it caused them a significant injury in fact in that it had substituted a simple method of imposing registration and reporting requirements for a more burdensome and less certain method of accomplishing that result, and, although expressing concern that the Supreme Court's policy of avoiding the premature adjudication of constitutional issues counselled postponement of any decision on the validity of the rule until after the Church's status as a religious organization within the meaning of the statute is finally resolved, stated that reaching the merits was consistent with the court's policy of strict necessity in disposing of constitutional issues and that a resolution of the question that had been fully considered by the District Court and by the Court of Appeals and had been fully briefed and argued in the court was consistent with the orderly administration of justice.

WHITE, J., joined by REHNQUIST, J., dissenting, expressed the view that the exemption provision of the statute did not violate the establishment clause, the court having concluded without an adequate factual basis that the provision deliberately preferred some religious denominations to others, it having rejected the justifications offered by the state without an adequate factual basis, and it having reached its conclusions by applying a legal standard different from that considered by either of the courts below.

REHNQUIST, J., joined by BURGER, Ch. J., and WHITE and O'CONNOR, JJ., dissented, expressing the view that the court erred when it found that the plaintiff had standing to challenge the constitutionality of the fifty percent rule, since although injured, they had not demonstrated that their injury was caused by the rule or would be redressed by its invalidation and that the case should be remanded to permit such proof and that until such time as the requirements of Article III had been satisfied, the court should refrain from rendering significant constitutional decisions.

COUNSEL

Larry Salustro argued the cause for appellants.
Barry A. Fisher argued the cause for appellees.

PULLMAN-STANDARD, A DIVISION OF
PULLMAN, INCORPORATED, Petitioner,

v

LOUIS SWINT and WILLIE JOHNSON, etc. (No.
80–1190)

UNITED STEELWORKERS OF AMERICA, AFL-
CIO, et al., Petitioners,

v

LOUIS SWINT and WILLIE JAMES JOHNSON
(No. 80–1193)

— US —, 72 L Ed 2d 66, 102 S Ct 1781

Argued January 19, 1982.
Decided April 27, 1982.

Decision: Federal Court of Appeals' reversal of
Federal District Court ruling as to legality of
seniority system under 42 USCS § 2000e-2(h),
held erroneous in view of court's independent
determination of allegations of discrimination.

SUMMARY

Certain black employees of a company manufac-
turing railway freight cars and parts brought suit
against the company and their union in the United
States District Court for the Northern District of
Alabama, charging that a seniority system maintained by the company and union violated Title VII
of the Civil Rights Act of 1964 (42 USCS §§ 2000e
et seq.). Under § 703(h) of Title VII (42 USCS
§ 2000e-2(h)), it is not an unlawful employment
240

practice for an employer to apply different compensation standards or different terms, conditions, or privileges of employment pursuant to a bona fide seniority system "provided that such differences are not the result of an intention to discriminate because of race." The District Court found that any differentials resulting from the seniority system were not the result of an intention to discriminate because of race or color, and held that the system satisfied the requirements of § 703(h) of Title VII. However, the United States Court of Appeals for the Fifth Circuit reversed, holding that the seniority system was not valid under § 703(h) because the differences in certain terms, conditions and standards of employment for black workers in the company resulted from an intent to discriminate. The Court of Appeals stated that Rule 52(a) of the Federal Rules of Civil Procedure requires that a District Court's findings of fact not be set aside unless "clearly erroneous," but it determined that a finding of discrimination under § 703(h) was a finding of "ultimate fact" that it would review by making an independent determination of the allegations of discrimination in the case (624 F2d 525).

On certiorari, the United States Supreme Court reversed and remanded. In an opinion by WHITE, J., joined by BURGER, Ch. J., and BRENNAN, POWELL, REHNQUIST, and O'CONNOR, JJ., it was held that the Court of Appeals erred in the course of its review of the District Court's judgment since (1) although recognizing the "clearly erroneous" standard of Rule 52(a), the court may have assumed that the District Court's finding on discriminatory intent was not subject to Rule 52(a) by concluding that a finding of discrimination under § 703(h) was a finding of "ultimate fact," (2) the Court of Appeals' acknowledgment of the controlling standard of Rule 52 came late in its opinion, and its conclusion strongly suggested that it was the product of the court's independent consideration of the totality of the circumstances it found in the record, (3) the Court of Appeals, after holding that the District Court had failed to consider relevant evidence and indicating that District Court might have come to a different conclusion had it considered that evidence, failed to remand for further proceedings as to the intent of a predecessor union and the significance, if any, of such a finding with respect to its successor.

STEVENS, J., concurring in part, joined in the court's opinion in the case at bar except to the extent that the court's preliminary comments on the burden of sustaining any challenge to a seniority system under Title VII are inconsistent with his separately expressed views in American Tobacco Co. v Patterson (1982) —— US ——, 71 L Ed 2d ——, 102 S Ct ——.

MARSHALL, J., joined (except as to point 1 below) by BLACKMUN, J., dissenting, expressed the view that (1) § 703(h) of Title VII does not immunize a seniority system that perpetuates past discrimination simply because those challenging the system are unable to demonstrate to the court's satisfaction that the system was adopted or maintained for an invidious purpose, and (2) the Court of Appeals did not ignore the clearly erroneous rule and make an independent determination of discriminatory purpose, but rather followed well-established legal principles both in rejecting the District Court's finding of no discriminatory purpose and in concluding that

242

a finding of such a purpose was compelled by all of the relevant evidence.

COUNSEL

Michael J. Gottesman argued the cause for petitioners.

Elaine R. Jones argued the cause for respondents.

CASPAR W. WEINBERGER, Secretary of Defense
et al., Petitioners,

v

CARLOS ROMERO-BARCELO et al.

— US —, 72 L Ed 2d 91, 102 S Ct 1798

Argued February 23, 1982.
Decided April 27, 1982.

Decision: Federal District Court relief of violations
of permit requirements of Federal Water Pollution Control Act (33 USCS §§ 1251 et seq.),
held not limited to immediate cessation orders.

SUMMARY

A number of persons, including the Governor of
Puerto Rico and residents of the island, filed an
action against the United States Navy in the United
States District Court for the District of Puerto Rico
to enjoin the Navy's use of an island off the Puerto
Rico coast for weapons training, alleging violations
of numerous federal environmental statutes and
various other laws, including the Federal Water
Pollution Control Act (33 USCS §§ 125] et seq.).
The District Court found that, under the explicit
terms of the Act, the Navy had violated the Act by
discharging ordnance into the water surrounding
the island without first obtaining a National Pollutant Discharge Elimination System permit from the
Environmental Protection Agency, and the District
Court ordered the Navy to apply for a permit, but
refused to enjoin Navy operations pending consideration of the permit application, concluding that an

injunction was not necessary to ensure suitably prompt compliance by the Navy (478 F Supp 646). On appeal, the United States Court of Appeals for the First Circuit vacated the District Court's order and remanded with instructions that the court order the Navy to cease the violation until it obtained a permit, concluding that the District erred in undertaking a traditional balancing of the parties' competing interests and that the Navy had an absolute statutory obligation to stop any discharges of pollutant until the permit procedure had been followed and the Administrator of the Environmental Protection Agency had granted a permit (643 F2d 835).

On certiorari, the United States Supreme Court reversed and remanded. In an opinion by WHITE, J., joined by BURGER, Ch. J., and BRENNAN, MARSHALL, BLACKMUN, POWELL, REHNQUIST, and O'CONNOR, JJ., it was held that the Federal Water Pollution Control Act does not require a Federal District Court to enjoin immediately all discharges that do not comply with the Act's permit requirements, but rather permits a District Court to order that relief it considers necessary to secure prompt compliance with the Act, such relief including, but not being limited to, an order of immediate cessation.

POWELL, J., concurring, expressed the view that the record clearly established that the District Court did not abuse its discretion by refusing to enjoin the immediate cessation of all discharges and would remand the case to the Court of Appeals with instructions that the decision of the District Court should be affirmed.

STEVENS, J., dissenting, expressed the view that while injunctions should not issue automatically or mechanically in every case an unpermitted discharge of a pollutant that occurs, Congress, by enacting the 1972 amendments to the Federal Water Pollution Control Act, circumscribed the District Courts' discretion on the question of remedies so narrowly that a general rule of immediate cessation must be applied in all but a narrow category of cases, and that the instant case did not present the kind of exceptional situation that justified a departure from the general rule.

COUNSEL

Elinor H. Stillman argued the cause for petitioners.

John A. Hodges argued the cause for respondents.

SOUTHERN PACIFIC TRANSPORTATION CO.,
Petitioner,

v

COMMERCIAL METALS CO.

— US —, 72 L Ed 2d 114, 102 S Ct 1815

Argued March 31, 1982.
Decided April 27, 1982.

Decision: Carrier's violation of Interstate Commerce Commission's credit regulations, held not to bar collection of lawful freight charges from consignor.

SUMMARY

A corporation, as consignor, sent three shipments of steel cobble by rail under the uniform straight bill of lading prescribed by the Interstate Commerce Commission (ICC). Each bill of lading included a "nonrecourse" clause, which rendered the consignor liable for freight charges unless it signed a statement that the carrier should not make delivery of the shipment without payment of all lawful charges, including freight. In each instance, the consignor failed to execute this nonrecourse clause. A common carrier released the first of the three cars to the consignee without collecting the freight charge in advance of delivery, and, without investigating the consignee's credit, mailed a bill to the consignee. After the second and third shipments, the carrier released the cars only after receiving checks from the consignee for the freight charges, but the checks were subsequently dishonored. After efforts to collect the unpaid freight charges from the consignee had proved fruitless, the carrier ultimately filed suit against the consignor in the United States District Court for the Northern District of Texas. The court ruled that the carrier had established a prima facie case for the recovery of the freight charges from the consignor, but went on to hold that the consignor had established a valid equitable defense to the carrier's collection of the charges by showing that the carrier had failed to comply with the ICC's credit regulations (49 CFR Part 1320) promulgated pursuant to the Interstate Commerce Act (current 49 USCS §§ 10101 et seq.). The United States Court of Appeals for the Fifth Circuit affirmed (641 F2d 235).

On certiorari, the United States Supreme Court reversed. In an opinion by BLACKMUN, J., expressing the unanimous view of the court, it was held that the common carrier's violation of the credit regulations issued by the ICC does not bar the carrier's collection of its lawful freight charge from the shipper-consignor since (1) the carrier established a prima facie case of the consignor's liability by proving that the consignor had failed to sign a "nonrecourse clause" in the applicable bills of lading, and (2) the carrier's violation of the credit regulations did not provide the consignor with an equitable, affirmative defense, such an interpretation being consistent with statutory and regulatory silence on the issue, the legislative and administrative history of the regulations, and public policy disfavoring judicial implication of such a defense.

COUNSEL

James H. Pipkin, Jr., argued the cause for petitioner.

David M. Sudbury argued the cause for respondent.

MERRILL LYNCH, PIERCE, FENNER & SMITH,
INC., Petitioner,

v

J.J. CURRAN and JACQUELYN L. CURRAN (No.
80–203)

———

NEW YORK MERCANTILE EXCHANGE et al.,
Petitioners,

v

NEIL LEIST, PHILIP SMITH and INCOMCO (No.
80–757)

———

CLAYTON BROKERAGE CO. OF ST. LOUIS,
INC., Petitioner,

v

NEIL LEIST, PHILIP SMITH and INCOMCO (No.
80–895)

———

HEINHOLD COMMODITIES, INC. et al.,
Petitioners,

v

NEIL LEIST et al. (No. 80–936)

— US —, 72 L Ed 2d 182, 102 S Ct 1825

Argued November 2, 1981.
Decided May 3, 1982.

Decision: Action for damages caused by violation of
Commodity Exchange Act (7 USCS §§ 1 et
seq.), held available to private parties.

SUMMARY

An investor in commodity futures contracts brought an action in the United States District Court for the Eastern District of Michigan, charging a futures commission merchant (i.e., a broker) with fraud in violation of § 4b of the Commodity Exchange Act (7 USCS § 6b). Additionally, three separate actions were filed in the United States District Court for the Southern District of New York against the New York Mercantile Exchange and its officials and various futures commission merchants, seeking damages under the Commodity Exchange Act (7 USCS §§ 1 et seq.) in connection with certain unlawful conspiracies to manipulate prices which proper enforcement of the Exchange's rules allegedly could have prevented. Although the Commodity Exchange Act regulates commodity futures trading, both it and the Commodity Futures Trading Commission Act of 1974 (88 Stat 1389), which substantially amended the Commodity Exchange Act, do not address the availability of a private right of action for damages caused by a violation of the Commodity Exchange Act. Following a District Court ruling adverse in both instances to those parties suing under the Commodity Exchange Act, the United States Court of Appeals for the Sixth Circuit (622 F2d 216) and the United States Court of Appeals for the Second Circuit (638 F2d 283) respectively ruled that an implied private right of action for damages exists under the Commodity Exchange Act.

On certiorari, the United States Supreme Court affirmed. In an opinion by STEVENS, J., joined by
251

BRENNAN, WHITE, MARSHALL, and BLACKMUN, JJ., it was held that (1) a private party may maintain an action for damages caused by a violation of the Commodity Exchange Act, and (2) purchasers and sellers of futures contracts have standing to assert both a claim that a broker violated prohibition against fraudulent and deceptive conduct in § 4b of the Act and claims that §§ 4a, 5(d), 5a(8) and 9(b) of the Act (7 USCS §§ 6a, 7(d), 7a(8), 13(b)), designed to prevent price manipulation, have been violated.

POWELL, J., joined by BURGER, Ch. J., REHNQUIST, J., and O'CONNOR, J., dissenting, expressed the view that (1) the theory that Congress endorsed the existence of a private right of action under the Commodity Exchange Act when it failed to amend the Act in 1974 in the face of erroneous federal court rulings upholding private rights of actions prior to 1974 is incompatible with the constitutional doctrine of the separation of powers and is without support in logic or law, (2) the court's finding in the case at bar that Congress in 1974 affirmatively manifested its intent to preserve private rights of action by adopting particular amendments to the Act was reached without even token deference to established tests for discerning congressional intent, and (3) courts should not condone the implication of any private right of action from a federal statute absent the most compelling evidence that Congress in fact intended such an action to exist, the evidence falling far short of the constitutionally appropriate standard in this particular case.

COUNSEL

Richard P. Saslow argued the cause for petitioner in No. 80-203.

Robert A. Hudson argued the cause for respondents in No. 80-203.

Barry Sullivan argued the cause for the Commodity Futures Trading Commission as amicus curiae, by special leave of court in No. 80-203.

William E. Hegarty argued the cause for petitioners in No. 80-757.

Gerard K. Sandweg, Jr., argued the cause for petitioners in Nos. 80-895 and 80-936.

Leonard Toboroff argued the cause for respondents in Nos. 80-757, 80-895, and 80-936.

WALTER ZANT, Warden, Petitioner,

v

ALPHA OTIS O'DANIEL STEPHENS

— US —, 72 L Ed 2d 222, 102 S Ct 1856

Argued February 24, 1982.
Decided May 3, 1982.

Decision: Questions as to what premises of state law support a conclusion that a death sentence was not impaired by the invalidity of one of the statutory aggravating circumstances found by the jury, certified to Georgia Supreme Court.

SUMMARY

An individual was convicted of murder in Superior Court, Bleckley County, Georgia, and the sentencing jury imposed the death penalty after finding three aggravating circumstances set forth in the Georgia death penalty statute. On direct appeal, the Supreme Court of Georgia affirmed, setting aside the second statutory aggravating circumstance found by the jury, but upholding the death sentence on the ground that in the case under review the evidence supported the jury's findings of the other statutory aggravating circumstances, so that the death sentence was not impaired (237 Ga 259, 227 SE2d 261). After exhausting his state post-conviction remedies, the prisoner applied for a writ of habeas corpus in the United States District Court for the Middle District of Georgia. The District Court denied relief, but the United States Court of Appeals for the Fifth Circuit reversed the District

Court's denial of habeas corpus relief insofar as it left standing the prisoner's death sentence and remanded for further proceedings (631 F2d 397, modified 648 F2d 446).

On certiorari, the United States Supreme Court, pursuant to a Georgia state statute, in a per curiam expressing the view of BURGER, Ch. J., and WHITE, BLACKMUN, REHNQUIST, STEVENS, and O'CONNOR, JJ., certified to the Supreme Court of Georgia the question what were the premises of state law that supported the conclusion that the death sentence in the case was not impaired by the invalidity of one of the statutory aggravating circumstances found by the jury, since despite the clarity of the state rule, there was considerable uncertainty about the state-law premises of that rule, and since the state-law premises of the Georgia Supreme Court's conclusion of state law were relevant to the constitutional issue at hand.

MARSHALL, J., joined by BRENNAN, J., dissented, expressing the view that (1) the death penalty is in all circumstances cruel and unusual punishment prohibited by the Eighth and Fourteenth Amendments, and (2) the prisoner's death sentence should be vacated and his case remanded to the Georgia state courts for resentencing, the Georgia Supreme Court's answer to the certified question not being determinative of the case, it being crucial that the jury's decision to impose the death sentence be guided by clear and appropriate instructions, and the argument in support of the state rule being patently contrary to the settled principle that if the jury has been instructed to consider several grounds for conviction, one of which proves to be unconstitutional, and the reviewing court is thereafter unable to determine from the record whether the jury relied on the unconstitutional ground, the verdict must be set aside.

POWELL, J., dissenting, stated his essential agreement with the views expressed by Marshall, J., in Part II of his dissenting opinion, and with his conclusion that the death sentence was imposed under instructions that could have misled the jury, but expressed the view that the case should not be remanded for resentencing by a jury, but rather to be left open for the Supreme Court of Georgia to decide whether it has authority to find that the instruction was harmless error beyond a reasonable doubt.

COUNSEL

Daryl A. Robinson argued the cause for petitioner.

John Charles Boger argued the cause for respondent.

JOHN O'DELL et al., Petitioners,

v

ANDREW ESPINOZA, etc., et al.

— US —, 72 L Ed 2d 237, 102 S Ct 1865

Argued April 26, 1982.
Decided May 4, 1982.

Decision: Writ of certiorari granted to the Colorado
Supreme Court in case where it had remanded
for trial, dismissed for want of jurisdiction.

SUMMARY

In a case involving the issue of whether the
Colorado wrongful death statute's limitation of
damages must be applied to an action under 42
USCS § 1983, the Supreme Court of Colorado, after
rendering its decision, remanded the case for trial.

On certiorari, the United States Supreme Court
dismissed for want of jurisdiction. In a per curiam
opinion expressing the unanimous view of the court,
it was held that the Colorado Supreme Court's
decision was not final under 28 USCS § 1257 as an
effective determination of the litigation, the state
court having remanded the case for trial, and that
the case did not fit into any of the limited set of
situations in which finality has been found as to the
federal issue despite the ordering of further proceedings in the lower state courts.

COUNSEL

Theodore S. Halaby argued the cause for petitioners.

Scott H. Robinson argued the cause for respondents.

———

DONALD FINNEGAN et al., Petitioners,

v

HAROLD D. LEU et al.

— US —, 72 L Ed 2d 239, 102 S Ct 1867

Argued February 24, 1982.

Decided May 17, 1982.

Decision: Discharge of union business agents by newly-elected president of local union, held not violative of Labor Management Reporting and Disclosure Act (29 USCS §§ 401 et seq.).

SUMMARY

Appointed union business agents who were discharged from their positions with a union local by a new union president after his election over a candidate supported by the business agents brought suit in the United States District Court for the Northern District of Ohio alleging that they had been terminated from their positions in violation of the Labor Management Reporting and Disclosure Act (29 USCS §§ 401 et seq.). Specifically, §§ 101(a)(1) and 101(a)(2) of the Act (29 USCS §§ 411(a)(1), 411(a)(2)) guarantee equal voting rights, and rights of speech and assembly, to "[e]very member of a labor organization." Also, § 609 of the Act (29 USCS § 529) renders it unlawful for a union or its representatives "to fine, suspend, expel, or otherwise discipline any of its members for exercising any right to which he is entitled" under the Act. The District Court granted summary judgment for the union local and its president, holding that the Labor

Management Reporting and Disclosure Act does not protect a union employee from discharge by the president of the union if the employee's rights as a union member are not affected. The United States Court of Appeals for the Sixth Circuit affirmed (652 F2d 58).

On certiorari, the United States Supreme Court affirmed. In an opinion by BURGER, Ch. J., expressing the unanimous view of the court, it was held that the appointed union business agents had failed to establish a violation of the Labor Management Reporting and Disclosure Act arising from their discharge, since (1) Title I of the Act (29 USCS §§ 411 et seq.) does not restrict the freedom of an elected union leader to choose a staff whose views are compatible with his own, it being rank and file union members, not union officers or employees, whom Congress sought to protect, and (2) removal from appointive union employment is not within the scope of those union sanctions explicitly prohibited by § 609 of the Act, the term "discipline" as used in § 609 referring only to retaliatory actions affecting a union member's rights or status as a member of the union.

BLACKMUN, J., joined by BRENNAN, J., concurring, expressed the view that the court's decision in the case at bar does not extend to nonpolicymaking, rank and file employees.

COUNSEL

Samuel G. Bolotin argued the cause for petitioner.

Theodore M. Iorio argued the cause for respondents.

JOSEPH GREENE, et al., Appellants,

v

LINNIE LINDSEY, et al.

— US —, 72 L Ed 2d 249, 102 S Ct 1874

Argued February 23, 1982.

Decided May 17, 1982.

Decision: Kentucky statute applicable to forcible entry and detainer actions permitting service of process by posting summons on door of premises, held violative of due process.

SUMMARY

A Kentucky statute provides that in forcible entry and detainer actions, service of process may be made by posting a summons on the door of a tenant's apartment if the tenant or a member of his family over 16 years of age is not on the premises to receive it. Tenants in a housing project were served in this manner regarding detainer actions seeking repossession of their apartments. The tenants claimed never to have seen the posted summonses and stated that they did not learn of the eviction proceedings until they were served with writs of possession, executed after default judgments had been entered against them, and after their opportunity for appeal had lapsed. They filed a class action suit in the United States District Court for the Western District of Kentucky alleging that the notice procedure failed to afford them the due process of law guaranteed by the Fourteenth Amendment. The District Court granted summary judgment against the tenants, but the United States Court of Appeals for the Sixth Circuit reversed, finding the notice provision constitutionally deficient (649 F2d 425).

On appeal, the United States Supreme Court affirmed. In an opinion by BRENNAN, J., joined by WHITE, MARSHALL, BLACKMUN, POWELL, and STEVENS, JJ., it was held that the statute failed to afford the tenants the notice of proceedings initiated against them required by the due process clause of the Fourteenth Amendment since, in a significant number of instances, reliance on posting pursuant to provisions of the statute resulted in a failure to provide actual notice to the tenants concerned, the state—in failing to afford the tenants adequate notice of the proceedings against them before issuing the final orders of eviction—having deprived them of property without due process of law.

O'CONNOR, J., joined by BURGER, Ch. J., and REHNQUIST, J., dissented, expressing the view that (1) insofar as the state's forcible entry and detainer action is a summary proceeding, it requires prompt and certain service of process, a need met by the statute in question, and (2) the court in the case at bar has chosen to overturn the state's procedures on the basis of a wholly inadequate record, holding that the Federal Constitution prefers the use of the postal service to posted notice.

COUNSEL

William L. Hoge, III argued the cause for petitioner.

Robert Frederick Smith argued the cause for respondent.

ROBIN KREMER, Petitioner,

v

CHEMICAL CONSTRUCTION CORPORATION

— US —, 72 L Ed 2d 262, 102 S Ct 1883

Argued December 7, 1981.

Decided May 17, 1982.

Decision: Giving of preclusive effect to state court's review of state agency's action on job bias claim upon later action in federal court on such claim under similar federal law, held required by 28 USCS § 1738.

SUMMARY

Following his layoff from employment and failure to be rehired despite several applications, an engineer filed a charge with the Equal Employment Opportunity Commission asserting that his discharge and failure to be rehired were due to his national origin (Polish) and his religion (Jewish) and were therefore violative of Title VII of the Civil Rights Act of 1964 (42 USCS §§ 2000e et seq.). The Commission referred his charges to the New York State Division of Human Rights, the state agency which enforces the New York law prohibiting job discrimination, pursuant to the requirement in Title VII that the Commission may not consider a claim until a state agency has had at least 60 days to resolve the matter (42 USCS § 2000e-5(c)). After investigating the complaint, the state agency concluded that there was no probable cause to believe that the employer had engaged in the alleged discriminatory practices, and this determination was upheld in an administrative appeal and in an appeal to the Appellate Division of the New York Supreme Court. The complainant could have, but did not seek review by the New York Court of Appeals. Later, a District Director of the Commission ruled that there was no reasonable cause to believe that the charge of discrimination was true, and the Commission issued a right-to-sue notice to the complainant pursuant to § 706(f) of Title VII (42 USCS § 2000e-5(f)). After the complainant's request for reconsideration was refused by the Commission, the complainant brought suit under Title VII in the United States District Court for the Southern District of New York claiming discrimination on the basis of national origin and religion. The District Court ultimately dismissed the complaint on grounds of res judicata (447 F Supp 587), and the United States Court of Appeals for the Second Circuit affirmed (623 F2d 786) and denied a motion for rehearing en banc.

On certiorari, the United States Supreme Court affirmed. In an opinion by WHITE, J., joined by BURGER, Ch. J., and POWELL, REHNQUIST, and O'CONNOR, JJ., it was held that the District Court was required under 28 USCS § 1738—which directs all United States courts to afford the same full faith and credit to state court judgments that would apply in the state's own courts—to give preclusive effect to the state-court decision upholding the state administrative agency's rejection of the job discrimination claim as meritless, such decision precluding under the state's law any other action, civil or criminal, based upon the same grievance in the state's courts, nothing in Title VII showing a clear and manifest legislative purpose to deny res judicata or collateral estoppel effect to a state-court judgment affirming that a job discrimination claim is unproved, and the procedures provided in New York for the determination of job discrimination claims offering a full and fair opportunity to litigate the merits and therefore being sufficient under the due process clause of the Fourteenth Amendment.

BLACKMUN, J., joined by BRENNAN and MARSHALL, JJ., dissenting, expressed the view that (1) when Congress referred to state "proceedings" in Title VII, it referred to both state agency proceedings and state judicial review of those agency proceedings, (2) Title VII directs that the outcomes of such state proceedings be given only "substantial weight" and not "preclusive effect" in subsequent federal proceedings, and (3) a New York court does not pass upon the merits of a discrimination claim when it reviews an action of the New York State Division of Human Rights on such a claim, so that it does not consider the subject matter of a Title VII suit in federal court on such a review and the principle of collateral estoppel embodied in 28 USCS § 1738 is therefore inapplicable to its decision.

STEVENS, J., dissenting, expressed the view that if the character of the judicial review to which a state antidiscrimination agency's decision is subjected is the equivalent of a de novo trial on the merits, then 28 USCS § 1738 forecloses a second lawsuit in a federal court, but that that was not the character of the relevant judicial review in New York, it rather being simply a part of the "proceedings" that are entitled to "substantial weight" under Title VII in a subsequent de novo trial in federal court.

COUNSEL

David A. Barrett argued the cause for petitioner.

Lawrence G. Wallace argued the cause for the United States and the Equal Employment Opportunity Commission as amici curiae, by special leave of Court.

Robert Layton argued the cause for respondent.

———————

NORTH HAVEN BOARD OF EDUCATION, et al.,
Petitioners,

v

TERREL H. BELL, Secretary, Department of
Education, et al.

— US —, 72 L Ed 2d 299, 102 S Ct 1912

Argued December 9, 1981.
Decided May 17, 1982.

Decision: Regulations prohibiting federally funded
education programs from discriminating on basis of sex in employment, held valid under Title
IX of Education Amendments of 1972 (20
USCS §§ 1681 et seq.).

SUMMARY

Two local boards of education filed suit in the
United States District Court for the District of Connecticut challenging regulations (34 CFR §§ 106.51
et seq.) promulgated by the then Department of
Health, Education, and Welfare under §§ 901(a) and
902 of Title IX of the Education Amendments of
1972 (20 USCS §§ 1681(a), 1682). Section 901(a)
prohibits sex discrimination in any federally funded
education program. Section 902 authorizes agencies
which award federal funds to any education program to promulgate regulations ensuring that recipients comply with § 901(a) and provides for termination of federal funds to any particular program in
which noncompliance is found. The regulations prohibited sex discrimination with respect to employment in such federally funded programs. The Dis-
267

trict Court granted summary judgment to each school board, holding that Title IX was not intended to apply to employment practices. It also invalidated the regulations and enjoined the Department from terminating funds to education programs in each school district for noncompliance with the regulations. The cases were consolidated on appeal, and the United States Court of Appeals for the Second Circuit reversed and remanded, concluding that § 901 was intended to prohibit employment discrimination, and finding the regulations consistent with both §§ 901(a) and 902 (629 F2d 773).

On certiorari, the United States Supreme Court affirmed and remanded. In an opinion by BLACKMUN, J., joined by BRENNAN, WHITE, MARSHALL, STEVENS, and O'CONNOR, JJ., it was held that employment discrimination comes within the prohibition of § 901(a), that section's broad directive that "no person" may be discriminated against on the basis of gender including employees as well as students, and that the regulations at issue are therefore valid and are also consistent with the program-specific limitation of §§ 901 and 902 of Title IX, the authority of an agency to terminate funds being limited to particular programs found to have violated Title IX's ban against discrimination in federally funded education programs.

POWELL, J., joined by BURGER, Ch. J., and REHNQUIST, J., dissented, expressing the view that the interpretation that Title IX authorizes regulations prohibiting discrimination in employment is neither consistent with the statutory language nor supported by its legislative history, Title IX—under a plain reading of the statute—prohibiting discrimination only against beneficiaries of federally funded

268

programs and activities, not all employment discrimination by recipients of federal funds.

COUNSEL

Susan K. Krell argued the cause for petitioner North Haven Board of Education.

Paul E. Knag argued the cause for petitioner Trumbull Board of Education.

Solicitor General Rex E. Lee argued the cause for federal respondents.

Beverly J. Hodgson argued the cause for respondent Linda Potz.

———————

AMERICAN SOCIETY OF MECHANICAL
ENGINEERS, INC., Petitioner,

v

HYDROLEVEL CORPORATION

— US —, 72 L Ed 2d 330, 102 S Ct 1935

Argued January 13, 1982.
Decided May 17, 1982.

Decision: Nonprofit association of mechanical engineers responsible for promulgation of industry
codes, held civilly liable under antitrust laws for
antitrust violations of its agents committed with
apparent authority.

SUMMARY

Shortly after the manufacturer of a low-water fuel
cutoff, a safety device for heating boilers, secured an
important customer, the company which had domi-
nated the market for low-water fuel cutoffs became
concerned. The vice-president of the dominant
manufacturer, who was also vice-chairman of the
subcommittee of the association of mechanical engineers which, among other things, promulgated and
published codes and standards for areas of engineering and industry, including the code applicable
to cutoffs, and several company officials met with
the chairman of that subcommittee. They decided to
send an inquiry to the association's committee concerned with boilers asking whether a fuel cutoff with
a time delay—which was employed by the new
manufacturer, but not employed in the dominant
manufacturer's product—satisfied the requirements
270

of the applicable association-promulgated code. The two individuals, as vice-chairman and chairman, respectively, of the relevant subcommittee cooperated in drafting a letter, one they thought would elicit a negative response. Following the association's standard routine, the chairman prepared a response which, in effect, declared the competitor's product unsafe. Salesmen of the dominant manufacturer used the response to discourage customers from buying the competitor's product, so that the manufacturer successfully used his position within the association in an effort to thwart the competitor's challenge. The competitor subsequently sought a correction from the association of the response, but continued to suffer marked resistance after the pertinent committee replied. After the vice-chairman's part in drafting the original letter of inquiry became public, the competitor filed an action in the United States District Court for the Eastern District of New York against the association, and other parties, alleging that their actions had violated §§ 1 and 2 of the Sherman Act (15 USCS §§ 1, 2). After the other parties settled, the lawsuit proceeded to trial against the association, as the remaining defendant. The competitor requested that the trial court instruct the jury that the association could be held liable under the antitrust laws for its agents' conduct if the agents acted within the scope of their apparent authority. The District Court rejected this approach and instead, at the association's suggestion, charged the jury that the association could be held liable only if it had ratified its agents' actions or the agents had acted in pursuit of the association's interests. The jury, nonetheless, returned a verdict for the competitor. The United States Court of Appeals for the Second Circuit concluded that the association could be held liable if its agents had acted within the scope of their apparent authority, and since the District Court had delivered a charge that was more favorable to the defendant than the law requires, affirmed the jury's finding that the association was liable under § 1 of the Sherman Act for its agents' actions (635 F2d 118).

On certiorari, the United States Supreme Court affirmed. In an opinion by BLACKMUN, J., joined by BRENNAN, MARSHALL, STEVENS, and O'CONNOR, JJ., it was held that the association was civilly liable under the antitrust laws for the antitrust violations of its agents committed with apparent authority, this being consistent with the congressional intent to encourage competition, the imposition of treble damages not being inconsistent with the purposes of the antitrust laws and principles of agency law on the grounds that such damages are punitive and that under traditional agency law the courts do not employ apparent authority to impose punitive damages upon a principal for the acts of its agents, and the fact that the association was a nonprofit organization not weakening the force of the antitrust and agency principles that indicate that the association should be held liable for the competitor's antitrust injuries.

BURGER, Ch. J., concurred in the judgment, agreeing that the judgment against the association should be affirmed since the association permitted itself to be used to further the scheme which caused injury to the competitor and at no time disavowed the challenged conduct of its members who misused their position in the association, and that under the instructions approved by the association and given by the District Court, the jury found that the association had ratified or adopted the conduct in question.

POWELL, J., joined by WHITE and REHNQUIST, JJ., dissenting, expressed the view that the holding that standard-setting organizations may be held liable for the acts of their agents even though the organization never ratified, authorized, or derived any benefit whatsoever from the fraudulent activity of the agent and even though the agent acted solely for his private employer's gain, and the imposition of the potentially crippling burden of treble damages, was, at least as applied to nonprofit organizations, inconsistent with the weight of precedent and the intent of Congress, unsupported by the rules of agency law, and irrelevant to the achievement of the goals of the antitrust laws.

COUNSEL

Harold R. Tyler, Jr., argued the cause for petitioner.

Carl W. Schwarz argued the cause for respondent.

Stephen M. Shapiro argued the cause for the United States as amicus curiae, by special leave of Court.

UNITED STATES DEPARTMENT OF STATE, et
al., Petitioners,

v

THE WASHINGTON POST COMPANY

— US —, 72 L Ed 2d 358, 102 S Ct 1957

Argued March 31, 1982.
Decided May 17, 1982.

Decision: Citizenship information on foreign nationals, held to satisfy "similar files" requirement of Exemption 6 of Freedom of Information Act (5 USCS § 552(b)(6)).

SUMMARY

A newspaper filed a request under the Freedom
of Information Act (FOIA) (5 USCS § 552) for
certain documents from the United States Department of State. The request was for documents
indicating whether two Iranian nationals living in
Iran held valid U.S. passports, or for any other
records indicating whether either individual was an
American citizen. The State Department denied the
newspaper's request stating that the release of the
requested information would be a clearly unwarranted invasion of personal privacy, and was therefore exempt from disclosure under Exemption 6 of
the FOIA (5 USCS § 552(b)(6)), which exempts
from disclosure "personnel and medical files and
similar files the disclosure of which would constitute
a clearly unwarranted invasion of personal privacy."
The newspaper brought an action in the United
States District Court for the District of Columbia to
enjoin the Department from withholding the re-

quested documents. The District Court granted the newspaper's motion for summary judgment. The United States Court of Appeals for the District of Columbia Circuit affirmed, holding that the citizenship status of the Iranian nationals was less intimate than information normally contained in personnel and medical files, and accordingly was not contained in "similar files" for purposes of Exemption 6. In view of this finding, the Court of Appeals ruled that there was no need to consider whether disclosure of the information would constitute a clearly unwarranted invasion of personal privacy. (647 F2d 197).

On certiorari, the United States Supreme Court reversed and remanded. In an opinion by REHNQUIST, J., joined by BURGER, Ch. J., and BRENNAN, WHITE, MARSHALL, BLACKMUN, POWELL, and STEVENS, JJ., it was held that the documents satisfied the "similar files" requirement of Exemption 6, and therefore the State Department's denial of the request should have been sustained upon a showing by the government that release of the information would constitute a clearly unwarranted invasion of personal privacy, the phrase "similar files" not being limited to files containing "intimate details" and "highly personal" information.

O'CONNOR, J., concurred in the judgment.

COUNSEL

Kenneth S. Geller argued the cause for petitioners.

David E. Kendall argued the cause for respondent.

JOSEPH S. HOPPER, Commissioner, Alabama
Department of Corrections and JAMES D. WHITE,
Warden, Petitioners,

v

JOHN LOUIS EVANS, III

— US —, 72 L Ed 2d 367, 102 S Ct 2049

Argued March 24, 1982.
Decided May 24, 1982.

Decision: Preclusion of jury instructions on lesser
included offense in capital case, held not to
require new trial where defendant's own evidence negates possibility that such instruction
was warranted.

SUMMARY

An individual was convicted in the Circuit Court
of Mobile County, Alabama, of the capital offense of
intentional killing during a robbery, and was sentenced to death. The defendant confessed to the
crime and testified that he intended to kill his
victim. The trial judge, applying an Alabama statute
which provides that a jury hearing a capital case is
precluded from considering lesser included offenses,
instructed the jury to either impose the death sentence if it found the defendant guilty or else return
a verdict of not guilty. The defendant's conviction
and death sentence were affirmed on automatic
appeal by the Court of Criminal Appeals of Alabama
(361 So 2d 654) and the Supreme Court of Alabama
(361 So 2d 666), and the United States Supreme
Court denied certiorari (59 L Ed 2d 486). The

defendant then sought a writ of habeas corpus in the United States District Court for the Southern District of Alabama, alleging, among other things, that he had been sentenced under a statute which unconstitutionally precluded consideration of lesser included offenses. The District Court rejected the defendant's arguments and denied habeas relief (472 F Supp 707). Subsequently, the United States Supreme Court held, in Beck v Alabama (1980) 447 US 625, 65 L Ed 2d 392, 100 S Ct 2382, that a death sentence could not be imposed after a jury verdict of guilt of a capital offense when the jury was not permitted to consider a verdict of guilt of a lesser included non-capital offense, provided the evidence would have supported such a verdict. Relying on the Beck decision, the United States Court of Appeals for the Fifth Circuit reversed, concluding that the mere existence of the state preclusion clause so "infected" the defendant's trial that he must be retried so that he may have the opportunity to introduce evidence of some lesser included offense. (628 F2d 400, modified 639 F2d 221).

On certiorari, the United States Supreme Court reversed. In an opinion by BURGER, Ch. J., joined by WHITE, BLACKMUN, POWELL, REHNQUIST, STEVENS, and O'CONNOR, JJ., it was held that the Alabama preclusion law did not require a new trial where the defendant's own evidence that he intended to kill his victim during a robbery negated the possibility that an instruction on the offense of unintentional killing during the robbery was warranted, due process requiring that a lesser included offense instruction be given only in cases in which the evidence would have supported such a verdict and the mere existence of the Alabama preclusion law not prejudicing the defendant in any way which would have warranted a new trial, where he suggested no plausible claim which he might conceivably have made, had there been no preclusion law, which was not contradicted by his own testimony at trial.

BRENNAN, J., joined by MARSHALL, J., concurred in part and dissented in part, expressing the view that the death penalty is in all circumstances cruel and unusual punishment prohibited by the Eighth and Fourteenth Amendments.

COUNSEL

Edward E. Carnes argued the cause for petitioners.

John L. Carroll argued the cause for respondent.

———————

FEDERAL BUREAU OF INVESTIGATION et al.,
Petitioners,

v

HOWARD S. ABRAMSON

— US —, 72 L Ed 2d 376, 102 S Ct 2054

Aruged January 11, 1982.
Decided May 24, 1982.

Decision: Exemption 7 of Freedom of Information
Act (5 USCS § 552(b)(7)), held to exempt information originally contained in law enforcement
records but incorporated into document not
compiled for law enforcement purposes.

SUMMARY

A journalist filed a request pursuant to the Freedom of Information Act (5 USCS § 552) for specific
documents relating to the transmittal from the FBI
to the White House in 1969 of information concerning particular individuals who had criticized the
Administration. The FBI denied the request on
grounds that the information was exempt from
disclosure pursuant to Exemption 7(C) of the Act (5
USCS § 552(b)(7)(C))—which exempts from disclosure "investigatory records compiled for law-enforcement purposes" when the release of such records would "constitute an unwarranted invasion of
personal privacy". After an unsuccessful administrative appeal, the journalist filed suit in United States
District Court for the District of Columbia to enjoin
the FBI from withholding the requested records.
While the suit was pending, the FBI provided the

journalist with certain documents—some intact and some with deletions. In light of the released material, the journalist modified his request seeking only the material from a one-page memorandum from the FBI to the White House, together with approximately 63 pages of "name check" summaries and attached documents. The "name check" summaries contained information, culled from existing FBI files, on 11 public figures. The District Court found that the FBI had failed to show that the information was compiled for "law enforcement" rather than political purposes, but went on to rule that Exemption 7(C) was validly invoked by the government because disclosure of the withheld materials would constitute an "unwarranted invasion of personal privacy." Accordingly, the court granted the government's motion for summary judgment. The United States Court of Appeals for the District of Columbia Circuit reversed, holding that with the exception of those documents attached to the summaries that may have been duplicates of original FBI files, the government had failed to sustain its burden of demonstrating that the documents were compiled for law enforcement purposes. According to the court, Exemption 7(C) was unavailable even though disclosure would constitute an unwarranted invasion of personal privacy. The Court of Appeals rejected the government's claim that Exemption 7(C) was applicable because the "name check" summaries contained information taken from documents in FBI files that had been created for law enforcement purposes (658 F2d 806).

On certiorari, the United States Supreme Court reversed and remanded. In an opinion by WHITE, J., joined by BURGER, Ch. J., and POWELL, REHNQUIST, and STEVENS, JJ., it was held that information initially contained in a record made for law-enforcement purposes continues to meet the threshold requirements of Exemption 7 when the recorded information is reproduced or summarized in a new document prepared for a non-law-enforcement purpose.

BLACKMUN, J., joined by BRENNAN, J., dissenting, expressed the view that, in the case at Bar, the court has substituted the word "information" for the word "records" in Exemption 7, and that Congress, as the legislative history reveals, chose the term "records" rather than the word "information" advisedly, the court having presented no reason why its deviation from the statutory language is necessary or desirable.

O'CONNOR, J., joined by MARSHALL, J., dissenting, expressed the view that the majority has redrafted the statutory phrase "investigatory records compiled for law enforcement purposes" to exempt investigatory records that were not compiled for law enforcement purposes, an interpretation unsupported by any of the usual grounds of statutory construction.

COUNSEL

Kenneth S. Geller argued the cause for petitioner.
Sharon T. Nelson argued the cause for respondent.

WOELKE & ROMERO FRAMING, INC., Petitioner,

v

NATIONAL LABOR RELATIONS BOARD et al.
(No. 80–1798)

———

PACIFIC NORTHWEST CHAPTER OF THE
ASSOCIATED BUILDERS & CONTRACTORS,
INC., Petitioner,

v

NATIONAL LABOR RELATIONS BOARD et al.
(No. 80–1808)

———

OREGON-COLUMBIA CHAPTER, The Associated
General Contractors of America, Inc., Petitioner,

v

NATIONAL LABOR RELATIONS BOARD et al.
(No. 81–91)

— US —, 72 L Ed 2d 398, 102 S Ct 2071

Argued March 3, 1982.
Decided May 24, 1982.

Decision: Union signatory subcontracting clauses
sought or negotiated in context of collective
bargaining relationship, held protected by construction industry proviso to 29 USCS § 158(e).

SUMMARY

This case presented the question whether union
signatory subcontracting clauses that are sought or
negotiated in the context of a collective bargaining

relationship are protected by the construction industry proviso to § 8(e) of the National Labor Relations
Act (29 USCS § 158(e)). Section 8(e) prohibits "secondary" agreements between unions and employers
which require an employer to cease doing business
with another party, but the construction industry
proviso to § 8(e) exempts from this proscription
agreements between a union and an employer in the
construction industry over the contracting or subcontracting of work to be performed at a construction site. In one instance, a construction industry
subcontractor, during collective bargaining negotiations, reached an impasse with a union over the
union's demand that the contract include a union
signatory subcontracting clause barring subcontracting except to firms who are signatories to agreements with particular unions. In support of their
demands for a subcontracting clause, union locals
picketed the subcontractor's construction site causing work stoppages, but the subcontractor filed
unfair labor practice charges with the National Labor Relations Board asserting that the clause violated § 8(e) of the Act. It was further argued that
because the clause violated § 8(e), the picketing
violated § 8(b)(4)(A) of the Act (29 USCS
§ 158(b)(4)(A)), which forbids coercion "to enter
into any agreement which is prohibited by" § 8(e).
The Board ruled that the union signatory subcontracting clause at issue was saved by the construction industry proviso, and rejected the contention
that the proviso sheltered subcontracting clauses
only if the clauses were limited in application to
particular job sites at which both union and nonunion workers were employed. According to the
Board, such clauses are lawful when sought or
negotiated in the context of collective bargaining

283

relationships, and therefore picketing to obtain the clause was permitted under § 8(b)(4)(A) (239 NLRB 241). A second dispute involved unfair labor practice charges filed against a union by a member of an association of construction industry employers asserting that a contract between the association and the union containing a union signatory subcontracting clause violated § 8(e). The Board held that such clauses were protected by the proviso (239 NLRB 274). The subcontractor, the industry association, and the association member sought review of the Board's orders in the United States Court of Appeals for the Ninth Circuit which, after consolidating the cases, ultimately enforced the orders. The court ruled that union signatory subcontracting clauses are protected so long as they are sought or negotiated in the context of a collective bargaining relationship, and that economic pressure may be used to obtain a subcontracting agreement, but that it may not be employed to enforce a subcontracting agreement (654 F2d 1301).

On certiorari, the United States Supreme Court affirmed in part, vacated in part, and remanded. In an opinion by MARSHALL, J., expressing the unanimous view of the court, it was held that (1) the construction industry proviso to § 8(e) of the National Labor Relations Act ordinarily shelters union signatory subcontracting clauses sought or negotiated in the context of a collective bargaining relationship, even when not limited in application to particular job sites at which both union and nonunion workers are employed, and (2) the Court of Appeals was without jurisdiction to consider whether a union violates § 8(b)(4)(A) of the Act when it pickets to obtain a lawful subcontracting clause since the issue was not raised during proceedings before the National Labor Relations Board by either the Board's General Counsel or the party bringing the unfair labor practice charge.

COUNSEL

John W. Prager, Jr., argued the cause for petitioner in 80-1798.

Lewis K. Scott argued the cause for petitioners in 80-1808 and 81-91.

Norton J. Come argued the cause for respondent NLRB.

Laurence Gold argued the cause for respondent unions.

_____

OREGON, Petitioner,

v

BRUCE ALAN KENNEDY

— US —, 72 L Ed 2d 416, 102 S Ct 2083

Argued March 29, 1982.
Decided May 24, 1982.

Decision: Second trial of defendant who successfully moves for mistrial because of prosecutorial
misconduct, held barred by double jeopardy
clause only if prosecutor intended to provoke
defendant to move for mistrial.

SUMMARY

On redirect examination of a prosecution witness
in the Oregon state trial of an individual charged
with theft, the prosecutor, after having obtained the
information that the witness had never done business with the defendant, asked if that was because
the defendant was a crook. The trial court then
granted the defendant's motion for a mistrial. Subsequently, the state sought to retry the defendant in
the Circuit Court, Multnomah County, Oregon, and
the defendant moved to dismiss the charges because
of double jeopardy. After a hearing in which the
prosecutor testified, the trial court found as a fact
that it was not the intention of the prosecutor in the
case to cause a mistrial and, on the basis of this
finding, held that double jeopardy principles did not
bar retrial. The defendant was then tried and convicted. On appeal, the Court of Appeals of Oregon

286

sustained the double jeopardy claim, accepting the trial court's finding that it was not the intent of the prosecutor to cause a mistrial, but holding that retrial was barred because the prosecutor's conduct in the case constituted what it viewed as overreaching (49 Ore App 415, 619 P2d 948).

On certiorari, the United States Supreme Court reversed and remanded. In an opinion by REHNQUIST, J., joined by BURGER, Ch. J., and WHITE, POWELL, and O'CONNOR, JJ., it was held that a criminal defendant who successfully moves for a mistrial because of prosecutorial or judicial misconduct may not invoke the bar of the double jeopardy clause of the Fifth and Fourteenth Amendments against a second trial except in those cases in which the prosecutorial or judicial conduct giving rise to the successful motion for a mistrial was intended to provoke the defendant into moving for a mistrial.

POWELL, J., concurring, expressed the view that because subjective intent often may be unknowable, a court, in considering a double jeopardy motion based upon the intention of a prosecutor, should rely primarily upon the objective facts and circumstances of the particular case, and that in the instant case relevant facts and circumstances strongly supported the view that prosecutorial intent to cause a mistrial was absent.

BRENNAN, J., joined by MARSHALL, J., concurred in the judgment, noting that nothing in the court's holding prevented the state courts, on remand, from concluding that the defendant's retrial would violate the provision of the Oregon Constitution prohibiting double jeopardy, as that provision has been interpreted by the state courts.

STEVENS, J., joined by BRENNAN, MARSHALL, and BLACKMUN, JJ., concurred in the judgment, expressing the view that an exception to the rule that a defendant's motion for a mistrial removes any double jeopardy bar to retrial should remain available for prosecutorial overreaching or harassment, in addition to the intentional provocation of a mistrial.

COUNSEL

David B. Frohnmayer argued the cause for petitioner.

Samuel A. Alito, Jr., argued the cause for the United States as amicus curiae, by special leave of Court.

Donald C. Walker argued the cause for respondent.

INSURANCE CORP. OF IRELAND, LTD. et al.,
Petitioner,

v

COMPAGNIE DES BAUXITES DE GUINEA

— US —, 72 L Ed 2d 492, 102 S Ct 2099

Argued March 23, 1982.
Decided June 1, 1982.

Decision: District Court's action in establishing personal jurisdiction as sanction for failure to comply with discovery order under Rule 37 of Federal Rules of Civil Procedure, held not violative of due process.

SUMMARY

A mining company, which was partially owned by a corporation operating in Pennsylvania, purchased business interruption insurance to cover its operations in a foreign country. Part of this insurance was obtained in the London insurance market. The mining company allegedly experienced mechanical problems in its foreign operation, resulting in a business interruption loss. Contending that the loss was covered under its policies, the company brought suit when the insurers refused to indemnify it for the loss. The company brought suit in United States District Court for the Western District of Pennsylvania, asserting jurisdiction based on diversity of citizenship. The foreign insurers raised a number of defenses, including lack of in personam jurisdiction. The mining company filed a discovery request in an attempt to establish jurisdictional facts. After the

289

insurers failed to comply with discovery orders for the requested information, the court gave the insurers sixty more days to produce the requested information, and warned them that it would assume jurisdiction if they did not do so. Five months later, the court, after concluding that the requested material had not been produced, imposed the threatened sanction that the foreign insurers were subject to the in personam jurisdiction of the court under the authority of Rule 37(b)(2)(A) of the Federal Rules of Civil Procedure, which provides that a Federal District Court, as a sanction for failure to comply with discovery orders, may order that the matters regarding which the orders were made shall be taken as established for purposes of the action in question. The United States Court of Appeals for the Third Circuit affirmed, concluding that the sanction was not violative of due process, and that its imposition did not constitute an abuse of the court's discretion under Rule 37(b)(2)(A). (651 F2d 877).

On certiorari, the United States Supreme Court affirmed. In an opinion by WHITE, J., joined by BURGER, Ch. J., and BRENNAN, MARSHALL, BLACKMUN, REHNQUIST, STEVENS and O'CONNOR, JJ., it was held that (1) Rule 37(b)(2)(A) of the Federal Rules of Civil Procedure does not violate due process when applied to enable a District Court, as a sanction for failure to comply with a discovery order directed at establishing jurisdictional facts, to proceed on the basis that personal jurisdiction over the recalcitrant party has been established, and (2) the District Court did not abuse its discretion in applying Rule 37(b)(2) of the Federal Rules of Civil Procedure to support a finding of personal jurisdiction since (a) the defendant's course of behavior in failing to provide requested material on jurisdictional facts, coupled with ample warnings of a possible sanction, demonstrates that the sanction was "just" for purposes of the Rule, and (b) the sanction imposed by the District Court was specifically related to the "claim" at issue in the discovery order, the sanction having taken as established the jurisdictional facts that the plaintiff was seeking to establish through discovery.

POWELL, J., concurring in the judgment, expressed the view that (1) where a plaintiff has made a prima facie showing of minimum contacts, its showing is sufficient to warrant a District Court's entry of discovery orders, and where a defendant then fails to comply with these orders, the prima facie showing may be held adequate to sustain the court's finding that minimum contacts exist, either under Rule 37 or under a theory of "presumption" or "waiver", and (2) in the case at bar, the facts alone —unaided by broad jurisdictional theories—more than amply demonstrate that the District Court possessed personal jurisdiction to impose sanctions under Rule 37 and otherwise to adjudicate the case.

COUNSEL

Edmund K. Trent argued the cause for petitioners.

Cloyd R. Mellott argued the cause for respondent.

SUMMIT VALLEY INDUSTRIES, Petitioner,

v

LOCAL 112, UNITED BROTHERHOOD OF
CARPENTERS AND JOINERS OF AMERICA

— US —, 72 L Ed 2d 511, 102 S Ct 2112

Argued April 28, 1982.
Decided June 1, 1982.

Decision: Attorney's fees incurred during proceedings before National Labor Relations Board,
held not proper element of damages under
§ 303(b) of Labor Management Relations Act
(29 USCS § 187(b)).

SUMMARY

Following unfair labor practice proceedings in
which the National Labor Relations Board found
that a union had violated § 8(b)(4) of the National
Labor Relations Act (29 USCS § 158(b)(4)) by conducting an illegal secondary boycott of an employer,
the employer filed an action in the United States
District Court for the District of Montana under
§ 303(b) of the Labor Management Relations Act
(29 USCS § 187(b)), seeking damages resulting from
business losses suffered from the union's boycott
and attorney's fees incurred by the employer in the
proceedings before the Board. The District Court
awarded the employer an amount representing its
business losses, but concluded that the employer
was not entitled to attorney's fees as part of its
damages (475 F Supp 665). The United States

Court of Appeals for the Ninth Circuit affirmed (652 F2d 65).

On certiorari, the United States Supreme Court affirmed. In an opinion by MARSHALL, J., expressing the unanimous view of the court, it was held that attorney's fees are not a proper element of damages under § 303(b), neither the language nor the legislative history of § 303 supporting the contention that the section provides statutory authorization for attorney's fees and the allowance of attorney's fees not being justified on the ground that it would further Congress' intent to protect employers from the adverse effects of a union's illegal secondary activity.

COUNSEL

Donald C. Robinson argued the cause for petitioner.

David S. Paull argued the cause for respondent.

ARMY AND AIR FORCE EXCHANGE SERVICE,
Petitioner,

v

ARTHUR EDWARD SHEEHAN

— US —, 72 L Ed 2d 520, 102 S Ct 2118

Argued February 23, 1982.
Decided June 1, 1982.

Decision: Federal court jurisdiction over action for
monetary damages brought by discharged military exchange employee, held not conferred by
Tucker Act (28 USCS § 1346(a)(2)) in absence
of express or implied contract.

SUMMARY

An employee of a military exchange received
written notice of separation from the exchange for
cause following his guilty plea to state drug law
violations. The employee's administrative appeal of
his discharge was denied by military authorities.
While the matter was pending before the Air Force
Judge Advocate General, the former employee filed
suit against the exchange in the United States District Court for the Northern District of Texas, alleging that his discharge was unlawful and seeking
reinstatement and damages. The District Court dismissed the complaint for want of subject matter
jurisdiction. The United States Court of Appeals for
the Fifth Circuit reversed, holding that the Tucker
Act (28 USCS § 1346(a)(2)), which gives the federal
courts jurisdiction over certain suits against the
United States founded upon express or implied

contracts, provided a basis for jurisdiction over the claims for monetary relief (619 F2d 1132).

On certiorari, the United States Supreme Court reversed. In an opinion by BLACKMUN, J., joined by BRENNAN, WHITE, MARSHALL, POWELL, REHNQUIST, STEVENS, and O'CONNOR, JJ., it was held that the Tucker Act did not confer jurisdiction over the former employee's claims for monetary relief, since (1) his employment with the exchange was the result of an appointment rather than an employment contract, and (2) the military exchange's regulations governing dismissal of employees did not specifically authorize awards of monetary damages and thus did not create an implied-in-fact contract.

BURGER, Ch. J., concurred in the judgment.

COUNSEL

Samuel A. Alito, Jr., argued the cause for petitioner.

Ira E. Tobolowsky argued the cause for respondent.

FEDERAL ENERGY REGULATORY
COMMISSION, et. al., Appellants,

v

MISSISSIPPI et al.

— US —, 72 L Ed 2d 532, 102 S Ct 2126

Argued January 19, 1982.
Decided June 1, 1982.

Decision: Provisions of Public Utility Regulatory
Policies Act (15 USCS §§ 3201 et seq.; 16
USCS §§ 824a-3, 2611 et seq.), held not viola-
tive of commerce clause (Art I, § 8, cl 3) and
Tenth Amendment.

SUMMARY

The state of Mississippi and the Mississippi Public
Service Commission filed an action in the United
States District Court for the Southern District of
Mississippi against the Federal Energy Regulatory
Commission and the Secretary of Energy, seeking a
declaratory judgment that Titles I and III and § 210
of Title II of the Public Utility Regulatory Policies
Act of 1978 (16 USCS §§ 2611 et seq.; 15 USCS
§§ 3201 et seq.; 16 USCS § 824a-3) were unconstitutional as being beyond the scope of congressional
power under the commerce clause of the United
States Constitution (Art I, § 8, cl 3) and as constituting an invasion of state sovereignty in violation of
the Tenth Amendment. Titles I and III of the Act
require state utility regulatory commissions to consider federal rate design and regulatory standards
and require state commissions to follow certain
296

notice and comment procedures when acting on the proposed federal standards, and § 210 of the Act seeks to encourage the development of cogeneration and small power production facilities by authorizing the Federal Energy Regulatory Commission to exempt qualified power facilities from state laws and regulations and by requiring that state authorities implement the Commission's rules developed to carry out this goal. On cross-motions for summary judgment, the District Court held that in enacting the Act Congress had exceeded its powers under the commerce clause and that the challenged provisions of the Act trenched on state sovereignty and were therefore void because they constituted a direct intrustion on integral and traditional functions of the state of Mississippi.

On direct appeal, the United States Supreme Court reversed. In an opinion by BLACKMUN, J., joined by BRENNAN, WHITE, MARSHALL, and STEVENS, JJ., it was held that (1) Titles I and III and § 210 of the Act were within Congress' power under the commerce clause, Congress' specific finding that the regulated activities have an immediate effect on interstate commerce having a rational basis, (2) § 210 of the Act did not trench on state sovereignty in violation of the Tenth Amendment, § 210's authorization of the Federal Energy Regulatory Commission to exempt qualified power facilities from state laws and regulations doing nothing more than preempting conflicting state enactments in the traditional way, and § 210's requirement that state authorities implement the Commission's rules simply requiring state authorities to adjudicate disputes under the statute, the very type of activity customarily engaged in by these authorities, and (3) Titles

297

I and III of the Act did not trench on state sovereignty in violation of the Tenth Amendment, the provisions of these titles requiring state utility regulatory commissions to. consider federal standards not invoking the compelled exercise of a state's sovereign powers nor setting a mandatory agenda to be considered in all events by state legislative or administrative decisionmakers, but simply establishing requirements for continued state activity in an otherwise preemptible field, and the provisions requiring state commissions to adopt certain procedures also not compelling the exercise of a state's sovereign power and not purporting to set standards to be followed in all areas of the state commission's endeavors.

POWELL, J., concurring and dissenting, agreed that the substantive provisions of the Act were constitutional on their face, but stated that the Act, to the extent that it did not simply ask states to consider quasi-legislative matters the Congress believed they would do well to adopt, but also prescribed administrative and judicial procedures that states must follow in deciding whether to adopt the proposed standards, violated the Tenth Amendment.

O'CONNOR, J., joined by BURGER, Ch. J., and REHNQUIST, J., concurred in part in the judgment and dissented in part, expressing the view that Titles I and III of the Act conscripted state utility commissions into the national bureaucratic army contrary to the principles of the Tenth Amendment, antithetical to the values of federalism, and inconsistent with United States constitutional history.

COUNSEL

Solicitor General Rex E. Lee argued the cause for appellants.

Alex A. Alston, Jr., argued the cause for appellees.

UNITED STATES, Petitioner,

v

ALBERT ROSS, Jr.

— US —, 72 L Ed 2d 572, 102 S Ct 2157

Argued March 1, 1982.
Decided June 1, 1982.

Decision: Authority to conduct warrantless search
of motor vehicle based on probable cause, including compartments and containers, held
coextensive with authority based on magistrate's
issuance of warrant.

SUMMARY

Police officers, acting on information from an
informant who previously had proved reliable, drove
to a location specified by the informant and discovered a particular automobile which the informant
had alleged contained narcotics in the trunk. After a
brief period had elapsed, the officers, noting that
the automobile's driver matched a description provided by the informant, stopped the car and opened
its trunk. A closed paper bag was discovered which
contained a white powder subsequently determined
to be heroin. After a police officer drove the auto to
headquarters, he thoroughly searched the car without obtaining a warrant, finding a zippered pouch
containing $3200 in cash. The driver was convicted
of possession of heroin with intent to distribute
after the United States District Court for the District
of Columbia denied his motion to suppress the
heroin and currency. The United States Court of
300

Appeals for the District of Columbia Circuit eventually reversed, holding that the police should not have opened either container without first obtaining a warrant and rejecting the contention that it was reasonable for the police to open both the paper bag and pouch because they were entitled to conduct a warrantless search of the entire vehicle (655 F2d 1159).

On certiorari, the United States Supreme Court reversed and remanded. In an opinion by STEVENS, J., joined by BURGER, Ch. J., and BLACKMUN, POWELL, REHNQUIST, and O'CONNOR, JJ., it was held that police officers who have legitimately stopped an automobile and who have probable cause to believe that contraband is concealed somewhere within may conduct a warrantless search of the vehicle, including compartments and containers within the vehicle whose contents are not in plain view, that is as thorough as a magistrate could authorize in a warrant particularly describing the place to be searched, the scope of the warrantless search authorized by the so-called "automobile exception" being no broader and no narrower than a magistrate could legitimately authorize by warrant, so that if probable cause justifies the search of a lawfully stopped vehicle, it justifies the search of every part of the vehicle and its contents that may conceal the object of the search.

BLACKMUN, J., concurring, expressed his dissatisfaction with the Supreme Court's vacillation in prior cases regarding the troubled area of automobile searches, and joined in the court's opinion and judgment in the case at bar in order to have an authoritative ruling on the subject.

POWELL, J., concurring, expressed the view that one's reasonable expectation of privacy, which is limited with respect to automobiles in general, may be a decisive factor in a search case, and joined the court's opinion in order to have a ruling in automobile search cases that provides specific guidance to police and courts in this reoccurring situation.

WHITE, J., dissenting, stated that he would not have overruled Robbins v California (1981) 453 US 420, 69 L Ed 2d 744, 101 S Ct 2841, and would have affirmed the opinion of the Court of Appeals in the case at bar.

MARSHALL, J., joined by BRENNAN, J., dissenting, expressed the view that the court's opinion in the case at bar utterly disregards the value of a neutral and detached magistrate by equating a police officer's estimation of probable cause with the magistrate's, thereby repealing the Fourth Amendment warrant requirement in an opinion which shows contempt for Fourth Amendment values, ignores precedent, is internally inconsistent, and produces anomalous and unjust consequences.

COUNSEL

Andrew L. Frey argued the cause for petitioner.

William J. Garber argued the cause for respondent.

INWOOD LABORATORIES, INC., et. al.,

v

IVES LABORATORIES, INC. (No. 80–2182)

DARBY DRUG CO., INC., et al.

v

IVES LABORATORIES, INC. (No. 81–11)

— US —, 72 L Ed 2d 606, 102 S Ct 2182

Argued February 22, 1982.
Decided June 1, 1982.

Decision: Federal Court of Appeals' reversal of
District Court's findings as to trademark infringement by generic drug manufacturers, held
error where "clearly erroneous" standard of
FRCP 52 not followed.

SUMMARY

A drug manufacturer patented a certain drug
which it marketed under a registered trademark.
After the patent expired, several generic drug manufacturers began marketing the drug and intentionally copied the appearance of the trademarked drug
capsules. The holder of the trademarked drug instituted an action in the United States District Court
for the Eastern District of New York under, among
other things, § 32 of the Trademark Act of 1946
(Lanham Act) (15 USCS § 1114), alleging infringement of trademark. The District Court found that
the generic drug manufacturers had not suggested,
even by implication, that pharmicists should dis-

pense generic drugs incorrectly identified under the trademark name of the original patent holder of the drug and entered judgment for the generic drug manufacturers. (488 F Supp 394). Without expressly stating that the District Court's findings were clearly erroneous, the United States Court of Appeals Second Circuit concluded, on appeal, that the generic drug manufacturers had violated § 32 (638 F2d 538).

On certiorari, the United States Supreme Court reversed and remanded. In an opinion by O'CON-NOR, J., joined by BURGER, Ch. J., and BRENNAN, BLACKMUN, POWELL, and STEVENS, JJ., it was held that on review of the District Court's finding that generic drug manufacturers were not vicariously liable for infringement of the trademark by pharmacists of a trademark drug where the pharmacists dispensed a generic drug under the trademark, the Court of Appeals erred in setting aside findings of fact that were not clearly erroneous since the Court of Appeals is bound by the "clearly erroneous" standard of Rule 52(a), Federal Rules of Civil Procedure and a Court of Appeals may not reject a District Court's findings simply because it would have given more weight to certain evidence than the trial courts since if the trial court's findings are not clearly erroneous, they should not be disturbed.

WHITE, J., joined by MARSHALL, J., concurring in the judgment, expressed the view that the Court of Appeals erred in holding that the generic drug manufacturers could be held liable for trademark infringement under § 32 merely for a failure to "reasonably anticipate" that a legal substitution by some pharmacists was likely instead of applying the proper standard that, to be liable for trademark infringement, the manufacturers must have intended illegal substitution or knowingly continued to supply pharmacists who illegally substituted.

REHNQUIST, J., concurring in the judgment, expressed the view that since the Court of Appeals set aside the factual findings of the District Court without having found them to be clearly erroneous as required by Rule 52(a), the case should have been remanded to the Court of Appeals to determine whether the findings were clearly erroneous.

COUNSEL

Milton A. Bass argued the cause for petitioners.

Jerrold J. Ganzfried argued the cause for the United States as amicus curiae, by special leave of Court.

Marie V. Driscoll argued the cause for respondent.

JESUS RIVERA-RODRIGUEZ et al., Appellants

v

POPULAR DEMOCRATIC PARTY et al.

457 US 1, 72 L Ed 2d 628, 102 S Ct 2194

Argued March 22, 1982.
Decided June 7, 1982.

Decision: Puerto Rico law vesting in political party authority to appoint replacement for member who vacates seat on legislature, held not violative of United States Constitution.

SUMMARY

Due to the death of a member of the Puerto Rico House of Representatives, the Governor of Puerto Rico called for a "by-election" open to all qualified voters in the former legislator's district. The political party in which the former legislator was a member filed suit in the Superior Court of Puerto Rico, alleging that a Puerto Rico statute authorized only candidates and electors affiliated with the former legislator's party to participate in the by-election. The Superior Court agreed and ordered that participation in the by-election be limited to that party's members. The Supreme Court of Puerto Rico modified the Superior Court's judgment, holding that the statute in question required a by-election only in the event that the party of the vacating legislator fails to designate a replacement within 60 days after the vacancy occurs and that if such a designation is made the candidate is automatically elected to fill the vacancy, rendering a by-election unnecessary, the court rejecting a claim by nonparty-members, who were voters in the subject district, that this procedure violated the United States Constitution.

On appeal, the United States Supreme Court affirmed. In an opinion by BURGER, Ch. J., expressing the unanimous view of the court, it was held that the interim appointment provision did not violate the United States Constitution, the statute not restricting access to the electoral process or affording unequal treatment to different classes of voters or political parties, the appointment provision plainly serving a legitimate purpose of ensuring that vacancies are filled promptly, without the necessity of the expense and inconvenience of a special election, the provision not being rendered constitutionally defective by virtue of the fact that the interim appointment power is given to the political party with which the previous incumbent was affiliated rather than to the Governor or some other elected official, and the fact that the appointing party excluded nonmembers from the selection process not violating the nonmembers' rights of association nor depriving them of equal protection of the laws.

COUNSEL

Philip Lacovara argued the cause for appellants.
Abe Fortas argued the cause for appellees.

JACKSON TRANSIT AUTHORITY, et al.,
Petitioners,

v

LOCAL DIVISION 1285, AMALGAMATED
TRANSIT UNION, AFL-CIO-CLC

— US —, 72 L Ed 2d 639, 102 S Ct 2202

Argued April 21, 1982.
Decided June 7, 1982.

Decision: Section 13(c) of Urban Mass Transportation Act of 1964 (49 USCS § 1609(c)), held not
to create federal cause of action for breach of
§ 13(c) agreement or collective bargaining contract between local transit authority and union.

SUMMARY

A city applied for federal aid to convert a failing
private bus company into a public transit authority.
In order to satisfy § 13(c) of the Urban Mass Transportation Act of 1964 (49 USCS § 1609(c))—which
requires a state or local government to make arrangements to preserve transit workers' existing
collective bargaining rights before that government
may receive federal financial assistance under the
Act—the authority entered into a "§ 13(c) agreement" with a transit union to protect collective
bargaining rights. The authority's unionized workers
were subsequently covered by a series of collective
bargaining agreements. Six months after a new 3-
year collective bargaining agreement was signed, the
authority notified the union that it no longer considered itself bound by that contract. The union filed
suit in the United States District Court for the
308

Western District of Tennessee, alleging that the authority had breached the § 13(c) agreement and the collective bargaining contract, and seeking damages and injunctive relief. The District Court held that it lacked subject matter jurisdiction to hear the suit because the complaint rested on contract rights that should be enforced only in a state court (447 F Supp 88). The United States Court of Appeals for the Sixth Circuit reversed, holding that (1) it had subject matter jurisdiction under 28 USCS § 1331, and (2) § 13(c) implicitly provides a federal private right of action (650 F2d 1379).

On certiorari, the United States Supreme Court reversed and remanded. In an opinion by BLACKMUN, J., expressing the unanimous view of the court, it was held that § 13(c) does not create federal causes of action for breaches of § 13(c) agreements and collective bargaining contracts between aid recipients and transit unions, the legislative history indicating that Congress intended those contracts to be governed by state law applied in state courts.

POWELL, J., joined by O'CONNOR, J., concurred, expressing the view that the court should not condone the implication of federal jurisdiction over contract claims in the absence of an unambiguous expression of congressional intent.

COUNSEL

Joseph S. Kaufman argued the cause for petitioner.

Linda R. Hirshman argued the cause for respondent.

DELBERT LEE TIBBS, Petitioner,

v

FLORIDA

— US —, 72 L Ed 2d 652, 102 S Ct 2211

Argued March 2, 1982.
Decided June 7, 1982.

Decision: Florida Supreme Court's reversal of murder and rape conviction at jury trial based on weight of evidence, held not to bar retrial under double jeopardy clause of Fifth and Fourteenth Amendments.

SUMMARY

An individual was convicted of rape and murder by a jury in the Circuit Court of Lee County, Florida, and was sentenced to death. On appeal, the Supreme Court of Florida reversed, finding several weaknesses in the state's case against the defendant, holding that these weaknesses left the court in considerable doubt that the defendant was the man who committed the crimes for which he had been convicted, and ordering a new trial (337 So 2d 788). On remand, the trial court dismissed the indictment, concluding that retrial would violate the double jeopardy clause of the Fifth and Fourteenth Amendments. The District Court of Appeal of Florida, Second District, disagreed and remanded the case for trial (370 So 2d 386). The Supreme Court of Florida affirmed the latter decision, classifying its prior reversal of the defendant's conviction as resting on the weight of the evidence, as opposed to insufficient evidence, and concluding that under
310

such circumstances retrial was not barred (397 So 2d 1120).

On certiorari, the United States Supreme Court affirmed. In an opinion by O'CONNOR, J., joined by BURGER, Ch. J., and POWELL, REHNQUIST, and STEVENS, JJ., it was held that the double jeopardy clause did not bar the retrial of the defendant; since the conviction was set aside on the ground that the verdict was against "the weight of the evidence," as opposed to insufficient evidence, such a reversal, unlike one based on insufficient evidence, not meaning that acquittal was the only proper verdict, and it, occurring only after the state both has presented evidence to support conviction and has persuaded the jury to convict, affording the defendant a second opportunity to seek a favorable judgment and thus hardly amounting to governmental pressure the sort against which the double jeopardy clause was intended to protect.

WHITE, J., joined by BRENNAN, MARSHALL and BLACKMUN, JJ., dissented, expressing the view that, given the fact that the only point of a second trial would be to allow the state to present additional evidence to bolster its case and that, if it has no additional evidence, retrial would serve no purpose other than harassment, reprosecution under these circumstances would offend the double jeopardy clause.

COUNSEL

Louis R. Beller argued the cause for petitioner.
Michael A. Palecki argued the cause for respondent.

_____

KATHY SUE JOHNSON, etc., et al.

v

BOARD OF EDUCATION OF THE CITY OF
CHICAGO et al.

— US —, 72 L Ed 2d 668, 102 S Ct 2223

Decided June 7, 1982.

Decision: Case challenging voluntary adoption by
municipal board of education of racial quotas
on enrollment, held not moot, and ordered
consolidated with related case.

SUMMARY

Plaintiffs filed suit in a United States District
Court challenging the voluntary adoption by a municipal board of education of racial quotas on enrollment at two high schools. The District Court
upheld the plan, and the United States Court of
Appeals for the Seventh Circuit affirmed. The
United States Supreme Court, vacated the judgment
and remanded the case for further consideration in
the light of a subsequent development involving the
entry of a consent decree in a related case and the
board's announcement that it had abandoned use of
the quotas at the schools (449 US 915, 66 L Ed 2d
162, 101 S Ct 339). The Court of Appeals remanded to the District Court to consider the suggestion of mootness. The District Court concluded
that the case was not moot, since the board had
readopted the quotas. The Court of Appeals, agreeing that the case was not moot and relying upon the
doctrine of the law of the case, affirmed without

reconsidering the challenge to the quotas in light of the subsequent development that the board argued eliminated or reduced any discriminatory effects of the quotas.

Granting certiorari, the United States Supreme Court vacated and remanded. In a per curiam opinion, expressing the view of BURGER, Ch. J., and BLACKMUN, POWELL, STEVENS, and O'CONNOR, JJ., it was held that (1) the case was not moot and the subsequent development did not undermine the Court of Appeals' original decision upholding the racial quotas and (2) the case would be consolidated with the related case so that the court could decide the challenge to the quotas on the basis of a complete factual record.

BRENNAN, J., would have granted the petition for a writ of certiorari and set the case for oral argument.

REHNQUIST, J., joined by MARSHALL, J., dissented, expressing the view that (1) nothing in the record suggested any reason why the court should order consolidation of the instant case with another pending action in the District Court, a function more properly exercised by the Court of Appeals or by the District Court, and (2) the court should have more clearly specified its reasons for its disposition of the case.

WHITE, J., did not participate.

RONALD M. ZOBEL and PATRICIA L. ZOBEL,
Appellants,

v

THOMAS WILLIAMS, Commissioner of Revenue,
and ALASKA

— US —, 72 L Ed 2d 672, 102 S Ct —

Argued October 7, 1981.
Decided June 14, 1982.

Decision: Alaska statute distributing income derived from state's natural resources to state's citizens in varying amounts based on length of each citizen's residency, held to violate equal protection clause.

SUMMARY

Alaska adopted a constitutional amendment establishing a fund into which the state must deposit at least 25 percent of its mineral income each year. The Alaska legislature enacted a dividend program to distribute annually a portion of the fund's earnings directly to the state's adult residents. Under the plan, each citizen 18 years of age or older would receive one dividend unit for each year of residency subsequent to 1959, the first year of statehood. Plaintiffs, residents of Alaska since 1978, brought suit challenging the dividend distribution plan. The Superior Court for Alaska's Third Judicial District granted summary judgment in favor of the plaintiffs, holding that the plan violated the rights of interstate travel and equal protection. The Supreme Court of

Alaska reversed and upheld the statute (619 P2d 448).

On appeal, the United States Supreme Court reversed and remanded. In an opinion by BURGER, Ch. J., joined by BRENNAN, WHITE, MARSHALL, BLACKMUN, POWELL, and STEVENS, JJ., it was held that the Alaska dividend distribution plan violated the equal protection clause of the Fourteenth Amendment, since the state had shown no valid state interests which were rationally served by the distinction it made between citizens who established residency before 1959 and those who have become residents since then.

BRENNAN, J., joined by MARSHALL, BLACKMUN, and POWELL, JJ., concurred, expressing the view that the right to travel—or, more precisely, the federal interest in free interstate migration—was affected by the Alaska dividend-distribution law, and that this threat to free interstate migration provided an independent rationale for holding that law unconstitutional.

O'CONNOR, J., concurred in the judgment, expressing the view that the Alaska law should be measured against the principles implementing the privileges and immunities clause, and that this analysis supplies a needed foundation for many of the "right to travel" claims discussed in the court's prior opinions.

REHNQUIST, J., dissented, expressing the view that the Alaska distribution scheme was rationally based, and that the Fourteenth Amendment gives the federal courts no power to impose upon the states their view of what constitutes wise economic or social policy.

COUNSEL

Mark A. Sandberg argued the cause for appellants.

Avrum M. Gross argued the cause for appellees.

KENNETH CORY, Controller of the State of
California, et al., Petitioners,

v

MARK WHITE, Attorney General of the State of
Texas, et al.

— US —, 72 L Ed 2d 694, 102 S Ct —

Argued January 18, 1982.
Decided June 14, 1982.

Decision: Action under Federal Interpleader Act (28
USCS § 1335) to resolve inconsistent death tax
claims on estate of Howard Hughes by officials
of two states, held barred by Eleventh Amendment.

SUMMARY

The administrator of the estate of Howard
Hughes filed a statutory interpleader action under
28 USCS § 1335 in the United States District Court
for the Western District of Texas, asserting that the
officials of two states (California and Texas) were
seeking to tax the estate on the basis of inconsistent
claims that each state was Hughes' domicile at
death. The District Court entered a temporary restraining order prohibiting the California and Texas
officials from pursuing domicile-based inheritance
tax claims in any other forum, including their own
state courts. The District Court then dismissed the
action for lack of subject matter jurisdiction for
failure to satisfy the requirement of 28 USCS § 1335
that there be diversity of citizenship between at least
two adverse claimants. The United States Court of

317

Appeals for the Fifth Circuit reversed the order of dismissal, holding that the requisite diversity was present, and rejecting the states' claim that although the suit was nominally against state officials, it was in effect a suit against two states barred by the Eleventh Amendment (629 F2d 397).

On certiorari, the United States Supreme Court reversed. In an opinion by WHITE, J., joined by BURGER, Ch. J., and BLACKMUN, REHNQUIST, and O'CONNOR, JJ., it was held that the Eleventh Amendment barred the statutory interpleader sought in the instant case.

BRENNAN, J., concurring in the judgment, expressed the view that (1) an interpleader suit in the District Court is not a practical solution to the problem of potential double taxation presented in cases such as the instant case, and (2) it would be appropriate for the Supreme Court to exercise its original jurisdiction to decide the controversy.

POWELL, J., joined by MARSHALL and STEVENS, JJ., dissented, expressing the view that the due process clause provides the right to be free of multiple taxation of intangibles based on domicile, and that the Federal Interpleader Act provides the remedy.

COUNSEL

Jerome B. Falk, Jr., argued the cause for petitioners.

O. Clayton Lilienstern argued the cause for respondents Lummis, et al.

Rick Harrison argued the cause for respondents White and Bullock.

UNITED STEELWORKERS OF AMERICA, AFL-
CIO-CLC, Petitioner,

v

EDWARD SADLOWSKI, JR., et al.

— US —, 72 L Ed 2d 707, 102 S Ct —

Argued March 31, 1982.
Decided June 14, 1982.

Decision: Union "outsider rule," held not violative
of Labor-Management Reporting and Disclosure Act's "free speech and assembly" or "right
to sue" provisions (29 USCS § 411(a)(2), (4)).

SUMMARY

An unsuccessful candidate for union office and
several other individuals brought an action in the
United States District Court for the District of Columbia challenging a union "outsider rule"—which
prohibited candidates for union office from accepting campaign contributions from nonmembers—on
the ground that the rule violated the members'
"right to sue" under § 101(a)(4) of the Labor-Management Reporting and Disclosure Act of 1959 (29
USCS § 411(a)(4)), the candidate contending that
the rule prohibited outside contributions to finance
campaign-related litigation. The District Court
found that the rule violated the "right to sue"
provision (507 F Supp 623). The United States
Court of Appeals for the District of Columbia Circuit affirmed, agreeing that the rule violated the
"right to sue" provision and further accepting the
candidate's argument, first raised on appeal, that the

319

outsider rule also violated the "free speech and assembly" guarantee of § 101(a)(2) of the Act (29 USCS § 411(a)(2)). The Court of Appeals rejected the union's contention that even if the rule interfered with rights protected by the Act it was sheltered by the proviso to § 101(a)(2), which gives a union authority to adopt "reasonable" rules regarding the responsibilities of its members (207 App DC 189, 645 F2d 1114).

On certiorari, the United States Supreme Court reversed and remanded. In an opinion by MARSHALL, J., joined by POWELL, REHNQUIST, STEVENS, and O'CONNOR, JJ., it was held that (1) the "outsider rule" did not violate § 101(a)(2), although it may interfere with rights Congress intended to protect, since it was rationally related to a legitimate and protected interest in reducing outsider interference with union affairs and was thus sheltered by the proviso to § 101(a)(2), and (2) the "outsider rule" did not violate a member's statutory "right to sue" under § 101(a)(4), the rule simply not applying where a member uses funds from outsiders to finance litigation.

WHITE, J., joined by BURGER, Ch. J., and BRENNAN and BLACKMUN, JJ., dissented, expressing the view that the intent of Congress when it passed § 101(a)(2) of the Act was to ensure "union democracy" by protecting the union member's right to seek higher office within the union, and that Congress never intended that a union be permitted to impose a limitation which would confine a challenger to financial support garnered within the union.

COUNSEL

Michael H. Gottesman argued the cause for petitioner.

Joseph L. Raush, Jr., argued the cause for respondents.

BARBARA BLUM, etc., Appellant,

v

JEANNE BACON, etc., et al.

— US —, 72 L Ed 2d 728, 102 S Ct —

Argued April 28, 1982.
Decided June 14, 1982.

Decision: State emergency assistance program precluding furnishing assistance to AFDC recipients, held invalid under supremacy clause (Art VI, cl 2) as in conflict with valid federal regulation.

SUMMARY

New York established an Emergency Assistance Program receiving substantial federal funding under Title IV-A of the Social Security Act (42 USCS § 603(a)(5)). In establishing its program, New York excluded recipients of Aid to Families with Dependent Children (AFDC) from emergency assistance in the form of cash and excluded public assistance recipients, including AFDC recipients, from reimbursement for lost or stolen grants, even though it provided such reimbursement to other public benefit recipients. A number of AFDC recipients brought a class action in the United States District Court for the Southern District of New York to enjoin enforcement of the state law insofar as it denied Emergency Assistance pursuant to the no-cash provision and the loss-or-theft provision, arguing that the law conflicts with the Social Security Act and violated equal protection because it arbitrarily discriminated against AFDC recipients. Following a remand of its initial decision invalidating the provisions under the supremacy clause of the United States Constitution (Art VI, cl 2) (437 F Supp 1371, affirmed 508 F2d 1044), the District Court held that the state law was not inconsistent with § 406(e) of the Social Security Act (42 USCS § 606(e)), and upheld the loss-or-theft provision, but invalidated the no-cash provision as a violation of equal protection (493 F Supp 865). On appeal, the United States Court of Appeals for the Second Circuit concluded that both the no-cash and the loss-or-theft provisions violated equal protection (648 F2d 801).

On appeal, the United States Supreme Court affirmed. In an opinion by MARSHALL, J., expressing the unanimous view of the court, it was held that the state rules conflicted with a valid federal regulation (45 CFR § 233.10) promulgated by the Secretary of Health, Education, and Welfare which proscribes inequitable treatment of individuals or groups under Emergency Assistance program, and thus were invalid under the supremacy clause of the Constitution, the Secretary's decision to apply the "equitable treatment" regulation so as to forbid a state to exclude AFDC recipients from its program being eminently reasonable and deserving judicial deference.

COUNSEL

Robert S. Hammer argued the cause for appellant.

Martin A. Schwartz argued the cause for appellees.

GENERAL TELEPHONE COMPANY OF THE
SOUTHWEST, Petitioner,

v

MARIANO S. FALCON

— US —, 72 L Ed 2d 740, 102 S Ct —

Argued April 26, 1982.
Decided June 14, 1982.

Decision: Mexican-American employee who was denied promotion, held not entitled to maintain
class action on behalf of Mexican-American
applicants for employment who were not hired.

SUMMARY

A Mexican-American employee who was denied a
promotion filed a charge with the Equal Employment Opportunity Commission alleging national
origin discrimination, and received a right to sue
letter from the Commission. The employee brought
a class action against his employer under Title VII
of the Civil Rights Act of 1964 (42 USCS § 2000e et
seq.) in the United States District Court for the
Northern District of Texas. The District Court certified a class including Mexican-American employees
and Mexican-American applicants for employment
who had not been hired. The District Court found
that the employer had not discriminated against the
employee in hiring, but that it had discriminated
against him in its promotion practices. With regard
to the class, the court conversely found no discrimination in promotion practices, but concluded that
the employer had discriminated against Mexican-

Americans in its hiring practices at the facility in question. (463 F Supp 315). The United States Court of Appeals for the Fifth Circuit held that the District Court's class certification was proper under its "across-the-board" rule, under which it is permissible for an employee complaining of one employment practice to represent another complaining of another practice, if the plaintiff and the members of the class suffer from essentially the same injury. On the merits, the Court of Appeals upheld the employee's promotion claim, but held that the District Court's findings were insufficient to support recovery on behalf of the class (626 F2d 369). Eventually, on remand from the United States Supreme Court, the Court of Appeals vacated its ruling as to the employee's promotion claim, but approved the District Court's class certification (647 F2d 633).

On certiorari, the United States Supreme Court reversed and remanded. In an opinion by STEVENS, J., joined by BRENNAN, WHITE, MARSHALL, BLACKMUN, POWELL, REHNQUIST, and O'CONNOR, JJ., it was held that, for purposes of permitting the employee to maintain a class action on behalf of the job applicants, it was error for the District Court to presume that the employee's claim was typical of other claims against the employer by other Mexican-American employees and applicants for employment, in the absence of any specific presentation identifying the questions of law or fact that were common to the claims of the employee and of the members of the class he sought to represent, the employee's complaint providing an insufficient basis for concluding that the adjudication of his claim of discrimination in promotion would require the decision of any common question concerning the failure of the employer to hire more Mexican-Americans.

Burger, Ch. J., concurred in part and dissented in part, expressing the view that, although the Court's decision correctly stated the general principles which apply in determining whether a class should have been certified under Rule 23 of the Federal Rules of Civil Procedure, it was not necessary to remand for further proceedings since it was entirely clear on the record that no class should have been certified in the case at bar.

COUNSEL

Noyes Thompson Powers argued the cause for petitioner.

Frank R. Hernandez argued the cause for respondent.

STATE OF CALIFORNIA

v

STATE OF TEXAS, et al.

— US —, 72 L Ed 2d 755, 102 S Ct —

Decided June 14, 1982.

Decision: California's motion for leave to file bill of complaint against Texas to decide whether Howard Hughes was domiciled in California or Texas at time of death, granted as properly invoking Supreme Court's original jurisdiction.

SUMMARY

California sought leave to file a complaint against Texas under the United States Supreme Court's original jurisdiction, renewing a motion which the Supreme Court had denied in a prior decision (California v Texas (1978) 437 US 601, 57 L Ed 2d 464, 98 S Ct 3107). The proposed complaint asked the Supreme Court to decide whether Howard Hughes was domiciled in California or Texas at the time of his death, a decision which could determine which state was entitled to levy death taxes on Hughes' estate.

On the motion, the United States Supreme Court granted California leave to file its bill of complaint. In a per curiam opinion expressing the view of BURGER, Ch. J., and BRENNAN, WHITE, BLACKMUN, and O'CONNOR, JJ., it was held that the Supreme Court's original jurisdiction was properly invoked, since (1) California's bill of complaint stated a "controversy" between two states within the exclusive jurisdiction of the Supreme Court under 28 USCS § 1251(a), and (2) it was appropriate to exercise the Supreme Court's jurisdiction in the instant case, the precondition for the exercise of original jurisdiction having been met after its decision in Cory v White (1982) — US ——, 72 L Ed 2d ——, 102 S Ct ——, that a statutory interpleader action could not be brought in federal court which would be binding on both states.

POWELL, J., joined by MARSHALL, REHNQUIST, and STEVENS, JJ., dissented, expressing the view that the mere possibility of inconsistent state determinations of domicile, resulting in a still more remote possibility of the estate's being insufficient to satisfy the competing claims, did not give rise to a case or controversy in the constitutional sense.

———————

SUMITOMO SHOJI AMERICA, INC., Petitioner,

v

LISA M. AVAGLIANO et al. (No. 80–2070)

LISA M. AVAGLIANO, et al., Petitioners,

v

SUMITOMO SHOJI AMERICA, INC. (No. 81–24)

— US —, 72 L Ed 2d 765, 102 S Ct —

Argued April 26, 1982.
Decided June 15, 1982.

Decision: Employment practices of a New York corporation that is wholly-owned subsidiary of Japanese firm, held not exempted from Title VII of Civil Rights Act (42 USCS §§ 2000e et seq.) by treaty between the United States and Japan.

SUMMARY

Several past and present female secretarial employees of a New York corporation, which is a wholly-owned subsidiary of a Japanese general trading company, brought a class action in the United States District Court for the Southern District of New York against the corporation, claiming that its alleged practice of hiring only male Japanese citizens to fill executive, managerial, and sales positions violated Title VII of the Civil Rights Act of 1964 (42 USCS §§ 2000e et seq.). Without admitting the alleged practice, the corporation moved to dismiss the complaint on the ground that its employment

329

practices were protected from Title VII scrutiny by Article VIII(1) of the Treaty of Friendship, Commerce, and Navigation between the United States and Japan, which provides that the "companies of either Party shall be permitted to engage, within the territories of the other Party, accountants and other technical experts, executive personnel, attorneys, agents and other specialists of their choice," Article XXII(3) of the Treaty defining "companies" as "companies constituted under the applicable laws and regulations within the territories of either Party." The District Court refused to dismiss, holding that because the corporation was incorporated in the United States, it was not covered by Article VIII(1), but the court then certified for interlocutory appeal to the United States Court of Appeals for the Second Circuit the question whether the terms of the Treaty exempted the corporation from Title VII's provision (473 F Supp 506). The Court of Appeals reversed in part, holding that Article VIII(1) was intended to cover locally incorporated subsidiaries of foreign companies, but that the Treaty language did not insulate the corporation's employment practices from Title VII scrutiny (638 F2d 552).

On certiorari, the United States Supreme Court reversed and remanded. In an opinion by BURGER, Ch. J., expressing the unanimous view of the court, it was held that the corporation was not a company of Japan and thus was not covered by Article VIII(1) of the Treaty, nor shielded thereby from Title VII scrutiny, the corporation being a company of the United States since it was "constituted under the applicable laws and regulations" of New York and the rights provided in Article VIII(1) being available only to companies of Japan operating in the United

States and to companies of the United States operating in Japan.

COUNSEL

Abram Chayes argued the cause for Sumitomo Shoji America, Inc.

Lewis M. Steel argued the cause for Avagliano, et al.

Lawrence G. Wallace argued the cause for the United States as amicus curiae by special leave of Court.

———————

VICTOR P. DIEDRICH et ux., Petitioners,

v

COMMISSIONER OF INTERNAL REVENUE

———

UNITED MISSOURI BANK OF KANSAS

v

COMMISSIONER OF INTERNAL REVENUE

— US —, 72 L Ed 2d 777, 102 S Ct —

Argued February 24, 1982.
Decided June 15, 1982.

Decision: Donor making gift of property on condition that donee pay resulting gift tax, held to realize taxable income to extent that gift tax paid by donee exceeds donor's adjusted basis in property.

SUMMARY

In two separate cases, individual taxpayers made a gift of property on condition that the donee pay the resulting gift tax. In both cases the Commissioner of Internal Revenue determined, after an audit, that the taxpayers had realized taxable income to the extent that the gift tax paid by the donee exceeds the taxpayer's adjusted basis in the property transferred, and the taxpayers filed petitions in the United States Tax Court for redetermination of deficiencies. The Tax Court held for the taxpayers, concluding that no income had been realized. The United States Court of Appeals for the Eighth Circuit consolidated the two appeals and reversed,
332

concluding that to the extent the gift taxes paid by the donees exceeded the donors' adjusted bases in the property transferred, the donors realized taxable income (643 F2d 499).

On certiorari, the United States Supreme Court affirmed. In an opinion by BURGER, Ch. J., joined by BRENNAN, WHITE, MARSHALL, BLACKMUN, POWELL, STEVENS, and O'CONNOR, JJ., it was held that a donor who makes a gift of property on condition that the donee pay the resulting gift tax realizes taxable income to the extent that the gift tax paid by the donee exceeds the donor's adjusted basis in the property.

REHNQUIST, J., dissenting, expressed the view that although Congress could determine that the payment of the gift tax by the donee constitutes income to the donor, the relevant statutes do not affirmatively indicate that Congress has made such a determination.

COUNSEL

Norman E. Beal argued the cause for petitioners.
Stuart A. Smith argued the cause for respondent.

JAMES PLYLER, Superintendent of the Tyler
Independent School District and its Board of
Trustees et al., Appellants,

v

J. and R. DOE et al. (No. 80–1538)

_____

TEXAS, et al., Appellants,

v

CERTAIN NAMED and UNNAMED
UNDOCUMENTED ALIEN CHILDREN et al. (No.
80–1934)

— US —, 72 L Ed 2d 786, 102 S Ct —

Argued December 1, 1981.
Decided June 15, 1982.

Decision: Texas statute withholding funds from
local school districts for education of children
not legally admitted into United States and
authorizing districts to deny enrollment to such
children, held to violate equal protection clause.

SUMMARY

The Texas legislature enacted a statute which
withholds from local school districts any state funds
for the education of children who were not "legally
admitted" into the United States and which authorizes local school districts to deny enrollment in
their public schools to such children. Constitutional
challenges were made to the provisions by a number
of parties. One case was a class action filed in the
United States District Court for the Eastern District
334

of Texas on behalf of certain school-aged children of Mexican origin residing in Smith County, Texas, who could not establish that they had been legally admitted into the United States, against the Superintendent and members of the Board of Trustees of the Tyler Independent School District, complaining of the exclusion of the plaintiff children from the public schools of the School District. After making extensive findings of fact, the District Court held that illegal aliens were entitled to the protection of the equal protection clause of the Fourteenth Amendment, and that the Texas statute violated that clause (458 F Supp 569). The United States Court of Appeals for the Fifth Circuit upheld an injunction issued by the District Court, affirming in all essential respects the equal protection analysis of the District Court, concluding that the Texas statute was constitutionally infirm regardless of whether it was tested using a more rational basis standard or some more stringent test (658 F2d 448). A number of other actions filed in Federal District Courts in Texas were consolidated by the Judicial Panel on Multidistrict Litigation into a single action against state officials to be heard in the United States District Court for the Southern District of Texas. The District Court held that the Texas statute violated the equal protection clause of the Fourteenth Amendment, concluding that the statute was not carefully tailored to advance the asserted state interest in an acceptable manner (501 F Supp 544), and, apparently on the strength of its earlier decision, the Court of Appeals summarily affirmed the decision of the District Court.

On appeal, the United States Supreme Court affirmed. In an opinion by BRENNAN, J., joined by

335

MARSHALL, BLACKMUN, POWELL, and STEVENS, JJ., it was held that the Texas statute violated the equal protection clause of the Fourteenth Amendment, neither the undocumented status of the alien children vel non, nor the state's asserted interest in the preservation of its limited resources for the education of its lawful residents furthering some substantial goal of the state in order to establish a sufficient rational basis for the discrimination contained in the statute.

MARSHALL, J., concurring, emphasized his belief that an individual's interest in education is fundamental and that a class-based denial of public education is utterly incompatible with the equal protection clause of the Fourteenth Amendment.

BLACKMUN, J., concurring, expressed his view that the nature of the interest at stake in the case was crucial to its proper resolution, that when a state provides an education to some and denies it to others it immediately and inevitably creates class distinctions of a type fundamentally inconsistent with the purposes of the equal protection clause, and that whatever the state's power to classify deportable aliens, the statute at issue swept within it a substantial number of children who would in fact, and who may well be entitled to, remain in the United States.

POWELL, J., concurring, emphasized the unique character of the instant case and expressed his view that the state's denial of education to the children in the case bore no substantial relation to any substantial state interest.

BURGER, Ch. J., joined by WHITE, REHNQUIST, and O'CONNOR, JJ., dissented, expressing the view that the United States Supreme Court trespasses on the assigned function of the political branches under the stricture of limited and separate powers when it assumes a policymaking role as the court did in the case before it, and that the distinction that Texas had drawn was based not only upon its own legitimate interest but on classifications established by the federal government in its immigration laws and policies and was not unconstitutional.

COUNSEL

Richard L. Arnett argued the cause for appellants in 80-1934.

John C. Hardy argued the cause for appellants in 80-1538.

Peter A. Schey argued the cause for appellees in 80-1934.

Peter D. Roos argued the cause for appellees in 80-1538.

RALPH HATHORN, et al., Petitioners,

v

MRS. BOBBY LOVORN, et al.

— US —, 72 L Ed 2d 824, 102 S Ct —

Argued April 27, 1982.
Decided June 15, 1982.

Decision: Jurisdiction to decide whether § 5 of Voting Rights Act of 1965 (42 USCS § 1973c) applies to changes in local election procedures, held within power of state court.

SUMMARY

Several voters from Winston County, Mississippi, filed an action in the Chancery Court of Winston County, seeking to enforce a neglected state statute passed in 1964, which prescribed the composition and election procedures for members of boards of trustees of all municipal separate school districts. The statute also prescribed a separate procedure, applicable only to Winston County. The Chancery Court dismissed the voters' complaint, holding that the statute violated Mississippi's constitutional bar against local legislation. The Supreme Court of Mississippi reversed, striking only the specific reference which limited application of the special election procedure to Winston County, upholding the remainder of the statute, and remanding to the Chancery Court for further proceedings not inconsistent with its opinion (365 So 2d 947). Certain local county officials then filed a petition for rehearing, in which they argued for the first time that the

338

Chancery Court could not implement the reformed statute until the change had been precleared with the Attorney General of the United States pursuant to § 5 of the Voting Rights Act of 1965 (42 USCS § 1973c). The Supreme Court of Mississippi denied the petition without comment and the United States Supreme Court denied certiorari (60 L Ed 2d 1049). On remand, the Chancery Court ordered an election pursuant to the redacted statute and, agreeing that the changes in election procedure fell within § 5, directed that local officials submit the election plan to the Attorney General for preclearance. The Attorney General objected to the plan, arguing that the procedure requiring a runoff between the two leading candidates absent any candidate's receiving a majority of the vote had a discriminatory effect. The Chancery Court then ordered that its decree calling for an election remain in force subject to compliance with the Act. The voters again appealed to the Supreme Court of Mississippi, which observed that its prior decision was the law of the case and held that the Chancery Court properly enforced the law requiring runoffs but improperly conditioned the election on compliance with the Voting Rights Act (399 So 2d 1356).

On certiorari, the United States Supreme Court reversed and remanded. In an opinion by O'CONNOR, J., joined by BURGER, Ch. J., and BRENNAN, WHITE, MARSHALL, BLACKMUN, and STEVENS, JJ., it was held that (1) the Mississippi courts had the power to decide whether § 5 of the Voting Rights Act applied to a change in local election procedures, § 14(b) of the Act (42 USCS § 1973*l*(b))—which provides the United States District Court for the District of Columbia exclusive jurisdiction over declaratory judgments pursuant to § 5—governing only declaratory judgments approving proposed changes and voting procedures rather than the distinct question of whether a proposed change is subject to the Act, and nothing in either § 5, requiring an action thereunder to be heard by a three-judge Federal District Court, or § 12(f) of the Act (42 USCS § 1973j(f)), declaring that Federal District Courts have jurisdiction over proceedings involving violations of the Act, negating the presumption that, at least when the issue arises collaterally, state courts may decide whether a proposed change in election procedure requires preclearance under § 5.

REHNQUIST, J., dissenting, expressed the view that the provisions of §§ 5, 12(f), and 14(b) of the Voting Rights Act did not express any congressional intention that state courts play a role in the enforcement of that Act.

COUNSEL

James C. Mayo argued the cause for petitioners.

William Bradford Reynolds argued the cause for the United States, as amicus curiae, by special leave of Court.

Laurel G. Weir argued the cause for respondents.

STATE OF CALIFORNIA, ex rel., STATE LANDS
COMMISSION, Plaintiff,

v

UNITED STATES

— US —, 73 L Ed 2d 1, 102 S Ct —

Argued March 29, 1982.
Decided June 18, 1982.

Decision: United States, held entitled to oceanfront
accretions to Coast Guard reservation under
federal rule that accretions belong to upland
owner.

SUMMARY

California sued the United States in the Supreme
Court of the United States, seeking to quiet title to
184 acres of upland created near Humboldt Bay,
California, by a fairly rapid accretion on the ocean
side of a Coast Guard reservation as a result of the
United States' construction of two jetties at the bay
entrance. The Supreme Court granted leave for
California to file a bill of complaint.

The Supreme Court granted the United States'
motion for judgment on the Pleadings. In an opinion by WHITE, J., joined by BURGER, Ch. J., and
BRENNAN, MARSHALL, BLACKMUN, and POWELL, JJ., it
was held that (1) federal law governs a dispute over
accretions to oceanfront land where title rests with
or was derived from the federal government, under
the rule of Hughes v Washington (1967) 389 US
290, 19 L Ed 2d 530, 88 S Ct 438, that federal law
determines the boundary between state-owned tide-

lands and oceanfront property where accretions have extended the shoreline seaward, and under the rule of Wilson v Omaha Indian Tribe (1979) 442 US 653, 61 L Ed 2d 153, 99 S Ct 2529, that federal law governs the effect of accretive or avulsive changes in the course of a navigable stream where the dispute involves the United States as riparian owner, (2) title to the entire disputed land was vested in the United States under the federal rule that accretions, regardless of cause, accrue to the upland owner, and (3) the Submerged Lands Act does not affect the longstanding federal rule that accretions belong to the upland owner, and did not surrender title to the accretions to California.

REHNQUIST, J., joined by STEVENS and O'CONNOR, JJ., concurred in the judgment, stating that under the Wilson case, federal law resolved the dispute in favor of the government without considering the continuing vitality of the Hughes decision.

COUNSEL

Bruce S. Flushman argued the cause for plaintiff.
Louis F. Claiborne argued the cause for defendant.

MARK J. MILLS et al., Petitioners

v

RUBIE ROGERS et al.

— US —, 73 L Ed 2d 16, 102 S Ct —

Argued January 13, 1982.
Decided June 18, 1982.

Decision: Case presenting question whether state
involuntarily committed mental patients may
refuse certain drugs, vacated and remanded to
Federal Court of Appeals to consider intervening state court decision bearing on issue.

SUMMARY

Seven present or former mental patients at a state
hospital filed suit in the United States District for
the District of Massachusetts against various officials
and staff of the hospital, alleging that during their
period of institutionalization they had all been
forced to accept unwanted treatment with antipsychotic drugs, which violated rights protected by the
Constitution of the United States, and seeking compensatory and punitive damages and injunctive relief. The District Court, although denying relief in
damages, held that the mental patients enjoyed
constitutionally protected liberty and privacy interests in deciding for themselves whether to submit to
drug therapy (478 F Supp 1342). The United States
Court of Appeals for the First Circuit affirmed in
part and reversed in part and agreed that the mental patients had a constitutionally protected interest
in deciding for themselves whether to undergo

343

treatment with antipsychotic drugs (634 F2d 650). Five months after the Court of Appeals decided the case, and shortly after the United States Supreme Court granted certiorari, the Supreme Judicial Court of Massachusetts announced its decision in a case involving the right of a noninstitutionalized but mentally incompetent person to refuse treatment with antipsychotic drugs. Expressly resting its decision on the common law of Massachusetts as well as on the Federal Constitution, the Massachusetts court held that such a person had a protected liberty interest in deciding for himself whether to submit to the use of antipsychotic drugs (421 NE2d 40).

On certiorari, the United States Supreme Court vacated and remanded. In an opinion by POWELL, J., expressing the unanimous view of the court, it was held that the court would remand the case to the Court of Appeals to consider how the intervening state case may have changed the state law and how any changes may affect the instant case since the Court of Appeals has a greater familiarity both with the record and the state law.

COUNSEL

Stephen Schultz argued the cause for petitioners.
Richard Wayne Cole argued the cause for respondents.

DUANE YOUNGBERG, etc., et al., Petitioners,

v

NICHOLAS ROMEO, an incompetent, by his
mother and next friend, PAULA ROMEO

— US —, 73 L Ed 2d 28, 102 S Ct —

Argued January 11, 1982.
Decided June 18, 1982.

Decision: Involuntarily committed retarded person,
held to have due process liberty interests requiring state to provide minimally adequate
training to ensure safety and freedom from
undue restraint.

SUMMARY

The mother of a mentally retarded person, who
was involuntarily committed to a Pennsylvania state
institution upon her petition and who was injured
on numerous occasions while a patient at the institution, filed a complaint, as her son's next friend, in
the United States District Court for the Eastern
District of Pennsylvania under 42 USCS § 1983,
seeking damages against the institution's officials,
and alleging that these officials knew, or should
have known, that her son was suffering injuries and
that they failed to institute appropriate preventive
procedures, thereby violating his rights under the
Eighth and Fourteenth Amendments. A second
amended complaint was filed, alleging that the officials were restraining her son for prolonged periods
on a routine basis, and claiming damages for the
official's failure to provide him with appropriate

345

treatment or programs for his mental retardation. At the close of trial, the District Court instructed the jury on the assumption that the proper standard of liability was that of the Eighth Amendment, and verdict was returned for the officials. The United States Court of Appeals for the Third Circuit reversed and remanded for a new trial, holding that the Eighth Amendment was not an appropriate source for determining the rights of the involuntarily committed, but that the Fourteenth Amendment, and the liberty interest protected therein, provided the proper constitutional basis for these rights (644 F2d 147).

On certiorari, the United States Supreme Court vacated and remanded. In an opinion by POWELL, J., joined by BRENNAN, WHITE, MARSHALL, BLACKMUN, REHNQUIST, STEVENS, and O'CONNOR, JJ., it was held that the mentally retarded individual has liberty interests under the due process clause of the Fourteenth Amendment which require the state to provide him minimally adequate or reasonable training to ensure safety and freedom from undue restraint, and that the state is under a duty to provide him with such training as an appropriate professional would consider reasonable to ensure him safety and to facilitate his ability to function free from bodily restraints.

BLACKMUN, J., joined by BRENNAN and O'CONNOR, JJ., concurred, expressing the view that the court properly left unresolved, because of the less-than-fully developed record, the issues as to the constitutionality of a state's total failure to provide treatment to an individual committed under state law for care and treatment, and as to an involuntarily-committed mentally retarded person's independent court claim, grounded in the due process clause of the Fourteenth Amendment, to that habilitation or training necessary to preserve those self-care skills he possessed when he first entered the state institution.

BURGER, Ch. J., concurred in the judgment, stating that a mentally retarded person, involuntarily committed to a state institution, has no constitutional right to training, or habilitation, per se.

COUNSEL

David H. Allshouse argued the cause for petitioners.

Edmond A. Tiryak argued the cause for respondents.

_____

ARIZONA, Petitioner

v

MARICOPA COUNTY MEDICAL SOCIETY et al.

— US —, 73 L Ed 2d 48, 102 S Ct —

Argued November 4, 1981.
Decided June 18, 1982.

Decision: Agreement among competing physicians setting, by majority vote, maximum fees for payment from participants in specified insurance plans, held per se unlawful under § 1 of Sherman Act (15 USCS § 1).

SUMMARY

Two Arizona county medical societies formed two "foundations for medical care" organized for the purpose of promoting fee-for-service medicine and to provide the community with a competitive alternative to existing health insurance plans. The foundations performed three primary activities including establishing the schedule of maximum fees that participating doctors agreed to accept as payment in full for services performed for patients insured under plans approved by the foundations. The state of Arizona filed a civil complaint in the United States District Court for the District of Arizona against the two county medical societies and foundations alleging that they were engaged in illegal price-fixing conspiracies in violation of § 1 of the Sherman Act (15 USCS § 1). The state moved for partial summary judgment after conducting a limited amount of pretrial discovery, and the District Court denied the

motion but certified for interlocutory appeal the
question of whether the foundations' membership
agreements, which contained the promise to abide
by maximum fee schedules, are illegal per se under
§ 1 of the Sherman Act. The United States Court of
Appeals for the Ninth Circuit affirmed the District
Court's order refusing to enter partial summary
judgment, holding that the question could not be
answered without evaluating the actual purpose and
effect of the agreement at a full trial (643 F2d 553).

On certiorari, the United States Supreme Court
reversed. In an opinion by STEVENS, J., joined by
BRENNAN, WHITE, and MARSHALL, JJ., it was held
that the maximum fee agreements, as price-fixing
agreements, are per se unlawful under § 1 of the
Sherman Act, (1) the agreements not escaping per
se condemnation because they were horizontal and
fix maximum prices since horizontal agreements to
fix maximum prices are placed on the same legal
footing as agreements to fix minimum or uniform
prices, (2) the fact that doctors—rather than non-
professionals—were the parties to the price-fixing
agreement not precluding application of the per se
rule as the price-fixing agreements are not premised
on public service or ethical norms, (3) the fact that
the judiciary has had little antitrust experience in
the health care industry being insufficient reason for
not applying the per se rule, (4) the per se rule not
being inapplicable because the agreements were
alleged to have procompetitive justifications as the
anticompetitive potential inherent in all price-fixing
agreements justifies their facial invalidation even if
procompetitive justifications are offered for some,
and (5) the maximum-fee schedules not involving
price-fixing in only a literal sense since as agree-

ments among independent competing enterpreneurs, the agreements fit squarely into the horizontal price-fixing mold.

POWELL, J., joined by BURGER, Ch. J., and REHNQUIST, J., dissented, expressing the view that a decision on an incomplete record was not consistent with proper judicial resolution of an issue of this complexity, novelty, and importance to the public.

BLACKMUN and O'CONNOR, JJ., did not participate.

COUNSEL

Kenneth R. Reed argued the cause for petitioner.

Stephen M. Shapiro argued the cause for the United States, as amicus curiae, by special leave of Court.

Philip P. Berelson argued the cause for respondents.

UNITED STATES, Petitioner

v

LEARLEY REED GOODWIN

— US —, 73 L Ed 2d 74, 102 S Ct —

Argued April 21, 1982.

Decided June 18, 1982.

Decision: Fact that defendant was charged with
felony after refusing to plead guilty to misdemeanor charges, held not to warrant presumption of prosecutorial vindictiveness in violation
of due process.

SUMMARY

An individual charged with several federal misdemeanor and petty offenses at first expressed a desire
to engage in plea bargaining regarding these
charges. However, the defendant later refused to
plead guilty to the charges and instead requested a
jury trial. The government prosecutor thereupon
sought and received an indictment including one
felony count arising out of the same facts which
constituted the lesser offenses. The jury convicted
the defendant in the United States District Court for
the District of Maryland on the felony count. The
defendant then moved to set aside the verdict on
the ground of prosecutorial vindictiveness, contending that the felony indictment gave rise to an impermissible appearance of retaliation. The District
Court denied the motion, finding that the prosecutor had dispelled adequately any appearance of
retaliatory intent. The United States Court of Ap-

peals for the Fourth Circuit reversed, holding that although there was no actual vindictiveness the due process clause prohibits the government from bringing more serious charges against a defendant after he has involved his right to a jury trial, unless the prosecutor comes forward with objective evidence to show that the increased charges could not have been brought before the defendant exercised his rights (637 F2d 250).

On certiorari, the United States Supreme Court reversed and remanded. In an opinion by STEVENS, J., joined by BURGER, Ch. J., and WHITE, POWELL, REHNQUIST, and O'CONNOR, JJ., it was held that the presumption of prosecutorial vindictiveness was not warranted in this case and absent such a presumption no violation of the due process clause of the Fifth Amendment was established, since the presumption of an improper vindictive motive is applicable only where a reasonable likelihood of vindictiveness exists, a change in the prosecutor's charging decision made before trial is less likely to be improperly motivated than were such a decision made after an initial trial, the mere fact that the defendant refused to plead guilty and forced the government to prove its case was insufficient to warrant a presumption that subsequent changes in the charging decision were vindictive, and the fact that the defendant requested a jury trial did not compel a special presumption of prosecutorial vindictiveness.

BLACKMUN, J., concurring in the judgment, expressed the view that a realistic likelihood of vindictiveness arose in this case but that the prosecutor had overcome the presumption by explaining that he was unaware of objective information supporting the increased charge at the time the charges were initially filed.

BRENNAN, J., joined by MARSHALL, J., dissented, expressing the view that the facts of the case easily supported the inference of a realistic likelihood of vindictiveness.

COUNSEL

Andrew L. Frey argued the cause for petitioner.
Paul W. Spence argued the cause for respondent.

CALIFORNIA, et al., Appellants

v

GRACE BRETHREN CHURCH et al. (No. 81–31)

———

UNITED STATES, et al., Appellants

v

GRACE BRETHREN CHURCH et al. (No. 81–228)

———

GRACE BRETHREN CHURCH, et al., Appellants

v

UNITED STATES et al. (No. 81–455)

— US —, 73 L Ed 2d 93, 102 S Ct —

Argued March 30, 1982.
Decided June 18, 1982.

Decision: Tax Injunction Act (28 USCS § 1341), held to bar federal court jurisdiction to declare state tax unconstitutional.

SUMMARY

A number of California churches and religious schools sued the State of California and the Secretary of Labor in a state court and in the United States District Court for the Central District of California, to which the state case was removed and in which it was consolidated with the federal case for trial, challenging the constitutionality of a co-operative federal-state scheme of unemployment compensation which failed to exclude religious schools unaffiliated with any church. The District Court held the corresponding state statute unconstitutional and ruled that constitutional considerations barred application of the scheme to the unaffiliated schools, that the Tax Injunction Act (28 USCS § 1341) was no bar to its issuing injunctive relief inasmuch as state court relief was uncertain, and that the taxpayers could apply for injunctive relief against the Secretary of Labor if he should institute decertification proceedings against the state for failure to collect taxes on behalf of the taxpayers' employees.

On direct appeal, the United States Supreme Court vacated and remanded. In an opinion by O'Connor, J., joined by BURGER, Ch.J., and BRENNAN, WHITE, MARSHALL, POWELL, and REHNQUIST, JJ., it was held that (1) the Supreme Court had jurisdiction of the appeal, under 28 USCS § 1252, since the effect of the lower court's several opinions and orders was to make the Secretary of Labor bound by a holding of unconstitutionality, (2) the Tax Injunction Act deprived the District Court of jurisdiction to grant injunctive or declaratory relief, since the taxpayers had a plain, speedy and efficient state court remedy, and (3) the Supreme Court could not reach the taxpayers' constitutional claims, because no federal trial court had jurisdiction of the case.

STEVENS, J., joined by BLACKMUN, J., dissented, expressing the view that the Tax Injunction Act does not necessarily preclude declaratory relief in tax cases.

COUNSEL

Harriet S. Shapiro argued the cause for the United States, et al.

Jeffrey M. Vesely argued the cause for the State of California, et al.

William B. Ball argued the cause for Grace Brethren Church, et al.

MIDDLESEX COUNTY ETHICS COMMITTEE,
etc., Petitioner

v

GARDEN STATE BAR ASSOCIATION, et al.

—US —, 73 L Ed 2d 116, 102 S Ct—

Argued March 31, 1982.
Decided June 21, 1982.

Decision: Federal court abstention from considering
challenge to constitutionality of attorney disciplinary rules that were subject of pending state
disciplinary proceeding within jurisdiction of
New Jersey Supreme Court, held required.

SUMMARY

A local attorney ethics committee, appointed by
the New Jersey Supreme Court, served a formal
statement of charges on an attorney, alleging violations of certain disciplinary rules because of the
attorney's public statements criticizing a criminal
trial and a trial judge. Instead of filing an answer to
the charges in accordance with state bar disciplinary
procedures, the attorney and three organizations
filed suit in the United States District Court for the
District of New Jersey, contending that the disciplinary rules violated the plaintiffs' First Amendment
rights and were facially vague and overbroad. The
District Court granted the ethics committee's motion to dismiss, concluding that the principles of
comity and federalism dictated that the federal court
abstain and afford the state the opportunity to
interpret its rules in the face of a constitutional

challenge. The District Court reopened the case to allow the attorney and the other plaintiffs an opportunity to establish bad faith, harassment, or other extraordinary circumstances which would constitute an exception to the Younger abstention doctrine, but the District Court found no evidence to justify such an exception, and dismissed the federal court complaint. The United States Court of Appeals for the Third Circuit reversed on the ground that the state bar disciplinary proceedings did not provide a meaningful opportunity to adjudicate constitutional claims, the disciplinary proceedings being viewed by the Court of Appeals as different from the state judicial proceedings to which federal courts usually defer (643 F2d 119). On reconsideration, the Court of Appeals declined to alter its original decision, despite an affidavit from the clerk of the Supreme Court of New Jersey stating that the Supreme Court of New Jersey would directly consider the attorney's constitutional challenges and that the court would consider whether such a procedure should be made explicit in the court's rules (651 F2d 154). Pending review in the United States Supreme Court, the Supreme Court of New Jersey heard oral arguments on the constitutional challenges presented by the attorney and adopted a rule allowing for an aggrieved party in a disciplinary hearing to seek interlocutory review of a constitutional challenge to the proceedings.

On certiorari, the United States Supreme Court reversed and remanded. In an opinion by BURGER, Ch. J., joined by WHITE, POWELL, REHNQUIST, and O'CONNOR, JJ., it was held that the federal courts should abstain from considering the challenge to the constitutionality of the disciplinary rules that

358

were the subject of the pending state disciplinary proceeding within the jurisdiction of the Supreme Court of New Jersey, since (1) the state court considered its bar disciplinary proceedings as judicial in nature, (2) the state had an extremely important interest in maintaining and assuring the professional conduct of the attorneys it licenses, especially those involved in the administration of criminal justice, (3) the attorney had an opportunity to raise and have timely decided by a competent state tribunal the federal issues involved, and (4) no bad faith, harassment, or other exceptional circumstances dictated to the contrary.

BRENNAN, J., concurring in the judgment, expressed the view that (1) federal courts should show particular restraint before intruding into an ongoing disciplinary proceeding by a state court against a member of the state's bar, where there is an adequate opportunity to raise federal issues in that proceeding, and (2) the abstention doctrine applied by the court is in general inapplicable to civil proceedings.

MARSHALL, J., joined by BRENNAN, BLACKMUN, and STEVENS, JJ., concurred in the judgment, expressing the view that it was unclear whether, at the time the lower courts addressed the issue, there was an adequate opportunity in the state disciplinary proceedings to raise a constitutional challenge to the disciplinary rules, but that at the time of the United States Supreme Court's decision there were ongoing judicial proceedings in the Supreme Court of New Jersey in which the attorney had been given the opportunity to raise his constitutional challenges.

COUNSEL

Mary Ann Burgess argued the cause for petitioner.

Morton Stavis argued the cause for respondents.

CONNECTICUT, et al., Petitioners

v

WINNIE TEAL et al.

— US —, 73 L Ed 2d 130, 102 S Ct —

Argued March 29, 1982.
Decided June 21, 1982.

Decision: Prima facie case under 42 USCS § 2000e-2 in regard to test that bars promotion and disporportionately excludes blacks, held not precluded by nondiscriminatory "bottom line" result of employer's promotional process.

SUMMARY

Several black employees of a Connecticut state agency who were promoted provisionally to supervisors filed suit in the United States District Court for the District of Connecticut after they failed a written examination and were thereby excluded from the selection process for attaining permanent status as supervisors. They alleged that the state of Connecticut and certain state agencies and officials violated Title VII of the Civil Rights Act of 1964 (42 USCS § 2000e-2) by requiring as an absolute condition for consideration for promotion that applicants pass a written test that disproportionately excluded blacks and was not job related, the passing rate on the test for blacks being only 68 percent of the passing rate for whites. In the meantime, before trial, promotions were made from the eligibility list generated by the written examination, the overall result being that 22.9 percent of the black candidates and 13.5

361

percent of the white candidates were promoted. The District Court ruled that the "bottom line" percentages, more favorable to blacks than whites, precluded a finding of a Title VII violation. The United States Court of Appeals for the Second Circuit reversed, holding that the District Court erred in ruling that the examination results alone were insufficient to support a prima facie case of disparate impact in violation of Title VII (645 F2d 133).

On certiorari, the United States Supreme Court affirmed and remanded. In an opinion by BRENNAN, J., joined by WHITE, MARSHALL, BLACKMUN, and STEVENS, JJ., it was held that the nondiscriminatory "bottom line" results of the employer's selection process did not preclude the complainant employees from establishing a prima facie case of discrimination violative of Title VII nor did it provide the employer with a defense in such a case.

POWELL, J., joined by BURGER, Ch. J., REHNQUIST, J., and O'CONNOR, J., dissenting, expressed the view that when claims are made of disparate impact in violation of Title VII, the case can be decided only by reference to the impact of the total selection process upon the protected group.

COUNSEL

Bernard F. McGovern, Jr., argued the cause for petitioners.

Thomas W. Bucci argued the cause for respondents.

BLUE SHIELD OF VIRGINIA, et al., Petitioners

v

CAROL McCREADY

— US —, 73 L Ed 2d 149, 102 S Ct —

Argued March 24, 1982.
Decided June 21, 1982.

Decision: Health plan subscriber denied reimbursement for psychologist's fees, held to have standing to sue for conspiracy to exclude psychologists from psychotherapy market.

SUMMARY

A prepaid group health plan subscriber brought a private antitrust class action in the United States District Court for the Eastern District of Virginia against the plan and a psychiatric society, alleging an unlawful conspiracy to exclude and boycott clinical psychologists from receiving compensation under the plan, so as to restrain competition in the psychotherapy market, and further alleging that her claims for psychotherapy by a clinical psychologist were routinely denied because not billed through a physician. The District Court granted the defendants' motion to dismiss, on the grounds that the subscriber lacked standing to sue, and the United States Court of Appeals for the Fourth Circuit reversed (649 F2d 228).

On certiorari, the United States Supreme Court affirmed. In an opinion by BRENNAN, J., joined by WHITE, MARSHALL, BLACKMUN, and POWELL, JJ., it was held that the subscriber had suffered an injury

363

redressable under the antitrust laws because the harm to her was a necessary step in effecting the ends of the illegal conspiracy.

REHNQUIST, J., joined by BURGER, Ch. J., and O'CONNOR, J., dissented, stating that the subscriber lacked standing to sue because she did not suffer the type of harm which makes the challenged practice illegal.

STEVENS, J., dissented, expressing the view that the subscriber suffered no damages because she received psychological services presumably worth the payment made by her.

COUNSEL

Griffin B. Bell argued the cause for petitioners.

Warwick R. Furr, II argued the cause for respondent.

GEORGIA PATSY, Petitioner

v

BOARD OF REGENTS OF THE STATE OF
FLORIDA, etc.

— US —, 73 L Ed 2d 172, 102 S Ct —

Argued March 2, 1982.
Decided June 21, 1982.

Decision: Exhaustion of administrative remedies,
held not prerequisite to bringing action pursuant to 42 USCS § 1983.

SUMMARY

An employee filed an action in the United States
District Court for the Southern District of Florida
under 42 USCS § 1983 alleging that her employer, a
Florida university, had denied her employment opportunities solely on the basis of her race and sex.
The District Court granted the defendant Florida
Board of Regents' motion to dismiss because the
employee had not exhausted available administrative
remedies. On appeal, a panel of the United States
Court of Appeals for the Fifth Circuit reversed, and
remanded the case for further proceedings (612 F2d
946). The full Court of Appeals then granted the
Board's petition for rehearing and, vacating the
panel decision, held that a § 1983 plaintiff could be
required to exhaust administrative remedies if certain minimum conditions were met, and remanded
the case to the District Court to determine whether
exhaustion would be appropriate in the instant case
(634 F2d 900).

365

On certiorari, the United States Supreme Court reversed and remanded. In an opinion by MARSHALL, J., joined by BRENNAN, BLACKMUN, REHNQUIST, STEVENS, and O'CONNOR, JJ., and joined in pertinent part by WHITE, J., it was held that exhaustion of state administrative remedies is not a prerequisite to an action under 42 USCS § 1983, in view of the legislative history of § 1983 and of the Civil Rights of Institutionalized Persons Act (42 USCS § 1997e), which carves out a narrow exception to the general no-exhaustion rule to govern certain prisoner claims.

O'CONNOR, J., joined by REHNQUIST, J., concurred, expressing the view that considerations of sound policy suggest that a § 1983 plaintiff should be required to exhaust adequate state administrative remedies before filing his complaint, but that the court already had ruled that in the absence of additional congressional legislation, exhaustion of administrative remedies is not required in § 1983 actions.

WHITE, J., concurring in all but Part III-B of the court's opinion, expressed the view that (1) for nearly 20 years and on at least ten occasions, the Supreme Court had clearly held that no exhaustion of administrative remedies is required in a § 1983 suit, (2) the court had not previously misapprehended the meaning of the legislative history of § 1983 on the exhaustion issue, and (3) the court in the instant case unnecessarily and unwisely went further to find support for its holding, since the wisdom of a general no-exhaustion rule in § 1983 suits was not at issue when Congress enacted the Civil Rights of Institutionalized Persons Act.

366

POWELL, J., joined by BURGER, Ch. J., as to Part B of the opinion, dissenting, expressed the view that (1) the Eleventh Amendment and the principle of sovereign immunity barred the suit in the instant case, and (2) the requirement that plaintiffs exhaust available and adequate administrative remedies, subject to well-developed exceptions, is firmly established in virtually every area of law, and should apply to § 1983 actions where adequate state administrative remedies are available.

COUNSEL

Charles S. Sims argued the cause for petitioner.
Mitchell D. Franks argued the cause for respondent.

UNITED STATES, Petitioner

v

RAYMOND EUGENE JOHNSON

— US —, 73 L Ed 2d 202, 102 S Ct —

Argued February 24, 1982.
Decided June 21, 1982.

Decision: Rule of Payton v New York prohibiting warrantless, nonconsensual entry into suspect's home to make routine felony arrest, held to apply to case pending on direct appeal when Payton was decided.

SUMMARY

United States Secret Service agents arrested a suspect at his home without an arrest warrant. Before trial, the defendant sought to suppress his oral and written statements as fruits of an unlawful arrest not supported by probable cause. The United States District Court for the Central District of California found the arrest to be proper and admitted the evidence, and jury then convicted the defendant of a federal crime. The United States Court of Appeals for the Ninth Circuit affirmed the judgment of conviction. While the defendant's petition for rehearing was pending before the Court of Appeals, the United States Supreme Court decided Payton v New York (1980) 445 US 573, 63 L Ed 2d 639, 100 S Ct 1371, in which it was held that the Fourth Amendment prohibits the police from making a warrantless and nonconsensual entry into a suspect's home to make a routine felony arrest. The
368

Court of Appeals granted the defendant's petition for rehearing, withdrew its prior opinion, and on the strength of Payton v New York reversed the judgment of conviction (626 F2d 753). The government petitioned for rehearing, arguing that the principles of Payton should not apply retroactively to an arrest that had occurred before Payton was decided. The Court of Appeals disagreed, denied the petition for rehearing, and amended its opinion to clarify that Payton did apply retroactively.

On certiorari, the United States Supreme Court affirmed. In an opinion by BLACKMUN, J., joined by BRENNAN, MARSHALL, POWELL, and STEVENS, JJ., it was held that the rule announced in Payton v New York applies to a case which was pending on direct appeal when Payton was decided, Payton not having applied settled precedent to a new set of facts, not having announced an entirely new and unanticipated principle of law, nor having held either that the trial court lacked authority to convict the defendant nor that the Fourth Amendment immunized his conduct from punishment.

BRENNAN, J., concurring, expressed the view that the court's decision left undisturbed the court's retroactivity precedents as applied to convictions final at the time of decision.

WHITE, J., joined by BURGER, Ch. J., REHNQUIST, J., and O'CONNOR, J., dissenting, expressed the view that retroactive application of a new constitutional doctrine is appropriate when that doctrine's major purpose is to overcome an aspect of the criminal trial that substantially impairs its truth-finding function and so raises serious questions about the accuracy of guilty verdicts in past trials and that new extensions of the exclusionary rule do not serve this purpose and will not generally be applied retroactively, and that there was nothing extraordinary about the ruling in Payton to justify an exception to this general rule.

COUNSEL

Elliott Schulder argued the cause for petitioner.
John F. Walter argued the cause for respondent.

RICHARD S. SCHWEIKER, Secretary of Health
and Human Services, Appellant

v

GEORGE HOGAN, et al.

— US —, 73 L Ed 2d 227, 102 S Ct —

Argued March 24, 1982.
Decided June 21, 1982.

Decision: Medicaid eligibility provisions of Social
Security Act (42 USCS § 1396b(f)) as applied in
Massachusetts, held constitutional.

SUMMARY

A class of aged, blind, or disabled persons receiving Social Security benefits, themselves or through
their spouses, in an amount rendering them ineligible for Supplemental Security Income (SSI) benefits
or state supplementary benefits, brought suit in the
United States District Court for the District of Massachusetts, challenging the Medicaid eligibility rules
as applied in Massachusetts in that because they
must incur unreimbursable medical expenses before
they become eligible for Medicaid, they have less
income available for their non-medical needs than
SSI recipients. The District Court concluded that
this discrimination was irrational and that § 1903(f)
of the Social Security Act (42 USCS § 1396b(f)) was
unconstitutional (501 F Supp 1129).

On direct appeal, the United States Supreme
Court reversed and remanded. In an opinion by
STEVENS, J., expressing the unanimous view of the
court, it was held that the statute is constitutional,

371

as applied in Massachusetts, because the fact that the recipient of a government benefit may in some cases be better off after receiving the benefit than a wealthier person who did not qualify to receive it does not undermine the validity of the basis for determining eligibility.

COUNSEL

George W. Jones argued the cause for appellant, pro hac vice, by special leave of Court.

William H. Simon argued the cause for appellees.

JOHANN SCHMIDT and LELAND POLLARD, etc.,
Petitioners

v

OAKLAND UNIFIED SCHOOL DISTRICT et al.

— US —, 73 L Ed 2d 245, 102 S Ct —

Decided June 21, 1982.

Decision: Federal Court of Appeals' refusal to resolve pendent state-law claim in affirming affirmative action plan for contractors as constitutional, held abuse of discretion.

SUMMARY

A California statute requires school districts to
award any contracts for work involving more than
$12,000 to the lowest responsible bidder, and for
projects over $100,000, the Oakland, California,
school board requires that to be considered responsible, general contractors must use minority-owned
businesses for at least 25 percent of the dollar
amount of the total bid. Contractors which submitted the low bid for an advertised project but who
were disqualified under the school-board plan as not
being responsible, brought an action in Federal
District Court claiming damages and asserting that
the affirmative action plan violated not only the
Federal Constitution but state law. The District
Court upheld the plan on constitutional grounds,
and the United States Court of Appeals for the
Ninth Circuit affirmed the judgment, declining to
decide the state-law question—although acknowl-
edging that under one of its prior decisions, the

plan at issue might be invalid under state law—since it was a sensitive matter and the contractors could present it to the state courts.

Granting certiorari, the United States Supreme Court vacated and remanded. In a per curiam opinion expressing the unanimous view of the court, it was held that the Federal Court of Appeals abused its discretion in declining to resolve the pendent state law claim, since, if the plan was invalid under state law, the Court of Appeals need not have reached the federal constitutional issue.

———————

GLOBE NEWSPAPER COMPANY, Appellant

v

SUPERIOR COURT FOR THE COUNTY OF NORFOLK

— US —, 73 L Ed 2d 248, 102 S Ct —

Argued March 29, 1982.
Decided June 23, 1982.

Decision: State statute which requires, under all circumstances, exclusion of press and general public from courtroom during testimony of minor victim in sex-offense trial, held violative of First Amendment.

SUMMARY

A newspaper publisher in the Boston metropolitan area sought admission to the courtroom during a trial of a defendant charged with the rape of three minor girls, but the Massachusetts trial court ordered the exclusion of the press and public from the courtroom in reliance on a Massachusetts statute providing for exclusion of the general public from trials of specified sexual offenses involving a victim under the age of 18. The publisher challenged the exclusion order, and ultimately, after the trial had resulted in the defendant's acquittal, the Supreme Judicial Court of Massachusetts construed the Massachusetts statute as requiring, under all circumstances, the exclusion of the press and public during the testimony of a minor victim in a sex-offense trial (423 NE2d 773).

375

On appeal, the United States Supreme Court reversed. In an opinion by BRENNAN, J., joined by WHITE, MARSHALL, BLACKMUN, and POWELL, JJ., it was held that the Massachusetts statute, as construed by the Massachusetts Supreme Judicial Court, violated the First Amendment as applied to the states through the Fourteenth Amendment, and that the statute could not be justified on the basis of either the state's interest in protecting minor victims of sex crimes from further trauma and embarrassment or its interest in encouraging such victims to come forward and testify in a truthful and credible manner.

O'CONNOR, J., concurring, emphasized that the majority's decision carries no implications outside the context of criminal trials.

BURGER, Ch. J., joined by REHNQUIST, J., dissenting, expressed the view that the statute did not violate the First Amendment in light of a balancing of the competing interests of the media for instant access to a sex-offense trial against the interests of the state in protecting child rape victims from the trauma of public testimony.

STEVENS, J., dissenting, expressed the view that the appeal should have been dismissed because the challenged statute, as construed by the state's highest court, had never been applied in a live controversy, the governing state law being materially changed after the trial court's order had expired by its own terms.

COUNSEL

James F. McHugh, III, argued the cause for appellant.

Mitchell J. Sikora, Jr., argued the cause for appellee.

JAMES EDGAR, Appellant

v

MITE CORPORATION AND MITE HOLDINGS, INC.

— US —, 73 L Ed 2d 269, 102 S Ct —

Argued November 30, 1981.
Decided June 23, 1982.

Decision: Illinois business takeover statute, held unconstitutional under commerce clause (Art I, § 8, cl 3).

SUMMARY

A corporation which was organized under Delaware law and which had its principal office in Connecticut initiated a cash tender offer for all outstanding shares of an Illinois corporation by filing a certain schedule with the Securities and Exchange Commission in order to comply with the Williams Act (15 USCS §§ 78m(d)–(e) and 78n(d)–(f)). The corporation did not comply with the Illinois business takeover statute—which required that a takeover offer be registered with the Secretary of State if Illinois shareholder owned 10 percent or more of the target company and instead filed an action in the United States District Court for the Northern District of Illinois, asking for a declaratory judgment that the Illinois statute was preempted by the Williams Act and violated the commerce clause of the United States Constitution (Art I, § 8, cl 3). The corporation also sought a temporary restraining order and an injunction prohibiting the Illinois

Secretary of State from enforcing the Illinois statute. The District Court issued a preliminary injunction prohibiting enforcement of the statute against the tender offer, and the corporation then published its tender offer. Subsequently the District Court entered final judgment, declaring that the Illinois statute was preempted by the Williams Act and violated the commerce clause, and permanently enjoined enforcement of the statute against the corporation. The corporation and the target company then entered into an agreement whereby the corporation's tender offer and an offer made by the target company were withdrawn, under which agreement the corporation was either to make a tender offer at a certain price per share or decide not to acquire the target company. The corporation subsequently announced its decision not to make a tender offer. The United States Court of Appeals for the Seventh Circuit affirmed, agreeing with the District Court that several provisions of the Illinois statute were preempted by the Williams Act and that it unduly burdened interstate commerce in violation of the commerce clause (633 F2d 486).

On appeal, the United States Supreme Court affirmed. Although unable to agree on an opinion with respect to the preemption issue, five justices agreed that the Illinois statute violated the commerce clause. In an opinion (parts of which constituted the opinion of the court—Parts I, II, and V-B) by WHITE, J., joined by BURGER, Ch. J., and BLACKMUN (except for holding 2), POWELL (except for holding 1), STEVENS, and O'CONNOR, JJ., it was held that (1) the case was not moot, since the Illinois Secretary of State had indicated that he intended to enforce the Illinois statute against the corporation and since a reversal of the judgment of the District Court would thus expose the corporation to civil and criminal liability for making an offer in violation of the statutes, and (2) the Illinois statute imposed a substantial burden on interstate commerce which outweighed its putative local benefits, and thus was invalid under the commerce clause. WHITE, J., joined by BURGER, Ch. J., and BLACKMUN, J., also expressed the view that certain provisions of the Illinois statute were preempted by the Williams Act under the supremacy clause of the United States (Art VI, cl 2).

POWELL, J., concurring in part, expressed the view that the case was moot, but stated that in view of the decision of the majority of the court to reach the merits, he joined the court's commerce clause ruling because it left some room for state regulation of tender offers.

STEVENS, J., concurring in part and concurring in the judgment, stated that the United States Supreme Court had jurisdiction to consider whether the judgment and relief entered by the District Court were proper, and agreed with the court that the Illinois statute was invalid as a burden on interstate commerce.

O'CONNOR, J., concurring in part, expressed the view that (1) the case was not moot, (2) portions of the Illinois statute were invalid under the commerce clause, and (3) it was not necessary to reach the preemption issue.

MARSHALL, J., joined by Brennan, J., dissented, expressing the view that the case was moot, since even if the court had held the Illinois statute constitutional and had lifted the permanent injunction

380

restraining enforcement of the statute against the corporation, there would have been no basis for continued litigation.

REHNQUIST, J., dissenting, expressed the view that the case did not present a justiciable controversy, since the facts that gave rise to the instant controversy over the constitutionality of the anti-takeover statute no longer existed and it was unlikely that they would be repeated in the future.

COUNSEL

Russell C. Grimes, Jr., argued the cause for appellant.

Eugene D. Berman argued the cause for the State of New York as amicus curiae, by special leave of Court.

Richard W. Hulbert argued the cause for appellees.

Stephen M. Shapiro argued the cause for the SEC as amicus curiae, by special leave of Court.

FOREMOST INSURANCE COMPANY et al.,
Petitioners,

v

PANSY F. RICHARDSON et al.

— US —, 73 L Ed 2d 300, 102 S Ct —

Argued January 12, 1982.
Decided June 23, 1982.

Decision: Complaint alleging collision between two
pleasure boats on navigable waters, held to
state claim within federal admiralty jurisdiction.

SUMMARY

As a result of a collision of two pleasure boats on
the Amite River in Louisiana, causing the death of
one passenger, suit was brought in the United
States District Court for the Middle District of
Louisiana, alleging negligent operation of one boat
and predicating jurisdiction on admiralty jurisdiction
under 28 USCS § 1333(1). The District Court dismissed the complaint for lack of subject matter
jurisdiction because the collision did not involve any
commercial activity and therefore lacked the relationship with traditional maritime activity required
for admiralty jurisdiction (470 F Supp 699). The
United States Court of Appeals for the Fifth Circuit
reversed on the ground that two boats are engaged
in traditional maritime activity when a collision
between them occurs on navigable waters (641 F2d
314).

On certiorari, the United States Supreme Court
affirmed. In an opinion by MARSHALL, J., joined by
382

BRENNAN, WHITE, BLACKMUN, and STEVENS, JJ., it was held that although federal admiralty tort jurisdiction is limited by the requirement that the wrong must bear a significant relationship to traditional maritime activity, there is no requirement that the maritime activity be an exclusively commercial one, and a complaint alleging a collision between two vessels on navigable waters properly states a claim within federal admiralty jurisdiction.

POWELL, J., joined by BURGER, Ch. J., REHNQUIST, J., and O'CONNOR, J., dissented, stating that admiralty jurisdiction extends only to maritime commerce.

COUNSEL

Arthur H. Andrews argued the cause for petitioners.

Dorsey C. Martin, III argued the cause for respondents.

_____

OMAR TAYLOR, Petitioner

v

ALABAMA

— US —, 73 L Ed 2d 314, 102 S Ct —

Argued March 23, 1982.
Decided June 23, 1982.

Decision: Confession obtained through custodial interrogation after illegal arrest, held excluded where intervening events did not break causal connection between illegal arrest and confession.

SUMMARY

An individual was arrested, without a warrant, charged with robbing a grocery store, and given his Miranda warnings, after an informant's tip, which was insufficient to give the police probable cause, implicated him. At the police station, he was fingerprinted, readvised of his Miranda rights, questioned and placed in a line-up, in which the robbery victims were unable to identify him. Subsequently, the police told the suspect that his fingerprints matched those found at the scene of the crime, and after a short visit from his girlfriend and a male companion, he signed a waiver-of-rights form and a written confession, both of which were admitted to evidence. At trial, the defendant argued that his warrantless arrest was not supported by probable cause and that the confession must be suppressed as the fruit of this illegal arrest. The trial court overruled this objection and the accused was convicted. On appeal, the Alabama Court of Criminal Appeals reversed, holding that the confession should not have been admitted into evidence, but Supreme Court of Alabama reversed the Court of Criminal Appeals.

On certiorari, the United States Supreme Court reversed and remanded. In an opinion by MARSHALL, J., joined by BRENNAN, WHITE, BLACKMUN, and STEVENS, JJ., it was held that (1) a confession obtained through custodial interrogation, after an illegal arrest, should be excluded unless intervening events break the causal connection between the illegal arrest and the confession so that the confession is sufficiently an act of free will to purge the primary taint, and (2) there was no meaningful intervening event, and the defendant's confession was the fruit of his illegal arrest, where the state failed to explain how his five to ten minute visit with his girlfriend and a male companion, while he was in custody but before he confessed, and after which he immediately recanted his former statements that he knew nothing about the robbery and signed the confession, could possibly have contributed to his ability to consider carefully and objectively his options and to exercise his free will so as voluntarily to confess to the crime, and where the fact that the police did not physically abuse the suspect, or that the confession may have been voluntary for purposes of the Fifth Amendment—the defendant being given Miranda warnings three times—did not cure the illegality of the initial arrest.

O'CONNOR, J., joined by BURGER, Ch. J., POWELL, J., and REHNQUIST, J., dissenting, expressed the view that the defendant's confession was not proximately caused by his illegal arrest, but was the product of a decision based both on knowledge of his constitutional rights—Miranda warnings having been given to him three times—and on the discussion with his girlfriend and neighbor, which was initiated at his request after his Miranda warnings were given to him.

COUNSEL

Robert M. Beno argued the cause for petitioner.

Thomas R. Allison argued the cause for respondent.

———————

JACKSONVILLE BULK TERMINALS, INC. et al.,
Petitioners

v

INTERNATIONAL LONGSHOREMEN'S
ASSOCIATION et al.

— US —, 73 L Ed 2d 327, 102 S Ct 2673

Argued January 18, 1982.
Decided June 24, 1982.

Decision: Work stoppage to protest Soviet invasion
of Afghanistan, held subject to anti-injunction
provisions of Norris-LaGuardia Act (29 USCS
§§ 101 et seq.), and not enjoinable pending
arbitrator's decision as to whether strike violated collective-bargaining contract.

SUMMARY

Following President Carter's announcement that,
due to the Soviet Union's intervention in Afghanistan, certain trade with the Soviet Union would be
restricted, an international union announced that its
members would not handle any cargo bound to, or
coming from, the Soviet Union or carried on Russian ships. In accordance with the international
union's resolution, a local affiliate refused to load
certain chemicals, not included in the Presidential
embargo, bound for the Soviet Union aboard three
ships that arrived at a shipping terminal. In response to this work stoppage, the operator of the
shipping terminal, the manufacturer of the chemical,
and the parent corporation of both brought an
action in the United States District Court for the

387

Middle District of Florida pursuant to § 301(a) of the Labor Management Relations Act (29 USCS § 185(a)) against the international union, the local union, and its officers and agents, alleging that the union's work stoppage violated the collective-bargaining agreement between the union and the terminal operator and requesting a temporary restraining order and a preliminary injunction pending arbitration. The District Court ordered the union to process its grievance in accordance with the contractual grievance procedure and granted the employer's request for a preliminary injunction pending arbitration. The United States Court of Appeals for the Fifth Circuit affirmed the District Court's order to the extent that it required arbitration of the question whether the work stoppage violated the collective-bargaining agreement, but disagreed with the District Court's conclusion that the provisions of the Norris-LaGuardia Act (29 USCS §§ 101 et seq.) are inapplicable to politically motivated work stoppages and held that the employer was not entitled to an injunction pending arbitration because the underlying dispute was not arbitrable (626 F2d 455).

On certiorari, the United States Supreme Court affirmed. In an opinion by MARSHALL, J., joined by BRENNAN, WHITE, BLACKMUN, and REHNQUIST, JJ., it was held that (1) the anti-injunction provisions of the Norris-LaGuardia Act apply to an employer's action under § 301(a) of the Labor Management Relations Act to enforce the provisions of a collective-bargaining agreement allegedly violated by a union's work stoppage, such a case involving a "labor dispute" within the meaning of §§ 4(a) and 13(c) of the Norris-LaGuardia Act (29 USCS

§§ 104(a), 113(c)), even though the work stoppage is politically motivated, so that the employer was not entitled to an injunction pending arbitration in the instant case, the § 301 action having been brought with respect to the dispute over whether the no-strike pledge prohibited the work stoppage at issue, rather than with respect to the underlying political dispute triggering the work stoppage, and (2) the local union's work stoppage could not be enjoined pending an arbitrator's decision as to whether the strike violated the collective-bargaining agreement, since the underlying dispute to the work stoppage was not arbitrable under the agreement.

O'CONNOR, J., concurring in the judgment, expressed the view that the court correctly concluded that the case involved a labor dispute within the meaning of § 4 of the Norris-LaGuardia Act (29 USCS § 104) and correctly determined that under Buffalo Forge Company v United Steelworkers (1976) 428 US 397, 49 L Ed 2d 1022, 96 S Ct 3141, no injunction could issue pending arbitration because the underlying political dispute was not arbitrable under the collective bargaining agreement, and that unless the court was willing to overrule Buffalo Forge, the conclusion reached by the court was inescapable.

BURGER, Ch. J., joined by POWELL, J., dissented, expressing the view that there was no labor dispute under the Norris-LaGuardia Act in the case, since the dispute was a political dispute and had no relation to any controversy concerning terms or conditions of employment.

POWELL, J., dissenting, expressed the view that under the plain language of the collective-bargaining agreement of the parties, the strike should have been enjoined pending arbitration and that Buffalo Forge Company v United Steelworkers should be overruled, but so long as the court adheres to the analysis of Buffalo Forge, the dispute must be viewed as a political dispute outside the scope of the Norris-LaGuardia Act.

STEVENS, J., dissenting, cited the reasoning in Part I of the dissenting opinion of Burger, Ch. J., as well as the reasons stated in Part I of his own dissenting opinion in Buffalo Forge Company v United Steelworkers.

COUNSEL

Thomas P. Gies argued the cause for petitioners.

Ernest L. Mathews, Jr., argued the cause for respondents.

RICHARD NIXON, Petitioner

v

A. ERNEST FITZGERALD

— US —, 73 L Ed 2d 349, 102 S Ct 2690

Argued November 30, 1981.
Decided June 24, 1982.

Decision: President of the United States, held entitled to absolute immunity from damages liability predicated on his official acts.

SUMMARY

An individual lost his job as a management analyst with the Department of the Air Force. The
analyst complained to the Civil Service Commission,
alleging that his separation represented unlawful
retaliation for his truthful testimony before a congressional committee concerning cost overruns on a
certain airplane. The Commission found that the
analyst's dismissal had violated civil service regulations but that he had not suffered retaliation for his
congressional testimony. The analyst filed a suit for
damages in the United States District Court for the
District of Columbia against various Defense Department and White House officials. The District
Court dismissed the action as barred by the applicable statute of limitations (384 F Supp 688), and the
United States Court of Appeals for the District of
Columbia Circuit affirmed as to all but one defendant and remanded for further proceedings (553
F2d 220). The analyst filed an amended complaint,
in which for the first time he named former Presi-

dent Nixon as a defendant. The District Court held that the analyst had stated triable causes of action, and that the former President was not entitled to claim absolute presidential immunity. The former President took a collateral appeal of the immunity decision to the United States Court of Appeals for the District of Columbia Circuit, which dismissed summarily.

On certiorari, the United States Supreme Court reversed and remanded. In an opinion by POWELL, J., joined by BURGER, Ch. J., and REHNQUIST, STEVENS, and O'CONNOR, JJ., it was held that the former President was entitled to absolute immunity from damages liability predicated on his official acts, and that absolute presidential immunity from damages liability extends to all acts within the outer perimeter of the President's official responsibility.

BURGER, Ch. J., concurring, expressed the view that presidential immunity derives from and is mandated by the constitutional doctrine of separation of powers.

WHITE, J., joined by BRENNAN, MARSHALL, and BLACKMUN, JJ., dissenting, expressed the view that attaching absolute immunity to the office of the President, rather than to particular activities that the President might perform, places the President above the law, and is a reversion to the old notion that the King can do no wrong.

BLACKMUN, J., joined by BRENNAN and MARSHALL, JJ., dissenting, expressed the view that (1) the court left unanswered the unanswerable argument that no man, not even the President, is absolutely and fully above the law, and (2) the writ of certiorari should have been dismissed as having been improvidently granted in view of a settlement agreement entered into by the parties.

COUNSEL

Herbert J. Miller, Fr., argued the cause for petitioner.

John E. Nolan, Jr., argued the cause for respondents.

———————

BRYCE N. HARLOW and ALEXANDER P.
BUTTERFIELD, Petitioners

v

A. ERNEST FITZGERALD

— US —, 73 L Ed 2d 396, 102 S Ct 2727

Argued November 30, 1981.
Decided June 24, 1982.

Decision: Senior aides and advisers of President of
United States, held entitled to qualified immunity from civil damages suits insofar as their
conduct does not violate rights of which reasonable person would have known.

SUMMARY

A civilian employee of the Department of the Air
Force was terminated from his position. He instituted a suit for civil damages in the United States
District Court for the District of Columbia against
two senior aides and advisers of the President of the
United States, alleging that they participated in a
conspiracy to violate his constitutional and statutory
rights, and entered the conspiracy in their official
capacities, to effect his unlawful discharge. At the
conclusion of discovery, the supporting evidence
remained inferential, whereupon the aides moved
for summary judgment. In denying their motion, the
District Court also ruled that the aides were not
entitled to .absolute immunity. The aides appealed
the denial of their immunity defense to the United
States Court of Appeals for the District of Columbia, which dismissed the appeal.

On certiorari, the United States Supreme Court vacated and remanded. In an opinion by POWELL, J., joined by BRENNAN, WHITE, MARSHALL, BLACKMUN, REHNQUIST, STEVENS, and O'CONNOR, JJ., it was held that, in a suit for civil damages based upon their official acts, senior aides and advisers of the President of the United States are not entitled to a blanket protection of absolute immunity as an incident of their offices as Presidential aides either derivatively from the President's absolute immunity or from their special functions as Presidential aides, but are entitled to application of the qualified immunity standard that would permit the defeat of insubstantial claims without resort to trial, government officials performing discretionary functions generally being shielded from liability for civil damages insofar as their conduct does not violate clearly established statutory or constitutional rights of which a reasonable person would have known.

BRENNAN, J., joined by MARSHALL and BLACKMUN, JJ., concurred, expressing the view that, in suits for civil damages against public officials based upon their official acts, (1) some measure of discovery may sometimes be required to determine exactly what a public official defendant did know at the time of his actions, and (2) discovery of defendants' knowledge should be deferred by the trial judge pending decision of any motion of defendants for summary judgment on grounds that plaintiff cannot prove, as a threshold matter, that a violation of his constitutional rights actually occurred.

BRENNAN J., joined by WHITE, MARSHALL, and BLACKMUN, JJ., concurred, disassociating themselves from any implication in the court's opinion that

Nixon v Fitzgerald, —— US ——, 73 L Ed 2d ——, 102 S Ct ——, was correctly decided.

REHNQUIST, J., concurred, expressing the view that until such time as the majority is willing to re-examine its holding in Butz v Economou, 438 US 478, 57 L Ed 2d 895, 95 S Ct 2894, which he would join in with alacrity, he agrees that the court's opinion properly disposes of the issues presented.

BURGER, Ch. J., dissented, expressing the view that senior aides of the President of the United States have derivative absolute immunity from the President.

COUNSEL

Elliot L. Richardson argued the cause for petitioners.

John E. Nolan, Jr., argued the cause for respondent.

SHEILA RENDELL-BAKER, et al., Petitioners

v

SANDRA KOHN et al.

— US —, 73 L Ed 2d 418, 102 S Ct 2764

Argued April 19, 1982.
Decided June 25, 1982.

Decision: Private school whose income is derived primarily from public sources and which is regulated by public authorities, held not to have acted under color of state law for purposes of 42 USCS § 1983 when it discharged certain employees.

SUMMARY

Certain employees were discharged from a private school which specializes in dealing with troubled high school students referred to it by public school officials or by a state drug rehabilitation agency. Public funds account for at least 90 percent of the school's operating budget. The school has contracts with public school committees and with the state agency, and is subject to both state and local regulations. One of the discharged employees filed suit under 42 USCS § 1983 in the United States District Court for the District of Massachusetts, alleging that she had been discharged in violation of her constitutional rights. The District Court granted the school's motion for summary judgment, holding that the action of the school in discharging the employee could not be considered state action for purposes of § 1983. Five other discharged employ-

397

ees brought a separate suit under § 1983. In that suit a different judge of the same District Court held that the school had acted under color of state law, denied a motion to dismiss, and certified its order as immediately appealable pursuant to 28 USCS § 1292(b). The United States Court of Appeals for the First Circuit, consolidating the two actions, held that the District Court, in the action brought by the five employees, had erred in concluding that the school had acted under color of state law. The Court of Appeals affirmed the District Court's dismissal of the first employee's action, rejecting her claim that she was discharged under color of state law (641 F2d 14).

On certiorari, the United States Supreme Court affirmed. In an opinion by BURGER, Ch. J., joined by BLACKMUN, POWELL, REHNQUIST, STEVENS, and O'CONNOR, JJ., it was held that the private school did not act under color of state law when it discharged the employees, and therefore the employees did not state a claim for relief under 42 USCS § 1983, since (1) the decisions to discharge the employees were not compelled or even influenced by any state regulation, and (2) the school's fiscal relationship with the state was not different from that of many contractors performing services for the government, there being no "symbiotic relationship" between the school and the state.

WHITE, J., concurring in the judgment, expressed the view that the critical factor in the case was the absence of any allegation that the employment decision was itself based upon some rule of conduct or policy put forth by the state.

MARSHALL, J., joined by BRENNAN, J., dissented, expressing the view that the nexus between the school and the state was so substantial that the school's action had to be considered state action.

COUNSEL

Zachary R. Karol argued the cause for petitioners. Matthew H. Feinberg argued the cause for respondents.

———

BOARD OF EDUCATION, ISLAND TREES
UNION FREE SCHOOL DISTRICT NO. 26 et al.,
Petitioners

v

STEVEN A. PICO, by his next friend, FRANCES
PICO et al.

— US —, 73 L Ed 2d 435, 102 S Ct 2799

Argued March 2, 1982.
Decided June 25, 1982.

Decision: Federal District Court's entry of summary
judgment in case challenging local school
board's removal of library books as violative of
First Amendment, held erroneous where material issue of fact remained as to board's justifications.

SUMMARY

A local school board, characterizing a number of
books as "anti-American, anti-Christian, anti-Se-
mitic, and just plain filthy," directed their removal
from the libraries of a district high school and
junior high school. The board then appointed a
committee of parents and members of the school
staff to make recommendations about the books, but
it substantially rejected the committee's recommendations in deciding that nine books should be removed from elementary and secondary school libraries and from use in the curriculum. Several
students attending the junior high school and high
school brought an action under 42 USCS § 1983 in
the United States District Court for the Eastern
400

District of New York, alleging that the board's actions—taken because of offense to its social, political, and moral tastes—denied them their rights under the First Amendment and seeking declaratory and injunctive relief. The District Court granted summary judgment in favor of the board, finding that the board acted not on religious principles, but on its conservative education philosophy, in ordering the removal of the books and that, although the removal was content-based, there was no constitutional violation of the requisite magnitude (474 F Supp 387). The United States Court of Appeals for the Second Circuit reversed the judgment of the District Court and remanded the action for a trial on the students' allegations (638 F2d 404).

On certiorari, the United States Supreme Court affirmed. Although unable to agree on an opinion, five members of the court agreed that there was a material issue of fact that precluded summary judgment in favor of the school board.

BRENNAN, J., announced the judgment of the court and, in an opinion joined by MARSHALL and STEVENS, JJ., and joined in part (all except for statement 1 below) by BLACKMUN, J., expressed the view that (1) local school boards have broad discretion in the management of school affairs, but this discretion must be exercised in a manner that comports with the transcendent imperatives of the First Amendment, (2) the First Amendment rights of students may be directly and sharply implicated by the removal of books from the shelves of a school library, (3) local school boards may not remove books from school library shelves simply because they dislike the ideas contained in those books, and (4) the evidentiary materials that were before the

District Court, when construed most favorably to the students, raised a genuine issue of material fact as to whether the school board exceeded constitutional limitations in exercising its discretion to remove the books from the school libraries, such issue foreclosing summary judgment in favor of the school board.

BLACKMUN, J., concurring in part and concurring in the judgment, expressed the view that (1) school officials may not remove books for the purpose of restricting access to the political ideas or social perspectives discussed in them, when that action is motivated simply by the officials' disapproval of the ideas involved, and (2) this is a narrow principle, since school officials must be able to choose one book over another, without outside interference, when the first book is deemed more relevant to the curriculum, or better written, or when one of a host of other politically neutral reasons is present.

WHITE, J., concurring in the judgment, expressed the view that (1) the material issue of fact precluding summary judgment for the school board concerned the reasons underlying the school board's removal of the books, and (2) there was no necessity at this point to go further and issue a dissertation on the extent to which the First Amendment limits the discretion of a school board to remove books from a school library.

BURGER, Ch. J., joined by POWELL, REHNQUIST, and O'CONNOR, JJ., dissented, expressing the view that (1) in an attempt to deal with a problem in an area traditionally left to the states, a plurality of the court wrongly took the position that a school board's decision concerning what books are to be in the school library is subject to federal court review, (2) if the plurality's view were to become the law, the court would come perilously close to becoming a "super censor" of school board library decisions, and (3) the Constitution does not dictate that judges, rather than parents, teachers, and local school boards, must determine how the standards of morality and vulgarity are to be treated in the classroom.

POWELL, J., dissented, expressing the view that the states and locally elected school boards should have the responsibility for determining the educational policy of the public schools, school boards being uniquely local and democratic institutions.

REHNQUIST, J., joined by BURGER, Ch. J., and POWELL, J., dissented, expressing the view that (1) actions by the government as educator do not raise the same First Amendment concerns as actions by the government as sovereign, (2) a right to receive information, in the junior high school and high school setting, is wholly unsupported by the court's past decisions and is inconsistent with the necessarily selective process of elementary and secondary education, and (3) the statement in the plurality opinion that the Constitution does not permit the official suppression of ideas is not a useful analytical tool in solving difficult First Amendment problems.

O'CONNOR, J., dissented, expressing the view that (1) a school board can decide which books to discontinue or remove from the school library so long as it does not also interfere with the right of students to read the material and to discuss it, and (2) it is not the function of the courts to make the decisions that have been properly relegated to the elected members of school boards.

COUNSEL

George W. Lipp, Jr., argued the cause for petitioner.

Alan H. Levine argued the cause for respondents.

GILES M. LUGAR, Petitioner

v

EDMONDSON OIL COMPANY, INC. and
RONALD L. BARBOUR

— US —, 73 L Ed 2d 482, 102 S Ct 2744

Argued December 8, 1981.
Decided June 25, 1982.

Decision: Complaint against private creditor's prejudgment attachment, held to state cause of
action under 42 USCS § 1983 where state statute authorizing it is alleged to be procedurally
defective.

SUMMARY

A supplier of a lessee-operator of a truck stop
indebted to the supplier sued on the debt in state
court. Ancillary to that action and pursuant to state
law, the supplier sought prejudgment attachment of
certain of the operator's property. The prejudgment
attachment procedure required only that the creditor allege, in an ex parte petition, a belief that the
debtor was disposing of or might dispose of his
property in order to defeat his creditors. Acting
upon the petition, a clerk of the state court issued a
writ of attachment, which was then executed by the
county sheriff which effectively sequestered the
debtor's property, although it was left in his possession. Pursuant to the statute, a hearing on the
propriety of the attachment and levy was later conducted. Thirty-four days after the levy, a state trial
judge ordered the attachment dismissed because the

creditor had failed to establish the statutory grounds for attachment alleged in the petition. The debtor subsequently brought an action under 42 USCS § 1983 in the United States District Court for the Western District of Virginia against the creditor, alleging that in attaching his property the creditor had acted jointly with the state to deprive him of his property without due process of law. The District Court, construing the complaint as alleging a due process violation both from a misuse of the state procedure and from the statutory procedure itself, held that the alleged actions of the creditor did not constitute state action as required by the Fourteenth Amendment and that the complaint therefore did not state a claim upon which relief could be granted under § 1983. The United States Court of Appeals for the Fourth Circuit affirmed, holding that a private party acts under color of state law within the meaning of § 1983 only when there is a usurpation or corruption of official power by the private litigant or surrender of judicial power to the private litigant in such a way that the independence of the enforcing officer has been compromised to a significant degree (639 F2d 1058).

On certiorari, the United States Supreme Court affirmed in part, reversed in part, and remanded. In an opinion by WHITE, J., joined by BRENNAN, MARSHALL, BLACKMUN, and STEVENS JJ., it was held that (1) the constitutional requirements of due process apply to garnishment and prejudgment attachment procedures whenever state officers act jointly with a private creditor in securing the property in dispute and if the challenged conduct of the creditor constitutes state action, then that conduct is also action under color of state law and would support a suit under § 1983, and that (2) the allegation of the

406

creditor that deprivation of his property resulted from the creditor's misuse or abuse of state law did not state a cause of action under § 1983 but only challenged a private action, but the allegation that the deprivation of property resulted from a state statute that was procedurally defective under the due process clause stated a cause of action under 42 USCS § 1983 since the statutory scheme was a product of state action, as a private party's joint participation with state officials in the seizure of disputed property is sufficient to characterize that party as a "state actor" for purposes of the Fourteenth Amendment.

BURGER, Ch. J., dissenting, expressed the view that the inquiry for dealing with suits under § 1983 or suits brought pursuant to the Fourteenth Amendment is whether the claimed infringement of a federal right is fairly attributable to the state and, applying this standard, it cannot be said that the actions of the creditor here are fairly attributable to the state.

POWELL, J., joined by REHNQUIST and O'CONNOR, JJ., dissented, expressing the view that private "joint participants" with state officials do not themselves necessarily become state actors and, even when the inquiry is whether an action occured under color of law, the "joint participation" standard is not satisfied when a private citizen does no more than provoke a presumptively valid judicial process in pursuit only of legitimate private ends.

COUNSEL

Robert L. Morrison, Jr., argued the cause for petitioner.

James W. Haskins argued the cause for respondent.

———

WILLIAM P. CLEMENTS, JR., Governor of the
State of Texas, et al., Appellants

v

JOHN L. FASHING et al.

— US —, 73 L Ed 2d 508, 102 S Ct 2836

Argued January 12, 1982.
Decided June 25, 1982.

Decision: Provisions of Texas Constitution limiting
public official's ability to become candidate for
another public office, held not violative of First
Amendment or equal protection clause of Fourteenth Amendment.

SUMMARY

A section of the Texas Constitution provides that
no judge of any court, Secretary of State, Attorney
General, clerk of any court of record, or any person
holding a lucrative office under the United States,
Texas, or any foreign government shall during the
term for which he is elected or appointed be eligible
for the Texas legislature, such section being interpreted by the Texas courts to render an officeholder
ineligible for the legislature if his current term of
office will not expire until after the legislative term
to which he aspires begins. Another section of the
Texas Constitution provides that if any one of
certain specified state and county officers becomes a
candidate for any state or federal office other than
the office then held, at any time when the unexpired
term of the office then held shall exceed one year,
such candidacy shall constitute an automatic resig-

nation of the office then held. Four officeholders subject to the second provision brought suit in the United States District Court for the Western District of Texas, alleging that they were qualified under Texas law to be candidates for higher judicial office and that the reason they would not announce their candidacy was that such an announcement would constitute an automatic resignation from their current positions. One of the four officeholders also alleged that he could not become a candidate for the legislature because of the first provision. The other plaintiffs were 20 voters who alleged that they would vote for the officeholders if the officeholders were to become candidates. The District Court held that the two provisions denied the officeholders and voters equal protection (489 F Supp 471), and the United States Court of Appeals for the Fifth Circuit affirmed (631 F2d 731).

On appeal, the United States Supreme Court reversed. Although unable to agree on an opinion as to the equal protection issue, five members of the court agreed that the two sections of the Texas Constitution in question did not violate the First Amendment or the equal protection clause of the Fourteenth Amendment. In an opinion by REHNQUIST, J., part of which (Parts I, II, and V) constituted the opinion of the court, joined by BURGER, Ch. J., and POWELL, STEVENS, and O'CONNOR, JJ., it was held that the two sections of the Texas Constitution did not violate the First Amendment, since the state's interests were sufficient to warrant the de minimis interference with the officeholders' interests in candicacy and since the plaintiffs were elected state officeholders who contested restrictions on partisan political activity, the provisions in question
410

representing a far more limited restriction on political activity than the court had upheld with regard to civil servants. With regard to the equal protection issue, REHNQUIST, J., joined by BURGER, Ch. J., and POWELL and O'CONNOR, JJ., also expressed the view that (1) not all ballot access restrictions require heightened equal protection scrutiny, (2) the first provision discriminated neither on the basis of political affiliation nor on any factor not related to a candidate's qualifications to hold political office, and rested on a rational predicate, furthering the state's interests in maintaining the integrity of the state's Justices of the Peace, and (3) the second provision imposed even less burdens on candidacy then those imposed by the first provision, and did not serve the invidious purpose of denying access to the political process to identifiable classes of potential candidates.

STEVENS, J., concurring in part and concurring in the judgment, expressed the view that (1) the disparate treatment in the case was not inconsistent with any federal interest that was protected by the equal protection clause, and (2) with respect to the state action at issue, there was no federal requirement that the different classes be treated as though they were the same.

BRENNAN, J., joined by MARSHALL and BLACKMUN, JJ., and joined in part (as to 1 below) by White, J., dissenting, expressed the view that (1) neither of the two sections could survive even minimal equal protection scrutiny, and (2) the first section also violated the First Amendment, the section not being narrowly tailored to conform to the state's asserted interests and not furthering those interests in a meaningful way.

COUNSEL

James P. Allison argued the cause for appellants.
Raymond C. Caballero argued the cause for appellees.

BARBARA BLUM, Commissioner of the New York
State Department of Social Services, et al.,
Petitioners

v

WILLIAM YARETSKY et al.

— US —, 73 L Ed 2d 534, 102 S Ct 2777

Argued March 24, 1982.
Decided June 25, 1982.

Decision: Nursing homes' decisions to discharge or
transfer Medicaid patients to lower levels of
care, held not to involve state action for purposes of Fourteenth Amendment's due process
clause.

SUMMARY

As a participating state in the Medicaid program
established by Title XIX of the Social Security Act
(42 USCS §§ 1396 et seq.), New York provides
Medicaid assistance to eligible persons who receive
care in private nursing homes, which are designated
as either "skilled nursing facilities" (SNF's) or
"health related facilities" (HRF's), the latter providing less extensive, less expensive medical care than
the former. Nursing homes chosen by Medicaid
patients are directly reimbursed by the state for the
reasonable cost of health care services. Federal
regulations require each nursing home to establish a
utilization review committee (URC) of physicians
whose functions include periodically assessing
whether each patient is receiving the appropriate
level of care, and thus whether the patient's contin-

413

ued stay in the facility is justified. A New York nursing home's URC decided that two Medicaid patients did not need the care they were receiving in an SNF and should be transferred to a lower level of care in an HRF. New York City officials who administered the Medicaid program in the city were notified of this decision and prepared to reduce or terminate payments to the nursing home for the patients' care. Following administrative hearings, state officials affirmed the decision to discontinue benefits unless the patients accepted a transfer to an HRF providing a reduced level of care. The patients then brought suit in the United States District Court for the Southern District of New York, individually and on behalf of a class of Medicaid-eligible residents of New York nursing homes, alleging that the defendant state officials had not afforded them adequate notice of URC decisions or of their right to an administrative hearing, and claiming that these actions violated their rights under state and federal law, including the due process clause of the Fourteenth Amendment. The District Court certified a class and issued a preliminary injunction, and subsequently issued a pretrial order that identified a new claim raised by the patients that procedural safeguards should apply to URC decisions transfering a patient to a higher level of care as well as to a lower level of care. The District Court approved a consent judgment incorporating the relief previously awarded by the preliminary injunction, and later permanently enjoined the state officials, as well as all SNF's and HRF's in the state, from permitting or ordering the discharge of class members, or their transfer to a different level of care, without providing notice and a hearing. The United States Court of Appeals for the Second Circuit affirmed the

District Court's judgment in pertinent part, holding
that URC-initiated transfers from a lower level of
care to a higher one, and all discharges and transfers initiated by the nursing homes or attending
physicians, involved state action affecting constitutionally protected property and liberty interests (629
F2d 817).

On certiorari, the United States Supreme Court
reversed. In an opinion by REHNQUIST, J., joined by
BURGER, Ch. J., and BLACKMUN, POWELL, STEVENS,
and O'CONNOR, JJ., it was held that state action was
not established in the nursing homes' decisions to
discharge or transfer Medicaid patients to lower
levels of care, and therefore a violation of rights
secured by the Fourteenth Amendment was not
proven, even though the nursing homes were exten-
sively regulated by the state, the state responded to
the discharge or transfer decisions of the nursing
homes by adjusting the patients' Medicaid benefits,
the state required the completion of a certain form,
the state imposed penalties on nursing homes that
failed to discharge or transfer patients whose continued stay was inappropriate, the state subsidized
the operating and capital costs of the facilities, the
state paid the medical expenses of more than 90 per
cent of the patients in the facilities, and the state
licensed the facilities, the case involving decisions
ultimately turning on medical judgments made by
private parties according to professional standards
not established by the state, and the nursing homes
not performing a function that has traditionally
been the exclusive prerogative of the state.

WHITE, J., concurring in the judgment in an
opinion appearing in Rendell-Baker v Kohn, 73 L
Ed 2d, at page ——, supra, expressed the view that

to satisfy the state action requirement of the Fourteenth Amendment, the patients had to show that the transfer or discharge was made on the basis of some rule of decision for which the state was responsible, it not being enough to show that the state took certain actions in response to a private decision.

BRENNAN, J., joined by Marshall, J., dissented, expressing the view that the court failed to perceive the decisive involvement of the state in the private conduct challenged in the case.

COUNSEL

Judith A. Gordon argued the cause for petitioners.

John E. Kirklin argued the cause for respondents.

───────────

JOHN S. TOLL, President, University of Maryland
et al., Petitioners

v

JUAN CARLOS MORENO, et al.

458 US 1, 73 L Ed 2d 563, 102 S Ct —

Argued March 2, 1982.
Decided June 28, 1982.

Decision: State university's policy of denying in-
state status to domiciled nonimmigrant aliens
holding G-4 visas, held violative of supremacy
clause (Art VI, cl 2).

SUMMARY

A state-operated university granted preferential
treatment for purposes of tuition and fees to students with "in-state" status. Although citizens and
immigrant aliens could obtain in-state status upon a
showing of domicile within the state, nonimmigrant
aliens, even if domiciled, were not eligible for such
status. A number of university students who resided
with, and were financially dependent on, a parent
who was a nonimmigrant alien holding a "G-4" visa-
-issued to nonimmigrant aliens who are officers or
employees of certain international organizations described in 8 USCS § 1101(a)(15)(G)(iv), and to
members of their families—brought an action for
declaratory and injunctive relief against the university in the United States District Court for the
District of Maryland, contending that the university's policy violated various federal laws, including
the due process and equal protection clauses of the

417

Fourteenth Amendment and the supremacy clause of the Federal Constitution (Art VI, cl 2). During the course of the litigation, the university adopted a "clarifying resolution" concerning its in-state policy indicating that the university's policy, "insofar as it denies in-state status to nonimmigrant aliens, serves a number of substantial purposes and interests, whether or not it conforms to the generally or otherwise applicable definition of domicile." The District Court ultimately concluded that the revised in-state policy was constitutionally invalid, on grounds that the policy ran afoul of the equal protection clause and, alternatively, that the in-state policy violated the supremacy clause by encroaching upon Congress' prerogatives with respect to the regulation of immigration (489 F Supp 658), and the United States Court of Appeals for the Fourth Circuit affirmed (645 F2d 217).

On certiorari, the United States Supreme Court affirmed. In an opinion by BRENNAN, J., joined by WHITE, MARSHALL, BLACKMUN, POWELL, and STEVENS, JJ., it was held that the university's policy was invalid under the supremacy clause since, in light of Congress' decision in the Immigration and Nationality Act of 1952 (8 USCS §§ 1101 et seq.) to allow G-4 aliens to establish domicile in the United States, the state's decision to deny "in-state" status solely on account of the G-4 alien's immigration status amounted to an ancilliary "burden not contemplated by Congress" in admitting these aliens to the United States, and since, by imposing on undomiciled G-4 aliens higher tuition and fees than are imposed on other domiciliaries of the state, the university's policy frustrated the federal policies embodied in the special tax exemptions offered G-4 aliens by various treaties, international agreements, and federal statutes.

418

BLACKMUN, J., concurring in the judgment, expressed the view that the Supreme Court's decisions holding resident aliens to be a "suspect class" continue to be good law.

O'CONNOR, J., concurring in part and dissenting in part, expressed the view that a state may not charge out-of-state tuition to nonimmigrant aliens who, under federal law, are exempt from both state and federal taxes, and who are domiciled in the state, but that the supremacy clause does not prohibit the university from charging out-of-state tuition to those G-4 aliens who are exempted by federal law from federal taxes only and not from state taxation.

REHNQUIST, J., joined by BURGER, Ch J., dissenting, expressed the view that the court's actions are unjustified and unnecessary and its holding has the vice of foreclosing governmental autonomy in an area plainly within the state's judicial responsibilities —education—and acts, not in behalf of a disadvantaged minority, but at the behest of a group of individuals who have been accorded a status by the federal government superior to that of the average citizen, and in a case where the state has demonstrated, by virtue of its favorable treatment of resident aliens, that its policy is not the result of an invidious or irrational motive.

COUNSEL

Robert A. Zarnoch argued the cause for petitioners.

James R. Bieke argued the cause for respondents.

NORTHERN PIPELINE CONSTRUCTION CO.,
Appellant

v

MARATHON PIPE LINE COMPANY and UNITED
STATES (No. 81-150)

———

UNITED STATES, Appellant

v

MARATHON PIPE LINE CO. et al. (No. 81-546)

— US —, 73 L Ed 2d 598, 102 S Ct 2858

Argued April 27, 1982.
Decided June 28, 1982.

Decision: Bankruptcy Court's exercise of jurisdiction over state-law contract claims pursuant to 28 USCS § 1471, held violative of Article III.

SUMMARY

The Bankruptcy Act of 1978 (92 Stat 2549) established in each federal judicial district, as an adjunct to the Federal District Court for the District, a United States Bankruptcy Court whose judges are appointed to office for 14-year terms by the President, with the advice and consent of the Senate. The judges are subject to removal by the judicial council of the circuit on account of incompetence, misconduct, neglect of duty, or physical or mental disability, and their salaries are set by statute and are subject to adjustment. The Act grants the courts jurisdiction over all "civil proceedings arising under Title 11 or arising in or related to cases under Title
420

11" (28 USCS § 1471(b)). After a corporation filed a petition for reorganization in the United States Bankruptcy Court for the District of Minnesota, it filed in that court a suit against another corporation seeking damages for alleged breaches of contract and warranty, as well as for alleged misrepresentation, coercion, and duress. The defendant corporation sought dismissal of the suit, on the ground that the Act unconstitutionally conferred Article III judicial power upon judges who lacked life tenure and protection against salary diminution, but the bankruptcy judge denied the motion to dismiss. On appeal to the United States District Court for the District of Minnesota, the District Court entered an order granting the motion, on the ground that the delegation of authority in 28 USCS § 1471 to the bankruptcy judges to try cases otherwise relegated under the Constitution to Article III judges was unconstitutional (12 BR 946).

On direct appeal, the United States Supreme Court affirmed. Although unable to agree on an opinion, six members of the court agreed that the Bankruptcy Court's exercise of jurisdiction violated Article III of the United States Constitution, bankruptcy judges' tenure and salary protection not conforming to the requirements of Article III, and that this holding would apply prospectively only.

BRENNAN, J., announced the judgment of the court and in an opinion, joined by MARSHALL, BLACKMUN, and STEVENS, JJ., expressed the view that (1) the broad grant of jurisdiction to the Bankruptcy Courts contained in § 241(a) of the Bankruptcy Act of 1978 is unconstitutional, bankruptcy judges created by the Act not being Article III judges, Article III barring Congress from establishing under Article

I powers legislative courts to exercise jurisdiction over all matters arising under the bankruptcy laws, the establishment of such courts not falling within any of the historically recognized situations—courts of the territories of the United States or the District of Columbia, courts-martial, and courts created by Congress to adjudicate "public rights"—in which the general principle of independent adjudication commanded by Article III does not apply, nor there being any persuasive reason why the Bankruptcy Courts so established lie beyond the reach of Article III, and § 241(a) of the Bankruptcy Act having impermissibly removed most, if not all, of the essential attributes of judicial power from the Article III District Court and having vested those attributes in a non-Article III adjunct, which grant of jurisdiction cannot be sustained as an exercise of Congress' power to create adjuncts to Article III courts, and (2) the court's decision should apply only prospectively, since Congress' broad grant of judicial power to non-Article III bankruptcy judges presents an unprecedented question of interpretation of Article III, and retroactive application would not further the operation of the court's holding and would surely visit substantial injustice and hardship upon those litigants who relied upon the Act's vesting of jurisdiction in the Bankruptcy Courts.

REHNQUIST, J., joined by O'CONNOR, J., concurring in the judgment, expressed the view that so much of the Bankruptcy Act of 1978 as enables a Bankruptcy Court to entertain and decide the debtor corporation's lawsuit over the defendant corporation's objection should be held to be violative of Article III of the United States Constitution and that this grant of authority is not readily severable from the remaining grant of authority to Bankruptcy Courts under § 241(a), and agreed with the discussion of the plurality opinion respecting retroactivity and the staying of the court's judgment.

BURGER, Ch. J., dissenting, emphasized that, notwithstanding the plurality opinion, the court did not hold that Congress' broad grant of jurisdiction to the new bankruptcy courts is generally inconsistent with Article III of the Constitution, the court's holding being limited to the proposition that a traditional state common-law action, not made subject to a federal rule of decision, and related only peripherally to an adjudication of bankruptcy under federal law, must, absent the consent of the litigants, be heard by an Article III court if it is to be heard by any court or agency of the United States, and that it will not be necessary for Congress, in order to meet the requirements of the court's holding, to undertake a radical restruction of the present system of bankruptcy adjudication.

WHITE, J., joined by BURGER, Ch. J., and POWELL, J., dissenting, expressed the view that there was no basis for that part of the majority's argument that rests on the state-law character of the claim involved in the bankruptcy case, there was no difference in principle between the work that Congress may assign to an Article I court and that which the Constitution assigns to Article III courts, the inquiry focusing equally on the values furthered by Article III and asking whether and to what extent the legislative scheme accomodates them or, conversely, substantially undermines them, the burden on Article III values being then measured against the values Congress hopes to serve through the use of Article I courts, and that a scheme of Article I courts that provides for appellate review by Article III courts should be substantially less controversial than a legislative attempt entirely to avoid judicial review in a constitutional court and that as long as the proposed Article I courts are designed to deal with issues likely to be of little interest to the political branches, there being less reason to fear that such courts represent a dangerous accumulation of power in one of the political branches of government, and that the new Bankruptcy Courts established by the Bankruptcy Act of 1978 satisfied the standard, ample provision being made for appellate review by Article III courts, the Act not representing an attempt by the political branches of government to aggrandize themselves at the expense of the third branch or attempt to undermine the authority of constitutional courts in general, and the ends that Congress sought to accomplish by creating a system of non-Article III courts being at least as compelling as the ends found to be satisfactory in prior cases of the Supreme Court, or the ends that have traditionally justified the creation of legislative courts.

COUNSEL

Solicitor General Rex E. Lee argued the cause for the United States.

John L. Devney argued the cause for Northern Pipeline Construction Co.

Melvin I. Orenstein argued the cause for the Marathon Pipe Line Co.

UNION LABOR LIFE INSURANCE COMPANY, Petitioner

v

A. ALEXANDER PIRENO (No. 81–389)

— US —, 73 L Ed 2d 647, 102 S Ct —

Argued April 27, 1982.
Decided June 28, 1982.

Decision: Insurer use of peer review committee to determine reasonableness of chiropractor's fees, held not exempt from antitrust laws as "business of insurance" under McCarran-Ferguson Act (15 USCS § 1012(b)).

SUMMARY

A New York insurance company's health insurance policy covers certain policyholder claims for chiropractic treatment but certain of these policies limit the company's liability to "the reasonable charges" for "necessary medical care and services." Accordingly, when presented with a policyholder claim for reimbursement for chiropractic treatments, the insurance company must determine whether the treatments were necessary and whether the charges for them were reasonable. In making some of these determinations the company arranged with the New York chiropractic association to use the advice of the association's peer review committee. The committee was established by the association primarily to aid insurers in evaluating claims for chiropractic treatments and is composed of ten practicing chiropractors, who serve on a voluntary basis. On a number of occasions a certain chiropractor's treatments of the insurance company's policyholders, and his charges for those treatments, have been referred by the company to the committee, which sometimes concluded that his treatments were unnecessary or that his charges were unreasonable. The dispute over the charges deemed unreasonable resulted in the chiropractor bringing a suit in the United States District Court for the Southern District of New York, alleging that the peer review practices involved violated § 1 of the Sherman Act (15 USCS § 1). In particular, he claimed that the insurance company and others had used the peer review committee as the vehicle for a conspiracy to fix the prices that chiropractors would be permitted to charge for their services. After extensive discovery, the District Court dismissed the complaint, concluding that the insurance company's use of the peer review committee was exempted from antitrust scrutiny by the McCarran-Ferguson Act (15 USCS §§ 1011 et seq.), since the peer review practices constituted the "business of insurance" which was subject to an exemption under that Act. The United States Court of Appeals for the Second Circuit reversed, concluding that the District Court had erred in holding that the insurance company's use of the peer review committee constituted the "business of insurance" (650 F2d 387).

On certiorari, the United States Supreme Court affirmed. In an opinion by BRENNAN, J., joined by WHITE, MARSHALL, BLACKMUN, POWELL, and STEVENS, JJ., it was held that the alleged conspiracy was not exempt from federal antitrust law as part of the "business of insurance," since (1) the insurance company's use of the peer review committee played no part in the spreading and underwriting of a policyholder's risk, (2) the use of the peer review committee was not an integral part of the policy relationship between insurer and insured, and (3) although it could be assumed that the challenged peer review practices need not be denied the exemption under § 2(b) of the McCarran-Ferguson Act (15 USCS § 1012(b)), which operates so as to render the federal antitrust laws inapplicable to the "business of insurance" to the extent such business is regulated by state law, solely because they involved parties outside the insurance industry—namely the practicing chiropractors on the peer review committee—they could hardly be said to lie at the center of the Act's legislative concern and could prove contrary to the spirit as well as the letter of § 2(b), since they have the potential to restrain competition in non-insurance markets.

REHNQUIST, J., joined by BURGER, Ch. J., and O'CONNOR, J., dissenting, expressed the view that the claims adjustment function of the peer review committee is at the heart of the relationship between insurance companies and their policyholders and that, accordingly, such committees are clearly within the sphere of insurance activity which the McCarran-Ferguson Act intended to protect from the effect of the antitrust laws.

COUNSEL

T. Richard Kennedy argued the cause for petitioners.

Susan M. Jenkins argued the cause for respondent.

B. Barry Grossman argued the cause for the United States as amicus curiae, by special leave of Court.

————————

FIDELITY FEDERAL SAVINGS AND LOAN
ASSOCIATION, et al., Appellants

v

REGINALD D. de la CUESTA et al.

— US —, 73 L Ed 2d 664, 102 S Ct —

Argued April 28, 1982.
Decided June 28, 1982.

Decision: Federal Home Loan Bank Board regulation authorizing due-on-sale clauses in federal savings and loan instruments held to preempt state law.

SUMMARY

Purchasers of California real estate subject to deeds of trust issued by a federal savings and loan association, and containing due-on-sale clauses, sued the association in the Superior Court of California for Orange County for declaratory, injunctive, and damages relief against enforcement of the clauses. The Superior Court granted summary judgment against the purchasers, but the Court of Appeal for the Fourth Appellate District reversed on the ground that exercise of the clauses violated California's prohibition of unreasonable restraints on alienation (121 Cal App 3d 328, 175 Cal Rptr 467). The California Supreme Court denied a petition for review.

On appeal, the United States Supreme Court reversed. In an opinion by BLACKMUN, J., joined by BURGER, Ch. J., and BRENNAN, WHITE, MARSHALL, and O'CONNOR, JJ., it was held that the Home

Owners' Loan Act empowers the Federal Home Loan Bank Board to issue regulations authorizing due-on-sale clauses in the loan contracts of federal savings and loan associations, and that the regulation in question preempted conflicting state limitations on the due-on-sale practices of federal savings and loan associations.

O'CONNOR, J., while joining in the court's opinion, filed a concurring opinion emphasizing that the Federal Home Loan Bank Board cannot displace local laws, such as tax statutes and zoning ordinances, not directly related to savings and loan practices.

REHNQUIST, J., joined by STEVENS, J., dissented on the ground that the Home Owners' Loan Act does not empower the Federal Home Loan Bank Board to preempt state law as to due-on-sale clauses.

POWELL, J., did not participate.

COUNSEL

Ernest Leff argued the cause for appellants.

Stephen M. Shapiro argued the cause for FHLBB and FHLMC as amicus curiae, by special leave of Court.

Robert E. Boehmer argued the cause for appellees.

BOARD OF EDUCATION OF THE HENDRICK
HUDSON CENTRAL SCHOOL DISTRICT BD. OF
ED., WESTCHESTER COUNTY, et al., Petitioners

v

AMY ROWLEY, by her parents and natural
guardians, CLIFFORD and NANCY ROWLEY etc.

— US —, 73 L Ed 2d 690, 102 S Ct —

Argued March 23, 1982.
Decided June 28, 1982.

Decision: Deaf student held not entitled to sign-
language interpreter in public school classes,
under Education for All Handicapped Children
Act, where she was receiving adequate education and personalized instruction.

SUMMARY

A deaf student in a regular New York public
school sued local school officials in the United
States District Court for the Southern District of
New York, claiming that the administrators' denial
of a qualified sign-language interpreter in all of the
student's academic classes constituted a denial of
the "free appropriate public education" guaranteed
by the Education for All Handicapped Children Act
of 1975. The District Court ruled in her favor, and
the United States Court of Appeals for the Second
Circuit affirmed (632 F2d 945).

On certiorari, the United States Supreme Court
reversed and remanded. In an opinion by REHN-
QUIST, J., joined by BURGER, CH. J., and POWELL,
STEVENS, and O'CONNOR, JJ., it was held that a state

431

which receives federal funds to educate handicapped children need not provide a sign-language interpreter for a deaf student who is receiving an adequate education and personalized instruction and related services calculated by local school administrators to meet her educational needs.

BLACKMUN, J., concurred in the judgment on the ground that the student's program, as a whole, offered her an opportunity to understand and participate in the classroom that was substantially equal to that given her nonhandicapped classmates.

WHITE, J., joined by BRENNAN and MARSHALL, JJ., dissented on the ground that the Act intends to give handicapped children an educational opportunity commensurate with that given other children.

COUNSEL

Raymond G. Kuntz argued the cause for the petitioners.

Michael A. Chatoff argued the cause for the respondent.

Elliott Schulder argued the cause for the United States as amicus curiae, by special leave of Court.

FORD MOTOR COMPANY, Petitioner

v

EQUAL EMPLOYMENT OPPORTUNITY
COMMISSION

— US —, 73 L Ed 2d 721, 102 S Ct —

Argued April 20, 1982.
Decided June 28, 1982.

Decision: Employer's offer to discrimination claimant of job previously denied without offer of
retroactive seniority, held to toll continuing
accrual of backpay liability under 42 USCS
§ 2000e-5(g).

SUMMARY

Three women applied for jobs, for which they
were qualified, with an employer who did not hire
them but later filled three vacant positions with
men. One of the women filed a charge with the
Equal Employment Opportunity Commission, claiming that the employer had discriminated against her
because of her sex. About a year and one-half later,
the employer offered two of the women positions,
without seniority retroactive to their original application, which they refused. The Commission sued
the employer in the United States District Court for
the Western District of North Carolina, alleging that
the employer had violated Title VII of the Civil
Rights Act of 1964 (42 USCS §§ 2000e et seq.) by
refusing to hire the women. The District Court
found that the employer had discriminated against
the three women on the basis of their sex and

awarded them backpay from the time they were first denied employment until the time of the court order. The United States Court of Appeals for the Fourth Circuit affirmed the District Court's finding of unlawful discrimination as well as the court's award of backpay, suggesting that, had the employer promised retroactive seniority with its job offer, the offer would have cut off the employer's backpay liability (645 F2d 183).

On certiorari, the United States Supreme Court reversed and remanded. In an opinion by O'CON-NOR, J., joined by BURGER, Ch. J., and WHITE, POWELL, REHNQUIST and STEVENS, JJ., it was held that an employer charged with discrimination in hiring can toll the continuing accrual of backpay liability under § 706(g) of Title VII (42 USCS § 2000e-5(g)) by unconditionally offering the claimant the job previously denied, and need not offer seniority retroactive to the date of the alleged discrimination, since (1) such a rule well serves the objective of ending discrimination through voluntary compliance, for it gives an employer a strong incentive to hire the Title VII claimant, (2) an unemployed or underemployed claimant's statutory obligation to minimize damages under § 706(g) requires him or her to accept an unconditional job offer, even without retroactive seniority, (3) such a rule is consistent with the policy of full compensation when the claimant has had the good fortune to find a more attractive job than that offered by the employer charged with discrimination, because the availability of the better job terminates the ongoing ill effect of the latter's refusal to hire the claimant, (4) such a rule is consistent with Title VII's object of making injured claimants whole, in almost all circumstances, and (5) to require a retroactive seniority offer in addition to the unconditional job offer would threaten the interest of innocent incumbent employees by disrupting the established seniority hierarchy, with the attendant risk that an innocent employee would be unfairly laid off or disadvantaged because a Title VII claimant had been granted seniority.

BLACKMUN, J., joined by BRENNAN and MARSHALL, JJ., dissented, expressing the view that the court's rule provides employers who have engaged in unlawful hiring practices with a unilateral device to cut their backpay liability to the victims of their past discrimination and by so doing, the court not only supplants traditional Federal district court discretion to mold equitable relief, but also insures that the injured employees here will not be made whole for injury they indisputably have suffered.

COUNSEL

John R. Wester argued the cause for petitioner.

David A. Strauss argued the cause for respondent, pro hac vice, by special leave of Court.

MICHIGAN, Petitioner

v

LAMONT CHARLES THOMAS

— US —, 73 L Ed 2d 750, 102 S Ct —

Decided June 28, 1982.

Decision: Absence of "exigent circumstances," held not to preclude warrantless search of car conducted after police officers discovered contraband in justified inventory search of car.

SUMMARY

While an individual was the front-seat passenger in an automobile, the car was stopped for failing to signal a left turn. As two police officers approached the vehicle, they saw the individual bend forward so that his head was at or below the level of the dashboard. The officers then observed an open bottle of malt liquor standing upright on the floorboard between the individual's feet, and placed him under arrest for possession of open intoxicants in a motor vehicle. A truck was called to tow defendant's automobile, of which the defendant claimed ownership, and in searching the vehicle, pursuant to a departmental policy that impounded vehicles be searched prior to being towed, two bags of marijuana were found in the unlocked glove compartment, and a loaded revolver was found in a subsequent search of the air vent under the dashboard. The individual was subsequently convicted of possession of a concealed weapon. After the trial court denied a motion for a new trial on the basis of the
436

search, the Court of Appeals of Michigan reversed, holding that the warrantless search of the defendant's automobile violated the Fourth Amendment since there were no "exigent circumstances" justifying a warrantless search for contraband. (106 Mich App 601, 308 NW2d 170).

Granting certiorari, the United States Supreme Court reversed and remanded. In a per curiam opinion expressing the view of BURGER, Ch. J., and WHITE, BLACKMUN, POWELL, REHNQUIST, STEVENS, and O'CONNOR, JJ., it was held that the absence of "exigent circumstances" did not preclude the warrantless search of the rest of the car by the police officers when the officers were justified in conducting an inventory search of the car's glove compartment, which led to the discovery of the contraband.

BRENNAN and MARSHALL, JJ., would grant the petition for writ of certiorari and set the case for oral argument.

———————

UNITED STATES, Petitioner

v

HOLLYWOOD MOTOR CAR COMPANY, INC., et al.

— US —, 73 L Ed 2d 754, 102 S Ct —

Decided June 28, 1982.

Decision: Denial of motion to dismiss indictment on ground of prosecutorial vindictiveness, held not collateral order that can be appealed prior to judgment under 28 USCS § 1291.

SUMMARY

Certain individuals who were originally indicted in the Eastern District of Kentucky on two counts for violations of 18 USCS §§ 371 and 545 obtained a change of venue to the Central District of California. In the latter district the government secured a superseding indictment charging four new substantive counts of making false statements to Customs officers in violation of 18 USCS § 542, in addition to the two original counts. The government then obtained a voluntary dismissal of the original conspiracy count and two of the false statement counts. The defendants moved to dismiss the remaining counts on the ground that the superseding indictment manifested prosecutorial vindictiveness. The United States District Court for the Central District of California denied the defendants' motion, but stayed the commencement of the trial to permit an appeal. The United States Court of Appeals for the Ninth Circuit, ruling that the denial of a motion to
438

dismiss based on the ground of vindictive prosecution is immediately appealable as a final decision under 28 USCS § 1291, held that the defendants established a case of prosecutorial vindictiveness requiring dismissal of the superseding indictment (646 F2d 384).

Granting certiorari, the United States Supreme Court reversed. In a per curiam opinion expressing the view of BURGER, Ch. J., and WHITE, POWELL, REHNQUIST, STEVENS, and O'CONNOR, JJ., it was held that the denial of a motion to dismiss an indictment, when the motion is premised on a claim of prosecutorial vindictiveness, is not a collateral order that can be appealed prior to judgment under 28 USCS § 1291, a claim of prosecutorial vindictiveness not being one of a narrow group of claims which meet the test, under the collateral order doctrine, of being effectively unreviewable on appeal from a final judgment.

BLACKMUN, J., joined by BRENNAN and MARSHALL, JJ., dissented, expressing the view that (1) the substantial and controversial question raised in the case —whether an order denying a motion to dismiss based on prosecutorial vindictiveness is appealable before trial—did not lend itself to summary treatment, the issue not having been briefed or argued, and (2) the court's ruling was not compelled by the Supreme Court's prior cases and was not consistent with the clear weight of authority in the Courts of Appeals.

WILLIAM ARCHIE WILLIAMS, Petitioner

v

UNITED STATES

— US —, 73 L Ed 2d 767, 102 S Ct —

Argued April 20, 1982.
Decided June 29, 1982.

Decision: Deposit of bad check in federally insured bank, held not proscribed by 18 USCS § 1014.

SUMMARY

An individual embarked on a series of transactions that seemingly amounted to a case of "check kiting" between his accounts in federally insured banks, whereby he drew a check far in excess of his account balance in one bank, deposited it in his account in another bank, and then reversed the process between his accounts, thereby taking advantage of the several-day period required for the transmittal, processing, and payment of checks from accounts in different banks and receiving an interest-free loan for an extended period of time based on the provisional credit which the banks granted when the checks were deposited. He was convicted of violating 18 USCS § 1014—which makes it a crime to knowingly make any false statement, or willfully overvalue any property or security, for the purposes of influencing in any way the action of certain enumerated financial institutions—in the United States District Court for the Western District of Louisiana. The United States Court of Appeals for the Fifth Circuit affirmed (639 F2d 1311).

On certiorari, the United States Supreme Court reversed and remanded. In an opinion by BLACKMUN, J., joined by POWELL, REHNQUIST, STEVENS, and O'CONNOR, JJ., it was held that although the defendant deposited several checks that were not supported by sufficient funds, the deposit of a bad check in a federally insured bank is not proscribed by 18 USCS § 1014, since (1) that course of conduct does not involve the making of a false statement because a check is not a factual assertion at all, and therefore cannot be characterized as true or false, and (2) the defendant's actions cannot be regarded as overvaluing property or security, in that the face amounts of the checks were their values.

WHITE, J., joined by BRENNAN, J., dissented, expressing the view that it defies common sense and everyday practice to maintain, as the majority does, that a check carries with it no representation as to the drawer's account balance, and that if the majority really meant that the government failed to show that the defendant made a false statement or overvalued property or security, it would be unnecessary to explore the legislative history of 18 USCS § 1014 or to apply the rule of lenity.

MARSHALL, J., joined by BURGER, Ch. J., BRENNAN, J., and WHITE, J., dissented, expressing the view that the plain language of 18 USCS § 1014 covers the check kiting scheme practiced by the defendant, and nothing in the legislative history of the statute indicates that Congress intended to exclude this type of scheme from the coverage of the statute.

COUNSEL

Nickolas P. Chilivis argued the cause for petitioner.

Richard G. Wilkins argued the cause for respondent, pro hac vice, by special leave of Court.

ASARCO INCORPORATED, etc., Appellant,

v

IDAHO STATE TAX COMMISSION

— US —, 73 L Ed 2d 787, 102 S Ct —

Argued April 19, 1982.
Decided June 29, 1982.

Decision: Idaho's inclusion, within taxable income of nondomiciliary parent corporation doing business in state, of portion of intangible income parent receives from subsidiary having no other connection with state, held to violate due process.

SUMMARY

Idaho sought to levy corporate income taxes on a parent corporation which was incorporated in New Jersey and maintained its headquarters and commercial domicile in New York. The parent corporation's primary Idaho business was the operation of a silver mine. The case involved three types of intangible income—dividend payments, interest payments, and capital gains from the sale of stock—that the parent corporation received from subsidiary corporations having no other connection with Idaho. The Idaho State Tax Commission assessed tax deficiencies against the parent corporation. On the parent corporation's petition for review, the state district court upheld the Commission's unitized treatment of the subsidiaries but overruled the Commission's determination that the disputed dividends, interest, and capital gains constituted "business" income. The

Commission appealed to the Supreme Court of Idaho, which held that the trial court had erred by excluding from "business" income the parent corporation's receipt of dividends, interest, and capital gains as a result of its owning stock in the other corporations, and also held, in response to the parent corporation's constitutional arguments, that this tax treatment did not violate the commerce clause of the Federal Constitution (Art I, § 8, cl 3) or the due process clause of the Fourteenth Amendment (99 Idaho 924, 592 P2d 39). The United States Supreme Court vacated and remanded the case for reconsideration in light of an earlier decision of the United States Supreme Court, and the Supreme Court of Idaho then reinstated its previous opinion.

On appeal, the United States Supreme Court reversed. In an opinion by POWELL, J., joined by BURGER, Ch. J., and BRENNAN, WHITE, MARSHALL, and STEVENS, JJ., it was held that Idaho's inclusion, within the taxable income of the nondomiciliary parent corporation, of a portion of intangible income—dividend payments, interest payments, and capital gains from the sale of stock—that the parent received from subsidiary corporations having no other connection with Idaho violated the due process clause of the Fourteenth Amendment, the parent corporation having proven that the subsidiaries were not part of the parent corporation's unitary business but rather were discrete business enterprises.

BURGER, Ch. J., concurring, expressed the view that the court's holding did not preclude future congressional action in this area.

O'CONNOR, J., joined by BLACKMUN and REHNQUIST, JJ., dissented, expressing the view that (1)
444

without a well-founded constitutional mandate, the
court had straightjacketed the states' ability to develop fair systems of apportionment, and (2) the
court's error was compounded by its decision to
invoke the due process clause despite the ready
availability of the commerce clause, since unlike a
commerce clause ruling, which is susceptible to
repair by Congress, the court's due process decision
might be beyond Congress' power to correct.

COUNSEL

George W. Beatty argued the cause for appellant.

Theodore V. Spangler, Jr., argued the cause for
appellee.

F.W. WOOLWORTH CO., Appellant

v

TAXATION AND REVENUE DEPARTMENT OF
THE STATE OF NEW MEXICO

— US —, 73 L Ed 2d 819, 102 S Ct —

Argued April 19, 1982.
Decided June 29, 1982.

Decision: New Mexico's taxation of portion of dividends that corporation received from foreign subsidiaries that do no business in state, held to violate due process clause.

SUMMARY

New Mexico sought to tax a portion of dividends that a parent corporation, whose principal place of business and commercial domicile were in New York, received from foreign subsidiaries that did no business in New Mexico. New Mexico also sought to include within the parent corporation's apportionable New Mexico income a sum, commonly known as "gross-up," that the parent corporation calculated in order to claim a foreign tax credit on its federal income tax. The New Mexico Taxation and Revenue Department denied the corporation's protest, but this decision was reversed on appeal by the New Mexico Court of Appeals, which excluded from the corporation's apportionable New Mexico income the sums in question (95 NM 542, 624 P2d 51). The Supreme Court of New Mexico reversed, holding in favor of the state (95 NM 519, 624 P2d 28).
446

On appeal, the United States Supreme Court reversed. In an opinion by POWELL, J., joined by BURGER, Ch. J., and BRENNAN, WHITE, MARSHALL, and STEVENS, JJ., it was held that (1) New Mexico's taxation of a portion of dividends that the corporation received from foreign subsidiaries violated the due process clause of the Fourteenth Amendment, since each of the foreign subsidiaries operated a discrete business enterprise with an absence of any umbrella of centralized management and controlled interaction, the parent corporation's operations not being functionally integrated with its subsidiaries, and the subsidiaries not being a part of a unitary business, and (2) New Mexico violated the due process clause when it included within the corporation's apportionable New Mexico income the "gross-up" that the corporation calculated, since the foreign tax credit arose from the taxation by foreign nations of the corporation's foreign subsidiaries that had no unitary business relationship with the state.

BURGER, Ch. J., concurring in an opinion appearing in ASARCO Inc. v Idaho State Tax Comm'n, 73 L Ed 2d, at page ——, supra, expressed the view that the court's holding did not preclude future congressional action in this area.

O'CONNOR, J., joined by BLACKMUN and REHNQUIST, JJ., dissented, stating that she disagreed with the court's redefinition of the limits of a unitary business, and that the parent corporation's subsidiaries were simply not unrelated, discrete business enterprises having nothing to do with the activities of the parent corporation in New Mexico.

COUNSEL

William L. Goldman argued the cause for appellant.

Sarah E. Bennett argued the cause for appellee.

GENERAL BUILDING CONTRACTORS
ASSOCIATION, INC., Petitioner

v

PENNSYLVANIA et al. (No. 81–280)

———

UNITED ENGINEERS & CONSTRUCTORS, INC.,
Petitioner

v

PENNSYLVANIA et al. (No. 81–330)

———

CONTRACTORS ASSOCIATION OF EASTERN
PENNSYLVANIA and UNITED CONTRACTORS
ASSOCIATION, Petitioners

v

PENNSYLVANIA et al. (No. 81–331)

———

GLASGOW, INC., Petitioner

v

PENNSYLVANIA et al. (No. 81–332)

———

BECHTEL POWER CORPORATION, Petitioner

v

PENNSYLVANIA et al. (No. 81–333)

— US —, 73 L Ed 2d 835, 102 S Ct —

Argued March 3, 1982.
Decided June 29, 1982.

Decision: Proof of intentional discrimination, held
necessary for liability under 42 USCS § 1981;
vicarious liability under § 1981 of employers

449

and trade associations for discriminatory conduct of union, held not supportable.

SUMMARY

The Commonwealth of Pennsylvania and a class of racial minorities who were skilled or sought work as operating engineers in the construction industry in eastern Pennsylvania and Delaware brought an action in the United States District Court for the Eastern District of Pennsylvania under a variety of federal civil rights statutes, including 42 USCS § 1981, seeking to redress racial discrimination in the operation of an exclusive hiring hall established in contracts between a union and construction industry employers. The plaintiffs also alleged discrimination in the operation of an apprenticeship program established by the union and several construction trade associations. The defendants were the union, the trade associations, an apprenticeship and training committee, and a class of approximately 1,400 construction industry employers. The District Court, although finding that the plaintiffs had failed to prove that the associations or employers, as a class, were actually aware of the union's discrimination and that the plaintiffs had failed to show intent to discriminate by the employers as a class, nevertheless held the employers and associations liable under § 1981 for the purpose of imposing an injunctive remedy (469 F Supp 329). The United States Court of Appeals for the Third Circuit affirmed (648 F2d 923).

On certiorari, the United States Supreme Court reversed and remanded. In an opinion by REHN-

QUIST, J., joined by BURGER, Ch. J., and WHITE, BLACKMUN, POWELL, and O'CONNOR, JJ., and joined in part (all but holding 1 below) by STEVENS, J., it was held that (1) 42 USCS § 1981 can be violated only by intentional discrimination, the fact that the prohibitions of § 1981 encompass private as well as governmental action not suggesting that the statute reaches more than purposeful discrimination, whether public or private, (2) liability could not be vicariously imposed upon the employers and associations for the union's discrimination in its operation of the hiring hall or for the discriminatory conduct of the apprenticeship and training committee, there being no relationship of principal and agent or master and servant, (3) § 1981 did not impose a "nondelegable duty" on the employers and associations to see that discrimination did not take place in the selection of their work force, the statute not making the employers and associations the guarantors of the workers' rights as against third parties, and (4) absent a supportable finding of liability, the District Court did not have power, under either its traditional equitable authority or the All Writs Act (28 USCS § 1651(a)), to require the employers or associations to aid either in paying for the cost of a remedial program as a whole or in establishing and administering a training program, and did not have power to impose minority hiring quotas directly upon the employers and associations.

O'CONNOR, J., joined by BLACKMUN, J., concurring, expressed the view that (1) on remand nothing in the court's opinion would prevent the plaintiffs from litigating the question of the employers' liability under § 1981 by attempting to prove the traditional elements of respondeat superior, and (2) under appropriate circumstances some reports properly could be required of the employers to aid the court by charting the changes resulting from the injunction imposed on the union and the apprenticeship and training committee.

STEVENS, J., concurred in part and concurred in the judgment, expressing agreement with the conclusion reached by the court regarding the necessity of proving intentional discrimination in a § 1981 action insofar as that conclusion related to the statutory protection of equal opportunity, but adding that he would reach a different conclusion in a case challenging a denial of a citizen's civil rights.

MARSHALL, J., joined by BRENNAN, J., dissenting, expressed the view that (1) proof of intentional discrimination should not be required in order to find a violation of § 1981, in view of Congress' broad remedial purposes in enacting the statute and the paramount national policy of eradicating racial discrimination and its pernicious effects, and (2) even if he agreed with the court that intent must be proved in a § 1981 action, he could not agree with its conclusion that the associations should be immunized, even from injunctive liability, for the intentional discrimination practiced by the union hall to which they delegated a major portion of their hiring decisions.

COUNSEL

John J. McAleese, Jr., argued the cause for petitioners in 81-330, et al.

John G. Kester argued the cause for petitioners in 81-280, et al.

Harold I. Goodman argued the cause for respondents.

———————

JEAN LORETTO, on behalf of herself and all
others similarly situated, Appellant

v

TELEPROMPTER MANHATTAN CATV CORP. et
al.

— US —, 73 L Ed 2d 868, 102 S Ct —

Argued March 30, 1982.
Decided June 30, 1982.

Decision: New York law requiring landlords to
allow cable television facilities on property, held
to be "taking" of property compensable under
Fifth and Fourteenth Amendments.

SUMMARY

The State of New York enacted legislation to
facilitate tenant access to cable television (CATV).
The law provides that a landlord may not "interfere
with the installation of cable television facilities
upon his property or premises," and may not demand payment from any tenant for permitting
CATV, or demand payment from any CATV company "in excess of any amount which the [State
Commission on Cable Television] shall, by regulation, determine to be reasonable." The Commission
ruled that a one-time $1 payment is a normal fee to
which a landlord is entitled. A landlord brought suit
against a cable television company which has the
exclusive franchise for certain areas of Manhattan
and which had installed cables on the landlord's
building—both "crossovers" for serving other buildings and "noncrossovers" serving the landlord's
454

tenants—before the landlord acquired the buidling, alleging that the company's installation was a trespass and, insofar as it relied on the state law, a taking without just compensation. The City of New York, which granted the company the franchise intervened. The New York Supreme Court, Special Term, granted summary judgment to the company and the City, upholding the constitutionality of the state law, (98 Misc 2d 944, 415 NYS2d 180), and the New York Supreme Court, Appellate Division, First Department, affirmed (73 Ad 2d 849, 422 NYS2d 550). On appeal, the Court of Appeals of New York upheld the statute, ruling that the law served a legitimate public police power purpose and stating that the regulation did not have an excessive economic impact upon a landlord when measured against her aggregate property rights, and that it did not interfere with any reasonable investment-backed expectation and, accordingly, did not work the taking of the landlord's property (53 NY2d 124, 423 NE2d 320).

On appeal, the United States Supreme Court reversed and remanded. In an opinion by MARSHALL, J., joined by BURGER, Ch. J., and POWELL, REHNQUIST, STEVENS and O'CONNOR, JJ., it was held that the minor but permanent physical occupation of the owner's property authorized by the state law constituted a "taking" of property for which just compensation is due under the Fifth and Fourteenth Amendments of the Constitution, since when the character of the governmental action is a permanent physical occupation of real property, there is a taking to the extent of the occupation without regard to whether the action achieves an important public benefit or has only minimal economic impact on the owner, the cable installation in question constituting a physical occupation and taking since the installation occupied portions of a landlord's roof inside of her building, there being no constitutional difference between a crossover and noncrossover installation.

BLACKMUN, J., joined by BRENNAN and WHITE, JJ., dissenting, expressed the view that the court erected a strained and untenable distinction between temporary physical invasions, which constitutionality concededly is subject to a balancing process, and permanent physical occupations, which are takings, and adopted an approach that is potentially dangerous as well as misguided.

COUNSEL

Michael S. Gruen argued the cause for appellants.
Erwin N. Griswold argued the cause for appellees.

WASHINGTON, et al., Appellants

v

SEATTLE SCHOOL DISTRICT NO. 1, et al.

— US —, 73 L Ed 2d 896, 102 S Ct —

Argued March 22, 1982.
Decided June 30, 1982.

Decision: State initiative precluding school boards
from requiring attendance at other than neighborhood schools, held unconstitutional.

SUMMARY

Three Washington State school districts sued the
State in the United States District Court for the
Western District of Washington, challenging the
validity under the equal protection clause of a state
initiative known as Initiative 350, which provided
that no school board should require any student to
attend a school other than the school geographically
nearest or next nearest the student's place of residence and which offered the course of study pur-
sued by the student. The District Court held Initiative 350 to be unconstitutional (473 F Supp 996),
and the United States Court of Appeals for the
Ninth Circuit affirmed (633 F2d 1338).

On appeal, the United States Supreme Court
affirmed. In an opinion by BLACKMUN, J., joined by
BRENNAN, WHITE, MARSHALL, and STEVENS, JJ., it was
held that Initiative 350 violated the equal protection
clause because it used the racial nature of the issue
to define the governmental decisionmaking struc-

457

ture, and thus imposed substantial and unique burdens on racial minorities.

POWELL, J., JOINED BY BURGER, CH. J., REHNQUIST and O'CONNOR, JJ., dissented on the ground that the Fourteenth Amendment leaves the states free to decide school policy at the state level.

COUNSEL

Kenneth O. Eikenberry argued the cause for appellants.

Michael W. Hoge argued the cause for appellees.

MARJORIE LEHMAN, etc., Petitioner

v

LYCOMING COUNTY CHILDREN'S SERVICES
AGENCY

— US —, 73 L Ed 2d 928, 102 S Ct —

Argued March 30, 1982.
Decided June 30, 1982.

Decision: Habeas corpus statute (28 USCS
§ 2254(a)), held not to confer jurisdiction on
federal courts to consider collateral challenges
to state court judgments involuntarily terminating parental rights.

SUMMARY

The natural mother of three sons voluntarily
placed them in the legal custody of a county agency,
which then placed the children in foster homes.
Subsequently, the agency initiated parental termination proceedings, and a state court declared that the
mother's parental rights respecting the three sons
were terminated. The Pennsylvania Supreme Court
affirmed the termination order (497 Pa 322, 383
A2d 1228), and the United States Supreme Court
denied a petition for certiorari (58 L Ed 2d 192).
The mother then sought a writ of habeas corpus
under 28 USCS 2254(a)—which requires federal
courts to entertain an application for a writ of
habeas corpus in behalf of the person in custody
pursuant to the judgment of a state court—in the
United States District Court for the Middle District
of Pennsylvania. The District Court dismissed the

459

petition, concluding that the custody maintained by
the mother over her three children is not the type
of custody to which the federal habeas corpus remedy may be addressed, and the United States Court
of Appeals for the Third Circuit affirmed (648 F2d
135).

On certiorari, the United States Supreme Court
affirmed. In an opinion by POWELL, J., joined by
BURGER, Ch. J., and WHITE, REHNQUIST, STEVENS,
and O'CONNOR, JJ., it was held that 28 USCS
§ 2254(a) does not confer federal court jurisdiction
to challenge the constitutionality of a state statute
under which a state has obtained custody of children and has terminated involuntarily the parental
rights of their natural parent, the petitioner's children not being "in custody" of the state in the
sense in which the term has been used in determining the availability of the writ of habeas corpus, and
suffering no unusual restraints not imposed on
other children, and federalism concerns and the
exceptional need for finality in child custody disputes arguing strongly against the grant of a writ, in
that the state's interest in finality is unusually strong
in child custody disputes, and that extended uncertainty over whether the child is to remain in his
current home, under the care of his parents or
foster parents, is detrimental to the child's sound
development and would be inevitable if federal
courts had jurisdiction to relitigate state custody
decisions.

BLACKMUN, J., joined by BRENNAN and MARSHALL,
JJ., dissented, expressing the view that (1) courts
traditionally have asserted the power to issue common-law habeas writs in child custody disputes, and
the codification of the writ into federal law indicates

no congressional intent to contract its common-law scope, (2) the majority restrictively interprets prior decisions to refer only to criminal detention, not civil detention, (3) minor children, who as state wards are fully subject to state court custody orders, are sufficiently restrained to be deemed in custody for purposes of the habeas corpus statute, (4) federalism concerns and the exceptional need for finality in child custody disputes do not deprive federal courts of statutory jurisdiction to entertain habeas petitions, and (5) the District Court could have found, as a discretionary matter, that the mother had not made a sufficient showing that she acted in the interests of the children to warrant issuing her the writ as their next friend.

COUNSEL

Martin Guggenheim argued the cause for petitioner.

Charles F. Greevy, III, argued the cause for respondent.

MARY ELLEN CRAWFORD, a minor, etc., et al.,
Petitioners

v

BOARD OF EDUCATION OF THE CITY OF LOS
ANGELES et al.,

— US —, 73 L Ed 2d 948, 102 S Ct —

Argued March 22, 1982.
Decided June 30, 1982.

Decision: State constitutional amendment precluding state court-ordered school busing absent Fourteenth Amendment violation held constitutional.

SUMMARY

During California state court school desegregation litigation in the Los Angeles Unified School District, California voters ratified Proposition I, which amended the state court constitution by forbidding state courts to order mandatory pupil assignment or transportation unless a federal court would do so to remedy a violation of the Fourteenth Amendment's equal protection clause. The District asked the Superior Court to halt all mandatory reassignment and busing of pupils, but the court refused and instead ordered implementation of a revised desegregation plan substantially relying on mandatory pupil reassignment and transportation. The California Court of Appeal reversed on the ground that Proposition I applied and is constitutional (113 Cal App 3d 633). The California Supreme Court denied a hearing.

On certiorari, the United States Supreme Court affirmed. In an opinion by POWELL, J., joined by BURGER, CH. J., and BRENNAN, WHITE, BLACKMUN, REHNQUIST, STEVENS, and O'CONNOR, JJ., it was held that Proposition I is constitutional as not employing a racial classification and simply forbidding state courts from ordering pupil school assignment or transportation in the absence of a Fourteenth Amendment violation.

BLACKMUN, J., joined by BRENNAN, J., joined in the court's opinion but also filed a concurring opinion distinguishing Washington v Seattle School District No. 1, supra.

MARSHALL, J., dissented on the ground that Proposition I is an unconstitutional limitation on state judicial power to order busing as a remedy for de facto segregation.

COUNSEL

Laurence H. Tribe argued the cause for petitioners.

G. William Shea argued the cause for respondents.

Solicitor General Rex E. Lee argued the cause for the United States as amicus curiae, by special leave of Court.

DANNY L. GRIFFIN, Petitioner

v

OCEANIC CONTRACTORS, INC.

— US —, 73 L Ed 2d 973, 102 S Ct —

Argued April 26, 1982.
Decided June 30, 1982.

Decision: Limiting period during which wage penalty for failure to pay seamen promptly after discharge is assessed under 46 USCS § 596, held not within discretion of Federal District Courts.

SUMMARY

A seaman signed an employment contract with a shipper in New Orleans, agreeing to work as a senior pipeline welder on board vessels operated by the shipper in the North Sea. The contract provided that the employer would pay for transportation to and from the work site, but that if the seaman quit the job prior to its termination date, or if his services were terminated for cause, he would be charged with the cost of transportation back to the United States. The employer reserved the right to withhold $137.50 from each of the seaman's first four paychecks as a cash deposit for the payment of return transportation in the event the seaman should become obligated for its payment. While working on deck of a vessel in Antwerp, Belgium, the seaman suffered an injury and, two days later, underwent emergency surgery. After being discharged from the hospital, the seaman went to the employer's Antwerp office, where he spoke with the welding superintendent, and provided a physician's statement that he was not fit for duty. The superintendent refused to acknowledge that the seaman's injury was work-related and denied that the employer was liable for medical and hospital expenses, maintenance, or unearned wages. The superintendent also refused to furnish transportation back to the United States, and continued to retain $412.50 in earned wages that had been deducted from the seaman's first three paychecks for that purpose. The seaman returned to his home in Houston, Texas, the next day at his own expense and a month later began working as a welder for another company operating in the North Sea, after being examined by a physician who determined that he would be able to resume work at that time. He later brought suit in the United States District Court for the Eastern District of Texas against the employer under the Jones Act (46 USCS § 688) and under general maritime law, seeking damages for the employer's failure to pay maintenance, cure, unearned wages, repatriation expenses, and the value of certain personal effects lost on board the employer's vessel. He also sought penalty wages under 46 USCS § 596— which requires certain masters and vessel owners to pay seaman promptly after their discharge and authorizes seaman to recover double wages for each day that payment is delayed without sufficient cause —for the employer's failure to pay over the $412.50 in earned wages allegedly due upon discharge. The District Court found for the seaman and found that the employer's failure to pay the seaman the $412.50 in earned wages was "without sufficient cause" under § 596, but, holding that the period during which the penalty runs is to be determined

465

by the sound discretion of the District Court, limited the appropriate period for imposition of the penalty from the date of discharge to the date of the seaman's re-employment. The United States Court of Appeals for the Fifth Circuit affirmed (664 F2d 36).

On certiorari, the United States Supreme Court reversed and remanded. In an opinion by REHNQUIST, J., joined by BURGER, Ch. J., and BRENNAN, WHITE, MARSHALL, POWELL, and O'CONNOR, JJ., it was held that District Courts have no discretion to limit the period during which the wage penalty is assessed under 46 USCS § 596, since (1) the statute in straightforward terms provides for the payment of double wages, (2) the legislative history of the statute indicates that Congress intended the statute to mean exactly what its plain language says, and (3) the literal interpretation of § 596 is not precluded on the asserted ground that it would produce an absurd and unjust result which Congress could not have intended as awards made under the statute were not intended to be merely compensatory and it is in the nature of punitive remedies to authorize awards that may be out of proportion to actual injury.

STEVENS, J., joined by BLACKMUN, J., dissented, expressing the view that the qualifying language in 46 USCS § 596 supports a much narrower construction than the court adopted and an 1898 amendment to this statute, removing the 10-day limit on the scope of the trial judge's discretion to award pay, was not intended to be read as a command to award the absurd result the court sanctions.

COUNSEL

Robert A. Chaffin argued the cause for petitioner. Theodore Goller argued the cause for respondent.

ALFRED L. SNAPP & SON, INC., et al., Petitioners

v

PUERTO RICO, ex rel., PEDRO BAREZ, Secretary
of Labor and Human Resources

— US —, 73 L Ed 2d 995, 102 S Ct —

Argued April 20, 1982.
Decided July 1, 1982.

Decision: Commonwealth of Puerto Rico held to
have standing to sue as parens patriae to enjoin
applegrowers' discrimination against Puerto Rican migrant farmworkers.

SUMMARY

The Commonwealth of Puerto Rico sued in the
United States District Court for the Western District
of Virginia, as parens patriae for Puerto Rican
migrant farmworkers, and against Virginia applegrowers, to enjoin discrimination against Puerto
Ricans in favor of Jamaican workers in violation of
the Wagner-Peyser Act (29 USCS §§ 49 et seq.), the
Immigration and Nationality Act of 1952 (8 USCS
§§ 1101 et seq.), and implementing federal regulations. The District Court dismissed on the grounds
that the Commonwealth lacked standing to sue (469
F Supp 928), but the Court of Appeals for the
Fourth Circuit reversed (632 F2d 365).

On certiorari, the United States Supreme Court
affirmed. In an opinion by WHITE, J., joined by
BURGER, CH. J., and BRENNAN, MARSHALL, BLACK-
MUN, REHNQUIST, STEVENS, and O'CONNOR, JJ., it
was held that Puerto Rico has a claim to represent
468

its quasi-sovereign interests in federal court at least as strong as that of any state, and that it had parens patriae standing to sue to secure its residents from the harmful effects of discrimination and to obtain full and equal participation in the federal employment service scheme established pursuant to the Wagner-Peyser Act and the Immigration and Nationality Act of 1952.

BRENNAN, J., joined by MARSHALL, BLACKMUN, and STEVENS, JJ., joined in the court's opinion but also filed a concurring opinion emphasizing a state's prerogative to vindicate the federal rights of its citizens.

POWELL, J., did not participate.

COUNSEL

Thomas J. Bacas argued the cause for petitioners.
Paul A. Lenzini argued the cause for respondent.

QUENTIN ROGERS, et al., Appellants

v

HERMAN LODGE et al.

— US —, 73 L Ed 2d 1012, 102 S Ct —

Argued February 23, 1982.
Decided July 1, 1982.

Decision: At-large election system for large rural county with large black population held violative of equal protection clause.

SUMMARY

Eight black citizens of Burke County, Georgia, brought a class action in the United States District Court for the Southern District of Georgia, alleging that the county's system of at-large election of the five county commissioners violated the constitutional and statutory rights of the county's black citizens by diluting their voting power. The District Court found that the at-large system was being maintained for discriminatory purposes, and it ordered that the county be divided into five districts for the purpose of electing county commissioners. The Court of Appeals for the Fifth Circuit affirmed (639 F2d 1358).

On appeal, the United States Supreme Court affirmed. In an opinion by WHITE, J., joined by BURGER, CH. J., and BRENNAN, MARSHALL, BLACKMUN, and O'CONNOR, JJ., it was held that the doctrine of unconstitutional dilution of voting rights arising from an at-large election system applies to counties, that the evidence supported the District

Court's finding of intentional discrimination, and that the propriety of the remedy would not be considered because it was not questioned in the Court of Appeals.

POWELL, J., joined by REHNQUIST, J., dissented on the ground that discriminatory intent must be proved primarily by objective evidence.

STEVENS, J., dissented on the ground that subjective intent is not a valid criterion for constitutional adjudication.

COUNSEL

E. Freeman Leverett argued the cause for appellants.

David F. Walbert argued the cause for appellees.

BAXTER RICE, Director, Department of Alcohol
Beverage Control of California, Petitioner

v

NORMAN WILLIAMS COMPANY et al. (No. 80–
1012)

———

BOHEMIAN DISTRIBUTING COMPANY,
Petitioner

v

NORMAN WILLIAMS COMPANY et al. (No. 80–
1030)

———

WINE & SPIRITS WHOLESALERS OF
CALIFORNIA, Petitioner

v

NORMAN WILLIAMS COMPANY et al. (80–1052)

— US —, 73 L Ed 2d 1042, 102 S Ct —

Argued April 21, 1982.
Decided July 1, 1982.

Decision: State alcoholic beverage control law enforcing distiller's designation of wholesaler,
held not per se violation of Sherman Act (15
USCS §§ 1 et seq.).

SUMMARY

California amended its alcoholic beverage control
laws to prohibit a licensed importer from purchasing or accepting delivery of any brand of distilled

472

spirits unless he is designated as an authorized importer of such brand by the brand owner or his authorized agent. It apparently enacted this "designation statute" in response to the effects of Oklahoma's alcoholic beverage laws which were understood to require any distiller or brand owner selling its products to Oklahoma wholesalers to sell to all wholesalers on a nondiscriminatory basis. Because of the perceived extraterritorial effect of Oklahoma's "open-wholesaling" statutes, a licensed California importer who was unable to obtain distilled spirits through the distiller's established distribution system could obtain them from Oklahoma wholesalers. As a result, a distiller who desired to sell its products to Oklahoma wholesalers was unable to rely on contractual undertakings to determine which California wholesalers would handle its products. California's designation statute, therefore, sought to close off the "Oklahoma connection" to California importers not authorized by the distiller to deal in its products. Prior to the effective date of the designation statute, liquor importers who were benefiting from the Oklahoma connection, brought suit in the Court of Appeal of California, Third District, to enjoin enforcement of the designation statute. The Court of Appeal agreed with the importers that the designation statute on its face conflicted with § 1 of the Sherman Act (15 USCS § 1) and concluded that the designation statute was preempted by the Sherman Act (108 Cal App 3d 348, 166 Cal Rptr 563). The Supreme Court of California denied review.

On certiorari, the United States Supreme Court reversed and remanded. In an opinion by REHNQUIST, J., joined by BURGER, Ch.J., and BRENNAN, MARSHALL, BLACKMUN, POWELL, and O'CONNOR, JJ., it was held that the California statute was not per se illegal under the Sherman Act and, accordingly, on its face, was not invalid pursuant to the supremacy clause of the United States Constitution (Art VI, cl 2), since the statute merely enforced a distiller's decision to restrain intrabrand competition and did not require the distiller to impose vertical restraints of any kind and did not limit the number of importers which may be designated by the distillers, any anticompetitive effect the statute might have when applied in concrete factual situations being insufficient to declare the statute itself void on its face.

STEVENS, J., joined by WHITE, J., concurred in the judgment, expressing the view that the price-fixing cases do not require the invalidation of the designation statute and the question on remand should be whether the statute's provision to distillers of an additional club over California importers affords distillers an unreasonable degree of unsupervised power to regulate their distribution practices that they would not otherwise enjoy under a free market which cannot be determined without a more sophisticated inquiry.

COUNSEL

John R. McDonough argued the cause for petitioners in 80-1030 and 80-1052.

George J. Roth argued the cause for petitioner in 80-1012.

George G. Weickhardt argued the cause for respondents.

FLORIDA DEPARTMENT OF STATE, Petitioner

v

TREASURE SALVORS, INC., etc.

— US —, 73 L Ed 2d 1057, 102 S Ct —

Argued January 20, 1982.
Decided July 1, 1982.

Decision: Process issued by Federal District Court
to secure possession of property from state
officials in admiralty in rem action, held not
barred by Eleventh Amendment.

SUMMARY

A treasure salvage company located the site where
a Spanish ship sank in 1622, 40 nautical miles west
of what is today Key West, Florida. After the state
of Florida claimed that the ship belonged to the
state, the salvage company executed contracts with
the state that permitted the salvage company to
conduct underwater salvage operations on the vessel. The salvage company was successful in its attempt to salvage the ship's treasure. In unrelated
proceedings a final decree was entered providing
that, as against the state of Florida, the United
States was entitled to the lands, minerals, and other
natural resources in the area in which the remains
of the ship had been found. The salvage company
then filed a complaint in the United States District
Court for the Southern District of Florida seeking
title to the ship and its property, the complaint
invoking the court's admiralty and maritime jurisdiction, and, as an admiralty action in rem, naming the

ship as defendant. The United States intervened in the action as a party-defendant and filed a counterclaim seeking a declaratory judgment that the United States was the proper owner of the ship. The District Court entered judgment in favor of the salvage company against the United States and all other claimants (408 F Supp 907). The United States Court of Appeals for the Fifth Circuit affirmed the District Court's judgment as against the United States but modified its decree (569 F2d 330). The salvage company then filed a motion in District Court for an order commanding the United States Marshal to arrest and take custody of the ship's artifacts that remained in the custody of Florida officials. The District Court issued a warrant, addressed to two officers of the Florida division of archives, to arrest the property. The District Court denied the state's motion to quash the warrant, and, in proceedings in response to an order to show cause, the District Court rejected various arguments made by the state, including a defense based on the Eleventh Amendment (459 F Supp 507). The United States Court of Appeals for the Fifth Circuit affirmed, holding that the Eleventh Amendment did not prevent the court from resolving the controverted claims to ownership of the res, that the process in the case was proper, and that the state did not have a valid claim to the property (621 F2d 1340).

On certiorari, the United States Supreme Court affirmed in part and reversed in part. Although unable to agree on an opinion, five members of the court agreed that the Eleventh Amendment did not prohibit an execution of the warrant and transfer of the artifacts to the salvage company.

476

STEVENS, J., announced the judgment of the court, and in an opinion joined by BURGER, Ch. J., MARSHALL, J., and BLACKMUN, J., expressed the view that (1) the Eleventh Amendment did not prohibit an execution of the warrant and transfer of the artifacts to the salvage company, since the process was directed only at state officials and not at the state itself or any state agency, the state officials did not have a colorable claim to possession of the property, and the warrant of arrest sought possession of specific property, did not seek attachment of state funds, and imposed no burden on the state treasury, the action not being an in personam action brought to recover damages from the state, but (2) the Court of Appeals improperly adjudicated the state's right to the artifacts, since while such an adjudication would be justified if the state voluntarily advanced a claim to the artifacts, it could not be justified as part of the Eleventh Amendment analysis, the only issue before the Supreme Court.

BRENNAN, J., concurring in the judgment in part and dissenting in part, expressed the view that (1) the Eleventh Amendment prohibited neither an execution of the warrant nor a transfer of the artifacts to the salvage company, since the Eleventh Amendment does not bar federal court suits against a state when brought by its own citizens, and (2) the courts below did not err when they determined the state's ownership of the artifacts as part of their Eleventh Amendment analysis, the record plainly indicating that the state had a full opportunity to present its arguments respecting ownership of the artifacts at issue in the case when the action was in the District Court, and that the District Court held a full evidentiary hearing on the merits of these arguments.

WHITE, J., joined by POWELL,, REHNQUIST, and O'CONNOR, JJ., concurred in the judgment in part and dissented in part, expressing the view that the Eleventh Amendment barred the action since (1) it was a suit against the State of Florida, without its permission, and (2) alternatively, if the arrest of the artifacts was not, without more, a suit against the state, the action was nevertheless against state agents acting within their authority and holding property for the state under a colorable claim of right, the Eleventh Amendment barring actions which are in effect against the state even though the state is not the nominal party.

COUNSEL

Susan Gamble Smathers argued the cause for petitioner, pro hac vice, by special leave of Court.

David Paul Horan argued the cause for respondent.

MISSISSIPPI UNIVERSITY FOR WOMEN, et al.,
Petitioners

v

JOE HOGAN

— US —, 73 L Ed 2d 1090, 102 S Ct —

Argued March 22, 1982.
Decided July 1, 1982.

Decision: State-supported university's policy that
excludes males from enrolling in its professional nursing school, held violative of equal
protection clause of Fourteenth Amendment.

SUMMARY

The Mississippi University for Women, a state-
supported school in Alabama, has from its inception
limited its enrollment to women. A male registered
nurse who did not hold a baccalaureate degree in
nursing and had worked as a nursing supervisor in a
medical center in the city in which the University is
located applied for admission to the University
School of Nursing's baccalaureate program. Although he was otherwise qualified, he was denied
admission to the School of Nursing solely because
of his sex. School officials informed him that he
could audit the courses in which he was interested,
but could not enroll for credit. He then filed an
action in the United States District Court for the
Northern District of Mississippi, claiming the single-
sex admissions policy of the School of Nursing
violated the equal protection clause of the Fourteenth Amendment. Following a hearing, the Dis-

trict Court denied preliminary injunctive relief, concluding that the maintenance of the University as a single-sex school bore a rational relationship to the state's legitimate interest of providing the greatest practical range of educational opportunities for its female student population and stating that the admissions policy was not arbitrary because providing single-sex schools is consistent with the respected, though by no means universally accepted, educational theory that single-sex education affords unique benefits to students. The United States Court of Appeals for the Fifth Circuit reversed, holding that the policy excluding the male applicant because of his sex denies him equal protection of the laws (646 F2d 1116). On rehearing, the state contended that Congress, in enacting § 901(a)(5) of Title IX of the Education Amendments of 1972 (20 USCS § 1681(a)(5)), expressly had authorized the University to continue its single-sex admissions policy by exempting public undergraduate institutions that traditionally have used single-sex admissions policies from the discrimination prohibition of § 901 of Title IX (20 USCS § 1681(a)). Through that provision, the state argued, Congress limited the reach of the Fourteenth Amendment by exercising its power under § 5 of the Amendment. The Court of Appeals rejected the argument, holding that § 5 of the Fourteenth Amendment does not grant Congress power to authorize states to maintain practices otherwise violative of the Amendment (653 F2d 222).

On certiorari, the United States Supreme Court affirmed. In an opinion by O'CONNOR, J., joined by BRENNAN, WHITE, MARSHALL, and STEVENS, JJ., it was held (1) that the University's policy violated the
480

equal protection clause of the Fourteenth Amendment, the single-sex admissions policy not being justified on the grounds it compensates for discrimination against women as the policy tends to perpetuate the stereotyped view of nursing as an exclusively woman's job, and the state having made no showing that the gender-based classification is substantially and directly related to its proposed compensatory objective, to the contrary, the policy of permitting men to attend classes as auditors fatally undermining its claim that women are adversely affected by the presence of men in the classroom and, accordingly, the state having fallen far short of establishing the exceedingly persuasive justification needed to sustain the classification, and (2) the provisions of 20 USCS § 1681(a)(5) did not justify the policy since Congress' power under § 5 of the Fourteenth Amendment to enforce that Amendment is limited to adopting measures to enforce the guarantees of the Amendment and the section grants Congress no power to restrict, abrogate, or to dilute these guarantees.

BURGER, Ch. J., dissenting, expressed general agreement with Justice Powell's dissenting opinion and emphasized that the court's holding was limited to the context of a professional nursing school and that it suggested that a state might well be justified in maintaining, for example, the option of an all-women's business school or liberal arts program.

BLACKMUN, J., dissenting, expressed the view that since the state offers baccalaureate programs in nursing open to males at other state-supported colleges, the state has not closed the door of its educational system to males and that it is easy to go too far with rigid rules in this area of claimed sex discrimination, and to lose—indeed destroy—values that mean much to some people by forbidding the state from offering them a choice while not depriving others of an alternate choice.

POWELL, J., joined by REHNQUIST, J., dissenting, expressed the view that the court errs seriously by assuming that the equal protection standard generally applicable to sex discrimination was appropriate in the case, and that by applying heightened equal protection analysis, the court frustrates the liberating spirit of the equal protection clause by forbidding the states from providing women with an opportunity to choose the type of university they prefer.

COUNSEL

Hunter M. Gholson argued the cause for petitioners.

Wilbur O. Colom argued the cause for respondents.

_____

NEW YORK, Petitioner

v

PAUL IRA FERBER

— US —, 73 L Ed 2d 1113, 102 S Ct —

Argued April 27, 1982.

Decided July 2, 1982.

Decision: New York criminal statute prohibiting knowing promotion of sexual performances by children under 16, by distribution of material depicting such performances, held constitutional.

SUMMARY

The proprietor of a Manhattan bookstore was convicted in the Supreme Court, New York County of promoting a sexual performance of a child by selling two films which depicted young boys masturbating, in violation of a New York criminal statute prohibiting persons from knowingly promoting sexual performances by children under 16 by distributing material which depicts such performances, even if the materials were produced out of state; defining such promotion as producing, directing, or promoting any performance which includes sexual conduct by a child under 16; and defining sexual conduct to mean actual or simulated sexual intercourse, deviate sexual intercourse, sexual bestiality, masturbation, sado-masochistic abuse, or lewd exhibition of the genitals. The Appellate Division affirmed the conviction (424 NYS2d 967), but the New York Court of Appeals reversed on the ground that the statute

483

violated the First Amendment (52 NY2d 674, 422 NE2d 523).

On certiorari, the United States Supreme Court reversed and remanded. In an opinion by WHITE, J., joined by BURGER, CH. J., AND POWELL, REHNQUIST, and O'CONNOR, JJ., it was held that (1) child pornography, like obscenity, is unprotected by the First Amendment if it involves scienter and a visual depiction of sexual conduct by children without serious literary, artistic, political, or scientific value, (2) the New York statute sufficiently described a category of material the production and distribution of which was not entitled to First Amendment protection, and (3) the statute was not overbroad as forbidding the distribution of material with serious literary, scientific or educational value, or material not threatening the harms sought to be combated by the state.

O'CONNOR, J., while joining in the court's opinion, filed a concurring opinion stressing that New York need not except from its statute material with serious literary, scientific, or educational value.

BRENNAN, J., joined by MARSHALL, J., concurred in the judgment, stating that absent exposure or particular harm to juveniles or unconsenting adults, the state lacks power to suppress sexually oriented materials, and that the First Amendment protects depictions of children that have serious literary, artistic, scientific or medical value.

STEVENS, J., concurred in the judgment, expressing the view that the statute was constitutional as applied and that the question of constitutional overbreadth need not be reached.

BLACKMUN, J., concurred in the result.

COUNSEL

Robert M. Pitler argued the cause for petitioner.
Herald Price Fahringer argued the cause for respondent.

EARL ENMUND, Petitioner

v

FLORIDA

— US —, 73 L Ed 2d 1140, 102 S Ct —

Argued March 23, 1982.

Decided July 2, 1982.

Decision: Imposition of death penalty on person who aids and abets felony in course of which murder is committed by others but who does not himself kill, attempt to kill, or intend to kill, held to violate Eighth and Fourteenth Amendments.

SUMMARY

An individual and a codefendant, at a jury trial in a Florida court, were found guilty of murder and robbery of two elderly persons at their farmhouse, and both were sentenced to death. The Supreme Court of Florida affirmed the defendant's death sentence, holding that even though the record supported no more than the inference that he was in a car by the side of the road at the time of the killings, waiting to help the robbers (the codefendant and another) escape, this was enough under Florida law to make the defendant a constructive aider and abettor and hence a principal in first-degree murder upon whom the death penalty could be imposed, the court expressly rejecting the defendant's argument that because the evidence did not establish that he intended to take life, the death penalty was barred by the Eighth Amendment (399 So 2d 1362).

On certiorari, the United States Supreme Court reversed and remanded. In an opinion by WHITE, J., joined by BRENNAN, MARSHALL, BLACKMUN, and STEVENS, JJ., it was held that the Eighth and Fourteenth Amendments were violated by the imposition of the death penalty on the defendant, who aided and abetted a felony in the course of which a murder was committed by others but who did not himself kill, attempt to kill, intend to kill, or contemplate that life would be taken.

BRENNAN, J., concurred, expressing the view that the death penalty is in all circumstances cruel and unusual punishment prohibited by the Eighth and Fourteenth Amendments.

O'CONNOR, J., joined by BURGER, Ch. J., POWELL, J., and REHNQUIST, J., dissenting, expressed the view that (1) the court's holding that the Eighth Amendment prohibits a state from executing a convicted felony murderer was not supported by the analysis in the court's previous cases and interfered with state criteria for assessing legal guilt by recasting intent as a matter of federal constitutional law, and (2) in light of the Florida Supreme Court's rejection of critical factual findings, a remand was required for a new sentencing hearing.

COUNSEL

James S. Liebman argued the cause for petitioner, pro hac vice, by special leave of Court.

Lawrence A. Kaden argued the cause for respondent, pro hac vice, by special leave of Court.

RAMAH NAVAJO SCHOOL BOARD, INC., et al.,
Appellants

v

BUREAU OF REVENUE OF NEW MEXICO

— US —, 73 L Ed 2d 1174, 102 S Ct —

Argued April 28, 1982.
Decided July 2, 1982.

Decision: New Mexico tax imposed on gross receipts that non-Indian construction company
received from tribal school board for construction of school on reservation, held preempted
by federal law.

SUMMARY

A non-Indian construction company and a tribal
school board protested the imposition of a New
Mexico tax on the gross receipts that the company
received from the school board for the construction
of a school for Indian children on a reservation.
After exhausting administrative remedies, they filed
a refund action against the New Mexico Bureau of
Revenue in the New Mexico District Court. The trial
court entered judgment for the Bureau. The Court
of Appeals of New Mexico affirmed, concluding that
the tax was not preempted by federal law and did
not unlawfully burden tribal sovereignty (95 NM
708, 625 P2d 1225). The Court of Appeals denied a
petition for rehearing, and after initially granting
discretionary review, the Supreme Court of New
Mexico quashed the writ as improvidently granted
(96 NM 17, 627 P2d 412).

On appeal, the United States Supreme Court reversed and remanded. In an opinion by MARSHALL, J., joined by BURGER, Ch. J., and BRENNAN, BLACKMUN, POWELL and O'CONNOR, JJ., it was held that federal law—including the Indian Self-Determination and Education Assistance Act (25 USCS §§ 450 et seq.) and regulations promulgated thereunder (25 CFR §§ 274.1 et seq.), and the Indian Financing Act of 1974 (25 USCS §§ 1451 et seq.)—preempted the state tax in question, in view of the comprehensive federal regulatory scheme for the construction and financing of Indian educational institutions and the express federal policy of encouraging tribal self-sufficiency in the area of education, even though the federal statutes and regulations do not specifically express the intention to preempt this exercise of state authority.

REHNQUIST, J., joined by WHITE and STEVENS, JJ., dissented, stating that the court accorded a dependent Indian tribal organization greater tax immunity than the court accorded the sovereignty of the United States in an earlier case involving the precise state taxes at issue in the instant case.

COUNSEL

Michael P. Gross argued the cause for appellants.

Louis F. Claiborne argued the cause for the United States as amicus curiae, by special leave of Court.

Jan Unna argued the cause for appellees.

UNITED STATES, Petitioner

v

RICARDO VALENZUELA-BERNAL

— US —, 73 L Ed 2d 1193, 102 S Ct —

Argued April 20, 1982.
Decided July 2, 1982.

Decision: Government's deportation of alien witnesses, held not violative of Fifth and Sixth Amendments absent some showing evidence lost would be both material and favorable to defendant.

SUMMARY

An alien entered the United States illegally and was taken by smugglers to a house in Escondido, California. Six days later, in exchange for his not having to pay the smugglers for bringing him across the border, the alien agreed to drive himself and five other passengers to Los Angeles. During the course of this drive, the alien and three of his passengers were apprehended by the United States Border Patrol. Following their arrest, the alien and the other passengers were interviewed by criminal investigators. The alien and his three passengers admitted that they were illegally in the country and all of the passengers identified the alien as the driver of the car. An Assistant United States Attorney concluded that the passengers possessed no evidence material to the prosecution or defense of the alien-defendant for transporting illegal aliens, and two of the passengers were deported to Mexico,

490

while the third was detained to provide a non-hearsay basis for establishing that the defendant had transported an illegal alien in violation of 8 USCS § 1324(a)(2). On trial in the United States District Court for the Southern District of California, the defendant moved to dismiss the indictment, claiming that the government's deportation of two of the passengers violated his Fifth Amendment right to due process of law and his Sixth Amendment right to compulsory process for obtaining favorable witnesses, claiming that the deportation had deprived him of the opportunity to interview the two remaining passengers to determine whether they could aid in his defense. The District Court denied the defendant's motion and, following a bench trial on stipulated evidence, found the defendant guilty as charged. The United States Court of Appeals for the Ninth Circuit reversed the conviction holding that the government violated the Fifth and Sixth Amendments when it deported the alien witnesses before counsel had an opportunity to interview them (647 F2d 72).

On certiorari, the United States Supreme Court reversed. In an opinion by REHNQUIST, J., joined by BURGER, Ch. J., and WHITE, POWELL, and STEVENS, JJ., it was held that (1) the defendant failed t⌐ establish a violation of the Sixth Amendment which guarantees a criminal defendant the ri⌐ compulsory process for obtaining witnesse⌐ favor," but does not grant him the righ⌐ the attendance and testimony of any nesses — merely by showing that th⌐ the aliens deprived him of their t⌐ showing that the evidence lost v rial and favorable to the defe⌐

defendant in such a situation cannot be expected to render a detailed description of the lost testimony, the defendant is not relieved of the duty of making some showing of materiality, and (2) the defendant failed to establish a violation of the due process clause of the Fifth Amendment — which guarantees that a criminal defendant will be treated with that fundamental fairness essential to the very concept of justice — since such an absence of fairness is not made out by the government's deportation of witnesses to the crime unless there is some explanation of how their testimony would have been favorable and material.

BLACKMUN, J., concurring in the judgment, expressed the view that at least a plausible theory of how the testimony of the deported witnesses would be helpful to the defense must be offered and since none was advanced, the motion to dismiss the indictment was properly denied by the District Court.

O'CONNOR, J., concurring in the judgment, expressed the view that the proper standard should be that deportable aliens who are potential witnesses be detained for a very brief period to afford government and defense counsel the opportunity to interview them and, if, within that period, the defendant requests that certain aliens not be deported, a federal magistrate should hold a hearing to determine whether deportation of any of the witnesses should be deferred until after trial, and that since the defendant here made no plausible suggestion that the deported aliens possessed any material evidence that was not merely cumulative of other evidence, under that standard, the District Court properly denied the defendant's motion to dismiss the indictment.

Brennan, J., joined by Marshall, J., dissenting, expressed the view that a criminal defendant has a constitutional right under the compulsory process clause of the Sixth Amendment to interview eyewitnesses to his alleged crime before they are whisked out of the country by his prosecutor and the court's decision makes a mockery of that right.

COUNSEL

Carter G. Phillips argued the cause for petitioner.

Eugene G. Iredale argued the cause for respondent.

NATIONAL ASSOCIATION FOR THE
ADVANCEMENT OF COLORED PEOPLE, et al.,
Petitioners

v

CLAIBORNE HARDWARE COMPANY et al.

— US —, 73 L Ed 2d 1215, 102 S Ct —

Argued March 3, 1982.
Decided July 2, 1982.

Decision: First Amendment held to preclude state
court imposition of liability on participants in
black boycott of white businesses for losses
other than those caused by their own violence
or threats.

SUMMARY

Seventeen white merchants filed suit in the Chancery Court of Hinds County, Mississippi, for losses
sustained during a 7-year boycott of their businesses
by black individuals and organizations seeking racial
equality and integration, during which there were
marches, picketing, threats, and several significant
acts of boycott-related violence. The chancellor
granted injunctive relief and imposed damage liability for all the merchants' lost earnings during the 7-
year period, on the grounds of the tort of malicious
interference with the merchants' businesses, violation of the state statutory prohibition against secondary boycotts, and violation of the state antitrust
statute. The Mississippi Supreme Court affirmed in
part and reversed and remanded in part. It ruled
494

that the state secondary boycott statute and the state antitrust statute were inapplicable, but that there was common-law tort liability on the ground that the defendants had agreed to use force, violence, and threats to effectuate the boycott (393 So 2d 1290).

On certiorari, the United States Supreme Court reversed and remanded. In an opinion by STEVENS, J., joined by BURGER, CH. J., and BRENNAN, WHITE, BLACKMUN, POWELL, and O'CONNOR, JJ., it was held that (1) the First Amendment precluded imposition of liability on boycott participants for all damages resulting from the boycott, even though some of them engaged in violence and threats of violence, and even though such violence and threats contributed to the success of the boycott, because the boycott was otherwise nonviolent, politically-motivated, and designed to force governmental and economic change and to effectuate rights guaranteed by the Constitution itself, but (2) the First Amendment did not bar recovery from those who engaged in violence or threats of violence for losses proximately caused by their unlawful conduct.

REHNQUIST, J., concurred in the result.

MARSHALL, J., did not participate.

COUNSEL

Lloyd N. Cutler argued the cause for petitioners.
Grover Rees, III, argued the cause for respondents.

JOY SPORHASE and DELMER MOSS, etc.,
Appellants

v

NEBRASKA, ex rel. PAUL L. DOUGLAS, Attorney
General

— US —, 73 L Ed 2d 1254, 102 S Ct —

Argued March 30, 1982.
Decided July 2, 1982.

Decision: Nebraska statute forbidding withdrawal of ground water to foreign state which denies such privileges to Nebraska, held violative of commerce clause (Art I, § 8, cl 3).

SUMMARY

　　Landowners who owned contiguous tracts of land Nebraska and Colorado on which a well physically located on the Nebraska tract pumped ground water for irrigation of both the Nebraska Colorado tracts failed to apply for a permit required by Nebraska law which, among other things, stated that Nebraska would not provide a permit for the withdrawal of ground water for the use in another state if that state did not grant reciprocal rights to withdraw and transport ground water into Nebraska. The state of Colorado did not provide for reciprocity for the use of ground water. Nebraska brought an action to enjoin the landowners from transferring the water across the border without a permit in the District Court of Chase County, Nebraska, which granted an injunction, rejecting the defense that the statute
496

imposed an undue burden on interstate commerce. The Supreme Court of Nebraska affirmed, holding that ground water is not a marketable item freely transferable for value among private parties and therefore is not an article of commerce (208 Neb 703, 305 NW2d 614).

On appeal, the United States Supreme Court reversed and remanded. In an opinion by STEVENS, J., joined by BURGER, Ch. J., and BRENNAN, WHITE, MARSHALL, BLACKMUN, and POWELL, JJ., it was held that (1) ground water is an article of commerce and is therefore subject to congressional regulation, (2) the Nebraska reciprocity provisions violated the commerce clause (Art I, § 8, cl 3) as imposing an impermissible burden on interstate commerce, even though the three conditions set forth in the statute for granting a permit—that the withdrawal of the ground water be reasonable, not contrary to the conservation and use of ground water, and not otherwise detrimental to the public welfare—did not on their faces impermissibly burden interstate commerce, since the reciprocity provision operated as an explicit barrier to commerce between the state and adjoining states and where there was no evidence that the restriction is narrowly tailored to the asserted local purposes of conservation and preservation, and (3) Congress has not granted the states permission to engage in ground water regulation that would otherwise be impermissible, neither the fact that Congress has chosen not to create a federal water law to govern water rights involved in federal water projects nor the fact that Congress has been willing to let the states settle their differences over water rights with a mutual agreement, constituting persuasive evidence that Congress consented to the unilateral imposition of unreasonable burdens on commerce.

REHNQUIST, J., joined by O'CONNOR, J., dissented, expressing the view that since Nebraska recognizes only a limited right to use ground water on land owned by the appropriator, it cannot be said that commerce in ground water exists as far as Nebraska is concerned and therefore, it cannot be said that the statute either discriminates against, or burdens, interstate commerce.

COUNSEL

Richard A. Dudden argued the cause for appellants.

George Roderic Anderson argued the cause for appellee.

BOARD OF EDUCATION OF ROGERS,
ARKANSAS, et al.

v

PETE McCLUSKEY, by his next friend, SALLY
McCLUSKEY

— US —, 73 L Ed 2d 1273, 102 S Ct —

Decided July 2, 1982.

Decision: Federal courts' replacement of local
school board's construction of its own rules on
mandatory suspension in action under 42 USCS
§ 1983, held erroneous where board's construction was reasonable.

SUMMARY

   A tenth grade student left school without permission and, with four other students, consumed alcohol and became intoxicated. When he returned to
school later that day to go on a band trip, he was
notified that he was suspended from school. At a
hearing before the local school board, the board
voted to expel all five students for the remainder of
the semester. The student immediately sought injunctive relief under 42 USCS § 1983 in the United
States District Court for the Western District of
Arkansas, which decided that the school board had
violated the student's right to substantive due process. The District Court found that the board had
acted under one of its rules, which provides for
mandatory suspension of students who, on school
premises, use, sell, are under the influence of, or
possess narcotics or other hallucinogenics, drugs, or

controlled substances, and concluded that alcohol is not included in any of these categories and that, therefore, the board had acted unreasonably by suspending the student under the rule. The United States Court of Appeals for the Eighth Circuit affirmed (662 F2d 1263).

Granting certiorari, the United States Supreme Court reversed. In a per curiam opinion expressing the view of BURGER, Ch. J., and WHITE, BLACKMUN, POWELL, REHNQUIST, and O'CONNOR, JJ., it was held that the federal courts erred in replacing the school board's construction of its own rules with the courts' own notions, since the board's interpretation of its rule on mandatory suspension of students under the influence of drugs while on school premises to include the use of alcohol as a form of drug use was reasonable.

STEVENS, J., joined by BRENNAN, and MARSHALL, JJ., dissented, expressing the view that the court must continue to decide only those cases which present questions whose resolution will have immediate importance far beyond the particular facts and parties involved and that this case illustrates how ineffectively the court is supervising its discretionary docket as it exercises its power to enforce a school board's suspension of a tenth grade student who consumed too much alcohol and doubted that if the student had been unjustly suspended, it would consider the matter of sufficient national importance to require summary reversal.

GLOSSARY OF COMMON LEGAL TERMS

Abatement
The extinguishment of a lawsuit.

Abstention doctrine
The doctrine whereby a federal court may decline to exercise, or may postpone the exercise of, its jurisdiction, where a case involves a controlling question of state law.

Action
A lawsuit.

Administrative determination
A decision by a government board, agency or official, rather than by a court.

Administrator
One appointed by a court to settle the estate of a deceased person. The feminine form is "administratrix."

Admiralty
The body of law governing maritime cases.

Affidavit
A sworn written statement.

Amicus curiae
One who, not being a party to a lawsuit, assists the court in deciding the case.

Antitrust laws
Laws prohibiting restrictions on competition.

501

Appealable

That which may be taken to a higher court for review.

Appellant

One who appeals to a superior court from the order of an inferior court.

Appellee

A party against whom a case is appealed from an inferior court to a superior court.

Arbitration

The submission of a dispute to a selected person —not a court—for decision.

Arraign

To call a person before a judge or commissioner to answer criminal charges made against him.

Array

The whole body of persons, summoned to attend court, from whom a jury will be selected.

Assignee

One to whom property or a right is transferred.

Assignor

The transferor of property or a right.

Bill of Rights

The first ten amendments to the United States Constitution.

Brief

A written legal argument submitted to the court deciding the case.

Calendar

A list of cases awaiting decision in a court.

Capital crime
An offense punishable by death.

Cause of action
A right to legal redress.

Cease-and-desist order
An order to stop doing specified acts.

Certiorari
A superior court's order to a lower court to send up the record of a case for review by the superior court.

Choice of remedies
An election of which form of legal redress to seek.

Civil
Not criminal, as a civil lawsuit.

Class action
A lawsuit on behalf of persons too numerous to participate actively therein.

Commerce clause
The provision of the United States Constitution giving Congress power to regulate commerce with foreign nations, among the states.

Common law
The body of the law apart from constitutions, treaties, statutes, ordinances, and regulations.

Contempt
An exhibition of scorn or disrespect toward a judicial or legislative body.

Continuance
A postponement of proceedings.

Copyright
The exclusive privilege of publishing literary or artistic productions.

Coram nobis
A means of challenging a court's judgment, especially in criminal cases.

Court of Appeals
See United States Court of Appeals.

Cross Appeal
An appeal filed by the person against whom an appeal is taken.

De novo
Anew or over again, such as a trial de novo.

Devise
A will provision making a gift of land.

Disputes clause
A provision in a government contract for the settlement of disputes between the contractor and the government by decision of a government board or official.

District court
See United States District Court.

Diversity case
A case decided by a federal court because the parties are citizens of different states.

Double jeopardy
Placing a person twice in jeopardy of conviction for the same offense.

504

GLOSSARY

Due process clause

The provision of the United States Constitution that no person shall be deprived of life, liberty, or property without due process of law.

En banc

With all the judges of the court sitting.

Equal protection

The guaranty of the United States Constitution that no person or class of persons shall be denied the same protection of the laws that is enjoyed by other persons or classes of persons in like circumstances.

Establishment clause

The provision of the United States Constitution that Congress shall make no law respecting an establishment of religion.

Federal District Court

See District court.

Federal question jurisdiction

The jurisdiction of federal courts over cases presenting questions of federal law.

Felony

A crime punishable by death or by imprisonment in a state prison.

Forma pauperis

Without the payment of legal fees in advance.

Full faith and credit clause

The provision of the United States Constitution that full faith and credit shall be given in each state

505

to the public acts, records, and judicial proceedings of every other state.

Habeas corpus
A judicial inquiry into the legality of the restraint of a person.

Indictment
A grand jury's accusation of crime.

Interlocutory
That which settles an intervening matter but does not decide a case.

Intestate
One who dies without leaving a valid will.

Jurisdiction of subject matter
The power to decide a certain type of case.

Just compensation clause
The provision of the United States Constitution that no private property may be taken for public use without just compensation.

Laches
Delay barring the right to special forms of relief.

Legatee
One to whom personal property is given by will.

Lessee
A tenant.

Lessor
A landlord.

Libel
Written defamation; in maritime cases, a suit in court.

GLOSSARY

Lien

A charge upon property for the payment of a debt.

Local action

A lawsuit, especially one involving rights to land, which can be brought only in the place where the wrong was committed.

Maintenance and cure

The legal duty of a seaman's employer to care for him during his illness.

Mandamus

A judicial command to perform an official duty.

Misdemeanor

Any crime not punishable by death or by imprisonment in a state prison.

Patent

The exclusive right of manufacture, sale, or use secured by statute to one who invents or discovers a new and useful device or process.

Per curiam

By the court as a whole.

Per se

By itself.

Plaintiff

A person who brings a lawsuit.

Plenary

Full or complete.

Police power

The power inherent in the states as sovereigns and not derived uner any written constitution.

507

Prima facie
At first sight; with regard to evidence, that which, if unexplained or uncontradicted, is sufficient to establish a fact.

Privileges and immunities clause
The provision of the United States Constitution that no state shall make or enforce any law which abridges the privileges or immunities of citizens of the United States.

Pro hac vice
For this occasion.

Pro se
For himself; in his own behalf.

Proximate cause
The immediate cause of injury.

Public defender
A lawyer employed by the public to defend persons accused of crime.

Recognizance
A bail bond.

Remand
To order to be sent back.

Res judicata
The doctrine that a final judgment is binding on the parties to the lawsuit and the matter cannot be relitigated.

Respondent
The defendant in an action; with regard to appeals, the party against whom the appeal is taken.

Sanction
The penalty to be incurred by a wrongdoer.

Saving clause
A statutory provision preserving rights which would otherwise be annihilated by the statute.

Seaworthy
The reasonable fitness of a vessel to perform the service which she has undertaken to perform.

Statute of frauds
A statute rendering certain types of contracts unenforceable unless in writing.

Statute of limitations
A statute fixing a period of time within which certain types of lawsuits or criminal prosecutions must be begun.

Subpoena
Legal process to require the attendance of a witness.

Substantial federal question
A question of federal law of sufficient merit to warrant decision of the case by a federal court.

Substantive offense
An offense which is complete in itself and does not depend on the establishment of another offense.

Summary judgment
A judgment without a trial.

Supremacy clause
The provision of the United States Constitution that the Constitution, federal laws enacted pursuant thereto, and federal treaties shall be the supreme

law of the land, binding the judges in every state, notwithstanding any state law to the contrary.

Surety
One who binds himself with another, called the principal, for the performance of an obligation with respect to which the principal is already bound and primarily liable.

Surrogate
The judge of a court dealing largely with wills and decedents' estates.

Tort
A wrong independent of contract; a breach of duty which the law, as distinguished from a mere contract, has imposed.

Tortfeasor
One who commits a tort; a wrongdoer.

Transitory action
An action which may be brought wherever the defendant may be served with process.

Trespass
An injury intentionally inflicted on the person or property of another.

Trier of fact
One who decides questions of fact.

United States Code
The official compilation of statutes enacted by Congress.

United States Court of Appeals
The intermediate level of federal courts above the United States District Courts above the United

States District Courts but below the Supreme Court of the United States.

United States District Court
A federal trial court.

Unseaworthy
See Seaworthy.

USC
See United States Code.

USCS
The abbreviation for United States Code Service, Lawyers Edition, which is a publication annotating the federal laws, arranged according to the numbering of the United States Code.

Venue
The place where a case may be tried.

Writ of certiorari
See Certiorari.

Writ of error coram nobis
See Coram nobis.

TABLE OF CASES

TABLE OF CASES

514

TABLE OF CASES

TABLE OF CASES

TABLE OF CASES

TABLE OF CASES

518

TABLE OF CASES

TABLE OF CASES

TABLE OF CASES

TABLE OF CASES

TABLE OF CASES

TABLE OF CASES

INDEX

ABATEMENT OF NUISANCE
Obscenity: proof, in public nuisance abatement action by city against motion picture theater, that motion pictures in question were obscene beyond reasonable doubt, held not required, 70 L Ed 2d 262

ABSENCE AND PRESENCE
Deportation: government's deportation of alien witnesses, held not violative of Fifth and Sixth Amendments absent some showing evidence lost would be both material and favorable to defendant, 73 L Ed 2d 1193
Initiative: state initiative precluding school boards from requiring attendance at other than neighborhood schools, held unconstitutional, 73 L Ed 2d 896

ABSOLUTE IMMUNITY
Privileges and Immunities (this index)

ABSTENTION DOCTRINE
Attorney disciplinary rules: federal court abstention from considering challenge to constitutionality of attorney disciplinary rules that were subject of pending state disciplinary proceeding within jurisdiction of New Jersey Supreme Court held required, 73 L Ed 2d 116

ABUSE OF DISCRETION
Affirmative action plan: Federal Court of Appeals' refusal to resolve pendent state-law claim in affirming affirmative action plan for contractors as constitutional, held abuse of discretion, 73 L Ed 2d 245

ACADEMIC QUESTIONS
Moot Questions (this index)

ACCEPTANCE AND REJECTION
Trust beneficiary's disclaimer of contingent interest in testamentary trust, held taxable transfer of property by gift under 26 USCS §§ 2501(a)(1) and 2511(a), not excepted from tax by 26 CFR § 25.2511-1(c), 71 L Ed 2d 170

527

INDEX

ACCIDENTAL INJURY AND ACCIDENTS
Boats: complaint alleging collision between two pleasure boats on navigable waters, held to state claim within federal admiralty jurisdiction, 73 L Ed 2d 300

Compensable injury: presumption of compensability under § 20(a) of Longshoremen's and Harbor Workers' Compensation Act (33 USCS § 920(a)), held inapplicable to claimed injury at work where "injury" arose at home, 71 L Ed 2d 495

ACCRETIONS
United States held entitled to oceanfront accretions to Coast Guard reservation under federal rule that accretions belong to upland owner, 73 L Ed 2d 1

ACCRUAL OF ACTION
Limitation of actions: limitations period applicable to employment discrimination action under 42 USCS § 1983, held to run from time of notice that appointment would terminate rather than from termination date, 70 L Ed 2d 6

ACCRUAL OF LIABILITY
Backpay: employer's offer to discrimination claimant of job previously denied without offer of retroactive seniority, held to toll continuing accrual of backpay liability under 42 USCS § 2000e-6(g), 73 L Ed 2d 721

ACTIONS AND REMEDIES
Also see **Trials**

As to particular types of actions or remedies, see more specific topics

Cause of Action (this index)
Dismissal of Actions or Charges (this index)
Exhaustion of Remedies (this index)
Limitation of Actions (this index)
Pending Actions (this index)

"ACTUAL PREJUDICE"
Collateral relief: "cause and actual prejudice," rather than "plain error" of Rule 52(b) of Federal Rules of Criminal Procedure, held proper standard of review on motion for collateral relief under 28 USCS § 2255, 71 L Ed 2d 816

INDEX

ADDRESS LISTS
Disclosure: address lists compiled by Bureau of the Census, held not subject to disclosure under Freedom of Information Act (5 USCS § 552) or discovery provisions of Federal Rules of Civil Procedure, 71 L Ed 2d 199

ADJUDICATION OF RIGHTS
Full faith and credit: North Carolina courts' refusal to treat as res judicata Indiana rehabilitation court's adjudication of rights to insurance company's deposit posted in North Carolina, held violative of full faith and credit clause (Art IV, § 1), 71 L Ed 2d 558

ADJUSTED BASIS
Gift tax: donor making gift of property on condition that donee pay resulting gift tax, held to realize taxable income to extent that gift tax paid by donee exceeds donor's adjusted basis in property, 72 L Ed 2d 777

ADMINISTRATIVE LAW
Exhaustion of state administrative remedies, held not prerequisite to bringing action pursuant to 42 USCS § 1983, 73 L Ed 2d 172
Job bias: giving of preclusive effect to state court's review of state agency's action on job bias claim upon later action in federal court on such claim under similar federal law, held required by 28 USCS § 1738, 72 L Ed 2d 262

ADMIRALTY
Accidental Injury and Accidents (this index)
Longshoremen (this index)
Nuclear weapons: § 102 (2)(c) of the National Environmental Policy Act (42 USCS § 4332 (2)(c)), held not to require Navy to prepare and release "Hypothetical Environmental Impact Statement" regarding nuclear weapons storage, 70 L Ed 2d 298
Process issued by Federal District Court to secure possession of property from state officials in admiralty in rem action, held not barred by Eleventh Amendment, 73 L Ed 2d 1057
Wage penalty: limiting period during which wage penalty for failure to pay seamen promptly after discharge is assessed under 46 USCS § 596, held not within discretion of Federal District Courts, 73 L Ed 2d 973

ADMISSION AND ENROLLMENT

Illegal aliens: Texas statute withholding funds from local school districts for education of children not legally admitted into United States and authorizing districts to deny enrollment to such children, held to violate equal protection clause, 72 L Ed 2d 786

Sex discrimination: state-supported university's policy that excludes males from enrolling in its professional nursing school, held violative of equal protection clause of Fourteenth Amendment, 73 L Ed 2d 1090

ADOLESCENTS

Children and Minors (this index)

ADULTS

Youth Corrections Act (18 USCS §§ 5005 et seq.), held not to require that youth offender sentenced to adult term while serving youth term must receive youth treatment for remainder of youth term, 70 L Ed 2d 345

"ADVANCED FUNDING" PROCEDURES

Sales and use taxes: imposition of New Mexico's gross receipts and compensating use taxes on federal contractors doing business in state, held valid, 71 L Ed 2d 580

ADVERTISING

Attorneys: Missouri Supreme Court rule regulating attorney's advertising absent proof that regulated material was misleading, held violative of attorney's First Amendment rights, 71 L Ed 2d 64

Contributions and Solicitation of Funds (this index)

ADVISERS

Immunity: senior aides and advisers of President of United States, held entitled to qualified immunity from civil damages suits insofar as their conduct does not violate rights of which reasonable person would have known, 73 L Ed 2d 396

AFDC

Emergency assistance: state emergency assistance program precluding furnishing assistance to AFDC recipients, held invalid under supremacy clause (Art VI, cl 2) as in conflict with valid federal regulation, 72 L Ed 2d 728

INDEX

AFFIRMATIVE ACTION PLAN
Appeal: Federal Court of Appeals' refusal to resolve pendent state-law claim in affirming affirmative action plan for contractors as constitutional, held abuse of discretion, 73 L Ed 2d 245

AFGHANISTAN
Soviet Union (this index)

AGE
Children and Minors (this index)

AGENCIES OF GOVERNMENT
Job bias: giving of preclusive effect to state court's review of state agency's action on job bias claim upon later action in federal court on such claim under similar federal law, held required by 28 USCS § 1738, 72 L Ed 2d 262

AGENTS AND PRINCIPAL
Antitrust: nonprofit association of mechanical engineers responsible for promulgation of industry codes, held civilly liable under antitrust laws for antitrust violations of its agents committed with apparent authority, 72 L Ed 2d 330
Discharge of union business agent by newly-elected president of local union, held not violative of Labor Management Reporting and Disclosure Act (29 USCS §§ 401 et seq.), 72 L Ed 2d 239
Discrimination: proof of intentional discrimination, held necessary for liability under 42 USCS § 1981; vicarious liability under § 1981 of employers and trade associations for discriminatory conduct of union, held not supportable, 73 L Ed 2d 835

AGGRAVATING CIRCUMSTANCES
Death penalty: question as to what premises of state law support a conclusion that a death sentence was not impaired by the invalidity of one of the statutory aggravating circumstances found by the jury, certified to Georgia Supreme Court, 72 L Ed 2d 222

AGREEMENTS
Contracts and Agreements (this index)

AID
Funds and Funding (this index)

531

INDEX

AIDES AND ASSISTANTS
Immunity: senior aides and advisers of President of United States, held entitled to qualified immunity from civil damages suits insofar as their conduct does not violate rights of which reasonable person would have known, 73 L Ed 2d 396

AIDING AND ABETTING
Death penalty: imposition of death penalty on person who aids and abets felony in course of which murder is committed by others but who does not himself kill, attempt to kill, or intend to kill, held to violate Eight and Fourteenth Amendments, 73 L Ed 2d 1140

AID TO FAMILIES WITH DEPENDENT CHILDREN
Emergency assistance: state emergency assistance program precluding furnishing assistance to AFDC recipients, held invalid under supremacy clause (Art VI, cl 2) as in conflict with valid federal regulation, 72 L Ed 2d 728

ALASKA
Income distribution: Alaska statute distributing income derived from state's natural resources to state's citizens in varying amounts based on length of each citizen's residency, held to violate equal protection clause, 72 L Ed 2d 672

ALCOHOL
Schools: federal courts' replacement of local school board's construction of its own rules on mandatory suspension in action under 42 USCS § 1983, held erroneous where board's construction was reasonable, 73 L Ed 2d 1273

Sherman Act: state alcoholic beverage control law enforcing distiller's designation of wholesaler, held not per se violative of Sherman Act (15 USCS §§ 1 et seq.), 73 L Ed 2d 1042

ALIENATION
Sales and Transfers (this index)

ALIENS AND CITIZENS
Education: Texas statute withholding funds from local school districts for education of children not legally admitted into United States and authorizing districts to deny enrollment to such children, held to violate equal protection clause, 72 L Ed 2d 786

INDEX

ANTI-INJUNCTION PROVISIONS
Soviet invasion: work stoppage to protest Soviet invasion of Afghanistan, held subject to anti-injunction provisions of Norris-LaGuardia Act (29 USCS §§ 101 et seq.), and not enjoinable pending aribtrator's decision as to whether strike violated collective-bargaining contract, 73 L Ed 2d 327

ANTI-PASSTHROUGH PROVISIONS
Taxation: Temporary Emergency Court of Appeals' invalidation of anti-passthrough provision of state tax statute relating to oil company revenues, vacated and remanded in light of expiration of preempting federal price control authority, 71 L Ed 2d 120

ANTITRUST
Monopolies and Restraints of Trade (this index)

APARTMENTS
Discrimination: black "tester" given false information about housing availability and nonprofit, open housing organization, held to have standing to challenge racial steering under Fair Housing Act (42 USCS § 3612); Act's 180-day limitations period (42 USCS § 3612(a)), held not bar claims of continuing violation, even though some incidents alleged occur outside period, 71 L Ed 2d 214

APPARENT AUTHORITY
Antitrust: nonprofit association of mechanical engineers responsible for promulgation of industry codes, held civilly liable under antitrust laws for antitrust violations of its agents committed with apparent authority, 72 L Ed 2d 330

APPEAL AND REVIEW
Assistance of Counsel (this index)
"Cause and actual prejudice," rather than "plain error" of Rule 52(b) of Federal Rules of Criminal Procedure, held proper standard of review on motion for collateral relief under 28 USCS § 2255, 71 L Ed 2d 816
"Clearly Erroneous" Standard (this index)
Collateral Orders or Relief (this index)
Drugs and Narcotics (this index)
Employer and Employee (this index)
Job Discrimination (this index)

APPEAL AND REVIEW—Cont'd
Medicare and Medicaid (this index)
Moot Questions (this index)
Remand (this index)
Taxation (this index)

APPLEGROWERS
Discrimination: Commonwealth of Puerto Rico held to have standing to sue as parens patriae to enjoin applegrowers' discrimination against Puerto Rican migrant farmworkers, 73 L Ed 2d 995

APPLICATIONS AND PETITIONS
Habeas Corpus (this index)
Juror's submission, during criminal trial, of job application to prosecutor's office and failure of prosecution to disclose such fact during trial, held not violative of due process, 71 L Ed 2d 78
Licenses: ordinance directing city's police chief to consider applicant's "connection with criminal elements" in licensing amusement establishments, held not unconstitutionally vague, 71 L Ed 2d 152
Medicaid: state's unlimited deeming of Medicaid applicant's spouse's income as available to applicant in determining eligibility, held barred by 42 USCS § 1396a(a), 71 L Ed 2d 137
Reapportionment Plan (this index)
Resubmission (this index)
Stay. **Reapportionment Plan** (this index)

APPOINTED POSITIONS
Discharge of union business agent by newly-elected president of local union, held not violative of Labor Management Reporting and Disclosure Act (29 USCS §§ 401 et seq.), 72 L Ed 2d 239
Legislative seat: Puerto Rico law vesting in political party authority to appoint replacement for member who vacates seat on legislature, held not violative of United States Constitution, 72 L Ed 2d 628
Limitation of actions: limitations period applicable to employment discrimination action under 42 USCS § 1983, held to run from time of notice that appointment would terminate rather than from termination date, 70 L Ed 2d 6

APPOINTED POSITIONS—Cont'd

Military: federal court jurisdiction over action for monetary damages brought by discharged military exchange employee, held not conferred by Tucker Act (28 USCS § 1346(a)(2)) in absence of express or implied contract, 72 L Ed 2d 520

APPRENTICES

Discrimination: proof of intentional discrimination, held necessary for liability under 42 USCS § 1981; vicarious liability under § 1981 of employers and trade associations for discriminatory conduct of union, held not supportable, 73 L Ed 2d 835

ARBITRATION

Soviet invasion: work stoppage to protest Soviet invasion of Afghanistan, held subject to anti-injunction provisions of Norris-LaGuardia Act (29 USCS §§ 101 et seq.), and not enjoinable pending aribtrator's decision as to whether strike violated collective-bargaining contract, 73 L Ed 2d 327

ARMED FORCES

Insurance beneficiary: insured serviceman's beneficiary designation under life policy issued pursuant to Servicemen's Group Life Insurance Act (38 USCS §§ 765 et seq.), held to prevail over constructive trust imposed upon proceeds by state court, 70 L Ed 2d 39

Monetary damages: federal court jurisdiction over action for monetary damages brought by discharged military exchange employee, held not conferred by Tucker Act (28 USCS § 1346(a)(2)) in absence of express or implied contract, 72 L Ed 2d 520

Nuclear weapons: § 102 (2)(c) of the National Environmental Policy Act (42 USCS § 4332 (2)(c)), held not to require Navy to prepare and release "Hypothetical Environmental Impact Statement" regarding nuclear weapons storage, 70 L Ed 2d 298

Speedy trial: time between dismissal of military charges and subsequent indictment of individual on civilian charges held not to be considered in determining whether violation of right to speedy trial under Sixth Amendment has occurred, 71 L Ed 2d 696

INDEX

ARMED FORCES—Cont'd

Treaties: word "treaty" in 5 USCS § 7201 note, which excepts from certain employment discrimination requirements actions permitted by "treaty," held to include executive agreements, 71 L Ed 2d 715

ARMS AND WEAPONS

Nuclear weapons: § 102 (2)(c) of the National Environmental Policy Act (42 USCS § 4332 (2)(c)), held not to require Navy to prepare and release "Hypothetical Environmental Impact Statement" regarding nuclear weapons storage, 70 L Ed 2d 298

ARREST

Admiralty: process issued by Federal District Court to secure possession of property from state officials in admiralty in rem action, held not barred by Eleventh Amendment, 73 L Ed 2d 1057

Miranda Warnings (this index)

Private citizen's right to prevent state officials from presenting information that will assist magistrate in determining whether to issue arrest warrant, held not judicially cognizable, 70 L Ed 2d 65

Seizure: police officer's accompaniment of lawful arrestee to residence and subsequent seizure of contraband in plain view, held not violative of Fourth Amendment, 70 L Ed 2d 778

Warrant: rule of Payton v New York prohibiting warrantless, nonconsensual entry into suspect's home to make routine felony arrest, held to apply to case pending on direct appeal when Payton was decided, 73 L Ed 2d 202

ARTIFACTS

Admiralty: process issued by Federal District Court to secure possession of property from state officials in admiralty in rem action, held not barred by Eleventh Amendment, 73 L Ed 2d 1057

ARTISTIC VALUE

Sexual performances: New York criminal statute prohibiting knowing promotion of sexual performances by children under 16, by distribution of material depicting such performances, held constitutional, 73 L Ed 2d 1113

INDEX

ASSISTANCE
Funds and Funding (this index)

ASSISTANCE OF COUNSEL
Appeal: retained counsel's failure to timely file for discretionary review of state court convictions with state's highest court, held not to deprive defendant of effective assistance of counsel, 71 L Ed 2d 475
Habeas corpus: Federal Court of Appeals' consideration of issue of ineffective assistance of counsel of state defendant on federal habeas corpus petition, held erroneous where issue was not raised in state court or Federal District Court, 70 L Ed 2d 1

ASSISTANTS
Immunity: senior aides and advisers of President of United States, held entitled to qualified immunity from civil damages suits insofar as their conduct does not violate rights of which reasonable person would have known, 73 L Ed 2d 396

ASSOCIATION, FREEDOM OF
Speech, Assembly, and Press Freedom (this index)

ASSOCIATIONS AND ORGANIZATIONS
Antitrust: nonprofit association of mechanical engineers responsible for promulgation of industry codes, held civilly liable under antitrust laws for antitrust violations of its agents committed with apparent authority, 72 L Ed 2d 330
Constitutional challenges: trade associations and political action committees, held barred from invoking expedited constitutional challenge procedures of Federal Election Campaign Act (2 USCS § 437h), 71 L Ed 2d 432
Corporations (this index)
Discrimination: proof of intentional discrimination, held necessary for liability under 42 USCS § 1981; vicarious liability under § 1981 of employers and trade associations for discriminatory conduct of union, held not supportable, 73 L Ed 2d 835
Nonprofit Associations and Organizations (this index)

AT-LARGE ELECTION METHOD
Equal protection: at-large election system for large rural county with large black population held violative of equal protection clause, 73 L Ed 2d 1012

538

INDEX

AT-LARGE ELECTION METHOD—Cont'd
Referendum: letter to Attorney General advising of results of county referendum endorsing at-large method of electing county council, held to be request for reconsideration of Attorney General's prior objections to method and not preclearance request under Voting Rights Act (42 USCS § 1973c), 70 L Ed 2d 576

ATTACHMENT
Admiralty: process issued by Federal District Court to secure possession of property from state officials in admiralty in rem action, held not barred by Eleventh Amendment, 73 L Ed 2d 1057
Prejudgment attachment: complaint against private creditor's prejudgment attachment, held to state cause of action under 42 USCS § 1983 where statute authorizing it is alleged to be procedurally defective, 73 L Ed 2d 482

ATTEMPT
Death penalty: imposition of death penalty on person who aids and abets felony in course of which murder is committed by others but who does not himself kill, attempt to kill, or intend to kill, held to violate Eight and Fourteenth Amendments, 73 L Ed 2d 1140

ATTENDANCE
Absence and Presence (this index)

ATTORNEY GENERAL
At-Large Election method: letter to Attorney General advising of results of county referendum endorsing at-large method of electing county council, held to be request for reconsideration of Attorney General's prior objections to method and not preclearance request under Voting Rights Act (42 USCS § 1973c), 70 L Ed 2d 576
Reapportionment plan: Federal District Court effecting interim Texas congressional reapportionment for districts objected to by Attorney General, held without power to redraw other districts in absence of constitutional or statutory violation, 71 L Ed 2d 725

ATTORNEYS
Advertising: Missouri Supreme Court rule regulating attorney's advertising absent proof that regulated material was misleading, held violative of attorney's First Amendment rights, 71 L Ed 2d 64

539

INDEX

ATTORNEYS—Cont'd

Assistance of Counsel (this index)

"Color of state law": public defender performing lawyer's traditional functions, held not acting "under color of state law" for purposes of suit under 42 USCS § 1983, 70 L Ed 2d 509

Disciplinary rules: federal court abstention from considering challenge to constitutionality of attorney disciplinary rules that were subject of pending state disciplinary proceeding within jurisdiction of New Jersey Supreme Court held required, 73 L Ed 2d 116

District and Prosecuting Attorneys (this index)

Fees. **Attorney's Fees** (this index)

Pro se complaint: state prisoner's crudely written, pro se complaint alleging his placement in solitary confinement for one-week period without any notice of charges or any hearing, held sufficient to state cause of action, 70 L Ed 2d 551

ATTORNEY'S FEES

Damages: attorney's fees incurred during proceedings before National Labor Relations Board, held not proper element of damages under § 303(b) of Labor Management Relations Act (29 USCS § 187(b)), 72 L Ed 2d 511

Postjudgment request for attorney's fees under Civil Rights Attorney's Fees Awards Act (42 USCS § 1988), held not subject to 10-day timeliness standard of Rule 59(e) of Federal Rules of Civil Procedure, 71 L Ed 2d 325

AUTHORITY AND AUTHORIZATION

Legislative seat: Puerto Rico law vesting in political party authority to appoint replacement for member who vacates seat on legislature, held not violative of United States Constitution, 72 L Ed 2d 628

Search warrant: authority to conduct warrantless search of motor vehicle based on probable cause, including compartments and containers, held coextensive with authority based on magistrate's issuance of warrant, 72 L Ed 2d 572

Severance tax imposed on oil and gas removed from Indian reservation, held authorized by Tribe's inherent authority to tax as part of power of self-government, and held violative of commerce clause (Art I, § 8, cl 3), 71 L Ed 2d 21

INDEX

AUTOMOBILES
Search and Seizure (this index)

BACKPAY
Discrimination: employer's offer to discrimination claimant of job previously denied without offer of retroactive seniority, held to toll continuing accrual of backpay liability under 42 USCS § 2000e-6(g), 73 L Ed 2d 721

BAD CHECKS
Checks: deposit of bad check in federally insured bank, held not proscribed by 18 USCS § 1014, 73 L Ed 2d 767

BAIL
Sexual offenses: claim that Nebraska's prohibition of pretrial bail to person charged with sexual offenses violated Federal Constitution, held moot where defendant had already been convicted of offenses, 71 L Ed 2d 353

BALLOTS
Elections (this index)

BANKRUPTCY
Dismissal of Chapter XI petition filed under 1898 Bankruptcy Act in order to refile under Chapter 11 of 1978 Bankruptcy Code, held not authorized by Bankruptcy Rule 11-42(a) or § 403(a) of Bankruptcy Reform Act of 1978, 70 L Ed 2d 542

Employee protection provisions of Rock Island Transition and Employee Assistance Act (45 USCS §§ 1005 and 1008), held violative of bankruptcy clause (Art I, § 8, cl 4), 71 L Ed 2d 335

Jurisdiction: Bankruptcy Court's exercise of jurisdiction over state-law contract claims pursuant to 28 USCS § 1471, held violative of Article III, 73 L Ed 2d 598

BANKS
Certificate of deposit from federally regulated bank and business agreement arising from pledging of certificate as guarantee for loan, held not securities for purposes of 15 USCS § 78j(b), 71 L Ed 2d 409

Checks: deposit of bad check in federally insured bank, held not proscribed by 18 USCS § 1014, 73 L Ed 2d 767

BANKS—Cont'd

Due-on-sale clauses: Federal Home Loan Bank Board regulation authorizing due-on-sale clauses in federal savings and loan instruments held to preempt state law, 73 L Ed 2d 664

BARGAINING

Collective Bargaining (this index)

BASE LABOR AGREEMENT

Treaties: word "treaty" in 5 USCS § 7201 note, which excepts from certain employment discrimination requirements actions permitted by "treaty," held to include executive agreements, 71 L Ed 2d 715

BASIS

Gift tax: donor making gift of property on condition that donee pay resulting gift tax, held to realize taxable income to extent that gift tax paid by donee exceeds donor's adjusted basis in property, 72 L Ed 2d 777

BASTARDS

Paternity suits: Texas statute barring paternity suits brought on behalf of illegitimate children more than one year after their birth, held violative of equal protection, 71 L Ed 2d 770

BENEFICIARIES AND BENEFITS

Collective bargaining contract allocating health benefits among potential beneficiaries of employee trust fund, held not reviewable for reasonableness under Labor Management Relations Act (29 USCS § 186 (c)(5)), 71 L Ed 2d 419

Emergency assistance: state emergency assistance program precluding furnishing assistance to AFDC recipients, held invalid under supremacy clause (Art VI, cl 2) as in conflict with valid federal regulation, 72 L Ed 2d 728

First Amendment: Kentucky statute prohibiting candidates from offering benefits to voters in exchange for votes, held violative of First Amendment as applied to candidate who pledged to work at reduced salary, 71 L Ed 2d 732

Insured serviceman's beneficiary designation under life policy issued pursuant to Servicemen's Group Life Insurance Act (38 USCS §§ 765 et seq.), held to prevail over constructive trust imposed upon proceeds by state court, 70 L Ed 2d 39

BENEFICIARIES AND BENEFITS—Cont'd
Medicare and Medicaid (this index)
Social Security (this index)
Taxation: trust beneficiary's disclaimer of contingent interest in testamentary trust, held taxable transfer of property by gift under 26 USCS §§ 2501(a)(1) and 2511(a), not excepted from tax by 26 CFR § 25.2511-1(c), 71 L Ed 2d 170

BEVERAGES
Alcohol (this index)

BIAS AND PREJUDICE
Collateral relief: "cause and actual prejudice," rather than "plain error" of Rule 52(b) of Federal Rules of Criminal Procedure, held proper standard of review on motion for collateral relief under 28 USCS § 2255, 71 L Ed 2d 816
Discrimination (this index)
Juror's submission, during criminal trial, of job application to prosecutor's office and failure of prosecution to disclose such fact during trial, held not violative of due process, 71 L Ed 2d 78

BIDDING SYSTEMS
Leases: Interior Secretary's refusal to use non-cash-bonus bidding systems in leasing oil and gas tracts on outer continental shelf, held not violative of Outer Continental Shelf Lands Act Amendments, (43 USCS §§ 1331 et seq.), 70 L Ed 2d 309

BILL OF COMPLAINT
Decedents' estates: California's motion for leave to file bill of complaint against Texas to decide whether Howard Hughes was domiciled in California or Texas at time of death, granted as properly invoking Supreme Court's original jurisdiction, 72 L Ed 2d 755

BILLS OF LADING
Freight charges: carrier's violation of Interstate Commerce Commission's credit regulations, held not to bar collection of lawful freight charges from consignor, 72 L Ed 2d 114

INDEX

BLACK PERSONS
Boycotts: First Amendment held to preclude state court imposition of liability on participants in black boycott of white businesses for losses other than those caused by their own violence or threats, 73 L Ed 2d 1215
Racial Discrimination (this index)

BOARDS AND COMMISSIONS
Due-on-sale clauses: Federal Home Loan Bank Board regulation authorizing due-on-sale clauses in federal savings and loan instruments held to preempt state law, 73 L Ed 2d 664
School Boards (this index)

BOATS AND BOATING
Admiralty (this index)

BODILY RESTRAINTS
Mentally retarded person: involuntarily committed mentally retarded person, held to have due process liberty interests requiring state to provide minimally adequate training to insure safety and freedom from undue restraint, 73 L Ed 2d 28

BONDS
Securities (this index)

BOOKS
Summary judgment: Federal District Court's entry of summary judgment in case challenging local school board's removal of library books as violative of First Amendment, held erroneous where material issue of fact remained as to board's justifications, 73 L Ed 2d 435

BORDERS OR BOUNDARIES
Accretions: United States held entitled to oceanfront accretions to Coast Guard reservation under federal rule that accretions belong to upland owner, 73 L Ed 2d 1
Interstate Commerce (this index)

BOYCOTTS
First Amendment held to preclude state court imposition of liability on participants in black boycott of white businesses for losses other than those caused by their own violence or threats, 73 L Ed 2d 1215

BOYCOTTS—Cont'd

Secondary boycott: refusal by longshoremen's union to unload cargoes shipped from Soviet Union in protest against Afghanistan invasion, held illegal secondary boycott under 29 USCS § 158(b)(4), 72 L Ed 2d 21

BREACHES

Collective bargaining: section 13(c) of Urban Mass Transportation Act of 1964 (49 USCS § 1609(c)), held not to create federal cause of action for breach of § 13(c) agreement or collective bargaining contract between local transit authority and union, 72 L Ed 2d 639

BREAKS

Confession obtained through custodial interrogation after illegal arrest, held excluded where intervening events did not break causal connection between illegal arrest and confession, 73 L Ed 2d 314

"BROTHER-SISTER CONTROLLED GROUP"

Corporations: Treasury Regulation (26 CFR § 1.1563-1(a)(3)) implementing statutory definition of "brother-sister controlled group" of corporations (26 USCS § 1563(a)), held unreasonable, 70 L Ed 2d 792

BUILDINGS

Cable television: New York law requiring landlords to allow cable television facilities on property, held to be "taking" of property compensable under Fifth and Fourteenth Amendments, 73 L Ed 2d 868

Construction and Building (this index)

Dwellings (this index)

BURDEN OF PROOF

Presumptions and Burden of Proof (this index)

BUREAU OF THE CENSUS

Address lists compiled by Bureau of the Census, held not subject to disclosure under Freedom of Information Act (5 USCS § 552) or discovery provisions of Federal Rules of Civil Procedure, 71 L Ed 2d 199

BUSINESS AGENT

Discharge of union business agent by newly-elected president of local union, held not violative of Labor Management Reporting and Disclosure Act (29 USCS §§ 401 et seq.), 72 L Ed 2d 239

INDEX

BUSINESS AGREEMENT
Certificate of deposit from federally regulated bank and business agreement arising from pledging of certificate as guarantee for loan, held not securities for purposes of 15 USCS § 78j(b), 71 L Ed 2d 409

BUSINESSES
Boycotts: First Amendment held to preclude state court imposition of liability on participants in black boycott of white businesses for losses other than those caused by their own violence or threats, 73 L Ed 2d 1215

Corporations (this index)

"BUSINESS OF INSURANCE"
Fees: insurer use of peer review committee to determine reasonableness of chiropractor's fees, held not exempt from antitrust laws as "business of insurance" under McCarran-Ferguson Act (15 USCS § 1012(b)), 73 L Ed 2d 647

BUSING
Schools: state constitutional amendment precluding state court-ordered school busing absent Fourteenth Amendment violation held constitutional, 73 L Ed 2d 948

"BY-ELECTION"
Legislative seat: Puerto Rico law vesting in political party authority to appoint replacement for member who vacates seat on legislature, held not violative of United States Constitution, 72 L Ed 2d 628

CABLE TELEVISION
Landlords: New York law requiring landlords to allow cable television facilities on property, held to be "taking" of property compensable under Fifth and Fourteenth Amendments, 73 L Ed 2d 868

"State action" doctrine: ordinance enacted by home-rule municipality prohibiting expansion of cable television operator's business, held not to be "state action" eligible for exemption from federal antitrust laws, 70 L Ed 2d 810

CAMPAIGNS
Elections (this index)

546

INDEX

CANCELLATION OR TERMINATION
Discharge or Removal (this index)
Dismissal of Actions or Charges (this index)
Employer and Employee (this index)
Mineral interests: state statute extinguishing unused mineral
ment due process and equal protection, 70 L Ed 2d 738
Parents' Rights. **Children and Minors** (this index)
Parole: rescission without hearing of prisoner's parole by Ohio
Adult Parole Authority, held not violative of due process
Suspension (this index)

CANDIDATES
Elections (this index)

CANNABIS
Licenses: municipal ordinance requiring license to sell "items
71 L Ed 2d 362

CAPACITY AND INCAPACITY
Insane and Incompetent Persons (this index)

CAPITAL CASES
Death Penalty (this index)
Instructions to jury: preclusion of jury instructions on lesser
Murder (this index)

CAPITAL GAINS
Corporations: Idaho's inclusion within taxable income of non-

CARE OF PATIENTS
Medicaid: nursing homes' decisions to discharge or transfer Medicaid patients to lower levels of care, held not to involve state action for purposes of Fourteenth Amendment's due process clause, 73 L Ed 2d 534

CARGO
Secondary boycott: refusal by longshoremen's union to unload cargoes shipped from Soviet Union in protest against Afghanistan invasion, held illegal secondary boycott under 29 USCS § 158(b)(4), 72 L Ed 2d 21

CARRIERS
Collective bargaining: section 13(c) of Urban Mass Transportation Act of 1964 (49 USCS § 1609(c)), held not to create federal cause of action for breach of § 13(c) agreement or collective bargaining contract between local transit authority and union, 72 L Ed 2d 639

Freight charges: carrier's violation of Interstate Commerce Commission's credit regulations, held not to bar collection of lawful freight charges from consignor, 72 L Ed 2d 114

CARS
Search and Seizure (this index)

CAUSAL CONNECTION
Confession obtained through custodial interrogation after illegal arrest, held excluded where intervening events did not break causal connection between illegal arrest and confession, 73 L Ed 2d 314

"CAUSE AND ACTUAL PREJUDICE"
Collateral relief: "cause and actual prejudice," rather than "plain error" of Rule 52(b) of Federal Rules of Criminal Procedure, held proper standard of review on motion for collateral relief under 28 USCS § 2255, 71 L Ed 2d 816

CAUSE OF ACTION
Dismissal of Actions or Charges (this index)

Prejudgment attachment: complaint against private creditor's prejudgment attachment, held to state cause of action under 42 USCS § 1983 where statute authorizing it is alleged to be procedurally defective, 73 L Ed 2d 482

CAUSE OF ACTION—Cont'd

Pro se complaint: state prisoner's crudely written, pro se complaint alleging his placement in solitary confinement for one-week period without any notice of charges or any hearing, held sufficient to state cause of action, 70 L Ed 2d 551

CENSUS

Address lists compiled by Bureau of the Census, held not subject to disclosure under Freedom of Information Act (5 USCS § 552) or discovery provisions of Federal Rules of Civil Procedure, 71 L Ed 2d 199

CERTIFICATE OF DEPOSIT

Securities: certificate of deposit from federally regulated bank and business agreement arising from pledging of certificate as guarantee for loan, held not securities for purposes of 15 USCS § 78j(b), 71 L Ed 2d 409

CERTIFICATION OF CASE

Death penalty: question as to what premises of state law support a conclusion that a death sentence was not impaired by the invalidity of one of the statutory aggravating circumstances found by the jury, certified to Georgia Supreme Court, 72 L Ed 2d 222

CERTIORARI

Appeal and Review (this index)

CESSATION ORDERS

Pollution: Federal District Court relief of violations of permit requirements of Federal Water Pollution Control Act (33 USCS §§ 1251 et seq.), held not limited to immediate cessation orders, 72 L Ed 2d 91

CHANGE OR MODIFICATION

Attorney's fees: postjudgment request for attorney's fees under Civil Rights Attorney's Fees Awards Act (42 USCS § 1988), held not subject to 10-day timeliness standard of Rule 59(e) of Federal Rules of Civil Procedure, 71 L Ed 2d 325

Busing: state constitutional amendment precluding state court-ordered school busing absent Fourteenth Amendment violation held constitutional, 73 L Ed 2d 948

INDEX

INDEX

CHECKS

Deposit of bad check in federally insured bank, held not proscribed by 18 USCS § 1014, 73 L Ed 2d 767

CHIEF OF POLICE

Licenses: ordinance directing city's police chief to consider applicant's "connection with criminal elements" in licensing amusement establishments, held not unconstitutionally vague, 71 L Ed 2d 152

CHILDREN AND MINORS

Amusements: ordinance directing city's police chief to consider applicant's "connection with criminal elements" in licensing amusement establishments, held not unconstitutionally vague, 71 L Ed 2d 152

Education. **Schools and Education** (this index)

Emergency assistance: state emergency assistance program precluding furnishing assistance to AFDC recipients, held invalid under supremacy clause (Art VI, cl 2) as in conflict with valid federal regulation, 72 L Ed 2d 728

First Amendment: state statute which requires, under all circumstances, exclusion of press and general public from courtroom during testimony of minor victim in sex-offense trial, held violative of First Amendment, 73 L Ed 2d 248

Habeas corpus statute (28 USCS § 2254(a)), held not to confer jurisdiction on federal courts to consider collateral challenges to state court judgments involuntarily terminating parental rights, 73 L Ed 2d 928

Mitigation of penalty: state trial judge's refusal to consider defendant's family history and emotional disturbance in mitigation in death penalty sentencing hearing, held violative of Eighth and Fourteenth Amendments, 71 L Ed 2d 1

Parental termination proceeding: application of at least "clear and convincing evidence" standard of proof to state's parental rights termination proceeding, held required by Fourteenth Amendment due process clause, 71 L Ed 2d 599

Paternity suits: Texas statute barring paternity suits brought on behalf of illegitimate children more than one year after their birth, held violative of equal protection, 71 L Ed 2d 770

Schools and Education (this index)

CHILDREN AND MINORS—Cont'd

Sexual performances: New York criminal statute prohibiting knowing promotion of sexual performances by children under 16, by distribution of material depicting such performances, held constitutional, 73 L Ed 2d 1113

Youth Corrections Act (18 USCS §§ 5005 et seq.), held not to require that youth offender sentenced to adult term while serving youth term must receive youth treatment for remainder of youth term, 70 L Ed 2d 345

CHIROPRACTORS

Fees: insurer use of peer review committee to determine reasonableness of chiropractor's fees, held not exempt from antitrust laws as "business of insurance" under McCarran-Ferguson Act (15 USCS § 1012(b)), 73 L Ed 2d 647

CHOICE

Insurance beneficiary: insured serviceman's beneficiary designation under life policy issued pursuant to Servicemen's Group Life Insurance Act (38 USCS §§ 765 et seq.), held to prevail over constructive trust imposed upon proceeds by state court, 70 L Ed 2d 39

CHOICE OF LAW

Dismissal: plaintiff's showing that substantive law of alternative forum would be less favorable to plaintiff than that of chosen forum, held not to defeat motion to dismiss on ground of forum non conveniens, 70 L Ed 2d 419

CHURCHES

Religion and Religious Institutions (this index)

CITIES

Municipal Corporations and Other Political Subdivisions (this index)

CITIZENS

Aliens And Citizens (this index)

CIVIL DAMAGES

Privileges and Immunities (this index)

INDEX

CIVILIANS

Speedy trial: time between dismissal of military charges and subsequent indictment of individual on civilian charges held not to be considered in determining whether violation of right to speedy trial under Sixth Amendment has occurred, 71 L Ed 2d 696

CIVIL LIABILITY

Antitrust: nonprofit association of mechanical engineers responsible for promulgation of industry codes, held civilly liable under antitrust laws for antitrust violations of its agents committed with apparent authority, 72 L Ed 2d 330

CIVIL PROCEDURE

Federal Rules of Civil Procedure (this index)

CIVIL RIGHTS

Attorney's fees: postjudgment request for attorney's fees under Civil Rights Attorney's Fees Awards Act (42 USCS § 1988), held not subject to 10-day timeliness standard of Rule 59(e) of Federal Rules of Civil Procedure, 71 L Ed 2d 325

Bail: claim that Nebraska's prohibition of pretrial bail to person charged with sexual offenses violated Federal Constitution, held moot where defendant had already been convicted of offenses, 71 L Ed 2d 353

"Color of state law": public defender performing lawyer's traditional functions, held not acting "under color of state law" for purposes of suit under 42 USCS § 1983, 70 L Ed 2d 509

Discrimination (this index)

Job Discrimination (this index)

Racial Discrimination (this index)

Taxpayer's damages action under 42 USCS § 1983 for alleged unconstitutional administration of state tax system, held barred in federal court by principle of comity, 70 L Ed 2d 271

CIVIL SERVICE

Public Officers and Employees (this index)

INDEX

CLAIM STATEMENTS
Mineral interests: state statute extinguishing unused mineral interests after 20 years unless owner files statement of claim, held not violative of contract clause, Fifth Amendment just compensation clause, and Fourteenth Amendment due process and equal protection, 70 L Ed 2d 738

CLASS ACTIONS
Promotion: Mexican-American employee who was denied promotion, held not entitled to maintain class action on behalf of Mexican-American applicants for employment who were not hired, 72 L Ed 2d 740

CLASS AND CLASSIFICATION
Constitutional challenges: trade associations and political action committees, held barred from invoking expedited constitutional challenge procedures of Federal Election Campaign Act (2 USCS § 437h), 71 L Ed 2d 432
Discrimination (this index)

CLEAR AND CONVINCING EVIDENCE
Parental termination proceeding: application of at least "clear and convincing evidence" standard of proof to state's parental rights termination proceeding, held required by Fourteenth Amendment due process clause, 71 L Ed 2d 599

"CLEARLY ERRONEOUS" STANDARD
Seniority: Federal Court of Appeals' reversal of Federal District Court ruling as to legality of seniority system under 42 USCS § 2000e-5(h), held erroneous in view of court's independent determination of allegations of discrimination, 72 L Ed 2d 66
Trademark: Federal Court of Appeals' reversal of District Court's findings as to trademark infringement by generic drug manufacturers, held error where "clearly erroneous" standard of FRCP 52 not followed, 72 L Ed 2d 606

COAL
Welfare fund: coal producer sued on promise to contribute to union welfare funds based on "purchased coal," held entitled to plead and have adjudicated illegality defense, 70 L Ed 2d 833

INDEX

COAST GUARD
Accretions: United States held entitled to oceanfront accretions to Coast Guard reservation under federal rule that accretions belong to upland owner, 73 L Ed 2d 1

CODES OF INDUSTRY
Antitrust: nonprofit association of mechanical engineers responsible for promulgation of industry codes, held civilly liable under antitrust laws for antitrust violations of its agents committed with apparent authority, 72 L Ed 2d 330

COLLATERAL CHALLENGES
Habeas corpus statute (28 USCS § 2254(a)), held not to confer jurisdiction on federal courts to consider collateral challenges to state court judgments involuntarily terminating parental rights, 73 L Ed 2d 928

COLLATERAL ESTOPPEL
Job bias: giving of preclusive effect to state court's review of state agency's action on job bias claim upon later action in federal court on such claim under similar federal law, held required by 28 USCS § 1738, 72 L Ed 2d 262

COLLATERAL ORDERS OR RELIEF
Appeals: denial of motion to dismiss indictment on ground of prosecutorial vindictiveness, held not collateral order that can be appealed prior to judgment under 28 USCS § 1291, 73 L Ed 2d 754
"Cause and actual prejudice," rather than "plain error" of Rule 52(b) of Federal Rules of Criminal Procedure, held proper standard of review on motion for collateral relief under 28 USCS § 2255, 71 L Ed 2d 816

COLLECTIONS
Freight charges: carrier's violation of Interstate Commerce Commission's credit regulations, held not to bar collection of lawful freight charges from consignor, 72 L Ed 2d 114

COLLECTIVE BARGAINING
Confidential employees: National Labor Relations Board's "labor nexus" test for determining eligibility of confidential employees for inclusion in collective bargaining units, held to have reasonable basis in law, 70 L Ed 2d 323

COLLECTIVE BARGAINING—Cont'd

Employer's unilateral withdrawal from multiemployer bargaining unit, held not justified by bargaining impasse, 70 L Ed 2d 656

Health benefits: collective bargaining contract allocating health benefits among potential beneficiaries of employee trust fund, held not reviewable for reasonableness under Labor Management Relations Act (29 USCS § 186(c) (5)), 71 L Ed 2d 419

Jurisdiction: filing of timely charge with Equal Employment Opportunity Commission held not jurisdictional prerequisite to suit under Title VII of Civil Rights Act of 1964 (42 USCS §§ 2000e et seq.), 71 L Ed 2d 234

Soviet invasion: work stoppage to protest Soviet invasion of Afghanistan, held subject to anti-injunction provisions of Norris-LaGuardia Act (29 USCS §§ 101 et seq.), and not enjoinable pending aribtrator's decision as to whether strike violated collective-bargaining contract, 73 L Ed 2d 327

Subcontracting: union signatory subcontracting clauses sought or negotiated in context of collective bargaining relationship, held protected by construction industry proviso to 29 USCS § 158(e), 72 L Ed 2d 398

Transportation: section 13(c) of Urban Mass Transportation Act of 1964 (49 USCS § 1609(c)), held not to create federal cause of action for breach of § 13(c) agreement or collective bargaining contract between local transit authority and union, 72 L Ed 2d 639

Welfare fund: coal producer sued on promise to contribute to union welfare funds based on "purchased coal," held entitled to plead and have adjudicated illegality defense, 70 L Ed 2d 833

COLLEGES

Universities and Colleges (this index)

COLLISIONS

Boats: complaint alleging collision between two pleasure boats on navigable waters, held to state claim within federal admiralty jurisdiction, 73 L Ed 2d 300

COLOR OF STATE LAW

Prejudgment attachment: complaint against private creditor's prejudgment attachment, held to state cause of action under 42 USCS § 1983 where statute authorizing it is alleged to be procedurally defective, 73 L Ed 2d 482

Private school whose income is derived primarily from public sources and which is regulated by public authorities, held not to have acted under color of state law for purposes of 42 USCS § 1983 when it discharged certain employees, 73 L Ed 2d 418

Public defender performing lawyer's traditional functions, held not acting "under color of state law" for purposes of suit under 42 USCS § 1983, 70 L Ed 2d 509

COMITY

Also see **Full Faith and Credit Clause** (this index)

Habeas corpus: state prisoner's habeas corpus petition filed under 28 USCS § 2254, held required to be dismissed by Federal District Court when it contains both exhausted and unexhausted claims, 71 L Ed 2d 379

Taxpayer's damages action under 42 USCS § 1983 for alleged unconstitutional administration of state tax system, held barred in federal court by principle of comity, 70 L Ed 2d 271

COMMERCE

Bankruptcy: employee protection provisions of Rock Island Transition and Employee Assistance Act (45 USCS §§ 1005 and 1008), held violative of bankruptcy clause (Art I, § 8, cl 4), 71 L Ed 2d 335

Carriers (this index)

Interstate Commerce (this index)

Secondary boycott: refusal by longshoremen's union to unload cargoes shipped from Soviet Union in protest against Afghanistan invasion, held illegal secondary boycott under 29 USCS § 158(b)(4), 72 L Ed 2d 21

Statute of limitations: New Jersey statute tolling limitation period for actions against unrepresented foreign corporations, held not violative of Fourteenth Amendment's equal protection clause, 71 L Ed 2d 250

COMMERCIAL PAPER

Banks (this index)

COMMERCIAL SPEECH
Licenses: municipal ordinance requiring license to sell "items designed or marketed for use with illegal cannabis or drugs," held not unconstitutionally vague or overbroad, 71 L Ed 2d 362

COMMISSIONS
Boards and Commissions (this index)

COMMITMENT
Insane and Incompetent Persons (this index)

COMMITTEES
Elections (this index)

COMMODITY EXCHANGE ACT
Damages: action for damages caused by violation of Commodity Exchange Act (7 USCS §§ 1 et seq.), held available to private parties, 72 L Ed 2d 182

COMMON CARRIER
Carriers (this index)

COMMUNICATION SYSTEMS
Entertainment and Amusements (this index)

COMPARTMENTS
Search warrant: authority to conduct warrantless search of motor vehicle based on probable cause, including compartments and containers, held coextensive with authority based on magistrate's issuance of warrant, 72 L Ed 2d 572

COMPENSABLE INJURY
Presumption of compensability under § 20(a) of Longshoremen's and Harbor Workers' Compensation Act (33 USCS § 290(a)), held inapplicable to claimed injury at work where "injury" arose at home, 71 L Ed 2d 495

COMPENSATING USE TAX
Federal contractors: imposition of New Mexico's gross receipts and compensating use taxes on federal contractors doing business in state, held valid, 71 L Ed 2d 580

COMPENSATION AND INCOME
Attorney's Fees (this index)

INDEX

COMPENSATION AND INCOME—Cont'd

Backpay: employer's offer to discrimination claimant of job previously denied without offer of retroactive seniority, held to toll continuing accrual of backpay liability under 42 USCS § 2000e-6(g), 73 L Ed 2d 721

Bankruptcy (this index)

Cable television: New York law requiring landlords to allow cable television facilities on property, held to be "taking" of property compensable under Fifth and Fourteenth Amendments, 73 L Ed 2d 868

Collective Bargaining (this index)

Contributions and Solicitation of Funds (this index)

Distribution: Alaska statute distributing income derived from state's natural resources to state's citizens in varying amounts based on length of each citizen's residency, held to violate equal protection clause, 72 L Ed 2d 672

First Amendment: Kentucky statute prohibiting candidates from offering benefits to voters in exchange for votes, held violative of First Amendment as applied to candidate who pledged to work at reduced salary, 71 L Ed 2d 732

Gift Tax (this index)

Income Tax (this index)

Just Compensation Clause (this index)

Medicare and Medicaid (this index)

Physicians and Surgeons (this index)

Presumption of compensability under § 20(a) of Longshoremen's and Harbor Workers' Compensation Act (33 USCS § 290(a)), held inapplicable to claimed injury at work where "injury" arose at home, 71 L Ed 2d 495

Private school whose income is derived primarily from public sources and which is regulated by public authorities, held not to have acted under color of state law for purposes of 42 USCS § 1983 when it discharged certain employees, 73 L Ed 2d 418

Seamen: limiting period during which wage penalty for failure to pay seamen promptly after discharge is assessed under 46 USCS § 596, held not within discretion of Federal District Courts, 73 L Ed 2d 973

Social Security (this index)

Taxation. **Income Tax** (this index)

559

INDEX

COMPENSATION AND INCOME—Cont'd
"Two-step" pay increase rule of 5 USCS § 5334(b), held not
to apply to federal employees promoted from prevailing
wage rate system (WS) to General Schedule (GS), 70 L Ed
2d 768

COMPETITION
Monopolies and Restraints of Trade (this index)

COMPLAINTS
Pleadings (this index)

CONCLUSIONS OF LAW
Death penalty: question as to what premises of state law
support a conclusion that a death sentence was not impaired by the invalidity of one of the statutory aggravating
circumstances found by the jury, certified to Georgia
Supreme Court, 72 L Ed 2d 222

CONDEMNATION
Eminent Domain or Condemnation (this index)

CONDUCT AND MISCONDUCT
Discipline (this index)
District and Prosecuting Attorneys (this index)
Immunity: senior aides and advisers of President of United
States, held entitled to qualified immunity from civil dam-
ages suits insofar as their conduct does not violate rights
of which reasonable person would have known, 73 L Ed
2d 396

CONFESSIONS
Arrests: confession obtained through custodial interrogation
after illegal arrest, held excluded where intervening events
did not break causal connection between illegal arrest and
confession, 73 L Ed 2d 314

CONFIDENTIALITY
Address lists compiled by Bureau of the Census, held not
subject to disclosure under Freedom of Information Act (5
USCS § 552) or discovery provisions of Federal Rules of
Civil Procedure, 71 L Ed 2d 199
"Labor nexus" test: National Labor Relations Board's "labor
nexus" test for determining eligibility of confidential employees for inclusion in collective bargaining units, held to
have reasonable basis in law, 70 L Ed 2d 323

INDEX

CONFINEMENT
Custody (this index)

CONFLICT OF LAWS
Dismissal: plaintiff's showing that substantive law of alternative forum would be less favorable to plaintiff than that of chosen forum, held not to defeat motion to dismiss on ground of forum non conveniens, 70 L Ed 2d 419

CONGRESS
Elections (this index)
Establishment clause: taxpayers' organization dedicated to separation of church and state, held to have no standing to challenge, as violative of First Amendment establishment clause, no-cost transfer of surplus United States property to religious educational institution, 70 L Ed 2d 700
Legislative History and Intent (this index)
Public Utilities Regulatory Policies Act: provisions of Public Utility Regulatory Policies Act (15 USCS §§ 3201 et seq.; 16 USCS §§ 824a-3, 2611 et seq.), held not violative of commerce clause (Art I, § 8, cl 3) and Tenth Amendment, 72 L Ed 2d 532
Reapportionment Plan (this index)

"CONNECTIONS WITH CRIMINAL ELEMENTS"
Licenses: ordinance directing city's police chief to consider applicant's "connection with criminal elements" in licensing amusement establishments, held not unconstitutionally vague, 71 L Ed 2d 152

CONSECUTIVE PRISON TERMS
Cruel and unusual punishment: sentence of two consecutive 20-year prison terms and two fines of $10,000 for convictions of possession and distribution of 9 ounces of marijuana, held not to constitute cruel and unusual punishment under Eighth Amendment, 70 L Ed 2d 556

CONSENT
Arrest: rule of Payton v New York prohibiting warrantless, nonconsensual entry into suspect's home to make routine felony arrest, held to apply to case pending on direct appeal when Payton was decided, 73 L Ed 2d 202

CONSERVATION AND POLLUTION
Environmental Law (this index)

561

CONSIGNMENTS

Freight charges: carrier's violation of Interstate Commerce Commission's credit regulations, held not to bar collection of lawful freight charges from consignor, 72 L Ed 2d 114

CONSOLIDATION OF ORDERS

Racial quotas: case challenging voluntary adoption by municipal board of education of racial quotas on enrollment, held not moot, and ordered consolidated with related case, 72 L Ed 2d 668

CONSPIRACY

Psychologist's fees: health plan subscriber denied reimbursement for psychologist's fees, held to have standing to sue for conspiracy to exclude psychologists from psychotherapy market, 73 L Ed 2d 149

CONSTITUTIONAL AMENDMENTS

Schools: state constitutional amendment precluding state court-ordered school busing absent Fourteenth Amendment violation held constitutional, 73 L Ed 2d 948

CONSTITUTIONAL LAW

As to particular areas of constitutional law, see more specific topics

CONSTRUCTION AND BUILDING

Collective bargaining: union signatory subcontracting clauses sought or negotiated in context of collective bargaining relationship, held protected by construction industry proviso to 29 USCS § 158(e), 72 L Ed 2d 398

Gross Receipts (this index)

CONSTRUCTIVE TRUSTS

Insurance beneficiary: insured serviceman's beneficiary designation under life policy issued pursuant to Servicemen's Group Life Insurance Act (38 USCS §§ 765 et seq.), held to prevail over constructive trust imposed upon proceeds by state court, 70 L Ed 2d 39

CONTAINERS

Search warrant: authority to conduct warrantless search of motor vehicle based on probable cause, including compartments and containers, held coextensive with authority based on magistrate's issuance of warrant, 72 L Ed 2d 572

INDEX

CONTEMPORANEOUS OBJECTION RULE
Habeas corpus: assertions of state prisoners in federal habeas corpus proceedings that jury instructions given at their trials violated due process, held barred where prisoners did not comply with state contemporaneous objection rule, 71 L Ed 2d 783

CONTINENTAL SHELF
Bidding system: Interior Secretary's refusal to use non-cash-bonus bidding systems in leasing oil and gas tracts on outer continental shelf, held not violative of Outer Continental Shelf Lands Act Amendments, (43 USCS §§ 1331 et seq.), 70 L Ed 2d 309

CONTINGENT INTERESTS
Taxation: trust beneficiary's disclaimer of contingent interest in testamentary trust, held taxable transfer of property by gift under 26 USCS §§ 2501(a)(1) and 2511(a), not excepted from tax by 26 CFR § 25.2511-1(c), 71 L Ed 2d 170

CONTINUING ACCRUAL OF LIABILITY
Backpay: employer's offer to discrimination claimant of job previously denied without offer of retroactive seniority, held to toll continuing accrual of backpay liability under 42 USCS § 2000e-6(g), 73 L Ed 2d 721

CONTINUING VIOLATION CLAIMS
Discrimination: black "tester" given false information about housing availability and nonprofit, open housing organization, held to have standing to challenge racial steering under Fair Housing Act (42 USCS § 3612); Act's 180-day limitations period (42 USCS § 3612(a)), held not bar claims of continuing violation, even though some incidents alleged occur outside period, 71 L Ed 2d 214

CONTRABAND
Search and Seizure (this index)

CONTRACT CLAUSE
Mineral interests: state statute extinguishing unused mineral interests after 20 years unless owner files statement of claim, held not violative of contract clause, Fifth Amendment just compensation clause, and Fourteenth Amendment due process and equal protection, 70 L Ed 2d 738

INDEX

CONTRACTORS

Also see **Construction and Building** (this index)

Affirmative action plan: Federal Court of Appeals' refusal to resolve pendent state-law claim in affirming affirmative action plan for contractors as constitutional, held abuse of discretion, 73 L Ed 2d 245

Sales and use taxes: imposition of New Mexico's gross receipts and compensating use taxes on federal contractors doing business in state, held valid, 71 L Ed 2d 580

CONTRACTS AND AGREEMENTS

Bankruptcy Court's exercise of jurisdiction over state-law contract claims pursuant to 28 USCS § 1471, held violative of Article III, 73 L Ed 2d 598

Certificate of deposit from federally regulated bank and business agreement arising from pledging of certificate as guarantee for loan, held not securities for purposes of 15 USCS § 78j(b), 71 L Ed 2d 409

Collective Bargaining (this index)

Commodity Exchange Act: action for damages caused by violation of Commodity Exchange Act (7 USCS §§ 1 et seq.), held available to private parties, 72 L Ed 2d 182

Due-on-sale clauses: Federal Home Loan Bank Board regulation authorizing due-on-sale clauses in federal savings and loan instruments held to preempt state law, 73 L Ed 2d 664

Military: federal court jurisdiction over action for monetary damages brought by discharged military exchange employee, held not conferred by Tucker Act (28 USCS § 1346(a)(2)) in absence of express or implied contract, 72 L Ed 2d 520

Price-fixing: agreement among competing physicians setting, by majority vote, maximum fees for payment from participants in specified insurance plans, held per se unlawful under § 1 of Sherman Act (15 USCS § 1), 73 L Ed 2d 48

Treaties: word "treaty" in 5 USCS § 7201 note, which excepts from certain employment discrimination requirements actions permitted by "treaty," held to include executive agreements, 71 L Ed 2d 715

INDEX

INDEX

CORPORATIONS—Cont'd
Foreign Corporations (this index)
Income Tax (this index)
Subsidiary Corporations (this index)
Takeover: Illinois business takeover statute, held unconstitutional under commerce clause (Art I, § 8, cl 3), 73 L Ed 2d 269

CORRECTIONAL INSTITUTIONS
Penal and Correctional Institutions (this index)

COSTS, EXPENSES, AND FEES
Attorney's Fees (this index)
Compensation and Income (this index)
Constitutional challenges: trade associations and political action committees, held barred from invoking expedited constitutional challenge procedures of Federal Election Campaign Act (2 USCS § 437h), 71 L Ed 2d 432
Freight charges: carrier's violation of Interstate Commerce Commission's credit regulations, held not to bar collection of lawful freight charges from consignor, 72 L Ed 2d 114
Interpreters: deaf student held not entitled to sign-language interpreter in public school classes, under Education for All Handicapped Children Act, where she was receiving adequate education and personalized instruction, 73 L Ed 2d 690
Medicaid: nursing homes' decisions to discharge or transfer Medicaid patients to lower levels of care, held not to involve state action for purposes of Fourteenth Amendment's due process clause, 73 L Ed 2d 534
Physicians and Surgeons (this index)

COUNCIL OF COUNTY
Election method: letter to Attorney General advising of results of county referendum endorsing at-large method of electing county council, held to be request for reconsideration of Attorney General's prior objections to method and not preclearance request under Voting Rights Act (42 USCS § 1973c), 70 L Ed 2d 576

COUNSEL
Attorneys (this index)
566

INDEX

COUNSELING SERVICES
Discrimination: black "tester" given false information about housing availability and nonprofit, open housing organization, held to have standing to challenge racial steering under Fair Housing Act (42 USCS § 3612); Act's 180-day limitations period (42 USCS § 3612(a)), held not bar claims of continuing violation, even though some incidents alleged occur outside period, 71 L Ed 2d 214

COUNTIES
Elections (this index)

COURT OF CLAIMS
Medicare: determinations by insurance carriers of amount of benefits payable under Part B of Medicare program (42 USCS §§ 1395j et seq.), held not reviewable in Court of Claims, 72 L Ed 2d 12

COURTROOM
First Amendment: state statute which requires, under all circumstances, exclusion of press and general public from courtroom during testimony of minor victim in sex-offense trial, held violative of First Amendment, 73 L Ed 2d 248

COURTS
As to particular courts or matters pertaining to courts, see more specific topics

CREDIT AND LOANS
Certificate of deposit from federally regulated bank and business agreement arising from pledging of certificate as guarantee for loan, held not securities for purposes of 15 USCS § 78j(b), 71 L Ed 2d 409

Due-on-sale clauses: Federal Home Loan Bank Board regulation authorizing due-on-sale clauses in federal savings and loan instruments held to preempt state law, 73 L Ed 2d 664

CREDITOR'S RIGHTS
Attachment (this index)

CREDITS
Freight charges: carrier's violation of Interstate Commerce Commission's credit regulations, held not to bar collection of lawful freight charges from consignor, 72 L Ed 2d 114

567

DAMAGES

Antitrust: nonprofit association of mechanical engineers responsible for promulgation of industry codes, held civilly liable under antitrust laws for antitrust violations of its agents committed with apparent authority, 72 L Ed 2d 330

Attorney's fees incurred during proceedings before National Labor Relations Board, held not proper element of damages under § 303(b) of Labor Management Relations Act (29 USCS § 187(b)), 72 L Ed 2d 511

Backpay: employer's offer to discrimination claimant of job previously denied without offer of retroactive seniority, held to toll continuing accrual of backpay liability under 42 USCS § 2000e-6(g), 73 L Ed 2d 721

Boycotts: First Amendment held to preclude state court imposition of liability on participants in black boycott of white businesses for losses other than those caused by their own violence or threats, 73 L Ed 2d 1215

Commodity Exchange Act: action for damages caused by violation of Commodity Exchange Act (7 USCS §§ 1 et seq.), held available to private parties, 72 L Ed 2d 182

Military: federal court jurisdiction over action for monetary damages brought by discharged military exchange employee, held not conferred by Tucker Act (28 USCS § 1346(a)(2)) in absence of express or implied contract, 72 L Ed 2d 520

Privileges and Immunities (this index)

DATE

Time and Date (this index)

DEAF STUDENTS

Interpreters: deaf student held not entitled to sign-language interpreter in public school classes, under Education for All Handicapped Children Act, where she was receiving adequate education and personalized instruction, 73 L Ed 2d 690

DEATH

Decedents' Estates (this index)

INDEX

DEATH PENALTY

Aiding and abetting: imposition of death penalty on person who aids and abets felony in course of which murder is committed by others but who does not himself kill, attempt to kill, or intend to kill, held to violate of Eighth and Fourteenth Amendments, 73 L Ed 2d 1140

Mitigation of penalty: state trial judge's refusal to consider defendant's family history and emotional disturbance in mitigation in death penalty sentencing hearing, held violative of Eighth and Fourteenth Amendments, 71 L Ed 2d 1

Question as to what premises of state law support a conclusion that a death sentence was not impaired by the invalidity of one of the statutory aggravating circumstances found by the jury, certified to Georgia Supreme Court, 72 L Ed 2d 222

DEATH TAX

Interpleader: action under Federal Interpleader Act (28 USCS § 1335) to resolve inconsistent death tax claims on estate of Howard Hughes by officials of two states, held barred by Eleventh Amendment, 72 L Ed 2d 694

DECEDENTS' ESTATES

Death tax claim: action under Federal Interpleader Act (28 USCS § 1335) to resolve inconsistent death tax claims on estate of Howard Hughes by officials of two states, held barred by Eleventh Amendment, 72 L Ed 2d 694

Domicile: California's motion for leave to file bill of complaint against Texas to decide whether Howard Hughes was domiciled in California or Texas at time of death, granted as properly invoking Supreme Court's original jurisdiction, 72 L Ed 2d 755

DECEIT

Fraud and Deceit (this index)

DECISIONS OF COURT

Judgments, Orders, and Decrees (this index)

DECLARATORY JUDGMENT

Elections: jurisdiction to decide whether § 5 of Voting Rights Act of 1965 (42 USCS § 1973c) applies to changes in local election procedures, held within power of state court, 72 L Ed 2d 824

INDEX

DECREASE
Compensation and Income (this index)

DECREES
Judgments, Orders, and Decrees (this index)

"DEEMING" OF SPOUSE'S INCOME
Medicaid: state's unlimited deeming of Medicaid applicant's spouse's income as available to applicant in determining eligibility, held barred by 42 USCS § 1396a(a), 71 L Ed 2d 137

DEFENSES
Welfare fund: coal producer sued on promise to contribute to union welfare funds based on "purchased coal," held entitled to plead and have adjudicated illegality defense, 70 L Ed 2d 833

DELAY
Speedy trial: time between dismissal of military charges and subsequent indictment of individual on civilian charges held not to be considered in determining whether violation of right to speedy trial under Sixth Amendment has occurred, 71 L Ed 2d 696

DELEGATION OF POWER
Cable television: ordinance enacted by home-rule municipality prohibiting expansion of cable television operator's business, held not to be "state action" eligible for exemption from federal antitrust laws, 70 L Ed 2d 810

DENIAL OR REFUSAL
District and Prosecuting Attorneys (this index)
In-state status: state university's policy of denying in-state status to domiciled nonimmigrant aliens holding G-4 visas, held violative of supremacy clause (Art VI, cl 2), 73 L Ed 2d 563
Mental patients: case presenting question whether state involuntarily committed patients may refuse certain drugs, vacated and remanded to Federal Court of Appeals, to consider intervening state decision opinion bearing on issue, 73 L Ed 2d 16
Secondary boycott: refusal by longshoremen's union to unload cargoes shipped from Soviet Union in protest against Afghanistan invasion, held illegal secondary boycott under 29 USCS § 158(b)(4), 72 L Ed 2d 21

INDEX

DENOMINATIONAL PREFERENCES

First Amendment: Minnesota statute exempting from certain registration and reporting requirements only religious organizations receiving more than 50% of contributions from members, held violative of First Amendment establishment clause, 72 L Ed 2d 33

DEPORTATION

Aliens: government's deportation of alien witnesses, held not violative of Fifth and Sixth Amendments absent some showing evidence lost would be both material and favoable to defendant, 73 L Ed 2d 1193

DEPOSITS

Checks: deposit of bad check in federally insured bank, held not proscribed by 18 USCS § 1014, 73 L Ed 2d 767

Full faith and credit: North Carolina courts' refusal to treat as res judicata Indiana rehabilitation court's adjudication of rights to insurance company's deposit posted in North Carolina, held violative of full faith and credit clause (Art IV, § 1), 71 L Ed 2d 558

DEPRIVATION OF PROPERTY

Eminent Domain or Condemnation (this index)

Just Compensation Clause (this index)

Prejudgment attachment: complaint against private creditor's prejudgment attachment, held to state cause of action under 42 USCS § 1983 where statute authorizing it is alleged to be procedurally defective, 73 L Ed 2d 482

DEPUTY PROBATION OFFICERS

Citizens: state statute requiring peace officers, including deputy probation officers, to be United States citizens, held not violative of equal protection clause of Fourteenth Amendment, 70 L Ed 2d 677

DILUTION

Elections: at-large election system for large rural county with large black population held violative of equal protection clause, 73 L Ed 2d 1012

INDEX

DIRECT APPEAL

Fair Labor Standards Act: appeal taken to Federal Court of Appeals of District Court decision finding application of Fair Labor Standards Act unconstitutional, held improper under 28 USCS §§ 1252 and 1291, and appeal to Supreme Court dismissed, 70 L Ed 2d 570

DISABLED PERSONS

Insane and Incompetent Persons (this index)

Interpreters: deaf student held not entitled to sign-language interpreter in public school classes, under Education for All Handicapped Children Act, where she was receiving adequate education and personalized instruction, 73 L Ed 2d 690

DISBARMENT

Attorney disciplinary rules: federal court abstention from considering challenge to constitutionality of attorney disciplinary rules that were subject of pending state disciplinary proceeding within jurisdiction of New Jersey Supreme Court held required, 73 L Ed 2d 116

DISCHARGE OR REMOVAL

Medicaid: nursing homes' decisions to discharge or transfer Medicaid patients to lower levels of care, held not to involve state action for purposes of Fourteenth Amendment's due process clause, 73 L Ed 2d 534

Military: federal court jurisdiction over action for monetary damages brought by discharged military exchange employee, held not conferred by Tucker Act (28 USCS § 1346(a)(2)) in absence of express or implied contract, 72 L Ed 2d 520

Schools and Education (this index)

Seamen: limiting period during which wage penalty for failure to pay seamen promptly after discharge is assessed under 46 USCS § 596, held not within discretion of Federal District Courts, 73 L Ed 2d 973

Union business agent: discharge of union business agent by newly-elected president of local union, held not violative of Labor Management Reporting and Disclosure Act (29 USCS §§ 401 et seq.), 72 L Ed 2d 239

573

DISCIPLINE

Attorney disciplinary rules: federal court abstention from considering challenge to constitutionality of attorney disciplinary rules that were subject of pending state disciplinary proceeding within jurisdiction of New Jersey Supreme Court held required, 73 L Ed 2d 116

Discharge of union business agent by newly-elected president of local union, held not violative of Labor Management Reporting and Disclosure Act (29 USCS §§ 401 et seq.), 72 L Ed 2d 239

DISCLAIMERS

Taxation: trust beneficiary's disclaimer of contingent interest in testamentary trust, held taxable transfer of property by gift under 26 USCS §§ 2501(a)(1) and 2511(a), not excepted from tax by 26 CFR § 25.2511-1(c), 71 L Ed 2d 170

DISCLOSURE AND DISCOVERY

Freedom of Information Act (this index)

Jurisdiction: District Court's action in establishing personal jurisdiction as sanction for failure to comply with discovery order under Rule 37 of of Federal Rules of Civil Procedure held not violative of due process, 72 L Ed 2d 492

Juror's submission, during criminal trial, of job application to prosecutor's office and failure of prosecution to disclose such fact during trial, held not violative of due process, 71 L Ed 2d 78

Search: absence of "exigent circumstances," held not to preclude warrantless search of car conducted after police officers discovered contraband in justified inventory search of car, 73 L Ed 2d 750

Union "outsider rule," held not violative of Labor-Management Reporting and Disclosure Act's "free speech and assembly" or "right to sue" provisions (29 USCS § 411(a)(2), (4)), 72 L Ed 2d 707

DISCOVERY

Disclosure and Discovery (this index)

574

DISCRETION

Address lists compiled by Bureau of the Census, held not subject to disclosure under Freedom of Information Act (5 USCS § 552) or discovery provisions of Federal Rules of Civil Procedure, 71 L Ed 2d 199

Affirmative action plan: Federal Court of Appeals' refusal to resolve pendent state-law claim in affirming affirmative action plan for contractors as constitutional, held abuse of discretion, 73 L Ed 2d 245

Immunity: senior aides and advisers of President of United States, held entitled to qualified immunity from civil damages suits insofar as their conduct does not violate rights of which reasonable person would have known, 73 L Ed 2d 396

DISCRIMINATION

Elections: jurisdiction to decide whether § 5 of Voting Rights Act of 1965 (42 USCS § 1973c) applies to changes in local election procedures, held within power of state court, 72 L Ed 2d 824

Employment. **Job Discrimination** (this index)

Hiring Practices (this index)

Job Discrimination (this index)

Limitation of Actions (this index)

Promotions (this index)

Racial Discrimination (this index)

Reapportionment Plan (this index)

Religion and Religious Institutions (this index)

Schools and Education (this index)

Seniority (this index)

Severance tax imposed on oil and gas removed from Indian reservation, held authorized by Tribe's inherent authority to tax as part of power of self-government, and held violative of commerce clause (Art I, § 8, cl 3), 71 L Ed 2d 21

Sex Discrimination (this index)

Treaties: employment practices of a New York corporation that is wholly-owned subsidiary of Japanese firm, held not exempted from Title VII of Civil Rights Act (42 USCS §§ 2000e et seq.) by treaty between the United States and Japan, 72 L Ed 2d 765

INDEX

DISMISSAL OF ACTIONS OR CHARGES

Bail: claim that Nebraska's prohibition of pretrial bail to person charged with sexual offenses violated Federal Constitution, held moot where defendant had already been convicted of offenses, 71 L Ed 2d 353

Bankruptcy: dismissal of Chapter XI petition filed under 1898 Bankruptcy Act in order to refile under Chapter 11 of 1978 Bankruptcy Code, held not authorized by Bankruptcy Rule 11-42(a) or § 403(a) of Bankruptcy Reform Act of 1978, 70 L Ed 2d 542

Fair Labor Standards Act: appeal taken to Federal Court of Appeals of District Court decision finding application of Fair Labor Standards Act unconstitutional, held improper under 28 USCS §§ 1252 and 1291, and appeal to Supreme Court dismissed, 70 L Ed 2d 570

Forum non conveniens: plaintiff's showing that substantive law of alternative forum would be less favorable to plaintiff that that of chosen forum, held not to defeat motion to dismiss on ground of forum non conveniens, 70 L Ed 2d 419

Habeas corpus: state prisoner's habeas corpus petition filed under 28 USCS § 2254, held required to be dismissed by Federal District Court when it contains both exhausted and unexhausted claims, 71 L Ed 2d 379

Indictment and Information (this index)

Jurisdiction (this index)

DISQUALIFICATION

Qualification and Disqualification (this index)

DISTILLERS OF ALCOHOL

State alcoholic beverage control law enforcing distiller's designation of wholesaler, held not per se violative of Sherman Act (15 USCS §§ 1 et seq.), 73 L Ed 2d 1042

DISTRIBUTION

Drugs and Narcotics (this index)

Income distribution: Alaska statute distributing income derived from state's natural resources to state's citizens in varying amounts based on length of each citizen's residency, held to violate equal protection clause, 72 L Ed 2d 672

Sexual performances: New York criminal statute prohibiting knowing promotion of sexual performances by children under 16, by distribution of material depicting such performances, held constitutional, 73 L Ed 2d 1113

INDEX

DISTRICT AND PROSECUTING ATTORNEYS

DISTRICT COURTS

DISTRICTS

DIVERSITY OF CITIZENSHIP

DIVIDENDS

DRUGS AND NARCOTICS—Cont'd

Licenses: municipal ordinance requiring license to sell "items designed or marketed for use with illegal cannabis or drugs," held not unconstitutionally vague or overbroad, 71 L Ed 2d 362

Mental patients: case presenting question whether state involuntarily committed patients may refuse certain drugs, vacated and remanded to Federal Court of Appeals, to consider intervening state decision opinion bearing on issue, 73 L Ed 2d 16

Schools: federal courts' replacement of local school board's construction of its own rules on mandatory suspension in action under 42 USCS § 1983, held erroneous where board's construction was reasonable, 73 L Ed 2d 1273

Search and Seizure (this index)

Trademark: Federal Court of Appeals' reversal of District Court's findings as to trademark infringement by generic drug manufacturers, held error where "clearly erroneous" standard of FRCP 52 not followed, 72 L Ed 2d 606

DUE-ON-SALE CLAUSES

Federal Home Loan Bank Board regulation authorizing due-on-sale clauses in federal savings and loan instruments held to preempt state law, 73 L Ed 2d 664

DUE PROCESS

District and Prosecuting Attorneys (this index)
Employer and Employee (this index)
Habeas Corpus (this index)
Income Tax (this index)

Instructions to jury: preclusion of jury instructions on lesser included offense in capital case, held not to require new trial where defendant's own evidence negates possibility that such instruction was warranted, 72 L Ed 2d 367

Jurisdiction: District Court's action in establishing personal jurisdiction as sanction for failure to comply with discovery order under Rule 37 of of Federal Rules of Civil Procedure held not violative of due process, 72 L Ed 2d 492

Licenses: municipal ordinance requiring license to sell "items designed or marketed for use with illegal cannabis or drugs," held not unconstitutionally vague or overbroad, 71 L Ed 2d 362

INDEX

DUE PROCESS—Cont'd
Medicare and Medicaid (this index)
Mineral interests: state statute extinguishing unused mineral interests after 20 years unless owner files statement of claim, held not violative of contract clause, Fifth Amendment just compensation clause, and Fourteenth Amendment due process and equal protection, 70 L Ed 2d 738
Parental termination proceeding: application of at least "clear and convincing evidence" standard of proof to state's parental rights termination proceeding, held required by Fourteenth Amendment due process clause, 71 L Ed 2d 599
Parole: rescission without hearing of prisoner's parole by Ohio Adult Parole Authority, held not violative of due process under Fourteenth Amendment, 70 L Ed 2d 13
Prejudgment attachment: complaint against private creditor's prejudgment attachment, held to state cause of action under 42 USCS § 1983 where statute authorizing it is alleged to be procedurally defective, 73 L Ed 2d 482
Service of process: Kentucky statute applicable to forcible entry and detainer actions permitting service of process by posting summons on door of premises, held violative of due process, 72 L Ed 2d 249

DWELLINGS
Also see **Residence and Domicile**
Compensable injury: presumption of compensability under § 20(a) of Longshoremen's and Harbor Workers' Compensation Act (33 USCS § 920(a)), held inapplicable to claimed injury at work where "injury" arose at home, 71 L Ed 2d 495
Discrimination: black "tester" given false information about housing availability and nonprofit, open housing organization, held to have standing to challenge racial steering under Fair Housing Act (42 USCS § 3612); Act's 180-day limitations period (42 USCS § 3612(a)), held not bar claims of continuing violation, even though some incidents alleged occur outside period, 71 L Ed 2d 214
Search and Seizure (this index)

EARNINGS
Compensation and Income (this index)
580

ECONOMIC CONDITIONS OR MATTERS

Cable television: New York law requiring landlords to allow cable television facilities on property, held to be "taking" of property compensable under Fifth and Fourteenth Amendments, 73 L Ed 2d 868

Private school whose income is derived primarily from public sources and which is regulated by public authorities, held not to have acted under color of state law for purposes of 42 USCS § 1983 when it discharged certain employees, 73 L Ed 2d 418

EDUCATION

Schools and Education (this index)

EEOC

Jurisdiction: filing of timely charge with Equal Employment Opportunity Commission held not jurisdictional prerequisite to suit under Title VII of Civil Rights Act of 1964 (42 USCS §§ 2000e et seq.), 71 L Ed 2d 234

EIGHTH AMENDMENT

Cruel and Unusual Punishment (this index)
Death Penalty (this index)

ELECTION OR CHOICE

Insurance beneficiary: insured serviceman's beneficiary designation under life policy issued pursuant to Servicemen's Group Life Insurance Act (38 USCS §§ 765 et seq.), held to prevail over constructive trust imposed upon proceeds by state court, 70 L Ed 2d 39

ELECTIONS

At-Large Election Methods (this index)
Attorney General (this index)
Benefits to voters: Kentucky statute prohibiting candidates from offering benefits to voters in exchange for votes, held violative of First Amendment as applied to candidate who pledged to work at reduced salary, 71 L Ed 2d 732
Contributions and Solicitation of Funds (this index)
Discharge of union business agent by newly-elected president of local union, held not violative of Labor Management Reporting and Disclosure Act (29 USCS §§ 401 et seq.), 72 L Ed 2d 239
Federal Election Campaign Act (this index)

ELECTIONS—Cont'd

Jurisdiction to decide whether § 5 of Voting Rights Act of 1965 (42 USCS § 1973c) applies to changes in local election procedures, held within power of state court, 72 L Ed 2d 824

Price-fixing: agreement among competing physicians setting, by majority vote, maximum fees for payment from participants in specified insurance plans, held per se unlawful under § 1 of Sherman Act (15 USCS § 1), 73 L Ed 2d 48

Public officer: provisions of Texas Constitution limiting public official's ability to become candidate for another public office, held not violative of First Amendment or equal protection clause of Fourteenth Amendment, 73 L Ed 2d 508

Reapportionment Plan (this index)

Stay. **Reapportionment Plan** (this index)

Union "outsider rule," held not violative of Labor-Management Reporting and Disclosure Act's "free speech and assembly" or "right to sue" provisions (29 USCS § 411(a)(2), (4)), 72 L Ed 2d 707

Vacating legislative seat: Puerto Rico law vesting in political party authority to appoint replacement for member who vacates seat on legislature, held not violative of United States Constitution, 72 L Ed 2d 628

ELECTRICITY

Public utility: state public utility commission's order requiring privately-owned and federally-licensed public utility to sell within state hydroelectric energy it had been exporting, held violative of commerce clause (Art I, § 8, cl 3), 71 L Ed 2d 188

ELEVENTH AMENDMENT

Admiralty: process issued by Federal District Court to secure possession of property from state officials in admiralty in rem action, held not barred by Eleventh Amendment, 73 L Ed 2d 1057

Death tax claim: action under Federal Interpleader Act (28 USCS § 1335) to resolve inconsistent death tax claims on estate of Howard Hughes by officials of two states, held barred by Eleventh Amendment, 72 L Ed 2d 694

ELIGIBILITY

Qualification and Disqualification (this index)

INDEX

EMBARRASSMENT
First Amendment: state statute which requires, under all circumstances, exclusion of press and general public from courtroom during testimony of minor victim in sex-offense trial, held violative of First Amendment, 73 L Ed 2d 248

EMERGENCY ASSISTANCE
Supremacy clause: state emergency assistance program precluding furnishing assistance to AFDC recipients, held invalid under supremacy clause (Art VI, cl 2) as in conflict with valid federal regulation, 72 L Ed 2d 728

EMERGENCY PETROLEUM ALLOCATION ACT
Taxation: Temporary Emergency Court of Appeals' invalidation of anti-passthrough provision of state tax statute relating to oil company revenues, vacated and remanded in light of expiration of preempting federal price control authority, 71 L Ed 2d 120

EMINENT DOMAIN OR CONDEMNATION
Cable television: New York law requiring landlords to allow cable television facilities on property, held to be "taking" of property compensable under Fifth and Fourteenth Amendments, 73 L Ed 2d 868

EMOTIONAL DISTURBANCE
Mitigation of penalty: state trial judge's refusal to consider defendant's family history and emotional disturbance in mitigation in death penalty sentencing hearing, held violative of Eighth and Fourteenth Amendments, 71 L Ed 2d 1

EMPLOYER AND EMPLOYEE
Affirmative action plan: Federal Court of Appeals' refusal to resolve pendent state-law claim in affirming affirmative action plan for contractors as constitutional, held abuse of discretion, 73 L Ed 2d 245

EMPLOYER AND EMPLOYEE—Cont'd
Contractors (this index)
Discharge or Removal (this index)
Discrimination. **Job Discrimination** (this index)
Elections (this index)
Fair Labor Standards Act: appeal taken to Federal Court of Appeals of District Court decision finding application of Fair Labor Standards Act unconstitutional, held improper under 28 USCS §§ 1252 and 1291, and appeal to Supreme Court dismissed, 70 L Ed 2d 570
Hearing: termination of Illinois fair employment practices act claimant's claim because of state's failure to convene hearing within 120 days, held violative of Fourteenth Amendment due process and equal protection, 71 L Ed 2d 265
Hiring Practices (this index)
Job Discrimination (this index)
Juror's submission, during criminal trial, of job application to prosecutor's office and failure of prosecution to disclose such fact during trial, held not violative of due process, 71 L Ed 2d 78
Labor Management Relations Act (this index)
Longshoremen (this index)
National Labor Relations Act or Board (this index)
Promotions (this index)
Public Officers and Employees (this index)
Railroads (this index)
Seniority (this index)
Sex Discrimination (this index)
Soviet Union (this index)
Treaties (this index)
Unfair Labor Practices (this index)
Union "outsider rule," held not violative of Labor-Management Reporting and Disclosure Act's "free speech and assembly" or "right to sue" provisions (29 USCS § 411(a)(2), (4)), 72 L Ed 2d 707

ENERGY
Power and Energy (this index)
584

INDEX

ENGINEERS

Antitrust: nonprofit association of mechanical engineers responsible for promulgation of industry codes, held civilly liable under antitrust laws for antitrust violations of its agents committed with apparent authority, 72 L Ed 2d 330

ENROLLMENT
Admission and Enrollment (this index)

ENTERTAINMENT AND AMUSEMENTS
Cable Television (this index)
Lewdness, Indecency, and Obscenity (this index)
Licenses: ordinance directing city's police chief to consider applicant's "connection with criminal elements" in licensing amusement establishments, held not unconstitutionally vague, 71 L Ed 2d 152

ENVIRONMENTAL LAW

Cessation orders: Federal District Court relief of violations of permit requirements of Federal Water Pollution Control Act (33 USCS §§ 1251 et seq.), held not limited to immediate cessation orders, 72 L Ed 2d 91

Nuclear weapons: § 102 (2)(c) of the National Environmental Policy Act (42 USCS § 4332 (2)(c)), held not to require Navy to prepare and release "Hypothetical Environmental Impact Statement" regarding nuclear weapons storage, 70 L Ed 2d 298

EQUAL EMPLOYMENT OPPORTUNITY COMMISSION

Jurisdiction: filing of timely charge with Equal Employment Opportunity Commission held not jurisdictional prerequisite to suit under Title VII of Civil Rights Act of 1964 (42 USCS §§ 2000e et seq.), 71 L Ed 2d 234

EQUAL HOUSING OPPORTUNITIES

Discrimination: black "tester" given false information about housing availability and nonprofit, open housing organization, held to have standing to challenge racial steering under Fair Housing Act (42 USCS § 3612); Act's 180-day limitations period (42 USCS § 3612(a)), held not bar claims of continuing violation, even though some incidents alleged occur outside period, 71 L Ed 2d 214

EQUAL PROTECTION
Aliens and Citizens (this index)

EQUAL PROTECTION—Cont'd

Elections (this index)

Employment hearing: termination of Illinois fair employment practices act claimant's claim because of state's failure to convene hearing within 120 days, held violative of Fourteenth Amendment due process and equal protection, 71 L Ed 2d 265

Foreign corporations: New Jersey statute tolling limitation period for actions against unrepresented foreign corporations, held not violative of Fourteenth Amendment's equal protection clause, 71 L Ed 2d 250

Income distribution: Alaska statute distributing income derived from state's natural resources to state's citizens in varying amounts based on length of each citizen's residency, held to violate equal protection clause, 72 L Ed 2d 672

Mineral interests: state statute extinguishing unused mineral interests after 20 years unless owner files statement of claim, held not violative of contract clause, Fifth Amendment just compensation clause, and Fourteenth Amendment due process and equal protection, 70 L Ed 2d 738

Paternity suits: Texas statute barring paternity suits brought on behalf of illegitimate children more than one year after their birth, held violative of equal protection, 71 L Ed 2d 770

Sex discrimination: state-supported university's policy that excludes males from enrolling in its professional nursing school, held violative of equal protection clause of Fourteenth Amendment, 73 L Ed 2d 1090

ERROR

Appeal and Review (this index)

ESTABLISHMENT CLAUSE

Religion and Religious Institutions (this index)

ESTATES

Decedents' Estates (this index)

EVICTION

Service of process: Kentucky statute applicable to forcible entry and detainer actions permitting service of process by posting summons on door of premises, held violative of due process, 72 L Ed 2d 249

EVIDENCE
Burden of proof. **Presumptions and Burden of Proof** (this index)

"Cause and actual prejudice," rather than "plain error" of Rule 52(b) of Federal Rules of Criminal Procedure, held proper standard of review on motion for collateral relief under 28 USCS § 2255, 71 L Ed 2d 816

"Clearly Erroneous" Standard (this index)

Confession obtained through custodial interrogation after illegal arrest, held excluded where intervening events did not break causal connection between illegal arrest and confession, 73 L Ed 2d 314

Deportation: government's deportation of alien witnesses, held not violative of Fifth and Sixth Amendments absent some showing evidence lost would be both material and favorable to defendant, 73 L Ed 2d 1193

Discrimination (this index)

First Amendment (this index)

Habeas corpus: federal court's order in habeas corpus proceeding that state trial court must grant habeas petitioner new criminal trial or explain reasons for its inconsistent verdicts, held erroneous, 70 L Ed 2d 530

Job Discrimination (this index)

Jury and Jury Trials (this index)

Miranda warnings: state prosecutor's cross-examination of defendant as to post-arrest silence, held not violative of Fourteenth Amendment due process in absence of Miranda warning assurances, 71 L Ed 2d 490

Mitigation of penalty: state trial judge's refusal to consider defendant's family history and emotional disturbance in mitigation in death penalty sentencing hearing, held violative of Eighth and Fourteenth Amendments, 71 L Ed 2d 1

Obscenity: proof, in public nuisance abatement action by city against motion picture theater, that motion pictures in question were obscene beyond reasonable doubt, held not required, 70 L Ed 2d 262

Parental termination proceeding: application of at least "clear and convincing evidence" standard of proof to state's parental rights termination proceeding, held required by Fourteenth Amendment due process clause, 71 L Ed 2d 599

Presumptions and Burden of Proof (this index)

EVIDENCE—Cont'd

Search and Seizure (this index)

Securities: statute (18 USCS § 2314) prohibiting transport of forged securities in "interstate commerce," held not to require proof securities were forged before being taken across state lines, 71 L Ed 2d 522

EXAMINATIONS AND TESTS

Discrimination: prima facie case under 42 USCS § 2000e-2 in regard to test that bars promotion and disproportionately excludes blacks, held not precluded by nondiscriminatory "bottom line" result of employer's promotional process, 73 L Ed 2d 130

EXCEPTIONS AND EXEMPTIONS

Cable television: ordinance enacted by home-rule municipality prohibiting expansion of cable television operator's business, held not to be "state action" eligible for exemption from federal antitrust laws, 70 L Ed 2d 810

"Cause and actual prejudice," rather than "plain error" of Rule 52(b) of Federal Rules of Criminal Procedure, held proper standard of review on motion for collateral relief under 28 USCS § 2255, 71 L Ed 2d 816

Confession obtained through custodial interrogation after illegal arrest, held excluded where intervening events did not break causal connection between illegal arrest and confession, 73 L Ed 2d 314

Discrimination: prima facie case under 42 USCS § 2000e-2 in regard to test that bars promotion and disproportionately excludes blacks, held not precluded by nondiscriminatory "bottom line" result of employer's promotional process, 73 L Ed 2d 130

Election method: letter to Attorney General advising of results of county referendum endorsing at-large method of electing county council, held to be request for reconsideration of Attorney General's prior objections to method and not preclearance request under Voting Rights Act (42 USCS § 1973c), 70 L Ed 2d 576

First Amendment (this index)

Freedom of Information Act (this index)

EXCEPTIONS AND EXEMPTIONS—Cont'd

Habeas corpus: assertions of state prisoners in federal habeas corpus proceedings that jury instructions given at their trials violated due process, held barred where prisoners did not comply with state contemporaneous objection rule, 71 L Ed 2d 783

Physicians and Surgeons (this index)

Reapportionment plan: Federal District Court effecting interim Texas congressional reapportionment for districts objected to by Attorney General, held without power to redraw other districts in absence of constitutional or statutory violation, 71 L Ed 2d 725

Social security: imposition of social security taxes on persons who object on religious grounds to receipt of public insurance benefits and to payment of taxes to support such benefits, held constitutional, 71 L Ed 2d 127

State university's refusal to grant student religious group access to university facilities generally open to other student groups, held unjustifiable, content-based exclusion of religious speech, 70 L Ed 2d 440

Taxation: trust beneficiary's disclaimer of contingent interest in testamentary trust, held taxable transfer of property by gift under 26 USCS §§ 2501(a)(1) and 2511(a), not excepted from tax by 26 CFR § 25.2511-1(c), 71 L Ed 2d 170

Treaties (this index)

EXCHANGES

Also see **Sales and Transfers**

Commodity Exchange Act: action for damages caused by violation of Commodity Exchange Act (7 USCS §§ 1 et seq.), held available to private parties, 72 L Ed 2d 182

EXCLUSIONS

Exceptions and Exemptions (this index)

EXCLUSIVE JURISDICTION

Decedents' estates: California's motion for leave to file bill of complaint against Texas to decide whether Howard Hughes was domiciled in California or Texas at time of death, granted as properly invoking Supreme Court's original jurisdiction, 72 L Ed 2d 755

INDEX

EXECUTION OF WARRANTS
Admiralty: process issued by Federal District Court to secure possession of property from state officials in admiralty in rem action, held not barred by Eleventh Amendment, 73 L Ed 2d 1057

EXECUTIVE AGREEMENTS
Treaties: word "treaty" in 5 USCS § 7201 note, which excepts from certain employment discrimination requirements actions permitted by "treaty," held to include executive agreements, 71 L Ed 2d 715

EXEMPLARY OR PUNITIVE DAMAGES
Antitrust: nonprofit association of mechanical engineers responsible for promulgation of industry codes, held civilly liable under antitrust laws for antitrust violations of its agents committed with apparent authority, 72 L Ed 2d 330

EXEMPTIONS
Exceptions and Exemptions (this index)

EXHAUSTION OF REMEDIES
Habeas corpus: state prisoner's habeas corpus petition filed under 28 USCS § 2254, held required to be dismissed by Federal District Court when it contains both exhausted and unexhausted claims, 71 L Ed 2d 379

Prerequisites: exhaustion of state administrative remedies, held not prerequisite to bringing action pursuant to 42 USCS § 1983, 73 L Ed 2d 172

EXIGENT CIRCUMSTANCES
Search: absence of "exigent circumstances," held not to preclude warrantless search of car conducted after police officers discovered contraband in justified inventory search of car, 73 L Ed 2d 750

EXPEDITED CONSTITUTIONAL CHALLENGE PROCEDURES
Trade associations and political action committees, held barred from invoking expedited constitutional challenge procedures of Federal Election Campaign Act (2 USCS § 437h), 71 L Ed 2d 432

EXPENSES
Costs, Expenses, and Fees (this index)

590

"EXPLANATORY INFORMATION"
Election method: letter to Attorney General advising of results of county referendum endorsing at-large method of electing county council, held to be request for reconsideration of Attorney General's prior objections to method and not preclearance request under Voting Rights Act (42 USCS § 1973c), 70 L Ed 2d 576

EXPORTS
Imports and Exports (this index)

EXPRESS CONTRACTS
Military: federal court jurisdiction over action for monetary damages brought by discharged military exchange employee, held not conferred by Tucker Act (28 USCS § 1346(a)(2)) in absence of express or implied contract, 72 L Ed 2d 520

EXTINGUISHMENT
Cancellation or Termination (this index)

FACTS
Removal of books: Federal District Court's entry of summary judgment in case challenging local school board's removal of library books as violative of First Amendment, held erroneous where material issue of fact remained as to board's justifications, 73 L Ed 2d 435

FAIR EMPLOYMENT PRACTICES ACTS
Hearing: termination of Illinois fair employment practices act claimant's claim because of state's failure to convene hearing within 120 days, held violative of Fourteenth Amendment due process and equal protection, 71 L Ed 2d 265

FAIR HOUSING ACT OF 1968
Discrimination: black "tester" given false information about housing availability and nonprofit, open housing organization, held to have standing to challenge racial steering under Fair Housing Act (42 USCS § 3612); Act's 180-day limitations period (42 USCS § 3612(a)), held not bar claims of continuing violation, even though some incidents alleged occur outside period, 71 L Ed 2d 214

FAIR LABOR STANDARDS ACT
Appeal taken to Federal Court of Appeals of District Court decision finding application of Fair Labor Standards Act unconstitutional, held improper under 28 USCS §§ 1252 and 1291, and appeal to Supreme Court dismissed, 70 L Ed 2d 570

FAIR TRIAL
Habeas corpus: federal court's order in habeas corpus proceeding that state trial court must grant habeas petitioner new criminal trial or explain reasons for its inconsistent verdicts, held erroneous, 70 L Ed 2d 530

Juror's submission, during criminal trial, of job application to prosecutor's office and failure of prosecution to disclose such fact during trial, held not violative of due process, 71 L Ed 2d 78

FALSE INFORMATION
Fraud and Deceit (this index)

FAMILY AND RELATIVES
Death penalty: state trial judge's refusal to consider defendant's family history and emotional disturbance in mitigation in death penalty sentencing hearing, held violative of Eighth and Fourteenth Amendments, 71 L Ed 2d 1

Emergency assistance: state emergency assistance program precluding furnishing assistance to AFDC recipients, held invalid under supremacy clause (Art VI, cl 2) as in conflict with valid federal regulation, 72 L Ed 2d 728

Husband and Wife (this index)

FARMWORKERS
Discrimination: Commonwealth of Puerto Rico held to have standing to sue as parens patriae to enjoin applegrowers' discrimination against Puerto Rican migrant farmworkers, 73 L Ed 2d 995

FATHERS
Paternity suits: Texas statute barring paternity suits brought on behalf of illegitimate children more than one year after their birth, held violative of equal protection, 71 L Ed 2d 770

FEDERAL AID
Funds and Funding (this index)

INDEX

FEDERAL CONTRACTORS

Sales and use taxes: imposition of New Mexico's gross receipts and compensating use taxes on federal contractors doing business in state, held valid, 71 L Ed 2d 580

FEDERAL COURTS

Admiralty (this index)

Appeal and Review (this index)

Cessation orders: Federal District Court relief of violations of permit requirements of Federal Water Pollution Control Act (33 USCS §§ 1251 et seq.), held not limited to immediate cessation orders, 72 L Ed 2d 91

"Clearly Erroneous" Standard (this index)

Elections (this index)

Habeas Corpus (this index)

Job Discrimination (this index)

Jurisdiction (this index)

Military: federal court jurisdiction over action for monetary damages brought by discharged military exchange employee, held not conferred by Tucker Act (28 USCS § 1346(a)(2)) in absence of express or implied contract, 72 L Ed 2d 520

Reapportionment Plan (this index)

Schools and Education (this index)

Taxpayer's damages action under 42 USCS § 1983 for alleged unconstitutional administration of state tax system, held barred in federal court by principle of comity, 70 L Ed 2d 271

FEDERAL ELECTION CAMPAIGN ACT

Campaign expenditures: designation by political party's state committees of national senatorial campaign committee as agent for purposes of making campaign expenditures, held not foreclosed by provision of Federal Election Campaign Act (2 USCS § 441a(d)(3)), 70 L Ed 2d 23

Trade associations and political action committees, held barred from invoking expedited constitutional challenge procedures of Federal Election Campaign Act (2 USCS § 437h), 71 L Ed 2d 432

FEDERAL EMPLOYEES

Public Officers and Employees (this index)

FEDERAL ENERGY REGULATORY COMMISSION
Public Utilities Regulatory Policies Act: provisions of Public
Utility Regulatory Policies Act (15 USCS §§ 3201 et seq.;
16 USCS §§ 824a-3, 2611 et seq.), held not violative of
commerce clause (Art I, § 8, cl 3) and Tenth Amendment,
72 L Ed 2d 532

FEDERAL FUNDS
Funds and Funding (this index)

FEDERAL GIFT TAXES
Gift Tax (this index)

FEDERAL HOME LOAN BANK BOARD
Due-on-sale clauses: Federal Home Loan Bank Board regulation authorizing due-on-sale clauses in federal savings and
loan instruments held to preempt state law, 73 L Ed 2d
664

FEDERAL INTERPLEADER ACT
Death tax claim: action under Federal Interpleader Act (28
USCS § 1335) to resolve inconsistent death tax claims on
estate of Howard Hughes by officials of two states, held
barred by Eleventh Amendment, 72 L Ed 2d 694

FEDERALLY-LICENSED UTILITIES
Hydroelectric energy: state public utility commission's order
requiring privately-owned and federally-licensed public
utility to sell within state hydroelectric energy it had been
exporting, held violative of commerce clause (Art I, § 8, cl
3), 71 L Ed 2d 188

FEDERAL POWER ACT
Hydroelectric energy: state public utility commission's order
requiring privately-owned and federally-licensed public
utility to sell within state hydroelectric energy it had been
exporting, held violative of commerce clause (Art I, § 8, cl
3), 71 L Ed 2d 188

FEDERAL PRICE AUTHORITY
Taxation: Temporary Emergency Court of Appeals' invalidation of anti-passthrough provision of state tax statute
relating to oil company revenues, vacated and remanded
in light of expiration of preempting federal price control
authority, 71 L Ed 2d 120

INDEX

FEDERAL RULES OF CIVIL PROCEDURE

Attorney's fees: postjudgment request for attorney's fees under Civil Rights Attorney's Fees Awards Act (42 USCS § 1988), held not subject to 10-day timeliness standard of Rule 59(e) of Federal Rules of Civil Procedure, 71 L Ed 2d 325

Disclosure and Discovery (this index)

Seniority: Federal Court of Appeals' reversal of Federal District Court ruling as to legality of seniority system under 42 USCS § 2000e-5(h), held erroneous in view of court's independent determination of allegations of discrimination, 72 L Ed 2d 66

Trademark: Federal Court of Appeals' reversal of District Court's findings as to trademark infringement by generic drug manufacturers, held error where "clearly erroneous" standard of FRCP 52 not followed, 72 L Ed 2d 606

FEDERAL RULES OF CRIMINAL PROCEDURE

"Cause and actual prejudice," rather than "plain error" of Rule 52(b) of Federal Rules of Criminal Procedure, held proper standard of review on motion for collateral relief under 28 USCS § 2255, 71 L Ed 2d 816

FEDERAL WATER POLLUTION CONTROL ACT

Cessation orders: Federal District Court relief of violations of permit requirements of Federal Water Pollution Control Act (33 USCS §§ 1251 et seq.), held not limited to immediate cessation orders, 72 L Ed 2d 91

FEES

Costs, Expenses, and Fees (this index)

FELONIES

Arrest: rule of Payton v New York prohibiting warrantless, nonconsensual entry into suspect's home to make routine felony arrest, held to apply to case pending on direct appeal when Payton was decided, 73 L Ed 2d 202

Capital Cases (this index)

Cruel and Unusual Punishment (this index)

Due process: fact that defendant was charged with felony after refusing to plead guilty to misdemeanor charges, held not to warrant presumption of prosecutorial vindictiveness in violation of due process, 73 L Ed 2d 74

INDEX

INDEX

FINES, PENALTIES, AND FORFEITURES
For related topic, see **Sentence and Punishment**
Cruel and Unusual Punishment (this index)
Death Penalty (this index)
Habeas corpus: assertions of state prisoners in federal habeas corpus proceedings that jury instructions given at their trials violated due process, held barred where prisoners did not comply with state contemporaneous objection rule, 71 L Ed 2d 783
Medicaid: nursing homes' decisions to discharge or transfer Medicaid patients to lower levels of care, held not to involve state action for purposes of Fourteenth Amendment's due process clause, 73 L Ed 2d 534
Seamen: limiting period during which wage penalty for failure to pay seamen promptly after discharge is assessed under 46 USCS § 596, held not within discretion of Federal District Courts, 73 L Ed 2d 973

FIRST AMENDMENT
Advertising: Missouri Supreme Court rule regulating attorney's advertising absent proof that regulated material was misleading, held violative of attorney's First Amendment rights, 71 L Ed 2d 64
Boycotts (this index)
Elections (this index)
Lewdness, Indecency, and Obscenity (this index)
Licenses: municipal ordinance requiring license to sell "items designed or marketed for use with illegal cannabis or drugs," held not unconstitutionally vague or overbroad, 71 L Ed 2d 362
Religion and Religious Institutions (this index)
Social security: imposition of social security taxes on persons who object on religious grounds to receipt of public insurance benefits and to payment of taxes to support such benefits, held constitutional, 71 L Ed 2d 127
Speech, Assembly, and Press Freedom (this index)

FORCIBLE ENTRY AND DETAINER
Service of process: Kentucky statute applicable to forcible entry and detainer actions permitting service of process by posting summons on door of premises, held violative of due process, 72 L Ed 2d 249

597

INDEX

FOREIGN CORPORATIONS
Full faith and credit: North Carolina courts' refusal to treat as res judicata Indiana rehabilitation court's adjudication of rights to insurance company's deposit posted in North Carolina, held violative of full faith and credit clause (Art IV, § 1), 71 L Ed 2d 558

Statute of limitations: New Jersey statute tolling limitation period for actions against unrepresented foreign corporations, held not violative of Fourteenth Amendment's equal protection clause, 71 L Ed 2d 250

Taxation: New Mexico's taxation of portion of dividends that corporation received from foreign subsidiaries that do no business in state, held to violate due process clause, 73 L Ed 2d 819

FOREIGN COUNTRIES OR STATES
Comity (this index)

Corporations. **Foreign Corporations** (this index)

Freedom of Information Act: citizenship information on foreign nationals, held to satisfy "similar files" requirement of Exemption 6 of Freedom of Information Act (5 USCS § 552(b)(6)), 72 L Ed 2d 358

Full Faith and Credit Clause (this index)

Imports and Exports (this index)

Puerto Rico (this index)

Soviet Union (this index)

Treaties: word "treaty" in 5 USCS § 7201 note, which excepts from certain employment discrimination requirements actions permitted by "treaty," held to include executive agreements, 71 L Ed 2d 715

Water: Nebraska statute forbidding withdrawal of ground water to foreign state which denies such privileges to Nebraska, held violative of Congress clause (Art 1, § 8 cl 3), 73 L Ed 2d 1254

FORFEITURES
Fines, Penalties, and Forfeitures (this index)

FORGERY
Securities: statute (18 USCS § 2314) prohibiting transport of forged securities in "interstate commerce," held not to require proof securities were forged before being taken across state lines, 71 L Ed 2d 522

INDEX

FORMER JEOPARDY
Double Jeopardy (this index)

FORUM NON CONVENIENS
Dismissal: plaintiff's showing that substantive law of alternative forum would be less favorable to plaintiff than that of chosen forum, held not to defeat motion to dismiss on ground of forum non conveniens, 70 L Ed 2d 419

FOURTEENTH AMENDMENT
Cable television: New York law requiring landlords to allow cable television facilities on property, held to be "taking" of property compensable under Fifth and Fourteenth Amendments, 73 L Ed 2d 868

Cruel and Unusual Punishment (this index)
Death Penalty (this index)
Double Jeopardy (this index)
Due Process (this index)
Equal Protection (this index)

First Amendment: state statute which requires, under all circumstances, exclusion of press and general public from courtroom during testimony of minor victim in sex-offense trial, held violative of First Amendment, 73 L Ed 2d 248

Mentally retarded person: involuntarily committed mentally retarded person, held to have due process liberty interests requiring state to provide minimally adequate training to insure safety and freedom from undue restraint, 73 L Ed 2d 28

Obscenity: proof, in public nuisance abatement action by city against motion picture theater, that motion pictures in question were obscene beyond reasonable doubt, held not required, 70 L Ed 2d 262

Schools and Education (this index)

FOURTH AMENDMENT
Search and Seizure (this index)

FRAUD AND DECEIT
Advertising: Missouri Supreme Court rule regulating attorney's advertising absent proof that regulated material was misleading, held violative of attorney's First Amendment rights, 71 L Ed 2d 64

Banks (this index)

INDEX

FULL FAITH AND CREDIT CLAUSE—Cont'd
Job bias: giving of preclusive effect to state court's review of state agency's action on job bias claim upon later action in federal court on such claim under similar federal law, held required by 28 USCS § 1738, 72 L Ed 2d 262
Res judicata: North Carolina courts' refusal to treat as res judicata Indiana rehabilitation court's adjudication of rights to insurance company's deposit posted in North Carolina, held violative of full faith and credit clause (Art IV, § 1), 71 L Ed 2d 558

FUNDS AND FUNDING
Admiralty: process issued by Federal District Court to secure possession of property from state officials in admiralty in rem action, held not barred by Eleventh Amendment, 73 L Ed 2d 1057
Collective bargaining: section 13(c) of Urban Mass Transportation Act of 1964 (49 USCS § 1609(c)), held not to create federal cause of action for breach of § 13(c) agreement or collective bargaining contract between local transit authority and union, 72 L Ed 2d 639
Contributions and Solicitation of Funds (this index)
Emergency assistance: state emergency assistance program precluding furnishing assistance to AFDC recipients, held invalid under supremacy clause (Art VI, cl 2) as in conflict with valid federal regulation, 72 L Ed 2d 728
Schools and Education (this index)
Union "outsider rule," held not violative of Labor-Management Reporting and Disclosure Act's "free speech and assembly" or "right to sue" provisions (29 USCS § 411(a)(2), (4)), 72 L Ed 2d 707

FUTURES CONTRACTS
Commodity Exchange Act: action for damages caused by violation of Commodity Exchange Act (7 USCS §§ 1 et seq.), held available to private parties, 72 L Ed 2d 182

GAMES
Entertainment and Amusements (this index)

GARNISHMENT
Attachment (this index)

GAS
Oil and Gas (this index)

601

INDEX

GENDER-BASED DISCRIMINATION
Sex Discrimination (this index)

GENERAL SCHEDULE
"Two-step" pay increase rule of 5 USCS § 5334(b), held not to apply to federal employees promoted from prevailing wage rate system (WS) to General Schedule (GS), 70 L Ed 2d 768

GENERIC DRUGS
Trademark: Federal Court of Appeals' reversal of District Court's findings as to trademark infringement by generic drug manufacturers, held error where "clearly erroneous" standard of FRCP 52 not followed, 72 L Ed 2d 606

GIFTS
Contributions and Solicitation of Funds (this index)
Taxation. **Gift Tax** (this index)

GIFT TAX
Adjusted basis: donor making gift of property on condition that donee pay resulting gift tax, held to realize taxable income to extent that gift tax paid by donee exceeds donor's adjusted basis in property, 72 L Ed 2d 777
Trust beneficiary's disclaimer of contingent interest in testamentary trust, held taxable transfer of property by gift under 26 USCS §§ 2501(a)(1) and 2511(a), not excepted from tax by 26 CFR § 25.2511-1(c), 71 L Ed 2d 170

GLOVE COMPARTMENT
Search: absence of "exigent circumstances," held not to preclude warrantless search of car conducted after police officers discovered contraband in justified inventory search of car, 73 L Ed 2d 750

GOVERNING LAW
Dismissal: plaintiff's showing that substantive law of alternative forum would be less favorable to plaintiff than that of chosen forum, held not to defeat motion to dismiss on ground of forum non conveniens, 70 L Ed 2d 419

GOVERNMENTAL AGENCIES
Job bias: giving of preclusive effect to state court's review of state agency's action on job bias claim upon later action in federal court on such claim under similar federal law, held required by 28 USCS § 1738, 72 L Ed 2d 262

INDEX

GOVERNMENTAL DECISIONS
Initiative: state initiative precluding school boards from requiring attendance at other than neighborhood schools, held unconstitutional, 73 L Ed 2d 896

GOVERNMENTAL OFFICERS AND EMPLOYEES
Public Officers and Employees (this index)

GRACE PERIOD
Mineral interests: state statute extinguishing unused mineral interests after 20 years unless owner files statement of claim, held not violative of contract clause, Fifth Amendment just compensation clause, and Fourteenth Amendment due process and equal protection, 70 L Ed 2d 738

GRATUITOUS SERVICES
First Amendment: Kentucky statute prohibiting candidates from offering benefits to voters in exchange for votes, held violative of First Amendment as applied to candidate who pledged to work at reduced salary, 71 L Ed 2d 732

GROSS RECEIPTS
Federal contractors: imposition of New Mexico's gross receipts and compensating use taxes on federal contractors doing business in state, held valid, 71 L Ed 2d 580

Schools: New Mexico tax imposed on gross receipts that non-Indian construction company received from tribal school board for construction of school on reservation, held preempted by federal law, 73 L Ed 2d 1174

GROUND WATER
Withdrawal: Nebraska statute forbidding withdrawal of ground water to foreign state which denies such privileges to Nebraska, held violative of Congress clause (Art 1, § 8 cl 3), 73 L Ed 2d 1254

GROUP INSURANCE
Beneficiary: insured serviceman's beneficiary designation under life policy issued pursuant to Servicemen's Group Life Insurance Act (38 USCS §§ 765 et seq.), held to prevail over constructive trust imposed upon proceeds by state court, 70 L Ed 2d 39

INDEX

INDEX

HANDICAPPED PERSONS
Disabled Persons (this index)

HEALTH AND HUMAN SERVICES SECRETARY
Emergency assistance: state emergency assistance program precluding furnishing assistance to AFDC recipients, held invalid under supremacy clause (Art VI, cl 2) as in conflict with valid federal regulation, 72 L Ed 2d 728
Medicare and Medicaid (this index)

HEALTH CARE AND INSURANCE
Coal producer sued on promise to contribute to union welfare funds based on "purchased coal," held entitled to plead and have adjudicated illegality defense, 70 L Ed 2d 833
Insurance (this index)
Medicare and Medicaid (this index)
Physicians and Surgeons (this index)

HEARINGS
Medicare: hearing procedures for claim disputes under Part B of Medicare program (42 USCS § 1395j), held not violative of due process, 72 L Ed 2d 1
Pro se complaint: state prisoner's crudely written, pro se complaint alleging his placement in solitary confinement for one-week period without any notice of charges or any hearing, held sufficient to state cause of action, 70 L Ed 2d 551

HIGHER EDUCATION
Universities and Colleges (this index)

HIRING PRACTICES
Backpay: employer's offer to discrimination claimant of job previously denied without offer of retroactive seniority, held to toll continuing accrual of backpay liability under 42 USCS § 2000e-6(g), 73 L Ed 2d 721
Liability: proof of intentional discrimination, held necessary for liability under 42 USCS § 1981; vicarious liability under § 1981 of employers and trade associations for discriminatory conduct of union, held not supportable, 73 L Ed 2d 835
Promotions (this index)

HISTORY
Legislative History and Intent (this index)

605

HISTORY—Cont'd
Mitigation of penalty: state trial judge's refusal to consider defendant's family history and emotional disturbance in mitigation in death penalty sentencing hearing, held violative of Eighth and Fourteenth Amendments, 71 L Ed 2d 1

HOME
Dwellings (this index)

HOME-RULE MUNICIPALITY
Cable television: ordinance enacted by home-rule municipality prohibiting expansion of cable television operator's business, held not to be "state action" eligible for exemption from federal antitrust laws, 70 L Ed 2d 810

HOMICIDE
Murder (this index)

HOSPITALS
Insane and Incompetent Persons (this index)

"HOST COUNTRY"
Treaties: word "treaty" in 5 USCS § 7201 note, which excepts from certain employment discrimination requirements actions permitted by "treaty," held to include executive agreements, 71 L Ed 2d 715

"HOT CARGO"
Welfare fund: coal producer sued on promise to contribute to union welfare funds based on "purchased coal," held entitled to plead and have adjudicated illegality defense, 70 L Ed 2d 833

HOUSING
Dwellings (this index)

HOWARD HUGHES
Decedents' Estates (this index)

HUSBAND AND WIFE
Children and Minors (this index)
Medicaid: state's unlimited deeming of Medicaid applicant's spouse's income as available to applicant in determining eligibility, held barred by 42 USCS § 1396a(a), 71 L Ed 2d 137

HYDROELECTRIC ENERGY

Export: state public utility commission's order requiring privately-owned and federally-licensed public utility to sell within state hydroelectric energy it had been exporting, held violative of commerce clause (Art I, § 8, cl 3), 71 L Ed 2d 188

"HYPOTHETICAL ENVIRONMENTAL IMPACT STATEMENT"

Nuclear weapons: § 102 (2)(c) of the National Environmental Policy Act (42 USCS § 4332 (2)(c)), held not to require Navy to prepare and release "Hypothetical Environmental Impact Statement" regarding nuclear weapons storage, 70 L Ed 2d 298

IDENTIFICATION

Habeas corpus: Federal Court of Appeals' decision holding 28 USCS § 2254(d) inapplicable to habeas petition challenging photographic identification procedures, remanded for failure to adhere to instructions of Supreme Court on prior remand, 71 L Ed 2d 480

ILLEGALITY DEFENSE

Welfare fund: coal producer sued on promise to contribute to union welfare funds based on "purchased coal," held entitled to plead and have adjudicated illegality defense, 70 L Ed 2d 833

ILLEGALLY SEIZED EVIDENCE

Search and Seizure (this index)

ILLEGITIMATE CHILDREN

Limitation of actions: Texas statute barring paternity suits brought on behalf of illegitimate children more than one year after their birth, held violative of equal protection, 71 L Ed 2d 770

IMMIGRATION

Deportation: government's deportation of alien witnesses, held not violative of Fifth and Sixth Amendments absent some showing evidence lost would be both material and favorable to defendant, 73 L Ed 2d 1193

Discrimination: Commonwealth of Puerto Rico held to have standing to sue as parens patriae to enjoin applegrowers' discrimination against Puerto Rican migrant farmworkers, 73 L Ed 2d 995

INDEX

IMMIGRATION—Cont'd
In-state status: state university's policy of denying in-state status to domiciled nonimmigrant aliens holding G-4 visas, held violative of supremacy clause (Art VI, cl 2), 73 L Ed 2d 563

IMMUNITY
Privileges and Immunities (this index)

IMPAIRMENT OF CONTRACT OBLIGATIONS
Mineral interests: state statute extinguishing unused mineral interests after 20 years unless owner files statement of claim, held not violative of contract clause, Fifth Amendment just compensation clause, and Fourteenth Amendment due process and equal protection, 70 L Ed 2d 738

IMPEACHMENT
Miranda warnings: state prosecutor's cross-examination of defendant as to post-arrest silence, held not violative of Fourteenth Amendment due process in absence of Miranda warning assurances, 71 L Ed 2d 490

IMPLIED ACTS AND MATTERS
Juror's submission, during criminal trial, of job application to prosecutor's office and failure of prosecution to disclose such fact during trial, held not violative of due process, 71 L Ed 2d 78
Military: federal court jurisdiction over action for monetary damages brought by discharged military exchange employee, held not conferred by Tucker Act (28 USCS § 1346(a)(2)) in absence of express or implied contract, 72 L Ed 2d 520
Presumptions and Burden of Proof (this index)

IMPORTS AND EXPORTS
Alcohol distillers: state alcoholic beverage control law enforcing distiller's designation of wholesaler, held not per se violative of Sherman Act (15 USCS §§ 1 et seq.), 73 L Ed 2d 1042
Hydroelectric energy: state public utility commission's order requiring privately-owned and federally-licensed public utility to sell within state hydroelectric energy it had been exporting, held violative of commerce clause (Art I, § 8, cl 3), 71 L Ed 2d 188

608

INDEX

IMPORTS AND EXPORTS—Cont'd
Secondary boycott: refusal by longshoremen's union to unload cargoes shipped from Soviet Union in protest against Afghanistan invasion, held illegal secondary boycott under 29 USCS § 158(b)(4), 72 L Ed 2d 21

IMPRISONMENT
Penal and Correctional Institutions (this index)

INCAPACITY
Insane and Incompetent Persons (this index)

INCARCERATION
Penal and Correctional Institutions (this index)

INCOME
Compensation and Income (this index)

INCOME TAX
"Brother-sister controlled group": Treasury Regulation (26 CFR § 1.1563-1(a) (3)) implementing statutory definition of "brother-sister controlled group" of corporations (26 USCS § 1563(a)), held unreasonable, 70 L Ed 2d 792
Gross Receipts (this index)
Idaho's inclusion within taxable income of nondomiciliary parent corporation doing some business in state, of portion of intangible income parent receives from subsidiary having no other connection with state, held to violate due process, 73 L Ed 2d 787

INCOMPETENT PERSONS
Insane and Incompetent Persons (this index)

INCONSISTENCIES
Verdict (this index)

INCREASE IN PAY
Compensation and Income (this index)

INDECENCY
Lewdness, Indecency, and Obscenity (this index)

INDIANS
Accretions: United States held entitled to oceanfront accretions to Coast Guard reservation under federal rule that accretions belong to upland owner, 73 L Ed 2d 1

INDIANS—Cont'd

Gross receipts: New Mexico tax imposed on gross receipts that non-Indian construction company received from tribal school board for construction of school on reservation, held preempted by federal law, 73 L Ed 2d 1174

Severance tax imposed on oil and gas removed from Indian reservation, held authorized by Tribe's inherent authority to tax as part of power of self-government, and held violative of commerce clause (Art I, § 8, cl 3), 71 L Ed 2d 21

INDICTMENT AND INFORMATION

Collateral order: denial of motion to dismiss indictment on ground of prosecutorial vindictiveness, held not collateral order that can be appealed prior to judgment under 28 USCS § 1291, 73 L Ed 2d 754

Speedy trial: time between dismissal of military charges and subsequent indictment of individual on civilian charges held not to be considered in determining whether violation of right to speedy trial under Sixth Amendment has occurred, 71 L Ed 2d 696

INDIGENTS

Emergency assistance: state emergency assistance program precluding furnishing assistance to AFDC recipients, held invalid under supremacy clause (Art VI, cl 2) as in conflict with valid federal regulation, 72 L Ed 2d 728

Medicare and Medicaid (this index)

INDIRECT TRANSFER OF PROPERTY

Taxation: trust beneficiary's disclaimer of contingent interest in testamentary trust, held taxable transfer of property by gift under 26 USCS §§ 2501(a)(1) and 2511(a), not excepted from tax by 26 CFR § 25.2511-1(c), 71 L Ed 2d 170

INDUSTRY CODES

Antitrust: nonprofit association of mechanical engineers responsible for promulgation of industry codes, held civilly liable under antitrust laws for antitrust violations of its agents committed with apparent authority, 72 L Ed 2d 330

INELIGIBILITY

Qualification and Disqualification (this index)

INDEX

INFANTS
Children and Minors (this index)

INFERENCES
Implied Acts and Matters (this index)

INFORMATION
Freedom of Information Act (this index)

INFRINGEMENT
Trademark: Federal Court of Appeals' reversal of District Court's findings as to trademark infringement by generic drug manufacturers, held error where "clearly erroneous" standard of FRCP 52 not followed, 72 L Ed 2d 606

INHERENT AUTHORITY
Severance tax imposed on oil and gas removed from Indian reservation, held authorized by Tribe's inherent authority to tax as part of power of self-government, and held violative of commerce clause (Art I, § 8, cl 3), 71 L Ed 2d 21

INHERITANCE TAX
Death tax claim: action under Federal Interpleader Act (28 USCS § 1335) to resolve inconsistent death tax claims on estate of Howard Hughes by officials of two states, held barred by Eleventh Amendment, 72 L Ed 2d 694

INITIATIVE
Schools: state initiative precluding school boards from requiring attendance at other than neighborhood schools, held unconstitutional, 73 L Ed 2d 896

INJUNCTIONS
Comity: taxpayer's damages action under 42 USCS § 1983 for alleged unconstitutional administration of state tax system, held barred in federal court by principle of comity, 70 L Ed 2d 271
Discrimination: Commonwealth of Puerto Rico held to have standing to sue as parens patriae to enjoin applegrowers' discrimination against Puerto Rican migrant farmworkers, 73 L Ed 2d 995
Jurisdiction: Tax Injunction Act (28 USCS § 1341) held to bar federal court jurisdiction to declare state tax unconstitutional, 73 L Ed 2d 93

611

INJUNCTIONS—Cont'd

Oil: Temporary Emergency Court of Appeals' invalidation of anti-passthrough provision of state tax statute relating to oil company revenues, vacated and remanded in light of expiration of preempting federal price control authority, 71 L Ed 2d 120

Pollution: Federal District Court relief of violations of permit requirements of Federal Water Pollution Control Act (33 USCS §§ 1251 et seq.), held not limited to immediate cessation orders, 72 L Ed 2d 91

Soviet invasion: work stoppage to protest Soviet invasion of Afghanistan, held subject to anti-injunction provisions of Norris-LaGuardia Act (29 USCS §§ 101 et seq.), and not enjoinable pending aribtrator's decision as to whether strike violated collective-bargaining contract, 73 L Ed 2d 327

INJURIES

Accidental Injury and Accidents (this index)

IN PERSONAM AND IN REM ACTIONS

Admiralty: process issued by Federal District Court to secure possession of property from state officials in admiralty in rem action, held not barred by Eleventh Amendment, 73 L Ed 2d 1057

Due process: District Court's action in establishing personal jurisdiction as sanction for failure to comply with discovery order under Rule 37 of Federal Rules of Civil Procedure, held not violative of due process, 72 L Ed 2d 492

Full faith and credit: North Carolina courts' refusal to treat as res judicata Indiana rehabilitation court's adjudication of rights to insurance company's deposit posted in North Carolina, held violative of full faith and credit clause (Art IV, § 1), 71 L Ed 2d 558

INSANE AND INCOMPETENT PERSONS

Drugs: case presenting question whether state involuntarily committed patients may refuse certain drugs, vacated and remanded to Federal Court of Appeals, to consider intervening state decision opinion bearing on issue, 73 L Ed 2d 16

Due process liberty: involuntarily committed mentally retarded person, held to have due process liberty interests requiring state to provide minimally adequate training to insure safety and freedom from undue restraint, 73 L Ed 2d 28

INDEX

INSURANCE—Cont'd
Collective bargaining contract allocating health benefits among potential beneficiaries of employee trust fund, held not reviewable for reasonableness under Labor Management Relations Act (29 USCS § 186 (c)(5)), 71 L Ed 2d 419
Full faith and credit: North Carolina courts' refusal to treat as res judicata Indiana rehabilitation court's adjudication of rights to insurance company's deposit posted in North Carolina, held violative of full faith and credit clause (Art IV, § 1), 71 L Ed 2d 558
Medicare and Medicaid (this index)
Physicians and Surgeons (this index)
Social Security (this index)

INSURED BANK
Checks: deposit of bad check in federally insured bank, held not proscribed by 18 USCS § 1014, 73 L Ed 2d 767

INTANGIBLE INCOME
Corporations: Idaho's inclusion within taxable income of non-domiciliary parent corporation doing some business in state, of portion of intangible income parent receives from subsidiary having no other connection with state, held to violate due process, 73 L Ed 2d 787

INTENT AND MOTIVE
Death penalty: imposition of death penalty on person who aids and abets felony in course of which murder is committed by others but who does not himself kill, attempt to kill, or intend to kill, held to violate Eight and Fourteenth Amendments, 73 L Ed 2d 1140
Discrimination (this index)
Due process: fact that defendant was charged with felony after refusing to plead guilty to misdemeanor charges, held not to warrant presumption of prosecutorial vindictiveness in violation of due process, 73 L Ed 2d 74
Legislative History and Intent (this index)

INTEREST
Corporations: Idaho's inclusion within taxable income of non-domiciliary parent corporation doing some business in state, of portion of intangible income parent receives from subsidiary having no other connection with state, held to violate due process, 73 L Ed 2d 787

614

INDEX

INTERIM APPOINTMENT
Legislative seat: Puerto Rico law vesting in political party authority to appoint replacement for member who vacates seat on legislature, held not violative of United States Constitution, 72 L Ed 2d 628

INTERIM REAPPORTIONNENT PLAN
Objections: Federal District Court effecting interim Texas congressional reapportionment for districts objected to by Attorney General, held without power to redraw other districts in absence of constitutional or statutory violation, 71 L Ed 2d 725

INTERIOR SECRETARY
Bidding system: Interior Secretary's refusal to use non-cash-bonus bidding systems in leasing oil and gas tracts on outer continental shelf, held not violative of Outer Continental Shelf Lands Act Amendments, (43 USCS §§ 1331 et seq.), 70 L Ed 2d 309

INTERNAL REVENUE CODE
Taxation (this index)

INTERNATIONAL AGREEMENTS
Treaties (this index)

INTERPLEADER
Decedents' Estates (this index)

INTERPRETERS
Sign-language: deaf student held not entitled to sign-language interpreter in public school classes, under Education for All Handicapped Children Act, where she was receiving adequate education and personalized instruction, 73 L Ed 2d 690

INTERSTATE COMMERCE
Business takeover: Illinois business takeover statute, held unconstitutional under commerce clause (Art I, § 8, cl 3), 73 L Ed 2d 269
Freight charges: carrier's violation of Interstate Commerce Commission's credit regulations, held not to bar collection of lawful freight charges from consignor, 72 L Ed 2d 114
Power and Energy (this index)

615

INDEX

INTERSTATE COMMERCE—Cont'd
Railroads: application of Railway Labor Act (29 USCS §§ 151 et seq.) to state-owned railroad engaged in interstate commerce, held not prohibited by Tenth Amendment, 71 L Ed 2d 547

Securities: statute (18 USCS § 2314) prohibiting transport of forged securities in "interstate commerce," held not to require proof securities were forged before being taken across state lines, 71 L Ed 2d 522

Severance tax imposed on oil and gas removed from Indian reservation, held authorized by Tribe's inherent authority to tax as part of power of self-government, and held violative of commerce clause (Art I, § 8, cl 3), 71 L Ed 2d 21

Water: Nebraska statute forbidding withdrawal of ground water to foreign state which denies such privileges to Nebraska, held violative of Congress clause (Art 1, § 8 cl 3), 73 L Ed 2d 1254

INTERVENING BREAKS
Confession obtained through custodial interrogation after illegal arrest, held excluded where intervening events did not break causal connection between illegal arrest and confession, 73 L Ed 2d 314

INTERVENING DECISIONS
Mental patients: case presenting question whether state involuntarily committed patients may refuse certain drugs, vacated and remanded to Federal Court of Appeals, to consider intervening state decision opinion bearing on issue, 73 L Ed 2d 16

INTOXICATING LIQUORS
Alcohol (this index)

INVALIDITY
Validity and Invalidity (this index)

INVASION
Soviet Union (this index)

INVASION OF PRIVACY
Seizure: police officer's accompaniment of lawful arrestee to residence and subsequent seizure of contraband in plain view, held not violative of Fourth Amendment, 70 L Ed 2d 778

616

INDEX

INVESTMENT SECURITIES

Forgery: statute (18 USCS § 2314) prohibiting transport of forged securities in "interstate commerce," held not to require proof securities were forged before being taken across state lines, 71 L Ed 2d 522

INVOLUNTARY COMMITMENT

Insane and Incompetent Persons (this index)

INVOLUNTARY TERMINATION OF RIGHTS

Children and Minors (this index)

ISSUES

Mental patients: case presenting question whether state involuntarily committed patients may refuse certain drugs, vacated and remanded to Federal Court of Appeals, to consider intervening state decision opinion bearing on issue, 73 L Ed 2d 16

Removal of books: Federal District Court's entry of summary judgment in case challenging local school board's removal of library books as violative of First Amendment, held erroneous where material issue of fact remained as to board's justifications, 73 L Ed 2d 435

JAIL

Penal and Correctional Institutions (this index)

JAPAN

Treaties: employment practices of a New York corporation that is wholly-owned subsidiary of Japanese firm, held not exempted from Title VII of Civil Rights Act (42 USCS §§ 2000e et seq.) by treaty between the United States and Japan, 72 L Ed 2d 765

JICARILLA APACHE TRIBE

Severance tax imposed on oil and gas removed from Indian reservation, held authorized by Tribe's inherent authority to tax as part of power of self-government, and held violative of commerce clause (Art I, § 8, cl 3), 71 L Ed 2d 21

JOB DISCRIMINATION

Giving of preclusive effect to state court's review of state agency's action on job bias claim upon later action in federal court on such claim under similar federal law, held required by 28 USCS § 1738, 72 L Ed 2d 262

JOB DISCRIMINATION—Cont'd
Hiring Practices (this index)
Limitations period applicable to employment discrimination action under 42 USCS § 1983, held to run from time of notice that appointment would terminate rather than from termination date, 70 L Ed 2d 6
Migrant farmworkers: Commonwealth of Puerto Rico held to have standing to sue as parens patriae to enjoin apple-growers' discrimination against Puerto Rican migrant farmworkers, 73 L Ed 2d 995
Promotions (this index)

JOBS
Employer and Employee (this index)

JUDGES
Also see **Magistrates**
Bankruptcy Court's exercise of jurisdiction over state-law contract claims pursuant to 28 USCS § 1471, held violative of Article III, 73 L Ed 2d 598
Elections: jurisdiction to decide whether § 5 of Voting Rights Act of 1965 (42 USCS § 1973c) applies to changes in local election procedures, held within power of state court, 72 L Ed 2d 824
Mitigation of penalty: state trial judge's refusal to consider defendant's family history and emotional disturbance in mitigation in death penalty sentencing hearing, held violative of Eighth and Fourteenth Amendments, 71 L Ed 2d 1

JUDGMENTS, ORDERS, AND DECREES
Appeal and Review (this index)
Attorney's fees: postjudgment request for attorney's fees under Civil Rights Attorney's Fees Awards Act (42 USCS § 1988), held not subject to 10-day timeliness standard of Rule 59(e) of Federal Rules of Civil Procedure, 71 L Ed 2d 325
Cessation orders: Federal District Court relief of violations of permit requirements of Federal Water Pollution Control Act (33 USCS §§ 1251 et seq.), held not limited to immediate cessation orders, 72 L Ed 2d 91
Collateral Orders or Relief (this index)
Elections: jurisdiction to decide whether § 5 of Voting Rights Act of 1965 (42 USCS § 1973c) applies to changes in local election procedures, held within power of state court, 72 L Ed 2d 824

JURISDICTION—Cont'd

INDEX

JURISDICTION—Cont'd
Military: federal court jurisdiction over action for monetary damages brought by discharged military exchange employee, held not conferred by Tucker Act (28 USCS § 1346(a)(2)) in absence of express or implied contract, 72 L Ed 2d 520
Tax Injunction Act (28 USCS § 1341) held to bar federal court jurisdiction to declare state tax unconstitutional, 73 L Ed 2d 93

JURY AND JURY TRIALS
Death penalty: question as to what premises of state law support a conclusion that a death sentence was not impaired by the invalidity of one of the statutory aggravating circumstances found by the jury, certified to Georgia Supreme Court, 72 L Ed 2d 222
Double jeopardy: Florida Supreme Court's reversal of murder and rape conviction at jury trial based on weight of evidence, held not to bar retrial under double jeopardy clause of Fifth and Fourteenth Amendments, 72 L Ed 2d 652
Instructions to Jury (this index)
Juror's submission, during criminal trial, of job application to prosecutor's office and failure of prosecution to disclose such fact during trial, held not violative of due process, 71 L Ed 2d 78
Verdict (this index)

JUST COMPENSATION CLAUSE
Bankruptcy: employee protection provisions of Rock Island Transition and Employee Assistance Act (45 USCS §§ 1005 and 1008), held violative of bankruptcy clause (Art I, § 8, cl 4), 71 L Ed 2d 335
Mineral interests: state statute extinguishing unused mineral interests after 20 years unless owner files statement of claim, held not violative of contract clause, Fifth Amendment just compensation clause, and Fourteenth Amendment due process and equal protection, 70 L Ed 2d 738

JUSTIFICATION
Removal of books: Federal District Court's entry of summary judgment in case challenging local school board's removal of library books as violative of First Amendment, held erroneous where material issue of fact remained as to board's justifications, 73 L Ed 2d 435

621

JUVENILES
Children and Minors (this index)

KILLING
Murder (this index)

KNOWLEDGE
Notice and Knowledge (this index)

LABOR
Employer and Employee (this index)

LABOR MANAGEMENT RELATIONS ACT
Attorney's fees incurred during proceedings before National Labor Relations Board, held not proper element of damages under § 303(b) of Labor Management Relations Act (29 USCS § 187(b)), 72 L Ed 2d 511
Collective bargaining contract allocating health benefits among potential beneficiaries of employee trust fund, held not reviewable for reasonableness under Labor Management Relations Act (29 USCS § 186 (c)(5)), 71 L Ed 2d 419

LABOR-MANAGEMENT REPORTING AND DISCLOSURE ACT
Union "outsider rule," held not violative of Labor-Management Reporting and Disclosure Act's "free speech and assembly" or "right to sue" provisions (29 USCS § 411(a)(2), (4)), 72 L Ed 2d 707

LABOR SECRETARY
Jurisdiction: Tax Injunction Act (28 USCS § 1341) held to bar federal court jurisdiction to declare state tax unconstitutional, 73 L Ed 2d 93

LACHES AND DELAY
Speedy trial: time between dismissal of military charges and subsequent indictment of individual on civilian charges held not to be considered in determining whether violation of right to speedy trial under Sixth Amendment has occurred, 71 L Ed 2d 696

LACK OF JURISDICTION
University rules: appeal of decision invalidating subsequently amended university rule, held moot as to university and without jurisdictional basis as to state which sought review but refused to take position on merits, 70 L Ed 2d 855

INDEX

LANDLORD AND TENANT
Leases (this index)

LAW ENFORCEMENT OFFICERS
Citizens: state statute requiring peace officers, including deputy probation officers, to be United States citizens, held not violative of equal protection clause of Fourteenth Amendment, 70 L Ed 2d 677

Exemption 7 of Freedom of Information Act (5 USCS § 552(b)(7)), held to exempt information originally contained in law enforcement records but incorporated into document not compiled for law enforcement purposes, 72 L Ed 2d 376

Licenses: ordinance directing city's police chief to consider applicant's "connection with criminal elements" in licensing amusement establishments, held not unconstitutionally vague, 71 L Ed 2d 152

Search and Seizure (this index)

LAWYERS
Attorneys (this index)

LEASES
Cable television: New York law requiring landlords to allow cable television facilities on property, held to be "taking" of property compensable under Fifth and Fourteenth Amendments, 73 L Ed 2d 868

Discrimination: black "tester" given false information about housing availability and nonprofit, open housing organization, held to have standing to challenge racial steering under Fair Housing Act (42 USCS § 3612); Act's 180-day limitations period (42 USCS § 3612(a)), held not bar claims of continuing violation, even though some incidents alleged occur outside period, 71 L Ed 2d 214

Oil and Gas (this index)

Service of process: Kentucky statute applicable to forcible entry and detainer actions permitting service of process by posting summons on door of premises, held violative of due process, 72 L Ed 2d 249

LEGISLATIVE HISTORY AND INTENT
Address lists compiled by Bureau of the Census, held not subject to disclosure under Freedom of Information Act (5 USCS § 552) or discovery provisions of Federal Rules of Civil Procedure, 71 L Ed 2d 199

623

LEGISLATIVE HISTORY AND INTENT—Cont'd

Antitrust: nonprofit association of mechanical engineers responsible for promulgation of industry codes, held civilly liable under antitrust laws for antitrust violations of its agents committed with apparent authority, 72 L Ed 2d 330

Attorney's fees incurred during proceedings before National Labor Relations Board, held not proper element of damages under § 303(b) of Labor Management Relations Act (29 USCS § 187(b)), 72 L Ed 2d 511

"Brother-sister controlled group": Treasury Regulation (26 CFR § 1.1563-1(a) (3)) implementing statutory definition of "brother-sister controlled group" of corporations (26 USCS § 1563(a)), held unreasonable, 70 L Ed 2d 792

Collective Bargaining (this index)

Exhaustion of state administrative remedies, held not prerequisite to bringing action pursuant to 42 USCS § 1983, 73 L Ed 2d 172

Medicare: determinations by insurance carriers of amount of benefits payable under Part B of Medicare program (42 USCS §§ 1395j et seq.), held not reviewable in Court of Claims, 72 L Ed 2d 12

Seamen: limiting period during which wage penalty for failure to pay seamen promptly after discharge is assessed under 46 USCS § 596, held not within discretion of Federal District Courts, 73 L Ed 2d 973

Severance tax imposed on oil and gas removed from Indian reservation, held authorized by Tribe's inherent authority to tax as part of power of self-government, and held violative of commerce clause (Art I, § 8, cl 3), 71 L Ed 2d 21

Treaties: word "treaty" in 5 USCS § 7201 note, which excepts from certain employment discrimination requirements actions permitted by "treaty," held to include executive agreements, 71 L Ed 2d 715

LEGISLATURE
Congress (this index)

LENGTH OF SENTENCE
Sentence and Punishment (this index)

LESSER INCLUDED OFFENSES
Instructions to jury: preclusion of jury instructions on lesser included offense in capital case, held not to require new trial where defendant's own evidence negates possibility that such instruction was warranted, 72 L Ed 2d 367

LETTERS
Election method: letter to Attorney General advising of results of county referendum endorsing at-large method of electing county council, held to be request for reconsideration of Attorney General's prior objections to method and not preclearance request under Voting Rights Act (42 USCS § 1973c), 70 L Ed 2d 576

LEVELS OF CARE
Medicaid: nursing homes' decisions to discharge or transfer Medicaid patients to lower levels of care, held not to involve state action for purposes of Fourteenth Amendment's due process clause, 73 L Ed 2d 534

LEWDNESS, INDECENCY, AND OBSCENITY
Business takeover: Illinois business takeover statute, held unconstitutional under commerce clause (Art I, § 8, cl 3), 73 L Ed 2d 269

Proof, in public nuisance abatement action by city against motion picture theater, that motion pictures in question were obscene beyond reasonable doubt, held not required, 70 L Ed 2d 262

Sexual performances: New York criminal statute prohibiting knowing promotion of sexual performances by children under 16, by distribution of material depicting such performances, held constitutional, 73 L Ed 2d 1113

LIABILITY
Privileges and Immunities (this index)
Vicarious Liability (this index)

LIBERTY
Custody (this index)

LIBRARIES
Removal of books: Federal District Court's entry of summary judgment in case challenging local school board's removal of library books as violative of First Amendment, held erroneous where material issue of fact remained as to board's justifications, 73 L Ed 2d 435

INDEX

LICENSES AND PERMITS

Amusements: ordinance directing city's police chief to consider applicant's "connection with criminal elements" in licensing amusement establishments, held not unconstitutionally vague, 71 L Ed 2d 152

Attorney disciplinary rules: federal court abstention from considering challenge to constitutionality of attorney disciplinary rules that were subject of pending state disciplinary proceeding within jurisdiction of New Jersey Supreme Court held required, 73 L Ed 2d 116

Cessation orders: Federal District Court relief of violations of permit requirements of Federal Water Pollution Control Act (33 USCS §§ 1251 et seq.), held not limited to immediate cessation orders, 72 L Ed 2d 91

Drug paraphernalia: municipal ordinance requiring license to sell "items designed or marketed for use with illegal cannabis or drugs," held not unconstitutionally vague or overbroad, 71 L Ed 2d 362

Hydroelectric energy: state public utility commission's order requiring privately-owned and federally-licensed public utility to sell within state hydroelectric energy it had been exporting, held violative of commerce clause (Art I, § 8, cl 3), 71 L Ed 2d 188

Water: Nebraska statute forbidding withdrawal of ground water to foreign state which denies such privileges to Nebraska, held violative of Congress clause (Art 1, § 8 cl 3), 73 L Ed 2d 1254

LIFE INSURANCE

Beneficiary designation: insured serviceman's beneficiary designation under life policy issued pursuant to Servicmen's Group Life Insurance Act (38 USCS §§ 765 et seq.), held to prevail over constructive trust imposed upon proceeds by state court, 70 L Ed 2d 39

LIMITATION OF ACTIONS

Discrimination (this index)

Foreign corporations: New Jersey statute tolling limitation period for actions against unrepresented foreign corporations, held not violative of Fourteenth Amendment's equal protection clause, 71 L Ed 2d 250

INDEX

LIMITATION OF ACTIONS—Cont'd
Mineral interests: state statute extinguishing unused mineral interests after 20 years unless owner files statement of claim, held not violative of contract clause, Fifth Amendment just compensation clause, and Fourteenth Amendment due process and equal protection, 70 L Ed 2d 738

Paternity suits: Texas statute barring paternity suits brought on behalf of illegitimate children more than one year after their birth, held violative of equal protection, 71 L Ed 2d 770

LIMITATIONS AND RESTRICTIONS
Advertising: Missouri Supreme Court rule regulating attorney's advertising absent proof that regulated material was misleading, held violative of attorney's First Amendment rights, 71 L Ed 2d 64

Alcohol distillers: state alcoholic beverage control law enforcing distiller's designation of wholesaler, held not per se violative of Sherman Act (15 USCS §§ 1 et seq.), 73 L Ed 2d 1042

Due-on-sale clauses: Federal Home Loan Bank Board regulation authorizing due-on-sale clauses in federal savings and loan instruments held to preempt state law, 73 L Ed 2d 664

Election contributions: municipal ordinance placing $250 limitation on contributions to committees formed to support or oppose ballot measures, held violative of First Amendment rights of association and speech, 70 L Ed 2d 492

Monopolies and Restraints of Trade (this index)

Public officer: provisions of Texas Constitution limiting public official's ability to become candidate for another public office, held not violative of First Amendment or equal protection clause of Fourteenth Amendment, 73 L Ed 2d 508

Seamen: limiting period during which wage penalty for failure to pay seamen promptly after discharge is assessed under 46 USCS § 596, held not within discretion of Federal District Courts, 73 L Ed 2d 973

LIQUOR
Alcohol (this index)

LIS PENDENS
Pending Actions (this index)

627

LISTS
Address lists compiled by Bureau of the Census, held not subject to disclosure under Freedom of Information Act (5 USCS § 552) or discovery provisions of Federal Rules of Civil Procedure, 71 L Ed 2d 199

LITERARY VALUE
Sexual performances: New York criminal statute prohibiting knowing promotion of sexual performances by children under 16, by distribution of material depicting such performances, held constitutional, 73 L Ed 2d 1113

LOANS
Credit and Loans (this index)

LOCAL ELECTIONS
Jurisdiction to decide whether § 5 of Voting Rights Act of 1965 (42 USCS § 1973c) applies to changes in local election procedures, held within power of state court, 72 L Ed 2d 824

LOCAL GOVERNMENT
Municipal Corporations and Other Political Subdivisions (this index)

LOCAL TAXATION
State and Local Taxation (this index)

LOCATION
Compensable injury: presumption of compensability under § 20(a) of Longshoremen's and Harbor Workers' Compensation Act (33 USCS § 920(a)), held inapplicable to claimed injury at work where "injury" arose at home, 71 L Ed 2d 495

LONG-ARM STATUTE
Statute of limitations: New Jersey statute tolling limitation period for actions against unrepresented foreign corporations, held not violative of Fourteenth Amendment's equal protection clause, 71 L Ed 2d 250

LONGSHOREMEN
Compensable injury: presumption of compensability under § 20(a) of Longshoremen's and Harbor Workers' Compensation Act (33 USCS § 920(a)), held inapplicable to claimed injury at work where "injury" arose at home, 71 L Ed 2d 495

LONGSHOREMEN—Cont'd
Secondary boycott: refusal by longshoremen's union to unload cargoes shipped from Soviet Union in protest against Afghanistan invasion, held illegal secondary boycott under 29 USCS § 158(b)(4), 72 L Ed 2d 21

LOSSES
Boycotts: First Amendment held to preclude state court imposition of liability on participants in black boycott of white businesses for losses other than those caused by their own violence or threats, 73 L Ed 2d 1215

LOST EVIDENCE
Deportation: government's deportation of alien witnesses, held not violative of Fifth and Sixth Amendments absent some showing evidence lost would be both material and favorable to defendant, 73 L Ed 2d 1193

MAGISTRATES
Arrest warrant: private citizen's right to prevent state officials from presenting information that will assist magistrate in determining whether to issue arrest warrant, held not judicially cognizable, 70 L Ed 2d 65
Search warrant: authority to conduct warrantless search of motor vehicle based on probable cause, including compartments and containers, held coextensive with authority based on magistrate's issuance of warrant, 72 L Ed 2d 572

MALES
Sex discrimination: state-supported university's policy that excludes males from enrolling in its professional nursing school, held violative of equal protection clause of Fourteenth Amendment, 73 L Ed 2d 1090

MALICE
"Cause and actual prejudice," rather than "plain error" of Rule 52(b) of Federal Rules of Criminal Procedure, held proper standard of review on motion for collateral relief under 28 USCS § 2255, 71 L Ed 2d 816

MANDATORY PAROLE
Habeas corpus: claims of habeas corpus petitioners seeking relief on ground that failure to be advised of mandatory parole before pleading guilty violated due process, held moot after parole terms expired, 71 L Ed 2d 508

MANDATORY SUSPENSION

Schools: federal courts' replacement of local school board's construction of its own rules on mandatory suspension in action under 42 USCS § 1983, held erroneous where board's construction was reasonable, 73 L Ed 2d 1273

MANIPULATION OF PRICE

Commodity Exchange Act: action for damages caused by violation of Commodity Exchange Act (7 USCS §§ 1 et seq.), held available to private parties, 72 L Ed 2d 182

MANSLAUGHTER

"Cause and actual prejudice," rather than "plain error" of Rule 52(b) of Federal Rules of Criminal Procedure, held proper standard of review on motion for collateral relief under 28 USCS § 2255, 71 L Ed 2d 816

MANUFACTURERS

Trademark: Federal Court of Appeals' reversal of District Court's findings as to trademark infringement by generic drug manufacturers, held error where "clearly erroneous" standard of FRCP 52 not followed, 72 L Ed 2d 606

MARIJUANA

Drugs and Narcotics (this index)

MARINE RESOURCES

Bidding system: Interior Secretary's refusal to use non-cash-bonus bidding systems in leasing oil and gas tracts on outer continental shelf, held not violative of Outer Continental Shelf Lands Act Amendments, (43 USCS §§ 1331 et seq.), 70 L Ed 2d 309

MARITIME LAW

Admiralty (this index)

MARKETING

Licenses: municipal ordinance requiring license to sell "items designed or marketed for use with illegal cannabis or drugs," held not unconstitutionally vague or overbroad, 71 L Ed 2d 362

INDEX

MASS TRANSIT
Collective bargaining: section 13(c) of Urban Mass Transportation Act of 1964 (49 USCS § 1609(c)), held not to create federal cause of action for breach of § 13(c) agreement or collective bargaining contract between local transit authority and union, 72 L Ed 2d 639

MASTER ADDRESS REGISTER
Address lists compiled by Bureau of the Census, held not subject to disclosure under Freedom of Information Act (5 USCS § 552) or discovery provisions of Federal Rules of Civil Procedure, 71 L Ed 2d 199

MASTER AND SERVANT
Discrimination: proof of intentional discrimination, held necessary for liability under 42 USCS § 1981; vicarious liability under § 1981 of employers and trade associations for discriminatory conduct of union, held not supportable, 73 L Ed 2d 835

MATERIAL ISSUE OF FACT
Removal of books: Federal District Court's entry of summary judgment in case challenging local school board's removal of library books as violative of First Amendment, held erroneous where material issue of fact remained as to board's justifications, 73 L Ed 2d 435

MAXIMUM FEES
Price-fixing: agreement among competing physicians setting, by majority vote, maximum fees for payment from participants in specified insurance plans, held per se unlawful under § 1 of Sherman Act (15 USCS § 1), 73 L Ed 2d 48

McCARRAN-FERGUSON ACT
Fees: insurer use of peer review committee to determine reasonableness of chiropractor's fees, held not exempt from antitrust laws as "business of insurance" under McCarran-Ferguson Act (15 USCS § 1012(b)), 73 L Ed 2d 647

MECHANICAL ENGINEERS
Antitrust: nonprofit association of mechanical engineers responsible for promulgation of industry codes, held civilly liable under antitrust laws for antitrust violations of its agents committed with apparent authority, 72 L Ed 2d 330

MEDIA
Entertainment and Amusements (this index)
First Amendment: state statute which requires, under all circumstances, exclusion of press and general public from courtroom during testimony of minor victim in sex-offense trial, held violative of First Amendment, 73 L Ed 2d 248

MEDICAL CARE AND TREATMENT
Health Care and Insurance (this index)

MEDICARE AND MEDICAID
Constitutionality: medicaid eligibility provisions of Social Security Act (42 USCS § 1396b(f)) as applied in Massachusetts, held constitutional, 73 L Ed 2d 227

Hearing procedures for claim disputes under Part B of Medicare program (42 USCS § 1395j), held not violative of due process, 72 L Ed 2d 1

Nursing homes' decisions to discharge or transfer Medicaid patients to lower levels of care, held not to involve state action for purposes of Fourteenth Amendment's due process clause, 73 L Ed 2d 534

Reviewability of benefits: determinations by insurance carriers of amount of benefits payable under Part B of Medicare program (42 USCS §§ 1395j et seq.), held not reviewable in Court of Claims, 72 L Ed 2d 12

Spouse's income: state's unlimited deeming of Medicaid applicant's spouse's income as available to applicant in determining eligibility, held barred by 42 USCS § 1396a(a), 71 L Ed 2d 137

MEN
Sex discrimination: state-supported university's policy that excludes males from enrolling in its professional nursing school, held violative of equal protection clause of Fourteenth Amendment, 73 L Ed 2d 1090

MENTAL PATIENTS
Insane and Incompetent Persons (this index)

MERCHANDISER
Licenses: municipal ordinance requiring license to sell "items designed or marketed for use with illegal cannabis or drugs," held not unconstitutionally vague or overbroad, 71 L Ed 2d 362

INDEX

INDEX

MIRANDA WARNINGS—Cont'd
Cross-examination: state prosecutor's cross-examination of defendant as to post-arrest silence, held not violative of Fourteenth Amendment due process in absence of Miranda warning assurances, 71 L Ed 2d 490

MISCONDUCT
Conduct and Misconduct (this index)

MISDEMEANORS
Due process: fact that defendant was charged with felony after refusing to plead guilty to misdemeanor charges, held not to warrant presumption of prosecutorial vindictiveness in violation of due process, 73 L Ed 2d 74

MISREPRESENTATION
Fraud and Deceit (this index)

MISTRIAL
Double jeopardy: second trial of defendant who successfully moves for mistrial because of prosecutorial misconduct, held barred by double jeopardy clause only if prosecutor intended to provoke defendant to move for mistrial, 72 L Ed 2d 416

MITIGATION OF PENALTY
State trial judge's refusal to consider defendant's family history and emotional disturbance in mitigation in death penalty sentencing hearing, held violative of Eighth and Fourteenth Amendments, 71 L Ed 2d 1

MODIFICATION
Change or Modification (this index)

MONETARY DAMAGES
Military: federal court jurisdiction over action for monetary damages brought by discharged military exchange employee, held not conferred by Tucker Act (28 USCS § 1346(a)(2)) in absence of express or implied contract, 72 L Ed 2d 520

MONOPOLIES AND RESTRAINTS OF TRADE
Cable television: ordinance enacted by home-rule municipality prohibiting expansion of cable television operator's business, held not to be "state action" eligible for exemption from federal antitrust laws, 70 L Ed 2d 810

634

INDEX

MONOPOLIES AND RESTRAINTS OF TRADE—Cont'd

Nonprofit association of mechanical engineers responsible for promulgation of industy codes, held civilly liable under antitrust laws for antitrust violations of its agents committed with apparent authority, 72 L Ed 2d 330

Physicians and Surgeons (this index)

Sherman Act (this index)

MOOT QUESTIONS

Bail: claim that Nebraska's prohibition of pretrial bail to person charged with sexual offenses violated Federal Constitution, held moot where defendant had already been convicted of offenses, 71 L Ed 2d 353

Business takeover: Illinois business takeover statute, held unconstitutional under commerce clause (Art I, § 8, cl 3), 73 L Ed 2d 269

Habeas corpus: claims of habeas corpus petitioners seeking relief on ground that failure to be advised of mandatory parole before pleading guilty violated due process, held moot after parole terms expired, 71 L Ed 2d 508

Schools and Education (this index)

MORATORIUM ORDINANCE

Cable television: ordinance enacted by home-rule municipality prohibiting expansion of cable television operator's business, held not to be "state action" eligible for exemption from federal antitrust laws, 70 L Ed 2d 810

MORTGAGES

Due-on-sale clauses: Federal Home Loan Bank Board regulation authorizing due-on-sale clauses in federal savings and loan instruments held to preempt state law, 73 L Ed 2d 664

MOTION PICTURES

Obscenity: proof, in public nuisance abatement action by city against motion picture theater, that motion pictures in question were obscene beyond reasonable doubt, held not required, 70 L Ed 2d 262

MOTIONS

Decedents' estates: California's motion for leave to file bill of complaint against Texas to decide whether Howard Hughes was domiciled in California or Texas at time of death, granted as properly invoking Supreme Court's original jurisdiction, 72 L Ed 2d 755

MOTIONS—Cont'd
Dismissal of Actions or Charges (this index)

MOTIVE
Intent and Motive (this index)

MOTOR VEHICLES
Transportation (this index)

MULTIEMPLOYER BARGAINING UNITS
Employer's unilateral withdrawal from multiemployer bargaining unit, held not justified by bargaining impasse, 70 L Ed 2d 656

MUNICIPAL CORPORATIONS AND OTHER POLITICAL SUBDIVISIONS
Elections (this index)
Entertainment and Amusements (this index)
Licenses and Permits (this index)
Racial quotas: case challenging voluntary adoption by municipal board of education of racial quotas on enrollment, held not moot, and ordered consolidated with related case, 72 L Ed 2d 668

MURDER
"Cause and actual prejudice," rather than "plain error" of Rule 52(b) of Federal Rules of Criminal Procedure, held proper standard of review on motion for collateral relief under 28 USCS § 2255, 71 L Ed 2d 816
Death Penalty (this index)
Double jeopardy: Florida Supreme Court's reversal of murder and rape conviction at jury trial based on weight of evidence, held not to bar retrial under double jeopardy clause of Fifth and Fourteenth Amendments, 72 L Ed 2d 652

MUTUAL EMPLOYER
Secondary boycott: refusal by longshoremen's union to unload cargoes shipped from Soviet Union in protest against Afghanistan invasion, held illegal secondary boycott under 29 USCS § 158(b)(4), 72 L Ed 2d 21

NARCOTICS
Drugs and Narcotics (this index)

INDEX

NATIONAL BANKS
Checks: deposit of bad check in federally insured bank, held not proscribed by 18 USCS § 1014, 73 L Ed 2d 767

NATIONAL ENVIRONMENTAL POLICY ACT
Nuclear weapons: § 102 (2)(c) of the National Environmental Policy Act (42 USCS § 4332 (2)(c)), held not to require Navy to prepare and release "Hypothetical Environmental Impact Statement" regarding nuclear weapons storage, 70 L Ed 2d 298

NATIONAL LABOR RELATIONS ACT OR BOARD
Attorney's fees incurred during proceedings before National Labor Relations Board, held not proper element of damages under § 303(b) of Labor Management Relations Act (29 USCS § 187(b)), 72 L Ed 2d 511
Collective Bargaining (this index)
Secondary boycott: refusal by longshoremen's union to unload cargoes shipped from Soviet Union in protest against Afghanistan invasion, held illegal secondary boycott under 29 USCS § 158(b)(4), 72 L Ed 2d 21

NATIONAL STOLEN PROPERTY ACT
Securities: statute (18 USCS § 2314) prohibiting transport of forged securities in "interstate commerce," held not to require proof securities were forged before being taken across state lines, 71 L Ed 2d 522

NATURAL FATHERS
Paternity suits: Texas statute barring paternity suits brought on behalf of illegitimate children more than one year after their birth, held violative of equal protection, 71 L Ed 2d 770

NATURAL RESOURCES
Mines and Minerals (this index)
Oil and Gas (this index)

NAVAL MATTERS
Admiralty (this index)

"NEGATIVE IMPLICATIONS"
Severance tax imposed on oil and gas removed from Indian reservation, held authorized by Tribe's inherent authority to tax as part of power of self-government, and held violative of commerce clause (Art I, § 8, cl 3), 71 L Ed 2d 21

NEGLECTED CHILDREN
Parental termination proceeding: application of at least "clear and convincing evidence" standard of proof to state's parental rights termination proceeding, held required by Fourteenth Amendment due process clause, 71 L Ed 2d 599

NEGOTIABLE INSTRUMENTS
Banks (this index)

NEGOTIATIONS
Collective Bargaining (this index)

NEIGHBORHOOD SCHOOLS
Initiative: state initiative precluding school boards from requiring attendance at other than neighborhood schools, held unconstitutional, 73 L Ed 2d 896

NEWS MEDIA
Media (this index)

NEW MEXICO
Gross Receipts (this index)

NEW TRIAL
Habeas corpus: federal court's order in habeas corpus proceeding that state trial court must grant habeas petitioner new criminal trial or explain reasons for its inconsistent verdicts, held erroneous, 70 L Ed 2d 530
Instructions to jury: preclusion of jury instructions on lesser included offense in capital case, held not to require new trial where defendant's own evidence negates possibility that such instruction was warranted, 72 L Ed 2d 367

NO-COST TRANSFERS
Establishment clause: taxpayers' organization dedicated to separation of church and state, held to have no standing to challenge, as violative of First Amendment establishment clause, no-cost transfer of surplus United States property to religious educational institution, 70 L Ed 2d 700

NON-CASH-BONUS BIDDING SYSTEM
Leases: Interior Secretary's refusal to use non-cash-bonus bidding systems in leasing oil and gas tracts on outer continental shelf, held not violative of Outer Continental Shelf Lands Act Amendments, (43 USCS §§ 1331 et seq.), 70 L Ed 2d 309

INDEX

NONDELEGABLE DUTIES
Discrimination: proof of intentional discrimination, held necessary for liability under 42 USCS § 1981; vicarious liability under § 1981 of employers and trade associations for discriminatory conduct of union, held not supportable, 73 L Ed 2d 835

NONDISCLOSURE
Disclosure and Discovery (this index)

NONDOMICILIARY CORPORATION
Taxation: Idaho's inclusion within taxable income of nondomiciliary parent corporation doing some business in state, of portion of intangible income parent receives from subsidiary having no other connection with state, held to violate due process, 73 L Ed 2d 787

NONIMMIGRANT ALIENS
In-state status: state university's policy of denying in-state status to domiciled nonimmigrant aliens holding G-4 visas, held violative of supremacy clause (Art VI, cl 2), 73 L Ed 2d 563

NONPROFIT ASSOCIATIONS AND ORGANIZATIONS
Antitrust: nonprofit association of mechanical engineers responsible for promulgation of industry codes, held civilly liable under antitrust laws for antitrust violations of its agents committed with apparent authority, 72 L Ed 2d 330
Discrimination: black "tester" given false information about housing availability and nonprofit, open housing organization, held to have standing to challenge racial steering under Fair Housing Act (42 USCS § 3612); Act's 180-day limitations period (42 USCS § 3612(a)), held not bar claims of continuing violation, even though some incidents alleged occur outside period, 71 L Ed 2d 214

NONRECOURSE CLAUSES
Freight charges: carrier's violation of Interstate Commerce Commission's credit regulations, held not to bar collection of lawful freight charges from consignor, 72 L Ed 2d 114

639

NUCLEAR WEAPONS—Cont'd
prepare and release "Hypothetical Environmental Impact Statement" regarding nuclear weapons storage, 70 L Ed 2d 298

NUISANCE
Obscenity: proof, in public nuisance abatement action by city against motion picture theater, that motion pictures in question were obscene beyond reasonable doubt, held not required, 70 L Ed 2d 262

NURSING HOMES
Medicaid: nursing homes' decisions to discharge or transfer Medicaid patients to lower levels of care, held not to involve state action for purposes of Fourteenth Amendment's due process clause, 73 L Ed 2d 534

NURSING SCHOOLS
Sex discrimination: state-supported university's policy that excludes males from enrolling in its professional nursing school, held violative of equal protection clause of Fourteenth Amendment, 73 L Ed 2d 1090

OBJECTIONS
Exceptions and Exemptions (this index)

OBSCENITY
Lewdness, Indecency, and Obscenity (this index)

OCCUPATION OF PROPERTY
Cable television: New York law requiring landlords to allow cable television facilities on property, held to be "taking" of property compensable under Fifth and Fourteenth Amendments, 73 L Ed 2d 868

OCEAN
Water and Waterways (this index)

OFFICERS
Medicare: hearing procedures for claim disputes under Part B of Medicare program (42 USCS § 1395j), held not violative of due process, 72 L Ed 2d 1
Public Officers and Employees (this index)

OFFICIAL ACTS
Privileges and Immunities (this index)

OFFICIALS
Public Officers and Employees (this index)

OIL AND GAS
Bidding system: Interior Secretary's refusal to use non-cash-bonus bidding systems in leasing oil and gas tracts on outer continental shelf, held not violative of Outer Continental Shelf Lands Act Amendments, (43 USCS §§ 1331 et seq.), 70 L Ed 2d 309
Income distribution: Alaska statute distributing income derived from state's natural resources to state's citizens in varying amounts based on length of each citizen's residency, held to violate equal protection clause, 72 L Ed 2d 672
Severance tax imposed on oil and gas removed from Indian reservation, held authorized by Tribe's inherent authority to tax as part of power of self-government, and held violative of commerce clause (Art I, § 8, cl 3), 71 L Ed 2d 21
Temporary Emergency Court of Appeals' invalidation of anti-passthrough provision of state tax statute relating to oil company revenues, vacated and remanded in light of expiration of preempting federal price control authority, 71 L Ed 2d 120

ORDERS
Judgments, Orders, and Decrees (this index)

ORDINANCES
Statutes and Ordinances (this index)

ORGANIZATIONS
Associations and Organizations (this index)

ORIGINAL JURISDICTION
Decedents' estates: California's motion for leave to file bill of complaint against Texas to decide whether Howard Hughes was domiciled in California or Texas at time of death, granted as properly invoking Supreme Court's original jurisdiction, 72 L Ed 2d 755

OUTER CONTINENTAL SHELF
Bidding system: Interior Secretary's refusal to use non-cash-bonus bidding systems in leasing oil and gas tracts on outer continental shelf, held not violative of Outer Continental Shelf Lands Act Amendments, (43 USCS §§ 1331 et seq.), 70 L Ed 2d 309

INDEX

"OUTSIDER RULE"
Union "outsider rule," held not violative of Labor-Management Reporting and Disclosure Act's "free speech and assembly" or "right to sue" provisions (29 USCS § 411(a)(2), (4)), 72 L Ed 2d 707

OVERBREADTH
Licenses and Permits (this index)

OVERVALUATION
Checks: deposit of bad check in federally insured bank, held not proscribed by 18 USCS § 1014, 73 L Ed 2d 767

OWNERSHIP
Title and Ownership (this index)

PACKAGES
Search warrant: authority to conduct warrantless search of motor vehicle based on probable cause, including compartments and containers, held coextensive with authority based on magistrate's issuance of warrant, 72 L Ed 2d 572

PARAPHERNALIA
Licenses: municipal ordinance requiring license to sell "items designed or marketed for use with illegal cannabis or drugs," held not unconstitutionally vague or overbroad, 71 L Ed 2d 362

PARENS PATRIAE
Discrimination: Commonwealth of Puerto Rico held to have standing to sue as parens patriae to enjoin applegrowers' discrimination against Puerto Rican migrant farmworkers, 73 L Ed 2d 995

PARENT AND CHILD
Children and Minors (this index)

PARENT AND SUBSIDIARY CORPORATIONS
Subsidiary Corporations (this index)

PAROLE
Habeas corpus: claims of habeas corpus petitioners seeking relief on ground that failure to be advised of mandatory parole before pleading guilty violated due process, held moot after parole terms expired, 71 L Ed 2d 508

INDEX

PENAL AND CORRECTIONAL INSTITUTIONS
"Cause and actual prejudice," rather than "plain error" of Rule 52(b) of Federal Rules of Criminal Procedure, held proper standard of review on motion for collateral relief under 28 USCS § 2255, 71 L Ed 2d 816

Habeas Corpus (this index)

Parole (this index)

Pro se complaint: state prisoner's crudely written, pro se complaint alleging his placement in solitary confinement for one-week period without any notice of charges or any hearing, held sufficient to state cause of action, 70 L Ed 2d 551

Sentence and Punishment (this index)

PENALTIES
Fines, Penalties, and Forfeitures (this index)

PENDING ACTIONS
Affirmative action plan: Federal Court of Appeals' refusal to resolve pendent state-law claim in affirming affirmative action plan for contractors as constitutional, held abuse of discretion, 73 L Ed 2d 245

Attorney disciplinary rules: federal court abstention from considering challenge to constitutionality of attorney disciplinary rules that were subject of pending state disciplinary proceeding within jurisdiction of New Jersey Supreme Court held required, 73 L Ed 2d 116

PENSION AND RETIREMENT FUNDS
Coal producer sued on promise to contribute to union welfare funds based on "purchased coal," held entitled to plead and have adjudicated illegality defense, 70 L Ed 2d 833

PERMANENT OCCUPATION OF PROPERTY
Cable television: New York law requiring landlords to allow cable television facilities on property, held to be "taking" of property compensable under Fifth and Fourteenth Amendments, 73 L Ed 2d 868

PERMITS
Licenses and Permits (this index)

"PERSONAL" INFORMATION
Freedom of Information Act (this index)

INDEX

PERSONALIZED INSTRUCTIONS
Interpreters: deaf student held not entitled to sign-language interpreter in public school classes, under Education for All Handicapped Children Act, where she was receiving adequate education and personalized instruction, 73 L Ed 2d 690

PERSONAL JURISDICTION
In Personam and In Rem Actions (this index)

PETITIONS
Applications and Petitions (this index)

PETROLEUM
Oil and Gas (this index)

PHARMACISTS
Trademark: Federal Court of Appeals' reversal of District Court's findings as to trademark infringement by generic drug manufacturers, held error where "clearly erroneous" standard of FRCP 52 not followed, 72 L Ed 2d 606

PHILIPPINES
Treaties: word "treaty" in 5 USCS § 7201 note, which excepts from certain employment discrimination requirements actions permitted by "treaty," held to include executive agreements, 71 L Ed 2d 715

PHOTOGRAPHS AND PICTURES
Identification: Federal Court of Appeals' decision holding 28 USCS § 2254(d) inapplicable to habeas petition challenging photographic identification procedures, remanded for failure to adhere to instructions of Supreme Court on prior remand, 71 L Ed 2d 480

Obscenity: proof, in public nuisance abatement action by city against motion picture theater, that motion pictures in question were obscene beyond reasonable doubt, held not required, 70 L Ed 2d 262

PHYSICIANS AND SURGEONS
Chiropractor's fees: insurer use of peer review committee to determine reasonableness of chiropractor's fees, held not exempt from antitrust laws as "business of insurance" under McCarran-Ferguson Act (15 USCS § 1012(b)), 73 L Ed 2d 647

646

PLEADINGS—Cont'd

Prejudgment attachment: complaint against private creditor's prejudgment attachment, held to state cause of action under 42 USCS § 1983 where statute authorizing it is alleged to be procedurally defective, 73 L Ed 2d 482

Promotion: Mexican-American employee who was denied promotion, held not entitled to maintain class action on behalf of Mexican-American applicants for employment who were not hired, 72 L Ed 2d 740

Pro se complaint: state prisoner's crudely written, pro se complaint alleging his placement in solitary confinement for one-week period without any notice of charges or any hearing, held sufficient to state cause of action, 70 L Ed 2d 551

Welfare fund: coal producer sued on promise to contribute to union welfare funds based on "purchased coal," held entitled to plead and have adjudicated illegality defense, 70 L Ed 2d 833

PLEAS

Due process: fact that defendant was charged with felony after refusing to plead guilty to misdemeanor charges, held not to warrant presumption of prosecutorial vindictiveness in violation of due process, 73 L Ed 2d 74

Habeas corpus: claims of habeas corpus petitioners seeking relief on ground that failure to be advised of mandatory parole before pleading guilty violated due process, held moot after parole terms expired, 71 L Ed 2d 508

PLEASURE BOATS

Collision: complaint alleging collision between two pleasure boats on navigable waters, held to state claim within federal admiralty jurisdiction, 73 L Ed 2d 300

PLEDGE

Promises (this index)

PLEDGES

Certificate of deposit from federally regulated bank and business agreement arising from pledging of certificate as guarantee for loan, held not securities for purposes of 15 USCS § 78j(b), 71 L Ed 2d 409

POLICE

Law Enforcement Officers (this index)

648

INDEX

POLICE POWER
Eminent Domain or Condemnation (this index)

POLITICAL ACTS AND MATTERS
Elections (this index)
Soviet Union (this index)

POLLUTION
Environmental Law (this index)

POOR PERSONS
Indigents (this index)

PORNOGRAPHY
Lewdness, Indecency, and Obscenity (this index)

POSSESSION OF PROPERTY
Admiralty: process issued by Federal District Court to secure possession of property from state officials in admiralty in rem action, held not barred by Eleventh Amendment, 73 L Ed 2d 1057
Drugs and Narcotics (this index)

POSSESSIONS AND TERRITORIES
Puerto Rico (this index)

POST-ARREST SILENCE
Miranda warnings: state prosecutor's cross-examination of defendant as to post-arrest silence, held not violative of Fourteenth Amendment due process in absence of Miranda warning assurances, 71 L Ed 2d 490

POSTING OF SUMMONS
Service of process: Kentucky statute applicable to forcible entry and detainer actions permitting service of process by posting summons on door of premises, held violative of due process, 72 L Ed 2d 249

POSTJUDMENT REQUESTS
Attorney's fees: postjudgment request for attorney's fees under Civil Rights Attorney's Fees Awards Act (42 USCS § 1988), held not subject to 10-day timeliness standard of Rule 59(e) of Federal Rules of Civil Procedure, 71 L Ed 2d 325

649

POWER AND ENERGY

Hydroelectric energy: state public utility commission's order requiring privately-owned and federally-licensed public utility to sell within state hydroelectric energy it had been exporting, held violative of commerce clause (Art I, § 8, cl 3), 71 L Ed 2d 188

Public Utilities Regulatory Policies Act: provisions of Public Utility Regulatory Policies Act (15 USCS §§ 3201 et seq.; 16 USCS §§ 824a-3, 2611 et seq.), held not violative of commerce clause (Art I, § 8, cl 3) and Tenth Amendment, 72 L Ed 2d 532

PRECLEARANCE

Elections (this index)

PRECLUSION

Emergency assistance: state emergency assistance program precluding furnishing assistance to AFDC recipients, held invalid under supremacy clause (Art VI, cl 2) as in conflict with valid federal regulation, 72 L Ed 2d 728

Instructions to jury: preclusion of jury instructions on lesser included offense in capital case, held not to require new trial where defendant's own evidence negates possibility that such instruction was warranted, 72 L Ed 2d 367

Job bias: giving of preclusive effect to state court's review of state agency's action on job bias claim upon later action in federal court on such claim under similar federal law, held required by 28 USCS § 1738, 72 L Ed 2d 262

PREEMPTION

Due-on-sale clauses: Federal Home Loan Bank Board regulation authorizing due-on-sale clauses in federal savings and loan instruments held to preempt state law, 73 L Ed 2d 664

Public Utilities Regulatory Policies Act: provisions of Public Utility Regulatory Policies Act (15 USCS §§ 3201 et seq.; 16 USCS §§ 824a-3, 2611 et seq.), held not violative of commerce clause (Art I, § 8, cl 3) and Tenth Amendment, 72 L Ed 2d 532

Taxation (this index)

PREFERENCES

Bias and Prejudice (this index)

PREFERENCES—Cont'd
Discrimination (this index)
First Amendment: Minnesota statute exempting from certain registration and reporting requirements only religious organizations receiving more than 50% of contributions from members, held violative of First Amendment establishment clause, 72 L Ed 2d 33

PREJUDGMENT ATTACHMENT
Complaint against private creditor's prejudgment attachment, held to state cause of action under 42 USCS § 1983 where state statute authorizing it is alleged to be procedurally defective, 73 L Ed 2d 482

PREJUDICE
Bias and Prejudice (this index)

PREPONDERANCE OF EVIDENCE
Parental termination proceeding: application of at least "clear and convincing evidence" standard of proof to state's parental rights termination proceeding, held required by Fourteenth Amendment due process clause, 71 L Ed 2d 599

PREREQUISITES
Exhaustion of state administrative remedies, held not prerequisite to bringing action pursuant to 42 USCS § 1983, 73 L Ed 2d 172
Jurisdiction: filing of timely charge with Equal Employment Opportunity Commission held not jurisdictional prerequisite to suit under Title VII of Civil Rights Act of 1964 (42 USCS §§ 2000e et seq.), 71 L Ed 2d 234

PRESENCE
Absence and Presence (this index)

PRESIDENT OF UNION
Discharge of union business agent by newly-elected president of local union, held not violative of Labor Management Reporting and Disclosure Act (29 USCS §§ 401 et seq.), 72 L Ed 2d 239

PRESIDENT OF UNITED STATES
Privileges and Immunities (this index)

INDEX

PRESIDENT OF UNITED STATES—Cont'd
Treaties: word "treaty" in 5 USCS § 7201 note, which excepts from certain employment discrimination requirements actions permitted by "treaty," held to include executive agreements, 71 L Ed 2d 715

PRESS
Speech, Assembly, and Press Freedom (this index)

PRESUMPTIONS AND BURDEN OF PROOF
"Cause and actual prejudice," rather than "plain error" of Rule 52(b) of Federal Rules of Criminal Procedure, held proper standard of review on motion for collateral relief under 28 USCS § 2255, 71 L Ed 2d 816

Compensable injury: presumption of compensability under § 20(a) of Longshoremen's and Harbor Workers' Compensation Act (33 USCS § 920(a)), held inapplicable to claimed injury at work where "injury" arose at home, 71 L Ed 2d 495

Due process: fact that defendant was charged with felony after refusing to plead guilty to misdemeanor charges, held not to warrant presumption of prosecutorial vindictiveness in violation of due process, 73 L Ed 2d 74

Elections: jurisdiction to decide whether § 5 of Voting Rights Act of 1965 (42 USCS § 1973c) applies to changes in local election procedures, held within power of state court, 72 L Ed 2d 824

Obscenity: proof, in public nuisance abatement action by city against motion picture theater, that motion pictures in question was obscene beyond reasonable doubt, held not required, 70 L Ed 2d 262

Photographic identification: Federal Court of Appeals' decision holding 28 USCS § 2254(d) inapplicable to habeas petition challenging photographic identification procedures, remanded for failure to adhere to instructions of Supreme Court on prior remand, 71 L Ed 2d 480

PRETRIAL ACTS AND MATTERS
Bail: claim that Nebraska's prohibition of pretrial bail to person charged with sexual offenses violated Federal Constitution, held moot where defendant had already been convicted of offenses, 71 L Ed 2d 353

PRETRIAL ACTS AND MATTERS—Cont'd

Photographic identification: Federal Court of Appeals' decision holding 28 USCS § 2254(d) inapplicable to habeas petition challenging photographic identification procedures, remanded for failure to adhere to instructions of Supreme Court on prior remand, 71 L Ed 2d 480

PREVAILING WAGE RATE SYSTEM

"Two-step" pay increase rule of 5 USCS § 5334(b), held not to apply to federal employees promoted from prevailing wage rate system (WS) to General Schedule (GS), 70 L Ed 2d 768

PRICES

Commodity Exchange Act: action for damages caused by violation of Commodity Exchange Act (7 USCS §§ 1 et seq.), held available to private parties, 72 L Ed 2d 182

Costs, Expenses, and Fees (this index)

Taxation: Temporary Emergency Court of Appeals' invalidation of anti-passthrough provision of state tax statute relating to oil company revenues, vacated and remanded in light of expiration of preempting federal price control authority, 71 L Ed 2d 120

PRIMA FACIE CASE

Discrimination: prima facie case under 42 USCS § 2000e-2 in regard to test that bars promotion and disproportionately excludes blacks, held not precluded by nondiscriminatory "bottom line" result of employer's promotional process, 73 L Ed 2d 130

PRINCIPAL

Agents and Principal (this index)

PRIORITIES

Preferences (this index)

PRISONS AND PRISONERS

Penal and Correctional Institutions (this index)

PRIVACY

Seizure: police officer's accompaniment of lawful arrestee to residence and subsequent seizure of contraband in plain view, held not violative of Fourth Amendment, 70 L Ed 2d 778

INDEX

PRIVATE INSURANCE CARRIERS
Medicare: determinations by insurance carriers of amount of benefits payable under Part B of Medicare program (42 USCS §§ 1395j et seq.), held not reviewable in Court of Claims, 72 L Ed 2d 12

PRIVATELY-OWNED UTILITIES
Hydroelectric energy: state public utility commission's order requiring privately-owned and federally-licensed public utility to sell within state hydroelectric energy it had been exporting, held violative of commerce clause (Art I, § 8, cl 3), 71 L Ed 2d 188

PRIVATE SCHOOLS
Income: private school whose income is derived primarily from public sources and which is regulated by public authorities, held not to have acted under color of state law for purposes of 42 USCS § 1983 when it discharged certain employees, 73 L Ed 2d 418

PRIVILEGED INFORMATION
Address lists compiled by Bureau of the Census, held not subject to disclosure under Freedom of Information Act (5 USCS § 552) or discovery provisions of Federal Rules of Civil Procedure, 71 L Ed 2d 199

PRIVILEGES AND IMMUNITIES
Arrest: rule of Payton v New York prohibiting warrantless, nonconsensual entry into suspect's home to make routine felony arrest, held to apply to case pending on direct appeal when Payton was decided, 73 L Ed 2d 202

Double jeopardy: Florida Supreme Court's reversal of murder and rape conviction at jury trial based on weight of evidence, held not to bar retrial under double jeopardy clause of Fifth and Fourteenth Amendments, 72 L Ed 2d 652

President of United States, held entitled to absolute immunity from damages liability predicated on his official acts, 73 L Ed 2d 349

Railroads: application of Railway Labor Act (29 USCS §§ 151 et seq.) to state-owned railroad engaged in interstate commerce, held not prohibited by Tenth Amendment, 71 L Ed 2d 547

PRIVILEGES AND IMMUNITIES—Cont'd

Senior aides and advisers of President of United States, held entitled to qualified immunity from civil damages suits insofar as their conduct does not violate rights of which reasonable person would have known, 73 L Ed 2d 396

Water: Nebraska statute forbidding withdrawal of ground water to foreign state which denies such privileges to Nebraska, held violative of Congress clause (Art 1, § 8 cl 3), 73 L Ed 2d 1254

PROBABLE CAUSE

Search warrant: authority to conduct warrantless search of motor vehicle based on probable cause, including compartments and containers, held coextensive with authority based on magistrate's issuance of warrant, 72 L Ed 2d 572

PROBATION OFFICERS

Citizens: state statute requiring peace officers, including deputy probation officers, to be United States citizens, held not violative of equal protection clause of Fourteenth Amendment, 70 L Ed 2d 677

PROCEDURE

Federal Rules of Civil Procedure (this index)

Prejudgment attachment: complaint against private creditor's prejudgment attachment, held to state cause of action under 42 USCS § 1983 where statute authorizing it is alleged to be procedurally defective, 73 L Ed 2d 482

PROCEEDS OF INSURANCE

Beneficiary: insured serviceman's beneficiary designation under life policy issued pursuant to Servicemen's Group Life Insurance Act (38 USCS §§ 765 et seq.), held to prevail over constructive trust imposed upon proceeds by state court, 70 L Ed 2d 39

PROCESS AND SERVICE OF PROCESS

Admiralty: process issued by Federal District Court to secure possession of property from state officials in admiralty in rem action, held not barred by Eleventh Amendment, 73 L Ed 2d 1057

Forcible entry and detainer: Kentucky statute applicable to forcible entry and detainer actions permitting service of process by posting summons on door of premises, held violative of due process, 72 L Ed 2d 249

INDEX

PROCESS AND SERVICE OF PROCESS—Cont'd

Statute of limitations: New Jersey statute tolling limitation period for actions against unrepresented foreign corporations, held not violative of Fourteenth Amendment's equal protection clause, 71 L Ed 2d 250

PROFESSIONAL CONDUCT
Conduct and Misconduct (this index)

PROMISES

First Amendment: Kentucky statute prohibiting candidates from offering benefits to voters in exchange for votes, held violative of First Amendment as applied to candidate who pledged to work at reduced salary, 71 L Ed 2d 732

Welfare fund: coal producer sued on promise to contribute to union welfare funds based on "purchased coal," held entitled to plead and have adjudicated illegality defense, 70 L Ed 2d 833

PROMOTIONS

Class actions: Mexican-American employee who was denied promotion, held not entitled to maintain class action on behalf of Mexican-American applicants for employment who were not hired, 72 L Ed 2d 740

Discrimination: prima facie case under 42 USCS § 2000e-2 in regard to test that bars promotion and disproportionately excludes blacks, held not precluded by nondiscriminatory "bottom line" result of employer's promotional process, 73 L Ed 2d 130

"Two-step" pay increase rule of 5 USCS § 5334(b), held not to apply to federal employees promoted from prevailing wage rate system (WS) to General Schedule (GS), 70 L Ed 2d 768

PROOF
Evidence (this index)

PROPERTY

Accretions: United States held entitled to oceanfront accretions to Coast Guard reservation under federal rule that accretions belong to upland owner, 73 L Ed 2d 1

Bankruptcy: employee protection provisions of Rock Island Transition and Employee Assistance Act (45 USCS §§ 1005 and 1008), held violative of bankruptcy clause (Art I, § 8, cl 4), 71 L Ed 2d 335

656

PROPERTY—Cont'd
Deprivation of Property (this index)
Eminent Domain or Condemnation (this index)
Gift Tax (this index)
Leases (this index)
Possession of Property (this index)
Sales and Transfers (this index)
Securities: statute (18 USCS § 2314) prohibiting transport of
forged securities in "interstate commerce," held not to
require proof securities were forged before being taken
across state lines, 71 L Ed 2d 522
Title and Ownership (this index)

PROPERTY CLAUSE

Establishment clause: taxpayers' organization dedicated to separation of church and state, held to have no standing to
challenge, as violative of First Amendment establishment
clause, no-cost transfer of surplus United States property
to religious educational institution, 70 L Ed 2d 700 ·

PRO SE

Complaint: state prisoner's crudely written, pro se complaint
alleging his placement in solitary confinement for one-
week period without any notice of charges or any hearing,
held sufficient to state cause of action, 70 L Ed 2d 551

PROSECUTING ATTORNEYS

District and Prosecuting Attorneys (this index)

PROSPECTIVE AND RETROACTIVE MATTERS

Arrest: rule of Payton v New York prohibiting warrantless,
nonconsensual entry into suspect's home to make routine
felony arrest, held to apply to case pending on direct
appeal when Payton was decided, 73 L Ed 2d 202
Backpay: employer's offer to discrimination claimant of job
previously denied without offer of retroactive seniority,
held to toll continuing accrual of backpay liability under
42 USCS § 2000e-6(g), 73 L Ed 2d 721
Jurisdiction: filing of timely charge with Equal Employment
Opportunity Commission held not jurisdictional prerequisite to suit under Title VII of Civil Rights Act of 1964 (42
USCS §§ 2000e et seq.), 71 L Ed 2d 234

INDEX

PROTECTION PROVISIONS
Bankruptcy: employee protection provisions of Rock Island Transition and Employee Assistance Act (45 USCS §§ 1005 and 1008), held violative of bankruptcy clause (Art I, § 8, cl 4), 71 L Ed 2d 335

PSYCHOLOGISTS
Reimbursement of fee: health plan subscriber denied reimbursement for psychologist's fees, held to have standing to sue for conspiracy to exclude psychologists from psychotherapy market, 73 L Ed 2d 149

PUBLIC
First Amendment: state statute which requires, under all circumstances, exclusion of press and general public from courtroom during testimony of minor victim in sex-offense trial, held violative of First Amendment, 73 L Ed 2d 248

PUBLIC AID OR FUNDS
Funds and Funding (this index)

PUBLIC AUTHORITY
Private school whose income is derived primarily from public sources and which is regulated by public authorities, held not to have acted under color of state law for purposes of 42 USCS § 1983 when it discharged certain employees, 73 L Ed 2d 418

PUBLIC DEFENDER
"Color of state law": public defender performing lawyer's traditional functions, held not acting "under color of state law" for purposes of suit under 42 USCS § 1983, 70 L Ed 2d 509

PUBLIC FUNDS
Funds and Funding (this index)

PUBLIC INSURANCE
Social Security (this index)

PUBLICITY
First Amendment: state statute which requires, under all circumstances, exclusion of press and general public from courtroom during testimony of minor victim in sex-offense trial, held violative of First Amendment, 73 L Ed 2d 248

INDEX

PUBLIC LANDS

Bidding system: Interior Secretary's refusal to use non-cash-bonus bidding systems in leasing oil and gas tracts on outer continental shelf, held not violative of Outer Continental Shelf Lands Act Amendments, (43 USCS §§ 1331 et seq.), 70 L Ed 2d 309

PUBLIC OFFICERS AND EMPLOYEES

Admiralty: process issued by Federal District Court to secure possession of property from state officials in admiralty in rem action, held not barred by Eleventh Amendment, 73 L Ed 2d 1057

Arrest warrant: private citizen's right to prevent state officials from presenting information that will assist magistrate in determining whether to issue arrest warrant, held not judicially cognizable, 70 L Ed 2d 65

"Color of state law": public defender performing lawyer's traditional functions, held not acting "under color of state law" for purposes of suit under 42 USCS § 1983, 70 L Ed 2d 509

Death tax claim: action under Federal Interpleader Act (28 USCS § 1335) to resolve inconsistent death tax claims on estate of Howard Hughes by officials of two states, held barred by Eleventh Amendment, 72 L Ed 2d 694

District and Prosecuting Attorneys (this index)

Elections (this index)

Law Enforcement Officers (this index)

Prejudgment attachment: complaint against private creditor's prejudgment attachment, held to state cause of action under 42 USCS § 1983 where statute authorizing it is alleged to be procedurally defective, 73 L Ed 2d 482

Privileges and Immunities (this index)

Sales and use taxes: imposition of New Mexico's gross receipts and compensating use taxes on federal contractors doing business in state, held valid, 71 L Ed 2d 580

"Two-step" pay increase rule of 5 USCS § 5334(b), held not to apply to federal employees promoted from prevailing wage rate system (WS) to General Schedule (GS), 70 L Ed 2d 768

PUBLIC SCHOOLS

Schools and Education (this index)

INDEX

PUBLIC SOURCES
Funds and Funding (this index)

PUBLIC TRANSIT
Collective bargaining: section 13(c) of Urban Mass Transportation Act of 1964 (49 USCS § 1609(c)), held not to create federal cause of action for breach of § 13(c) agreement or collective bargaining contract between local transit authority and union, 72 L Ed 2d 639

PUBLIC UTILITIES
Power and Energy (this index)

PUERTO RICO
Discrimination: Commonwealth of Puerto Rico held to have standing to sue as parens patriae to enjoin applegrowers' discrimination against Puerto Rican migrant farmworkers, 73 L Ed 2d 995
Legislative seat: Puerto Rico law vesting in political party authority to appoint replacement for member who vacates seat on legislature, held not violative of United States Constitution, 72 L Ed 2d 628

PUNISHMENT
Sentence and Punishment (this index)

PUNITIVE DAMAGES
Antitrust: nonprofit association of mechanical engineers responsible for promulgation of industry codes, held civilly liable under antitrust laws for antitrust violations of its agents committed with apparent authority, 72 L Ed 2d 330

PUPILS
Schools and Education (this index)

"PURCHASED COAL"
Welfare fund: coal producer sued on promise to contribute to union welfare funds based on "purchased coal," held entitled to plead and have adjudicated illegality defense, 70 L Ed 2d 833

PUTATIVE FATHERS
Paternity suits: Texas statute barring paternity suits brought on behalf of illegitimate children more than one year after their birth, held violative of equal protection, 71 L Ed 2d 770

INDEX

QUALIFICATION AND DISQUALIFICATION
"Labor nexus" test: National Labor Relations Board's "labor nexus" test for determining eligibility of confidential employees for inclusion in collective bargaining units, held to have reasonable basis in law, 70 L Ed 2d 323

Medicare and Medicaid (this index)

Prerequisites (this index)

QUESTIONS OF LAW OR FACT
Promotion: Mexican-American employee who was denied promotion, held not entitled to maintain class action on behalf of Mexican-American applicants for employment who were not hired, 72 L Ed 2d 740

QUOTAS
Racial quotas: case challenging voluntary adoption by municipal board of education of racial quotas on enrollment, held not moot, and ordered consolidated with related case, 72 L Ed 2d 668

RACIAL DISCRIMINATION
Elections: at-large election system for large rural county with large black population held violative of equal protection clause, 73 L Ed 2d 1012

Exhaustion of state administrative remedies, held not prerequisite to bringing action pursuant to 42 USCS § 1983, 73 L Ed 2d 172

Housing: black "tester" given false information about housing availability and nonprofit, open housing organization, held to have standing to challenge racial steering under Fair Housing Act (42 USCS § 3612); Act's 180-day limitations period (42 USCS § 3612(a)), held not to bar claims of continuing violation, even though some incidents alleged occur outside period, 71 L Ed 2d 214

Promotions (this index)

Schools
- Busing: state constitutional amendment precluding state court-ordered school busing absent Fourteenth Amendment violation held constitutional, 73 L Ed 2d 948
- Enrollment: case challenging voluntary adoption by municipal board of education of racial quotas on enrollment, held not moot, and ordered consolidated with related case, 72 L Ed 2d 668

INDEX

RACIAL DISCRIMINATION—Cont'd
Schools—Cont'd
– Initiative: state initiative precluding school boards from requiring attendance at other than neighborhood schools, held unconstitutional, 73 L Ed 2d 896
Seniority: Federal Court of Appeals' reversal of Federal District Court ruling as to legality of seniority system under 42 USCS § 2000e-5(h), held erroneous in view of court's independent determination of allegations of discrimination, 72 L Ed 2d 66

RADIO AND TELEVISION
Cable Television (this index)

RAILROADS
Application of Railway Labor Act (29 USCS §§ 151 et seq.) to state-owned railroad engaged in interstate commerce, held not prohibited by Tenth Amendment, 71 L Ed 2d 547
Bankruptcy: employee protection provisions of Rock Island Transition and Employee Assistance Act (45 USCS §§ 1005 and 1008), held violative of bankruptcy clause (Art I, § 8, cl 4), 71 L Ed 2d 335

RAPE
Double jeopardy: Florida Supreme Court's reversal of murder and rape conviction at jury trial based on weight of evidence, held not to bar retrial under double jeopardy clause of Fifth and Fourteenth Amendments, 72 L Ed 2d 652

REAL PROPERTY
Property (this index)

REAPPORTIONMENT PLAN
Objections: Federal District Court effecting interim Texas congressional reapportionment for districts objected to by Attorney General, held without power to redraw other districts in absence of constitutional or statutory violation, 71 L Ed 2d 725
Stay: application for stay of judgment of three-judge Federal District Court invalidating New Jersey congressional reapportionment plan as unconstitutional, granted by individual justice, 71 L Ed 2d 635

662

REASONABLE DOUBT
Obscenity: proof, in public nuisance abatement action by city against motion picture theater, that motion pictures in question were obscene beyond reasonable doubt, held not required, 70 L Ed 2d 262

RECEIPTS
Gross Receipts (this index)

RECEIVING STOLEN PROPERTY
Securities: statute (18 USCS § 2314) prohibiting transport of forged securities in "interstate commerce," held not to require proof securities were forged before being taken across state lines, 71 L Ed 2d 522

RECIPROCITY
Water: Nebraska statute forbidding withdrawal of ground water to foreign state which denies such privileges to Nebraska, held violative of Congress clause (Art 1, § 8 cl 3), 73 L Ed 2d 1254

RECONSIDERATION
Appeal and Review (this index)
Election method: letter to Attorney General advising of results of county referendum endorsing at-large method of electing county council, held to be request for reconsideration of Attorney General's prior objections to method and not preclearance request under Voting Rights Act (42 USCS § 1973c), 70 L Ed 2d 576

RECORDS AND REPORTS
First Amendment: Minnesota statute exempting from certain registration and reporting requirements only religious organizations receiving more than 50% of contributions from members, held violative of First Amendment establishment clause, 72 L Ed 2d 33
Freedom of Information Act (this index)
Union "outsider rule," held not violative of Labor-Management Reporting and Disclosure Act's "free speech and assembly" or "right to sue" provisions (29 USCS § 411(a)(2), (4)), 72 L Ed 2d 707
Welfare fund: coal producer sued on promise to contribute to union welfare funds based on "purchased coal," held entitled to plead and have adjudicated illegality defense, 70 L Ed 2d 833

REDISTRICTING
Reapportionment Plan (this index)

REDUCTION IN SALARY
Compensation and Income (this index)

REFERENDUM
Election method: letter to Attorney General advising of results of county referendum endorsing at-large method of electing county council, held to be request for reconsideration of Attorney General's prior objections to method and not preclearance request under Voting Rights Act (42 USCS § 1973c), 70 L Ed 2d 576

REFERRAL SERVICES
Discrimination: black "tester" given false information about housing availability and nonprofit, open housing organization, held to have standing to challenge racial steering under Fair Housing Act (42 USCS § 3612); Act's 180-day limitations period (42 USCS § 3612(a)), held not bar claims of continuing violation, even though some incidents alleged occur outside period, 71 L Ed 2d 214

REFILINGS
Resubmission (this index)

REFUSAL
Denial or Refusal (this index)

REGISTRATION
First Amendment: Minnesota statute exempting from certain registration and reporting requirements only religious organizations receiving more than 50% of contributions from members, held violative of First Amendment establishment clause, 72 L Ed 2d 33

REGULATIONS
Private school whose income is derived primarily from public sources and which is regulated by public authorities, held not to have acted under color of state law for purposes of 42 USCS § 1983 when it discharged certain employees, 73 L Ed 2d 418

INDEX

REHABILITATION
Full faith and credit: North Carolina courts' refusal to treat as res judicata Indiana rehabilitation court's adjudication of rights to insurance company's deposit posted in North Carolina, held violative of full faith and credit clause (Art IV, § 1), 71 L Ed 2d 558

REIMBURSEMENT
Psychologist's fees: health plan subscriber denied reimbursement for psychologist's fees, held to have standing to sue for conspiracy to exclude psychologists from psychotherapy market, 73 L Ed 2d 149

REJECTION OR ACCEPTANCE
Trust beneficiary's disclaimer of contingent interest in testamentary trust, held taxable transfer of property by gift under 26 USCS §§ 2501(a)(1) and 2511(a), not excepted from tax by 26 CFR § 25.2511-1(c), 71 L Ed 2d 170

RELATIVES
Family and Relatives (this index)

RELEASE
Also see Discharge or Removal

Freedom of Information Act: citizenship information on foreign nationals, held to satisfy "similar files" requirement of Exemption 6 of Freedom of Information Act (5 USCS § 552(b)(6)), 72 L Ed 2d 358

RELIGION AND RELIGIOUS INSTITUTIONS
Contributions: Minnesota statute exempting from certain registration and reporting requirements only religious organizations receiving more than 50% of contributions from members, held violative of First Amendment establishment clause, 72 L Ed 2d 33

Social security: imposition of social security taxes on persons who object on religious grounds to receipt of public insurance benefits and to payment of taxes to support such benefits, held constitutional, 71 L Ed 2d 127

State university's refusal to grant student religious group access to university facilities generally open to other student groups, held unjustifiable, content-based exclusion of religious speech, 70 L Ed 2d 440

RELIGION AND RELIGIOUS INSTITUTIONS—Cont'd

Transfer of property: taxpayers' organization dedicated to separation of church and state, held to have no standing to challenge, as violative of First Amendment establishment clause, no-cost transfer of surplus United States property to religious educational institution, 70 L Ed 2d 700

REMAND

Jurisdiction: writ of certiorari granted to the Colorado Supreme Court in case where it had remanded for trial, dismissed for want of jurisdiction, 72 L Ed 2d 237

Licenses: ordinance directing city's police chief to consider applicant's "connection with criminal elements" in licensing amusement establishments, held not unconstitutionally vague, 71 L Ed 2d 152

Mental patients: case presenting question whether state involuntarily committed patients may refuse certain drugs, vacated and remanded to Federal Court of Appeals, to consider intervening state decision opinion bearing on issue, 73 L Ed 2d 16

Photographic identification: Federal Court of Appeals' decision holding 28 USCS § 2254(d) inapplicable to habeas petition challenging photographic identification procedures, remanded for failure to adhere to instructions of Supreme Court on prior remand, 71 L Ed 2d 480

Taxation: Temporary Emergency Court of Appeals' invalidation of anti-passthrough provision of state tax statute relating to oil company revenues, vacated and remanded in light of expiration of preempting federal price control authority, 71 L Ed 2d 120

REMEDIAL PROGRAMS

Discrimination: proof of intentional discrimination, held necessary for liability under 42 USCS § 1981; vicarious liability under § 1981 of employers and trade associations for discriminatory conduct of union, held not supportable, 73 L Ed 2d 835

REMEDIES

Actions and Remedies (this index)

REMOVAL OR DISCHARGE

Discharge or Removal (this index)

INDEX

RESIDENCE AND DOMICILE—Cont'd

Decedents' estates: California's motion for leave to file bill of complaint against Texas to decide whether Howard Hughes was domiciled in California or Texas at time of death, granted as properly invoking Supreme Court's original jurisdiction, 72 L Ed 2d 755

Discrimination: Commonwealth of Puerto Rico held to have standing to sue as parens patriae to enjoin applegrowers' discrimination against Puerto Rican migrant farmworkers, 73 L Ed 2d 995

Income distribution: Alaska statute distributing income derived from state's natural resources to state's citizens in varying amounts based on length of each citizen's residency, held to violate equal protection clause, 72 L Ed 2d 672

Schools and Education (this index)

Seizure: police officer's accompaniment of lawful arrestee to residence and subsequent seizure of contraband in plain view, held not violative of Fourth Amendment, 70 L Ed 2d 778

RES JUDICATA

Full faith and credit: North Carolina courts' refusal to treat as res judicata Indiana rehabilitation court's adjudication of rights to insurance company's deposit posted in North Carolina, held violative of full faith and credit clause (Art IV, § 1), 71 L Ed 2d 558

Job bias: giving of preclusive effect to state court's review of state agency's action on job bias claim upon later action in federal court on such claim under similar federal law, held required by 28 USCS § 1738, 72 L Ed 2d 262

RESOURCES

Mines and Minerals (this index)
Oil and Gas (this index)

RESTRAINTS OF PERSON

Custody (this index)

RESTRAINTS OF TRADE

Monopolies and Restraints of Trade (this index)

RESTRICTIONS AND LIMITATIONS

Limitations and Restrictions (this index)

INDEX

RESUBMISSION

Bankruptcy: dismissal of Chapter XI petition filed under 1898 Bankruptcy Act in order to refile under Chapter 11 of 1978 Bankruptcy Code, held not authorized by Bankruptcy Rule 11-42(a) or § 403(a) of Bankruptcy Reform Act of 1978, 70 L Ed 2d 542

Habeas corpus: state prisoner's habeas corpus petition filed under 28 USCS § 2254, held required to be dismissed by Federal District Court when it contains both exhausted and unexhausted claims, 71 L Ed 2d 379

RETALIATORY ACTION

Discharge of union business agent by newly-elected president of local union, held not violative of Labor Management Reporting and Disclosure Act (29 USCS §§ 401 et seq.), 72 L Ed 2d 239

RETARDED PERSONS

Due process liberty: involuntarily committed mentally retarded person, held to have due process liberty interests requiring state to provide minimally adequate training to insure safety and freedom from undue restraint, 73 L Ed 2d 28

RETIREMENT FUNDS

Coal producer sued on promise to contribute to union welfare funds based on "purchased coal," held entitled to plead and have adjudicated illegality defense, 70 L Ed 2d 833

RETRIAL
Double Jeopardy (this index)

RETROACTIVE MATTERS
Prospective and Retroactive Matters (this index)

REVENUES
Compensation and Income (this index)

REVERSAL

Double jeopardy: Florida Supreme Court's reversal of murder and rape conviction at jury trial based on weight of evidence, held not to bar retrial under double jeopardy clause of Fifth and Fourteenth Amendments, 72 L Ed 2d 652

INDEX

REVERSAL—Cont'd
Trademark: Federal Court of Appeals' reversal of District Court's findings as to trademark infringement by generic drug manufacturers, held error where "clearly erroneous" standard of FRCP 52 not followed, 72 L Ed 2d 606

REVERSIONS
Mineral interests: state statute extinguishing unused mineral interests after 20 years unless owner files statement of claim, held not violative of contract clause, Fifth Amendment just compensation clause, and Fourteenth Amendment due process and equal protection, 70 L Ed 2d 738

REVIEW
Appeal and Review (this index)

REVOCATION
Cancellation or Termination (this index)

"RIGHT TO SUE"
Union "outsider rule," held not violative of Labor-Management Reporting and Disclosure Act's "free speech and assembly" or "right to sue" provisions (29 USCS § 411(a)(2), (4)), 72 L Ed 2d 707

RIPARIAN RIGHTS
Accretions: United States held entitled to oceanfront accretions to Coast Guard reservation under federal rule that accretions belong to upland owner, 73 L Ed 2d 1

ROCK ISLAND TRANSITION AND EMPLOYEE ASSISTANCE ACT
Bankruptcy: employee protection provisions of Rock Island Transition and Employee Assistance Act (45 USCS §§ 1005 and 1008), held violative of bankruptcy clause (Art I, § 8, cl 4), 71 L Ed 2d 335

RURAL COUNTY
Elections: at-large election system for large rural county with large black population held violative of equal protection clause, 73 L Ed 2d 1012

RUSSIA
Soviet Union (this index)

INDEX

SAFETY

Mentally retarded person: involuntarily committed mentally retarded person, held to have due process liberty interests requiring state to provide minimally adequate training to insure safety and freedom from undue restraint, 73 L Ed 2d 28

SALARY

Compensation and Income (this index)

SALES AND TRANSFERS

Establishment clause: taxpayers' organization dedicated to separation of church and state, held to have no standing to challenge, as violative of First Amendment establishment clause, no-cost transfer of surplus United States property to religious educational institution, 70 L Ed 2d 700

Hydroelectric energy: state public utility commission's order requiring privately-owned and federally-licensed public utility to sell within state hydroelectric energy it had been exporting, held violative of commerce clause (Art I, § 8, cl 3), 71 L Ed 2d 188

Licenses: municipal ordinance requiring license to sell "items designed or marketed for use with illegal cannabis or drugs," held not unconstitutionally vague or overbroad, 71 L Ed 2d 362

Taxation (this index)

SALES AND USE TAXES

Imposition of New Mexico's gross receipts and compensating use taxes on federal contractors doing business in state, held valid, 71 L Ed 2d 580

SALVAGE COMPANIES

Admiralty: process issued by Federal District Court to secure possession of property from state officials in admiralty in rem action, held not barred by Eleventh Amendment, 73 L Ed 2d 1057

SANCTIONS

Jurisdiction: District Court's action in establishing personal jurisdiction as sanction for failure to comply with discovery order under Rule 37 of of Federal Rules of Civil Procedure held not violative of due process, 72 L Ed 2d 492

671

SAVINGS AND LOAN INSTITUTIONS

Due-on-sale clauses: Federal Home Loan Bank Board regulation authorizing due-on-sale clauses in federal savings and loan instruments held to preempt state law, 73 L Ed 2d 664

"SAVINGS CLAUSE"

Hydroelectric energy: state public utility commission's order requiring privately-owned and federally-licensed public utility to sell within state hydroelectric energy it had been exporting, held violative of commerce clause (Art I, § 8, cl 3), 71 L Ed 2d 188

SCHOOL BOARDS

Initiative: state initiative precluding school boards from requiring attendance at other than neighborhood schools, held unconstitutional, 73 L Ed 2d 896

Racial quotas: case challenging voluntary adoption by municipal board of education of racial quotas on enrollment, held not moot, and ordered consolidated with related case, 72 L Ed 2d 668

Suspension: federal courts' replacement of local school board's construction of its own rules on mandatory suspension in action under 42 USCS § 1983, held erroneous where board's construction was reasonable, 73 L Ed 2d 1273

SCHOOLS AND EDUCATION

Admission and Enrollment (this index)

Board. **School Boards** (this index)

Book removal: Federal District Court's entry of summary judgment in case challenging local school board's removal of library books as violative of First Amendment, held erroneous where material issue of fact remained as to board's justifications, 73 L Ed 2d 435

Colleges. **Universities and Colleges** (this index)

Enrollment. **Admission and Enrollment** (this index)

Interpreters: deaf student held not entitled to sign-language interpreter in public school classes, under Education for All Handicapped Children Act, where she was receiving adequate education and personalized instruction, 73 L Ed 2d 690

Racial Discrimination (this index)

Religion and Religious Institutions (this index)

SCHOOLS AND EDUCATION—Cont'd
School Boards (this index)
Sex Discrimination (this index)
Sexual performances: New York criminal statute prohibiting knowing promotion of sexual performances by children under 16, by distribution of material depicting such performances, held constitutional, 73 L Ed 2d 1113
Taxation: New Mexico tax imposed on gross receipts that non-Indian construction company received from tribal school board for construction of school on reservation, held preempted by federal law, 73 L Ed 2d 1174
Training (this index)
Universities and Colleges (this index)

SCIENTIFIC VALUE
Sexual performances: New York criminal statute prohibiting knowing promotion of sexual performances by children under 16, by distribution of material depicting such performances, held constitutional, 73 L Ed 2d 1113

SEA
Water and Waterways (this index)

SEARCH AND SEIZURE
Arrest: rule of Payton v New York prohibiting warrantless, nonconsensual entry into suspect's home to make routine felony arrest, held to apply to case pending on direct appeal when Payton was decided, 73 L Ed 2d 202
"Exigent circumstances": absence of "exigent circumstances," held not to preclude warrantless search of car conducted after police officers discovered contraband in justified inventory search of car, 73 L Ed 2d 750
Police officer's accompaniment of lawful arrestee to residence and subsequent seizure of contraband in plain view, held not violative of Fourth Amendment, 70 L Ed 2d 778
Probable cause: authority to conduct warrantless search of motor vehicle based on probable cause, including compartments and containers, held coextensive with authority based on magistrate's issuance of warrant, 72 L Ed 2d 572

SECONDARY ACTIVITY
Attorney's fees incurred during proceedings before National Labor Relations Board, held not proper element of damages under § 303(b) of Labor Management Relations Act (29 USCS § 187(b)), 72 L Ed 2d 511

INDEX

SECONDARY BOYCOTTS
Refusal by longshoremen's union to unload cargoes shipped from Soviet Union in protest against Afghanistan invasion, held illegal secondary boycott under 29 USCS § 158(b)(4), 72 L Ed 2d 21

SECOND TRIAL
Double Jeopardy (this index)

SECRETARY OF HEALTH AND HUMAN SERVICES
Health and Human Services Secretary (this index)

SECRETARY OF INTERIOR
Bidding system: Interior Secretary's refusal to use non-cash-bonus bidding systems in leasing oil and gas tracts on outer continental shelf, held not violative of Outer Continental Shelf Lands Act Amendments, (43 USCS §§ 1331 et seq.), 70 L Ed 2d 309

SECRETARY OF LABOR
Jurisdiction: Tax Injunction Act (28 USCS § 1341) held to bar federal court jurisdiction to declare state tax unconstitutional, 73 L Ed 2d 93

SECURITIES
"Brother-sister controlled group": Treasury Regulation (26 CFR § 1.1563-1(a) (3)) implementing statutory definition of "brother-sister controlled group" of corporations (26 USCS § 1563(a)), held unreasonable, 70 L Ed 2d 792

Business takeover: Illinois business takeover statute, held unconstitutional under commerce clause (Art I, § 8, cl 3), 73 L Ed 2d 269

Commodity Exchange Act: action for damages caused by violation of Commodity Exchange Act (7 USCS §§ 1 et seq.), held available to private parties, 72 L Ed 2d 182

Forgery: statute (18 USCS § 2314) prohibiting transport of forged securities in "interstate commerce," held not to require proof securities were forged before being taken across state lines, 71 L Ed 2d 522

SEIZURE
Prejudgment attachment: complaint against private creditor's prejudgment attachment, held to state cause of action under 42 USCS § 1983 where statute authorizing it is alleged to be procedurally defective, 73 L Ed 2d 482

INDEX

SEIZURE—Cont'd
Search and Seizure (this index)

SELECTION PROCESS
Discrimination: prima facie case under 42 USCS § 2000e-2 in regard to test that bars promotion and disproportionately excludes blacks, held not precluded by nondiscriminatory "bottom line" result of employer's promotional process, 73 L Ed 2d 130

SELF-EMPLOYED PERSONS
Social security: imposition of social security taxes on persons who object on religious grounds to receipt of public insurance benefits and to payment of taxes to support such benefits, held constitutional, 71 L Ed 2d 127

SELF-GOVERNMENT
Severance tax imposed on oil and gas removed from Indian reservation, held authorized by Tribe's inherent authority to tax as part of power of self-government, and held violative of commerce clause (Art I, § 8, cl 3), 71 L Ed 2d 21

SELF-REPRESENTATION
Pro se complaint: state prisoner's crudely written, pro se complaint alleging his placement in solitary confinement for one-week period without any notice of charges or any hearing, held sufficient to state cause of action, 70 L Ed 2d 551

SENATE OF UNITED STATES
Congress (this index)

SENIOR AIDES
Immunity: senior aides and advisers of President of United States, held entitled to qualified immunity from civil damages suits insofar as their conduct does not violate rights of which reasonable person would have known, 73 L Ed 2d 396

SENIORITY
Backpay: employer's offer to discrimination claimant of job previously denied without offer of retroactive seniority, held to toll continuing accrual of backpay liability under 42 USCS § 2000e-6(g), 73 L Ed 2d 721

675

SENIORITY—Cont'd

Invalidation of system: 42 USCS § 2000e-2(h) requiring showing of discriminatory impact and discriminatory purpose to invalidate seniority system, held not limited to systems adopted by Title VII's effective date, 71 L Ed 2d 748

Jurisdiction: filing of timely charge with Equal Employment Opportunity Commission held not jurisdictional prerequisite to suit under Title VII of Civil Rights Act of 1964 (42 USCS §§ 2000e et seq.), 71 L Ed 2d 234

Legality: Federal Court of Appeals' reversal of Federal District Court ruling as to legality of seniority system under 42 USCS § 2000e-5(h), held erroneous in view of court's independent determination of allegations of discrimination, 72 L Ed 2d 66

SENTENCE AND PUNISHMENT

Arrest: rule of Payton v New York prohibiting warrantless, nonconsensual entry into suspect's home to make routine felony arrest, held to apply to case pending on direct appeal when Payton was decided, 73 L Ed 2d 202

"Cause and actual prejudice," rather than "plain error" of Rule 52(b) of Federal Rules of Criminal Procedure, held proper standard of review on motion for collateral relief under 28 USCS § 2255, 71 L Ed 2d 816

Cruel and Unusual Punishment (this index)

Death Penalty (this index)

Habeas Corpus (this index)

Youth Corrections Act (18 USCS §§ 5005 et seq.), held not to require that youth offender sentenced to adult term while serving youth term must receive youth treatment for remainder of youth term, 70 L Ed 2d 345

SEPARATION OF CHURCH AND STATE
Religion and Religious Institutions (this index)

SERVICEMEN
Armed Forces (this index)

SERVICE OF PROCESS
Process and Service of Process (this index)

SERVICES

First Amendment: Kentucky statute prohibiting candidates from offering benefits to voters in exchange for votes, held violative of First Amendment as applied to candidate who pledged to work at reduced salary, 71 L Ed 2d 732

SETTING ASIDE
Vacating and Setting Aside (this index)

SETTLEMENT AGREEMENTS
Jurisdiction: filing of timely charge with Equal Employment Opportunity Commission held not jurisdictional prerequisite to suit under Title VII of Civil Rights Act of 1964 (42 USCS §§ 2000e et seq.), 71 L Ed 2d 234

SEVERANCE TAX
Indians: severance tax imposed on oil and gas removed from Indian reservation, held authorized by Tribe's inherent authority to tax as part of power of self-government, and held not violative of commerce clause (Art I, § 8, cl 3), 71 L Ed 2d 21

SEX DISCRIMINATION
Education programs: regulations prohibiting federally funded education programs from discriminating on basis of sex in employment, held valid under Title IX of Education Amendments of 1972 (20 USCS §§ 1681 et seq.), 72 L Ed 2d 299
Exhaustion of state administrative remedies, held not prerequisite to bringing action pursuant to 42 USCS § 1983, 73 L Ed 2d 172
Jurisdiction: filing of timely charge with Equal Employment Opportunity Commission held not jurisdictional prerequisite to suit under Title VII of Civil Rights Act of 1964 (42 USCS §§ 2000e et seq.), 71 L Ed 2d 234
Nursing schools: state-supported university's policy that excludes males from enrolling in its professional nursing school, held violative of equal protection clause of Fourteenth Amendment, 73 L Ed 2d 1090
Private school whose income is derived primarily from public sources and which is regulated by public authorities, held not to have acted under color of state law for purposes of 42 USCS § 1983 when it discharged certain employees, 73 L Ed 2d 418

SEX OFFENSES
Bail: claim that Nebraska's prohibition of pretrial bail to person charged with sexual offenses violated Federal Constitution, held moot where defendant had already been convicted of offenses, 71 L Ed 2d 353

INDEX

SEX OFFENSES—Cont'd

Children: New York criminal statute prohibiting knowing promotion of sexual performances by children under 16, by distribution of material depicting such performances, held constitutional, 73 L Ed 2d 1113

First Amendment: state statute which requires, under all circumstances, exclusion of press and general public from courtroom during testimony of minor victim in sex-offense trial, held violative of First Amendment, 73 L Ed 2d 248

SHARES OF STOCK
Securities (this index)

SHERMAN ACT

Alcohol distillers: state alcoholic beverage control law enforcing distiller's designation of wholesaler, held not per se violative of Sherman Act (15 USCS §§ 1 et seq.), 73 L Ed 2d 1042

Price-fixing: agreement among competing physicians setting, by majority vote, maximum fees for payment from participants in specified insurance plans, held per se unlawful under § 1 of Sherman Act (15 USCS § 1), 73 L Ed 2d 48

Welfare fund: coal producer sued on promise to contribute to union welfare funds based on "purchased coal," held entitled to plead and have adjudicated illegality defense, 70 L Ed 2d 833

SHIPS AND SHIPPING
Admiralty (this index)
Commerce (this index)

SHORELINE

Accretions: United States held entitled to oceanfront accretions to Coast Guard reservation under federal rule that accretions belong to upland owner, 73 L Ed 2d 1

SIGNATORY CLAUSES

Collective bargaining: union signatory subcontracting clauses sought or negotiated in context of collective bargaining relationship, held protected by construction industry proviso to 29 USCS § 158(e), 72 L Ed 2d 398

678

INDEX

SIGN-LANGUAGE

Interpreters: deaf student held not entitled to sign-language interpreter in public school classes, under Education for All Handicapped Children Act, where she was receiving adequate education and personalized instruction, 73 L Ed 2d 690

SILENCE

Miranda warnings: state prosecutor's cross-examination of defendant as to post-arrest silence, held not violative of Fourteenth Amendment due process in absence of Miranda warning assurances, 71 L Ed 2d 490

"SIMILAR FILES" REQUIREMENT

Freedom of Information Act: citizenship information on foreign nationals, held to satisfy "similar files" requirement of Exemption 6 of Freedom of Information Act (5 USCS § 552(b)(6)), 72 L Ed 2d 358

SIXTH AMENDMENT

Deportation: government's deportation of alien witnesses, held not violative of Fifth and Sixth Amendments absent some showing evidence lost would be both material and favorable to defendant, 73 L Ed 2d 1193

Speedy trial: time between dismissal of military charges and subsequent indictment of individual on civilian charges held not to be considered in determining whether violation of right to speedy trial under Sixth Amendment has occurred, 71 L Ed 2d 696

SOCIAL SECURITY

Emergency assistance: state emergency assistance program precluding furnishing assistance to AFDC recipients, held invalid under supremacy clause (Art VI, cl 2) as in conflict with valid federal regulation, 72 L Ed 2d 728

Medicare and Medicaid (this index)

Religious objections: imposition of social security taxes on persons who object on religious grounds to receipt of public insurance benefits and to payment of taxes to support such benefits, held constitutional, 71 L Ed 2d 127

SOLICITATION OF FUNDS

Contributions and Solicitation of Funds (this index)

INDEX

SOLITARY CONFINEMENT

Pro se complaint: state prisoner's crudely written, pro se complaint alleging his placement in solitary confinement for one-week period without any notice of charges or any hearing, held sufficient to state cause of action, 70 L Ed 2d 551

SOVEREIGNTY

Discrimination: Commonwealth of Puerto Rico held to have standing to sue as parens patriae to enjoin applegrowers' discrimination against Puerto Rican migrant farmworkers, 73 L Ed 2d 995

Public Utilities Regulatory Policies Act: provisions of Public Utility Regulatory Policies Act (15 USCS §§ 3201 et seq.; 16 USCS §§ 824a-3, 2611 et seq.), held not violative of commerce clause (Art I, § 8, cl 3) and Tenth Amendment, 72 L Ed 2d 532

Railroads: application of Railway Labor Act (29 USCS §§ 151 et seq.) to state-owned railroad engaged in interstate commerce, held not prohibited by Tenth Amendment, 71 L Ed 2d 547

Sales and use taxes: imposition of New Mexico's gross receipts and compensating use taxes on federal contractors doing business in state, held valid, 71 L Ed 2d 580

SOVIET UNION

Secondary boycott: refusal by longshoremen's union to unload cargoes shipped from Soviet Union in protest against Afghanistan invasion, held illegal secondary boycott under 29 USCS § 158(b)(4), 72 L Ed 2d 21

Work stoppage to protest Soviet invasion of Afghanistan, held subject to anti-injunction provisions of Norris-LaGuardia Act (29 USCS §§ 101 et seq.), and not enjoinable pending arbitrator's decision as to whether strike violated collective-bargaining contract, 73 L Ed 2d 327

SPANISH NAMED PERSONS

Promotion: Mexican-American employee who was denied promotion, held not entitled to maintain class action on behalf of Mexican-American applicants for employment who were not hired, 72 L Ed 2d 740

INDEX

SPECIAL ELECTIONS

Legislative seat: Puerto Rico law vesting in political party authority to appoint replacement for member who vacates seat on legislature, held not violative of United States Constitution, 72 L Ed 2d 628

SPEECH, ASSEMBLY, AND PRESS FREEDOM

Book removal: Federal District Court's entry of summary judgment in case challenging local school board's removal of library books as violative of First Amendment, held erroneous where material issue of fact remained as to board's justifications, 73 L Ed 2d 435

Lewdness, Indecency, and Obscenity (this index)

Licenses: municipal ordinance requiring license to sell "items designed or marketed for use with illegal cannabis or drugs," held not unconstitutionally vague or overbroad, 71 L Ed 2d 362

Minors: state statute which requires, under all circumstances, exclusion of press and general public from courtroom during testimony of minor victim in sex-offense trial, held violative of First Amendment, 73 L Ed 2d 248

Union "outsider rule," held not violative of Labor-Management Reporting and Disclosure Act's "free speech and assembly" or "right to sue" provisions (29 USCS § 411(a)(2), (4)), 72 L Ed 2d 707

SPEEDY TRIAL

Military charges: time between dismissal of military charges and subsequent indictment of individual on civilian charges held not to be considered in determining whether violation of right to speedy trial under Sixth Amendment has occurred, 71 L Ed 2d 696

SPOUSE

Husband and Wife (this index)

SSI BENEFITS

Medicaid: state's unlimited deeming of Medicaid applicant's spouse's income as available to applicant in determining eligibility, held barred by 42 USCS § 1396a(a), 71 L Ed 2d 137

INDEX

STAGGERS ACT
Bankruptcy: employee protection provisions of Rock Island Transition and Employee Assistance Act (45 USCS §§ 1005 and 1008), held violative of bankruptcy clause (Art I, § 8, cl 4), 71 L Ed 2d 335

STANDARD OF REVIEW
"Cause and actual prejudice," rather than "plain error" of Rule 52(b) of Federal Rules of Criminal Procedure, held proper standard of review on motion for collateral relief under 28 USCS § 2255, 71 L Ed 2d 816

STANDING
Parties (this index)

"STATE ACTION" DOCTRINE
Cable television: ordinance enacted by home-rule municipality prohibiting expansion of cable television operator's business, held not to be "state action" eligible for exemption from federal antitrust laws, 70 L Ed 2d 810 .

STATE AND LOCAL TAXATION
Gross Receipts (this index)

Jurisdiction: Tax Injunction Act (28 USCS § 1341) held to bar federal court jurisdiction to declare state tax unconstitutional, 73 L Ed 2d 93

Oil revenues: Temporary Emergency Court of Appeals' invalidation of anti-passthrough provision of state tax statute relating to oil company revenues, vacated and remanded in light of expiration of preempting federal price control authority, 71 L Ed 2d 120

Taxpayer's damages action under 42 USCS § 1983 for alleged unconstitutional administration of state tax system, held barred in federal court by principle of comity, 70 L Ed 2d 271

STATE DEPARTMENT
Freedom of Information Act: citizenship information on foreign nationals, held to satisfy "similar files" requirement of Exemption 6 of Freedom of Information Act (5 USCS § 552(b)(6)), 72 L Ed 2d 358

INDEX

STATEMENT OF CLAIMS

Mineral interests: state statute extinguishing unused mineral interests after 20 years unless owner files statement of claim, held not violative of contract clause, Fifth Amendment just compensation clause, and Fourteenth Amendment due process and equal protection, 70 L Ed 2d 738

STATE OFFICIALS

Public Officers and Employees (this index)

STATES AND STATE COURTS

Accretions: United States held entitled to oceanfront accretions to Coast Guard reservation under federal rule that accretions belong to upland owner, 73 L Ed 2d 1

Alcohol distillers: state alcoholic beverage control law enforcing distiller's designation of wholesaler, held not per se violative of Sherman Act (15 USCS §§ 1 et seq.), 73 L Ed 2d 1042

Boycotts: First Amendment held to preclude state court imposition of liability on participants in black boycott of white businesses for losses other than those caused by their own violence or threats, 73 L Ed 2d 1215

Business takeover: Illinois business takeover statute, held unconstitutional under commerce clause (Art I, § 8, cl 3), 73 L Ed 2d 269

Children and Minors (this index)

Citizens: state statute requiring peace officers, including deputy probation officers, to be United States citizens, held not violative of equal protection clause of Fourteenth Amendment, 70 L Ed 2d 677

Collective bargaining: section 13(c) of Urban Mass Transportation Act of 1964 (49 USCS § 1609(c)), held not to create federal cause of action for breach of § 13(c) agreement or collective bargaining contract between local transit authority and union, 72 L Ed 2d 639

Colleges. **Universities and Colleges** (this index)

Color of State Law (this index)

Comity (this index)

Controversies Between States (this index)

Death penalty: question as to what premises of state law support a conclusion that a death sentence was not impaired by the invalidity of one of the statutory aggravating circumstances found by the jury, certified to Georgia Supreme Court, 72 L Ed 2d 222

STATES AND STATE COURTS—Cont'd

Decedents' Estates (this index)

District and Prosecuting Attorneys (this index)

Double jeopardy: Florida Supreme Court's reversal of murder and rape conviction at jury trial based on weight of evidence, held not to bar retrial under double jeopardy clause of Fifth and Fourteenth Amendments, 72 L Ed 2d 652

Elections (this index)

Emergency assistance: state emergency assistance program precluding furnishing assistance to AFDC recipients, held invalid under supremacy clause (Art VI, cl 2) as in conflict with valid federal regulation, 72 L Ed 2d 728

Exhaustion of state administrative remedies, held not prerequisite to bringing action pursuant to 42 USCS § 1983, 73 L Ed 2d 172

Foreign Countries or States (this index)

Full Faith and Credit (this index)

Habeas Corpus (this index)

Income Tax (this index)

Insane and Incompetent Persons (this index)

Insurance beneficiary: insured serviceman's beneficiary designation under life policy issued pursuant to Servicemen's Group Life Insurance Act (38 USCS §§ 765 et seq.), held to prevail over constructive trust imposed upon proceeds by state court, 70 L Ed 2d 39

Interstate Commerce (this index)

Job Discrimination (this index)

Jurisdiction (this index)

Medicare and Medicaid (this index)

Mines and Minerals (this index)

Preemption (this index)

Public Officers and Employees (this index)

Religion and Religious Institutions (this index)

Schools and Education (this index)

Taxation. **State and Local Taxation** (this index)

Universities and Colleges (this index)

STATUTE OF LIMITATIONS

Limitation of Actions (this index)

INDEX

STATUTES AND ORDINANCES

Alcohol distillers: state alcoholic beverage control law enforcing distiller's designation of wholesaler, held not per se violative of Sherman Act (15 USCS §§ 1 et seq.), 73 L Ed 2d 1042

Cable television: ordinance enacted by home-rule municipality prohibiting expansion of cable television operator's business, held not to be "state action" eligible for exemption from federal antitrust laws, 70 L Ed 2d 810

Citizens: state statute requiring peace officers, including deputy probation officers, to be United States citizens, held not violative of equal protection clause of Fourteenth Amendment, 70 L Ed 2d 677

Elections (this index)

First Amendment: Minnesota statute exempting from certain registration and reporting requirements only religious organizations receiving more than 50% of contributions from members, held violative of First Amendment establishment clause, 72 L Ed 2d 33

Lewdness, Indecency, and Obscenity (this index)

Licenses and Permits (this index)

Mineral interests: state statute extinguishing unused mineral interests after 20 years unless owner files statement of claim, held not violative of contract clause, Fifth Amendment just compensation clause, and Fourteenth Amendment due process and equal protection, 70 L Ed 2d 738

Prejudgment attachment: complaint against private creditor's prejudgment attachment, held to state cause of action under 42 USCS § 1983 where statute authorizing it is alleged to be procedurally defective, 73 L Ed 2d 482

Securities: statute (18 USCS § 2314) prohibiting transport of forged securities in "interstate commerce," held not to require proof securities were forged before being taken across state lines, 71 L Ed 2d 522

STAY

Reapportionment Plan (this index)

"STEERING" PRACTICES

Discrimination: black "tester" given false information about housing availability and nonprofit, open housing organization, held to have standing to challenge racial steering under Fair Housing Act (42 USCS § 3612); Act's 180-day

685

"STEERING" PRACTICES—Cont'd

limitations period (42 USCS § 3612(a)), held not bar claims of continuing violation, even though some incidents alleged occur outside period, 71 L Ed 2d 214

STOCK AND STOCKHOLDERS

Securities (this index)

STOPPAGE OF WORK

Soviet Union (this index)

STORAGE

Nuclear weapons: § 102 (2)(c) of the National Environmental Policy Act (42 USCS § 4332 (2)(c)), held not to require Navy to prepare and release "Hypothetical Environmental Impact Statement" regarding nuclear weapons storage, 70 L Ed 2d 298

STRIKES

Soviet invasion: work stoppage to protest Soviet invasion of Afghanistan, held subject to anti-injunction provisions of Norris-LaGuardia Act (29 USCS §§ 101 et seq.), and not enjoinable pending aribtrator's decision as to whether strike violated collective-bargaining contract, 73 L Ed 2d 327

STUDENTS

Schools and Education (this index)

SUBCONTRACTORS

Collective bargaining: union signatory subcontracting clauses sought or negotiated in context of collective bargaining relationship, held protected by construction industry proviso to 29 USCS § 158(e), 72 L Ed 2d 398

SUBJECT MATTER JURISDICTION

Full faith and credit: North Carolina courts' refusal to treat as res judicata Indiana rehabilitation court's adjudication of rights to insurance company's deposit posted in North Carolina, held violative of full faith and credit clause (Art IV, § 1), 71 L Ed 2d 558

SUBMERGED LANDS ACT

Accretions: United States held entitled to oceanfront accretions to Coast Guard reservation under federal rule that accretions belong to upland owner, 73 L Ed 2d 1

INDEX

SUBSCRIBERS
Psychologist's fees: health plan subscriber denied reimbursement for psychologist's fees, held to have standing to sue for conspiracy to exclude psychologists from psychotherapy market, 73 L Ed 2d 149

SUBSEQUENT TRIAL
Double jeopardy: second trial of defendant who successfully moves for mistrial because of prosecutorial misconduct, held barred by double jeopardy clause only if prosecutor intended to provoke defendant to move for mistrial, 72 L Ed 2d 416

SUBSIDIARY CORPORATIONS
Income Tax (this index)
Treaties: employment practices of a New York corporation that is wholly-owned subsidiary of Japanese firm, held not exempted from Title VII of Civil Rights Act (42 USCS §§ 2000e et seq.) by treaty between the United States and Japan, 72 L Ed 2d 765

SUBSTANTIVE LAW
Dismissal: plaintiff's showing that substantive law of alternative forum would be less favorable to plaintiff than that of chosen forum, held not to defeat motion to dismiss on ground of forum non conveniens, 70 L Ed 2d 419

SUMMARY JUDGMENTS
Removal of books: Federal District Court's entry of summary judgment in case challenging local school board's removal of library books as violative of First Amendment, held erroneous where material issue of fact remained as to board's justifications, 73 L Ed 2d 435

SUMMONS
Service of process: Kentucky statute applicable to forcible entry and detainer actions permitting service of process by posting summons on door of premises, held violative of due process, 72 L Ed 2d 249

SUPPLEMENTAL SECURITY INCOME
Medicaid: state's unlimited deeming of Medicaid applicant's spouse's income as available to applicant in determining eligibility, held barred by 42 USCS § 1396a(a), 71 L Ed 2d 137

INDEX

SUPPORT OF PERSONS
Paternity suits: Texas statute barring paternity suits brought on behalf of illegitimate children more than one year after their birth, held violative of equal protection, 71 L Ed 2d 770

SUPREMACY CLAUSE
Alcohol distillers: state alcoholic beverage control law enforcing distiller's designation of wholesaler, held not per se violative of Sherman Act (15 USCS §§ 1 et seq.), 73 L Ed 2d 1042

Emergency assistance: state emergency assistance program precluding furnishing assistance to AFDC recipients, held invalid under supremacy clause (Art VI, cl 2) as in conflict with valid federal regulation, 72 L Ed 2d 728

In-state status: state university's policy of denying in-state status to domiciled nonimmigrant aliens holding G-4 visas, held violative of supremacy clause (Art VI, cl 2), 73 L Ed 2d 563

SURGEONS
Physicians and Surgeons (this index)

SURPLUS PROPERTY
Establishment clause: taxpayers' organization dedicated to separation of church and state, held to have no standing to challenge, as violative of First Amendment establishment clause, no-cost transfer of surplus United States property to religious educational institution, 70 L Ed 2d 700

SURVEILLANCE
Seizure: police officer's accompaniment of lawful arrestee to residence and subsequent seizure of contraband in plain view, held not violative of Fourth Amendment, 70 L Ed 2d 778

SUSPECTS
Arrest: rule of Payton v New York prohibiting warrantless, nonconsensual entry into suspect's home to make routine felony arrest, held to apply to case pending on direct appeal when Payton was decided, 73 L Ed 2d 202

SUSPENSION
Also see **Discharge or Removal**

INDEX

SUSPENSION—Cont'd
Schools: federal courts' replacement of local school board's construction of its own rules on mandatory suspension in action under 42 USCS § 1983, held erroneous where board's construction was reasonable, 73 L Ed 2d 1273

SYMBIOTIC RELATIONSHIP
Private school whose income is derived primarily from public sources and which is regulated by public authorities, held not to have acted under color of state law for purposes of 42 USCS § 1983 when it discharged certain employees, 73 L Ed 2d 418

TAKEOVER OF BUSINESS
Illinois business takeover statute, held unconstitutional under commerce clause (Art I, § 8, cl 3), 73 L Ed 2d 269

"TAKING" OF PROPERTY
Deprivation of Property (this index)

TAXATION
Death tax claim: action under Federal Interpleader Act (28 USCS § 1335) to resolve inconsistent death tax claims on estate of Howard Hughes by officials of two states, held barred by Eleventh Amendment, 72 L Ed 2d 694
Gift Tax (this index)
Gross Receipts (this index)
Income Tax (this index)
Indians (this index)
Injunctions (this index)
In-state status: state university's policy of denying in-state status to domiciled nonimmigrant aliens holding G-4 visas, held violative of supremacy clause (Art VI, cl 2), 73 L Ed 2d 563
Oil and Gas (this index)
Social Security (this index)
State and Local Taxation (this index)

TEACHERS
Schools and Education (this index)

TELECOMMUNICATIONS
Cable Television (this index)

INDEX

TELEVISION
Cable Television (this index)

TEMPORARY EMERGENCY COURT OF APPEALS
Taxation: Temporary Emergency Court of Appeals' invalidation of anti-passthrough provision of state tax statute relating to oil company revenues, vacated and remanded in light of expiration of preempting federal price control authority, 71 L Ed 2d 120

TENANTS
Leases (this index)

10-DAY TIMELINESS STANDARD
Attorney's fees: postjudgment request for attorney's fees under Civil Rights Attorney's Fees Awards Act (42 USCS § 1988), held not subject to 10-day timeliness standard of Rule 59(e) of Federal Rules of Civil Procedure, 71 L Ed 2d 325

TENTH AMENDMENT
Public Utilities Regulatory Policies Act: provisions of Public Utility Regulatory Policies Act (15 USCS §§ 3201 et seq.; 16 USCS §§ 824a-3, 2611 et seq.), held not violative of commerce clause (Art I, § 8, cl 3) and Tenth Amendment, 72 L Ed 2d 532
Railroads: application of Railway Labor Act (29 USCS §§ 151 et seq.) to state-owned railroad engaged in interstate commerce, held not prohibited by Tenth Amendment, 71 L Ed 2d 547

TERMINATION
Cancellation or Termination (this index)

TERM OF SENTENCE
Sentence and Punishment (this index)

TERRITORIES
Puerto Rico (this index)

TESTAMENTARY TRUSTS
Taxation: trust beneficiary's disclaimer of contingent interest in testamentary trust, held taxable transfer of property by gift under 26 USCS §§ 2501(a)(1) and 2511(a), not excepted from tax by 26 CFR § 25.2511-1(c), 71 L Ed 2d 170

690

"TESTERS"

Discrimination: black "tester" given false information about housing availability and nonprofit, open housing organization, held to have standing to challenge racial steering under Fair Housing Act (42 USCS § 3612); Act's 180-day limitations period (42 USCS § 3612(a)), held not bar claims of continuing violation, even though some incidents alleged occur outside period, 71 L Ed 2d 214

TESTIMONY
Evidence (this index)

TESTS AND EXAMINATIONS

Discrimination: prima facie case under 42 USCS § 2000e-2 in regard to test that bars promotion and disproportionately excludes blacks, held not precluded by nondiscriminatory "bottom line" result of employer's promotional process, 73 L Ed 2d 130

THEATERS
Entertainment and Amusements (this index)

THREATS

Boycotts: First Amendment held to preclude state court imposition of liability on participants in black boycott of white businesses for losses other than those caused by their own violence or threats, 73 L Ed 2d 1215

THREE-JUDGE COURTS
Elections (this index)

TIDELANDS

Accretions: United States held entitled to oceanfront accretions to Coast Guard reservation under federal rule that accretions belong to upland owner, 73 L Ed 2d 1

TIME AND DATE

Appeal: retained counsel's failure to timely file for discretionary review of state court convictions with state's highest court, held not to deprive defendant of effective assistance of counsel, 71 L Ed 2d 475

Attorney's fees: postjudgment request for attorney's fees under Civil Rights Attorney's Fees Awards Act (42 USCS § 1988), held not subject to 10-day timeliness standard of Rule 59(e) of Federal Rules of Civil Procedure, 71 L Ed 2d 325

INDEX

TRADE ASSOCIATIONS
Associations and Organizations (this index)

TRADEMARKS
Infringement: Federal Court of Appeals' reversal of District Court's findings as to trademark infringement by generic drug manufacturers, held error where "clearly erroneous" standard of FRCP 52 not followed, 72 L Ed 2d 606

TRADE RESTRAINTS
Monopolies and Restraints of Trade (this index)

TRAINING
Discrimination: proof of intentional discrimination, held necessary for liability under 42 USCS § 1981; vicarious liability under § 1981 of employers and trade associations for discriminatory conduct of union, held not supportable, 73 L Ed 2d 835

Mentally retarded person: involuntarily committed mentally retarded person, held to have due process liberty interests requiring state to provide minimally adequate training to insure safety and freedom from undue restraint, 73 L Ed 2d 28

TRANSFERS
Medicaid: nursing homes' decisions to discharge or transfer Medicaid patients to lower levels of care, held not to involve state action for purposes of Fourteenth Amendment's due process clause, 73 L Ed 2d 534
Sales and Transfers (this index)

TRANSPORTATION
Busing: state constitutional amendment precluding state court-ordered school busing absent Fourteenth Amendment violation held constitutional, 73 L Ed 2d 948
Carriers (this index)
Collective bargaining: section 13(c) of Urban Mass Transportation Act of 1964 (49 USCS § 1609(c)), held not to create federal cause of action for breach of § 13(c) agreement or collective bargaining contract between local transit authority and union, 72 L Ed 2d 639
Commerce (this index)
Interstate Commerce (this index)
Search and Seizure (this index)

TRAUMA

First Amendment: state statute which requires, under all circumstances, exclusion of press and general public from courtroom during testimony of minor victim in sex-offense trial, held violative of First Amendment, 73 L Ed 2d 248

TREASURY REGULATION

"Brother-sister controlled group": Treasury Regulation (26 CFR § 1.1563-1(a) (3)) implementing statutory definition of "brother-sister controlled group" of corporations (26 USCS § 1563(a)), held unreasonable, 70 L Ed 2d 792

TREATIES

Civil rights: employment practices of a New York corporation that is wholly-owned subsidiary of Japanese firm, held not exempted from Title VII of Civil Rights Act (42 USCS §§ 2000e et seq.) by treaty between the United States and Japan, 72 L Ed 2d 765

Executive agreements: word "treaty" in 5 USCS § 7201 note, which excepts from certain employment discrimination requirements actions permitted by "treaty," held to include executive agreements, 71 L Ed 2d 715

TREBLE DAMAGES

Antitrust: nonprofit association of mechanical engineers responsible for promulgation of industry codes, held civilly liable under antitrust laws for antitrust violations of its agents committed with apparent authority, 72 L Ed 2d 330

TRIAL DE NOVO

New Trial (this index)

TRIALS

Double Jeopardy (this index)
Evidence (this index)
Exhaustion of Remedies (this index)
Fair Trial (this index)
First Amendment: state statute which requires, under all circumstances, exclusion of press and general public from courtroom during testimony of minor victim in sex-offense trial, held violative of First Amendment, 73 L Ed 2d 248
Judges (this index)
Jury and Jury Trials (this index)
New Trial (this index)

INDEX

UNCONSTITUTIONAL DILUTION
Elections: at-large election system for large rural county with large black population held violative of equal protection clause, 73 L Ed 2d 1012

UNDUE RESTRAINT
Mentally retarded person: involuntarily committed mentally retarded person, held to have due process liberty interests requiring state to provide minimally adequate training to insure safety and freedom from undue restraint, 73 L Ed 2d 28

UNEXHAUSTED CLAIMS
Exhaustion of Remedies (this index)

UNFAIR LABOR PRACTICES
Collective bargaining: union signatory subcontracting clauses sought or negotiated in context of collective bargaining relationship, held protected by construction industry proviso to 29 USCS § 158(e), 72 L Ed 2d 398

Discrimination: limitations period applicable to employment discrimination action under 42 USCS § 1983, held to run from time of notice that appointment would terminate rather than from termination date, 70 L Ed 2d 6

Employer's unilateral withdrawal from multiemployer bargaining unit, held not justified by bargaining impasse, 70 L Ed 2d 656

Nonprofit association of mechanical engineers responsible for promulgation of industy codes, held civilly liable under antitrust laws for antitrust violations of its agents committed with apparent authority, 72 L Ed 2d 330

UNFAIR TRADE PRACTICES
Monopolies and Restraints of Trade (this index)

UNILATERAL WITHDRAWAL
Employer's unilateral withdrawal from multiemployer bargaining unit, held not justified by bargaining impasse, 70 L Ed 2d 656

UNION OF SOVIET SOCIALIST'S REPUBLIC
Soviet Union (this index)

UNIONS
Employer and Employee (this index)

INDEX

UNITED STATES

Accretions: United States held entitled to oceanfront accretions to Coast Guard reservation under federal rule that accretions belong to upland owner, 73 L Ed 2d 1

Employees. **Public Officers and Employees** (this index)

Establishment clause: taxpayers' organization dedicated to separation of church and state, held to have no standing to challenge, as violative of First Amendment establishment clause, no-cost transfer of surplus United States property to religious educational institution, 70 L Ed 2d 700

Privileges and Immunities (this index)

Treaties (this index)

UNITED STATES ATTORNEY GENERAL

Election method: letter to Attorney General advising of results of county referendum endorsing at-large method of electing county council, held to be request for reconsideration of Attorney General's prior objections to method and not preclearance request under Voting Rights Act (42 USCS § 1973c), 70 L Ed 2d 576

UNIVERSITIES AND COLLEGES

Appeal of decision invalidating subsequently amended university rule, held moot as to university and without jurisdictional basis as to state which sought review but refused to take position on merits, 70 L Ed 2d 855

In-state status: state university's policy of denying in-state status to domiciled nonimmigrant aliens holding G-4 visas, held violative of supremacy clause (Art VI, cl 2), 73 L Ed 2d 563

Religion and Religious Institutions (this index)

Sex discrimination: state-supported university's policy that excludes males from enrolling in its professional nursing school, held violative of equal protection clause of Fourteenth Amendment, 73 L Ed 2d 1090

UNUSED MINERAL INTERESTS

Extinguishment of interest: state statute extinguishing unused mineral interests after 20 years unless owner files statement of claim, held not violative of contract clause, Fifth Amendment just compensation clause, and Fourteenth Amendment due process and equal protection, 70 L Ed 2d 738

INDEX

UPLAND OWNER

Accretions: United States held entitled to oceanfront accretions to Coast Guard reservation under federal rule that accretions belong to upland owner, 73 L Ed 2d 1

URBAN MASS TRANSPORTATION ACT

Collective bargaining: section 13(c) of Urban Mass Transportation Act of 1964 (49 USCS § 1609(c)), held not to create federal cause of action for breach of § 13(c) agreement or collective bargaining contract between local transit authority and union, 72 L Ed 2d 639

USE TAXES

Imposition of New Mexico's gross receipts and compensating use taxes on federal contractors doing business in state, held valid, 71 L Ed 2d 580

U.S.S.R.

Soviet Union (this index)

UTILITIES

Power and Energy (this index)

VACANCIES

Legislative seat: Puerto Rico law vesting in political party authority to appoint replacement for member who vacates seat on legislature, held not violative of United States Constitution, 72 L Ed 2d 628

VACATING AND SETTING ASIDE

"Cause and actual prejudice," rather than "plain error" of Rule 52(b) of Federal Rules of Criminal Procedure, held proper standard of review on motion for collateral relief under 28 USCS § 2255, 71 L Ed 2d 816

Double jeopardy: Florida Supreme Court's reversal of murder and rape conviction at jury trial based on weight of evidence, held not to bar retrial under double jeopardy clause of Fifth and Fourteenth Amendments, 72 L Ed 2d 652

Fair Labor Standards Act: appeal taken to Federal Court of Appeals of District Court decision finding application of Fair Labor Standards Act unconstitutional, held improper under 28 USCS §§ 1252 and 1291, and appeal to Supreme Court dismissed, 70 L Ed 2d 570

INDEX

VACATING AND SETTING ASIDE—Cont'd

Juror's submission, during criminal trial, of job application to prosecutor's office and failure of prosecution to disclose such fact during trial, held not violative of due process, 71 L Ed 2d 78

Mental patients: case presenting question whether state involuntarily committed patients may refuse certain drugs, vacated and remanded to Federal Court of Appeals, to consider intervening state decision opinion bearing on issue, 73 L Ed 2d 16

Taxation: Temporary Emergency Court of Appeals' invalidation of anti-passthrough provision of state tax statute relating to oil company revenues, vacated and remanded in light of expiration of preempting federal price control authority, 71 L Ed 2d 120

Trademark: Federal Court of Appeals' reversal of District Court's findings as to trademark infringement by generic drug manufacturers, held error where "clearly erroneous" standard of FRCP 52 not followed, 72 L Ed 2d 606

VAGUENESS

Licenses and Permits (this index)

VALIDITY AND INVALIDITY

Death penalty: question as to what premises of state law support a conclusion that a death sentence was not impaired by the invalidity of one of the statutory aggravating circumstances found by the jury, certified to Georgia Supreme Court, 72 L Ed 2d 222

Taxation: Temporary Emergency Court of Appeals' invalidation of anti-passthrough provision of state tax statute relating to oil company revenues, vacated and remanded in light of expiration of preempting federal price control authority, 71 L Ed 2d 120

VALUATION

Checks: deposit of bad check in federally insured bank, held not proscribed by 18 USCS § 1014, 73 L Ed 2d 767

VEHICLES

Transportation (this index)

VENDORS

Sales and Transfers (this index)

INDEX

VERDICT

Double jeopardy: Florida Supreme Court's reversal of murder and rape conviction at jury trial based on weight of evidence, held not to bar retrial under double jeopardy clause of Fifth and Fourteenth Amendments, 72 L Ed 2d 652

Habeas corpus: federal court's order in habeas corpus proceeding that state trial court must grant habeas petitioner new criminal trial or explain reasons for its inconsistent verdicts, held erroneous, 70 L Ed 2d 530

VERTICAL RESTRAINTS

Alcohol distillers: state alcoholic beverage control law enforcing distiller's designation of wholesaler, held not per se violative of Sherman Act (15 USCS §§ 1 et seq.), 73 L Ed 2d 1042

VESSELS

Admiralty (this index)

VETERANS

Insurance beneficiary: insured serviceman's beneficiary designation under life policy issued pursuant to Servicemen's Group Life Insurance Act (38 USCS §§ 765 et seq.), held to prevail over constructive trust imposed upon proceeds by state court, 70 L Ed 2d 39

VICARIOUS LIABILITY

Discrimination: proof of intentional discrimination, held necessary for liability under 42 USCS § 1981; vicarious liability under § 1981 of employers and trade associations for discriminatory conduct of union, held not supportable, 73 L Ed 2d 835

Trademark: Federal Court of Appeals' reversal of District Court's findings as to trademark infringement by generic drug manufacturers, held error where "clearly erroneous" standard of FRCP 52 not followed, 72 L Ed 2d 606

VINDICTIVENESS

District and Prosecuting Attorneys (this index)

VIOLENCE

Boycotts: First Amendment held to preclude state court imposition of liability on participants in black boycott of white businesses for losses other than those caused by their own violence or threats, 73 L Ed 2d 1215

INDEX

VISAS

In-state status: state university's policy of denying in-state status to domiciled nonimmigrant aliens holding G-4 visas, held violative of supremacy clause (Art VI, cl 2), 73 L Ed 2d 563

VOLUNTARY DISMISSAL

Bankruptcy: dismissal of Chapter XI petition filed under 1898 Bankruptcy Act in order to refile under Chapter 11 of 1978 Bankruptcy Code, held not authorized by Bankruptcy Rule 11-42(a) or § 403(a) of Bankruptcy Reform Act of 1978, 70 L Ed 2d 542

VOTING

Elections (this index)

WAGES

Compensation and Income (this index)

WAGNER-PEYSER ACT

Discrimination: Commonwealth of Puerto Rico held to have standing to sue as parens patriae to enjoin applegrowers' discrimination against Puerto Rican migrant farmworkers, 73 L Ed 2d 995

WANT OF JURISDICTION

University rules: appeal of decision invalidating subsequently amended university rule, held moot as to university and without jurisdictional basis as to state which sought review but refused to take position on merits, 70 L Ed 2d 855

WARRANTS

Arrest (this index)
Search and Seizure (this index)

WATER AND WATERWAYS

Accretions: United States held entitled to oceanfront accretions to Coast Guard reservation under federal rule that accretions belong to upland owner, 73 L Ed 2d 1
Admiralty (this index)
Bidding system: Interior Secretary's refusal to use non-cash-bonus bidding systems in leasing oil and gas tracts on outer continental shelf, held not violative of Outer Continental Shelf Lands Act Amendments, (43 USCS §§ 1331 et seq.), 70 L Ed 2d 309

701

INDEX

WATER AND WATERWAYS—Cont'd

Cessation orders: Federal District Court relief of violations of permit requirements of Federal Water Pollution Control Act (33 USCS §§ 1251 et seq.), held not limited to immediate cessation orders, 72 L Ed 2d 91

Hydroelectric energy: state public utility commission's order requiring privately-owned and federally-licensed public utility to sell within state hydroelectric energy it had been exporting, held violative of commerce clause (Art I, § 8, cl 3), 71 L Ed 2d 188

Longshoremen (this index)

Withdrawal: Nebraska statute forbidding withdrawal of ground water to foreign state which denies such privileges to Nebraska, held violative of Congress clause (Art 1, § 8 cl 3), 73 L Ed 2d 1254

WEAPONS

Nuclear weapons: § 102 (2)(c) of the National Environmental Policy Act (42 USCS § 4332 (2)(c)), held not to require Navy to prepare and release "Hypothetical Environmental Impact Statement" regarding nuclear weapons storage, 70 L Ed 2d 298

WEIGHT OF EVIDENCE

Double jeopardy: Florida Supreme Court's reversal of murder and rape conviction at jury trial based on weight of evidence, held not to bar retrial under double jeopardy clause of Fifth and Fourteenth Amendments, 72 L Ed 2d 652

WELFARE

Emergency assistance: state emergency assistance program precluding furnishing assistance to AFDC recipients, held invalid under supremacy clause (Art VI, cl 2) as in conflict with valid federal regulation, 72 L Ed 2d 728

Medicare and Medicaid (this index)

WHITE PERSONS

Boycotts: First Amendment held to preclude state court imposition of liability on participants in black boycott of white businesses for losses other than those caused by their own violence or threats, 73 L Ed 2d 1215

702

WHOLESALERS
Alcohol distillers: state alcoholic beverage control law enforcing distiller's designation of wholesaler, held not per se violative of Sherman Act (15 USCS §§ 1 et seq.), 73 L Ed 2d 1042

WIFE
Husband and Wife (this index)

WITHDRAWAL
Employer's unilateral withdrawal from multiemployer bargaining unit, held not justified by bargaining impasse, 70 L Ed 2d 656
Water: Nebraska statute forbidding withdrawal of ground water to foreign state which denies such privileges to Nebraska, held violative of Congress clause (Art 1, § 8 cl 3), 73 L Ed 2d 1254

WITNESSES
Evidence (this index)

WOMEN
Sex Discrimination (this index)

WORDS AND PHRASES
"Brother-sister controlled group"—within meaning of Treasury Regulation (26 CFR § 1.1563-1(a)(3)), 70 L Ed 2d 792
"Injury"—within meaning of Longshoremen's and Harbor Workers' Compensation Act (33 USCS § 920(a)), 71 L Ed 2d 495

WORK STOPPAGE
Soviet Union (this index)

YOUTH
Children and Minors (this index)